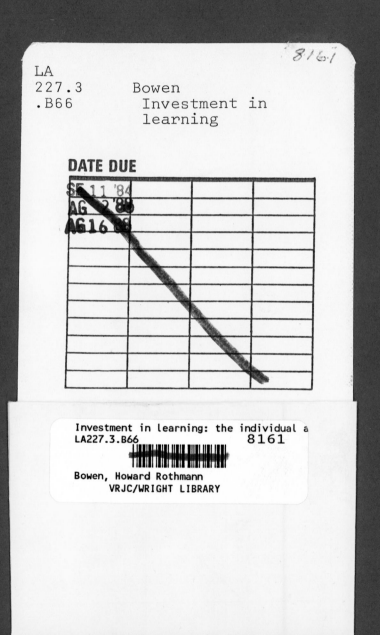

INVESTMENT IN LEARNING

*The Individual
and Social Value
of American Higher Education*

A REPORT PREPARED WITH THE SUPPORT
OF THE SLOAN FOUNDATION
AND ISSUED BY THE CARNEGIE COUNCIL
ON POLICY STUDIES IN HIGHER EDUCATION

Howard R. Bowen

with the collaboration of
Peter Clecak
Jacqueline Powers Doud
Gordon K. Douglass

INVESTMENT
IN LEARNING

*The Individual
and Social Value
of American Higher Education*

Jossey-Bass Publishers

San Francisco • Washington • London • 1978

INVESTMENT IN LEARNING
The Individual and/Social Value of American Higher Education
Howard R. Bowen *with the collaboration of* Peter Clecak,
Jacqueline Powers Doud, and Gordon K. Douglass

Library of Congress Catalogue Card Number LC 77-82069

International Standard Book Number ISBN 0-87589-341-4

Manufactured in the United States of America

DESIGN BY WILLI BAUM

FIRST EDITION
*First printing: September 1977
Second printing: February 1978*

Code 7740

The Carnegie Council Series

The Federal Role in Postsecondary
Education: Unfinished Business,
1975-1980
*The Carnegie Council on Policy
Studies in Higher Education*

More Than Survival: Prospects for
Higher Education in a Period
of Uncertainty
*The Carnegie Foundation for the
Advancement of Teaching*

Making Affirmative Action Work
in Higher Education: An Analysis
of Institutional and Federal Policies with Recommendations
*The Carnegie Council on Policy
Studies in Higher Education*

Presidents Confront Reality: From
Edifice Complex to University
Without Walls
*Lyman A. Glenny, John R. Shea,
Janet H. Ruyle, Kathryn H. Freschi*

Progress and Problems in Medical
and Dental Education: Federal
Support Versus Federal Control
*The Carnegie Council on Policy
Studies in Higher Education*

Faculty Bargaining in Public
Higher Education: A Report and
Two Essays
*The Carnegie Council on Policy
Studies in Higher Education,
Joseph W. Garbarino, David E.
Feller, Matthew W. Finkin*

Low or No Tuition: The Feasibility
of a National Policy for the First
Two Years of College
*The Carnegie Council on Policy
Studies in Higher Education*

Managing Multicampus Systems:
Effective Administration in an
Unsteady State
Eugene C. Lee, Frank M. Bowen

Challenges Past, Challenges
Present: An Analysis of American
Higher Education Since 1930
David D. Henry

The States and Higher Education:
A Proud Past and a Vital Future
*The Carnegie Foundation for the
Advancement of Teaching*

Educational Leaves for Employees:
European Experience for
American Consideration
*Konrad von Moltke,
Norbert Schneevoigt*

Investment in Learning: The
Individual and Social Value
of American Higher Education
*Howard R. Bowen
with the collaboration of Peter
Clecak, Jacqueline Powers Doud,
Gordon K. Douglass*

Contents

Foreword

In the last few years, the value of higher education has been under attack as seldom before in American history. We are being told of the "overeducated American," of the "case against college," and of the failure of education to contribute significantly to the reduction of inequality. The recent questioning of the value of college is associated with the less favorable job market that has faced recipients of bachelor's and more advanced degrees in the 1970s, compared with the exceptionally favorable 1960s. But this is by no means the whole story—some of the attacks come from those who argue that college is valuable chiefly for its credentialing function; some come from spokesmen of the "new left" eager to demonstrate that gross inequalities persist in capitalist America; some come from spokesmen of the right who are convinced that colleges harbor dangerously radical faculty members; and some come from persons who appear to have little conception of the values of advanced education.

In this environment, the publication of an exceptionally comprehensive and judicious analysis of all that has been learned (and not learned) about the consequences of American higher education comes at a most appropriate time. The range of relevant studies is enormous—from the outpouring of writings pro and con on human capital theory, to the analyses of how students' attitudes change from freshman to senior year, to the surveys of how alumni view their colleges, to the arguments back and forth about the measurability of the social benefits of higher education, and much more.

Through this vast array of studies Howard Bowen and his colleagues move with care and discrimination, producing a volume that covers the various aspects of the subject more fully than any study that has yet appeared. Those who have followed Howard Bowen's writings in recent years know that he is one of the optimists about the future of American higher education, but they are also aware that his optimism is based on profound knowledge of both the economic and noneconomic aspects of education. And, unlike some economists who would insist on strict cost-benefit accounting of expenditures on higher education in relation to pecuniary outcomes, Bowen argues that the nonmonetary benefits are so much greater than the monetary benefits that "individual and social decisions about the future of higher education should be made primarily on the basis of nonmonetary considerations, and only secondarily on the basis of monetary factors."

To those who fear that continued increases in the supply of college graduates aspiring to professional and managerial jobs beyond the capacity of the economy to employ them will lead to unemployment and discontent, Bowen responds that denying a large part of the population the opportunity for personal development through higher education would be indefensible and would condemn people to "lives of relative ignorance." And, lastly, he categorizes the notion that "blue collar work is in some sense inappropriate for educated men and women" as "a carry-over from an obsolete and aristocratic conception of both work and higher education." Bowen's emphasis on the importance of the nonpecuniary aspects of higher education may be especially salutary in the face of a danger that colleges and universities will overreact to what may be a temporarily unfavorable job market by deemphasizing the values of a liberal education in favor of narrow vocationalism. We wish to thank the author and the Sloan Foundation for the privilege of issuing their report as part of the Carnegie Council's series of publications on higher education. Howard Bowen is better prepared to survey the overall consequences of higher education in the United States than anyone else. Were proof needed, this volume is ample evidence.

Clark Kerr
Chairman, Carnegie Council on Policy
Studies in Higher Education

Preface

Are our colleges and universities worth what they cost? For generations, the American people have thought so. The idea has been widely accepted that higher education produces benefits for individuals in the form of personal development, economic opportunity, rich satisfactions, and benefits for society in the form of political, economic, and cultural advancement. These benefits have seemed ample to justify the mounting costs, including substantial public and philanthropic subsidies. Higher education has traditionally been rationalized in broad philosophical terms, often expressed in the glowing rhetoric of commencement exercises and institutional brochures.

Recently, however, the public has become more skeptical toward higher education and other social institutions as well. Many argue that the huge and costly enterprise of higher education is overextended, that the value of its outcomes does not justify the amount of resources employed, and that public subsidies should be curtailed. There are insistent calls for "accountability," meaning intelligible reporting of specific outcomes as well as formal accounting for expenditures.

The new demand for accountability places the higher educational community in an awkward position. Many of the outcomes—perhaps the most important ones—are intangible and therefore not easily identified or measured. Further, since higher education is only one of myriad influences in the development of individuals and the progress of society, it is extraordinarily difficult to single out its distinctive effects. Yet educators cannot reasonably ignore the call for accountability. Society needs facts and reliable judgments about the outcomes of higher education. If educators cannot meet this need, decisions about the allocation of resources to higher education will be made on the basis of incomplete criteria that are biased toward the tangible, the quantifiable, and perhaps the irrelevant.

Current knowledge of the consequences of higher education is substantial and is found in a vast literature derived mainly from research and scholarship in psychology, sociology, education, philosophy, social criticism, and economics. The literature is generally fragmentary, scattered, and of uneven quality and beset with many inconsistencies and unresolved issues. Nevertheless, it includes some solid studies that offer a great deal of information and insight into the consequences of American higher education. Much inquiry into the field is now in progress and the methodology is steadily improving. As yet the results of this extensive research effort are not readily accessible to administrators, governing boards, legislators, faculty members, or the general public. One purpose of this book is to build a bridge linking the world of higher educational research to the world of higher educational policy.

The time has come to gather the scattered knowledge of the outcomes of higher education, to interpret and evaluate this knowledge, to raise methodological questions, to provide analysis where empirical data are weak, to judge whether American higher education is worth what it costs, and to suggest policies that may flow from the conclusions. These are the agenda of this book. I cannot claim that these ambitious agenda have been fully achieved. But I hope that systematic exploration of the outcomes of American higher education will illuminate its many impacts upon American society.

I gratefully acknowledge the support of the Alfred P. Sloan Foundation and the encouragement of its president, Nils Wessell, and its executive vice president, Robert Kreidler. In the early stages of the project I was greatly benefited by a residency at the Villa Serbelloni as a guest of the Rockefeller Foundation. The facilities of the College Student Personnel Abstracts at Claremont and of the Roper Public Opinion Research Center at

Williams College were extremely helpful. I cannot exaggerate the important contributions of my "collaborators" and good friends: Peter Clecak of the University of California, Irvine; Jacqueline Powers Doud of La Verne College; and Gordon K. Douglass of Pomona College. Jacqueline Powers Doud prepared a doctoral dissertation in connection with the study, and all three made substantial contributions to the manuscript and were of enormous help as critics. (Copies of the dissertation, *An Inquiry into the Effects of a College Education on Attitudes, Competencies, and Behavior of Individuals,* by Jacqueline Powers Doud [Claremont Graduate School, 1976, 239 pp.], will be sent postpaid on request prior to December 31, 1978, with remittance of $5.00 paid in advance to Howard R. Bowen, Claremont Graduate School, Claremont, California 91711.) Jeannemarie Solak, a student at Claremont Graduate School, was helpful and astute in searching out data and in providing helpful criticisms. Special thanks go to Dorothy Pearson, executive secretary in my office, who helped to facilitate the project in a thousand ways, and to Janet Tanner for her skillful assistance in the manuscript preparation. Finally, I would acknowledge the helpful reviews of the manuscript made by Suzanne Estler, JB Lon Hefferlin, Paul Heist, Joseph B. Platt, Lewis C. Solmon, William Wadman, and by my son, Thomas G. Bowen.

Anyone who considers the outcomes of higher education for individual students is deeply indebted to several authors who have systematically assembled, summarized, and interpreted large portions of the scattered data. Above all, Kenneth A. Feldman and Theodore M. Newcomb in their monumental two-volume work, *The Impact of College on Students* (1969), have provided a solid base on which every worker in the field must build. In preparing that work, the two authors reviewed over 1,500 separate studies and summarized the results of many of them. Other basic sources of information are Nevitt Sanford (Ed.), *The American College* (1962); James W. Trent and Leland L. Medsker, *Beyond High School* (1968); Joe L. Spaeth and Andrew M. Greeley, *Recent Alumni and Higher Education* (1970); Stephen B. Withey and Associates, *A Degree and What Else?* (1971); Burton R. Clark, Paul Heist, T. R. McConnell,

Martin A. Trow, and George Yonge, *Students and Colleges: Interaction and Change* (1972); Lewis C. Solmon and Paul Taubman (Eds.), *Does College Matter?* (1973); F. Thomas Juster (Ed.), *Education, Income, and Human Behavior* (1975); Herbert H. Hyman, Charles R. Wright, and John Shelton Reed, *The Enduring Effects of College* (1975), and the many studies of Alexander W. Astin and his colleagues.

I am equally indebted to the pioneering economic studies of Theodore W. Schultz and Gary Becker; numerous studies sponsored by the Carnegie Commission on Higher Education; the remarkable bibliography prepared by Oscar T. Lenning, Leo M. Munday, O. Bernard Johnson, A. R. Vander Well, and Eldon J. Brue of the American College Testing Program (1974); and the illuminating studies of Arthur W. Chickering, Joseph Katz, and C. Robert Pace. Even though this list of important contributors to the field could be extended, I would be remiss in failing to acknowledge special indebtedness to these particular scholars and organizations.

I absolve all of these persons from responsibility for the faults of the book, yet I cannot deny that they were deeply implicated.

Claremont, California   Howard R. Bowen
July 1977

The Author

Howard R. Bowen is a native of Spokane, Washington. He attended Washington State University, received his Ph.D. in economics from the University of Iowa (1935), and was a postdoctoral student at Cambridge University and the London School of Economics (1937-38). He is an economist who in recent years has specialized in the economics of higher education.

His career has included service in business, government, and higher education. He was chief economist of the Joint Committee on Internal Revenue Taxation of the U.S. Congress (1942-1945) and economist of the Irving Trust Company, a Wall Street bank (1945-1947). He has taught at the University of Iowa, Williams College, and Claremont Graduate School. He served as Dean of the Business School at the University of Illinois and as president or chancellor of three institutions: Grinnell College (1955-1964), the University of Iowa (1964-1969), and Claremont University Center (1970-1974). Since resigning from the chancellorship at Claremont in 1974, he has been R. Stanton Avery Professor of Economics and Education at Claremont Graduate School.

He has served on the boards of many organizations and is currently a director or trustee of Grinnell College, Claremont University Center, Bankers Life Company, Teachers Insurance and Annuity Association, National Planning Association, Higher Education Research Institute, and *The Journal of Higher Education*. He has been president of the American Finance Association, the American Association for Higher Education, and the Western Economic Association and chairman of the National Citizens' Committee for Tax Revision and Reduction (1963) and of the National Commission on Technology, Automation, and Economic Progress. He has been a member of foreign missions to Japan, Thailand, and Yugoslavia. He has received numerous honorary degrees and awards, including special awards for educational leadership presented by the National Council of Independent Colleges and Universities, the New York Association of Colleges and Universities, and *Change* magazine.

Howard Bowen is the author or co-author of nine books and many articles and pamphlets. Among the books are *Toward Social Economy* (1948, reprinted 1977), *Social Responsibilities of the Businessman* (1953), *Graduate Education in Economics* (1954), *Automation and Economic Progress* (1966), *The Finance of Higher Education* (1969), and *Efficiency in Liberal Education* (1971). He is currently engaged in a three-year study of the costs of higher education, which is a sequel to the study reported in this book.

INVESTMENT IN LEARNING

*The Individual
and Social Value
of American Higher Education*

A REPORT PREPARED WITH THE SUPPORT
OF THE SLOAN FOUNDATION
AND ISSUED BY THE CARNEGIE COUNCIL
ON POLICY STUDIES IN HIGHER EDUCATION

Part One

The Setting

The two chapters of Part One serve as an introduction to later chapters that analyze the consequences of American higher education in detail. Chapter One describes the functions of the higher educational system, applies to it the idea of efficiency as a ratio between outcomes produced and resources employed, and considers methodological issues relating to the study of outcomes. Chapter Two examines the goals or intended outcomes of higher education and concludes with a catalogue of specific goals. This catalogue is regarded as a list of hypotheses about the outcomes of higher education. The remainder of the book investigates the degree to which each goal is in fact achieved.

1

Efficiency
and Accountability
in Higher Education

*If you think education is expensive,
try ignorance.*

Ann Landers

In 1977, American higher education was carried on in about 3,000 institutions, which employed a full-time equivalent instructional staff of about 500,000 persons and an additional 800,000 or more other workers. They served 11.3 million students; about 6.8 million were full-time. They spent annually about $42 billion for operating purposes and another $4 billion for capital improvements, or a total of $46 billion. To this cost must be added the forgone income (Bowen and Servelle, 1972, pp. 31-32; Carnegie Commission, 1973a, pp. 49-53) of the full-time students, which amounted to perhaps $34 billion and their transportation, books, and miscellaneous expenses of perhaps $4 to $5 billion. The grand total of all these institutional and student costs was around $85 billion, an amount equal to 5 percent of the GNP or nearly equal to the annual national defense outlays.

When an industry reaches such financial magnitude, many

people are bound to ask whether the outcomes are worth the cost. Today, this question is being asked with some insistence, not only by the general public, legislators, donors, and parents but also by students and even by educators themselves. This does not imply that higher education has lost the confidence of the public. As shown in many polls, it consistently ranks near the top in public confidence among major social institutions (Harris, 1974; Citicorp, 1975; U.S. Department of HEW, National Center for Education Statistics, 1976, p. 205; Procter and Gamble, 1976). Nevertheless, as people consider the state of our society, they are well aware that higher education has not yet brought on the millennium. America seemingly has not achieved the depth of learning, the richness of culture, the moral tone, the refinement of taste, the rise of economic productivity, the spread of responsible and enlightened citizenship, or the domestic tranquility that educators in their glowing rhetoric had promised. Ignorance appears to be rampant, values seem crassly materialistic, and wisdom is not equal to proliferating social problems. Moreover, especially since the student unrest of the 1960s and the change in campus mores, certain of the outcomes of higher education have been regarded by some as negative. A more immediate and explicit recent criticism of higher education is that it is educating more people than the economy can absorb in the kinds of jobs customarily reserved for college-educated men and women. A favorite journalistic theme is the alleged inability of college graduates to get jobs, or the failure of higher education to prepare its graduates for the world of work. And many legislators and other public leaders express deep skepticism about the social and economic value of higher education. These doubts have been reinforced by a series of scholarly and critical books and articles with rather flamboyant titles, among them, Paul Goodman's *Compulsory Miseducation* (1964); Ivar Berg's *Education and Jobs: The Great Training Robbery* (1970); Ivan Illich's *Deschooling Society* (1972); Kenneth Arrow's "Higher Education as a Filter" (1973); Caroline Bird's *The Case Against College* (1975); James O'Toole's "The Reserve Army of the Underemployed" (1975); Lester Thurow's *Generating Inequality* (1975); and Richard

Freeman's *The Overeducated American* (1976). Without exception, beneath these sensational titles lie useful as well as provocative analyses and critiques (though we do not subscribe to them *in toto*). American higher education faces real problems and it can benefit from constructive criticism. However, the recent public discussion of higher education has been one-sided. It has focused attention on problems and weaknesses and minimized or ignored the strengths and undoubted contributions to American society. In the present state of public opinion, evidence of the benefits of higher education—not rhetorical flourishes—is being demanded. The burden of proof is on the educators. The fashionable words are "efficiency" and "accountability."

Those who wish to hold colleges and universities accountable demand that the outcomes of higher education be identified, measured in dollars, and then compared with the costs. Obviously they are asking a lot, for the outcomes are extraordinarily hard to isolate and measure. Yet, without some reasonably reliable methods of defining and assessing outcomes, all questions relating to the efficiency of higher education, all judgments about its progress, and all efforts toward rational allocation of resources to the higher educational system become futile.

This book responds to the demand for efficiency and accountability. Its purpose is to assemble information about the outcomes of higher education and to reach reasonable judgments as to the value of these outcomes in relation to their cost (see, for example, Rossi and Williams, 1972).

American Higher Education as a System

We have chosen in this book to consider the outcomes of American higher education taken as a whole and considered as a consolidated *system*. The consequences of higher education may, of course, be explored at various levels of aggregation. For example, one may consider the outcomes from the work of a particular professor or department; explore the effects of different modes of instruction; assess the results achieved by a particular college or university; evaluate the outcomes of a particular class of institutions, such as research universities or community colleges; or attempt to appraise the outcomes of the entire higher educational system (Archibald, in Lumsden, 1974). The study of outcomes at each level has its uses, and complete knowledge of the subject would require simultaneous investigation at all levels. We have chosen the widest possible scope. We propose to concentrate on the broad significance of the entire system of higher education to the people whose lives it touches and to society at large. This approach leaves out much detail, but it does have major advantages. It facilitates direct consideration of the broad *social* impact of higher education. It adduces knowledge useful in considering state and national policy for higher education. And it provides perspective for the evaluation of particular institutions. Though the study of the entire system cannot substitute for the study of the parts, it is an essential aspect of the whole complex process of evaluating higher education.

In considering higher education as a nationwide *system*, we do not mean to imply that it is a tightly organized and monolithic structure. Institutions differ considerably in size, types of services rendered, sponsorship, and other characteristics. They range from two-year community colleges to major research universities and from tiny liberal arts colleges to great state colleges of 20,000 to 40,000 students. Their governance is widely diffused among independent private boards and quasi-independent public boards. There is much room for autonomy and variety. Nevertheless, American higher education is a *system* of considerable homogeneity. All the institutions are subject to varying degrees of control or influence by state governments, by various public coordinating agencies, and by the federal government. All of the institutions offer more or less comparable undergraduate instruction. They differ chiefly in the degree to which they are engaged in graduate and professional instruction, research, scholarship, artistic pursuits, and various public services. There is a well-established pattern of role models: Each institution tends to aspire to the status of the next higher institutions in the pecking order. Moreover, most faculty members bear the stamp of a graduate education dispensed by a few dozen leading universities. The institutions employ strikingly similar facilities and methods: The basic apparatus of libraries, laboratories,

studios, counselors, campus life, teaching methods, and curricula do not vary greatly over much of the system. Allowing
for differences in size, the campuses even look surprisingly
alike. The system of higher education is also held together by an
elaborate communications network consisting of voluntary
accreditation, professional associations, public licensing bodies,
statewide coordination, consortia, journals, innumerable academic meetings, easy mobility of students and faculty among
institutions, categorical grants from government and foundations, and commonality of interest in their relations with government. Finally, the many institutions are interlocked and
interdependent through a division of pedagogical and disciplinary labor that frees each institution from the responsibility
of trying to meet all conceivable educational and research needs
(Cremin, 1965, pp. 103-104).

Chapter Eight of this book is devoted to an exploration of
the differences and similarities of outcomes among diverse types
of institutions. As shown there, differences exist and are worth
investigating, but the differences are overshadowed by the similarities. The colleges and universities of the United States are
indeed a coherent system, not a disparate collection of unrelated enterprises and activities, and it is by no means absurd
to consider the outcomes of the system of American higher education as a whole. Indeed, a frequent criticism of American
higher education is that it is too standardized to meet the needs
of its diverse clientele.

Functions of Higher Education

Before exploring the outcomes of higher education, it may be
well to consider the higher educational system as an industry. It
is an industry that has, over time, acquired certain well-defined
functions. In performing these functions, it engages in "production." As in other industries, production in higher education
uses resources, which are transformed into end products called
outcomes. The efficiency of the system is measured by comparing the outcomes with the resources employed. And accountability is achieved when the outcomes, as well as the resources
used, are identified and measured.

American higher education engages in three principal functions: education, research, and public service. Education as here defined includes both the curricular and extracurricular influences on students. Its purpose is to change students in both the cognitive and affective aspects of their personalities and to prepare them for practical affairs. Research, broadly defined, includes the scholarly, scientific, philosophical, and critical activities of colleges and universities, as well as their creative contributions to the arts. The purpose of research is to preserve, acquire, disseminate, interpret, and apply knowledge, and to cultivate creative frontiers in arts and sciences. The clientele includes students, professional peers, various groups (such as government, business, farmers, labor unions, professional practitioners), and the general public. The public service activities include health care, consulting, off-campus lectures and courses, work performed by interns, artistic performances and exhibits, spectator sports, and so on.

The three functions of higher education are based mostly on a single unifying process—*learning. Learning,* in this sense, means knowing and interpreting the known (scholarship and criticism), discovering the new (research and related activities), and bringing about desired change in the cognitive and affective traits and characteristics of human beings (education). Learning is the chief stock-in-trade of higher education. It occurs in many subjects, it takes place in diverse settings, and it serves varied clienteles. As will be indicated later, learning yields important by-products that must be considered in judging the total outcomes of higher education.

Institutions tend to be categorized largely on the basis of their relative emphasis on the three functions of higher education. Community colleges focus on existing knowledge and dissemination through instruction; major universities emphasize new knowledge and dissemination to the professions and to the public. Other institutions, such as liberal arts colleges and four-year state colleges, lie between these extremes. But most institutions of all types engage in all three functions to some degree.

This multifunctional role of a college or university may be illustrated by the work of a typical faculty member. In a given week he or she may teach several classes, advise a graduate student on a research project, counsel with an undergraduate on a personal problem, discuss an intellectual issue with a colleague, invite a group of students to a social affair, write testimony for a legislative committee, give a talk to a local professional society, read a professional journal, record data from a laboratory experiment in progress, and block out a chapter in a new book. These varied activities represent efforts to learn the known and discover the new and to disseminate knowledge to students, the profession, and the general public. In the same way, an institution's administrative and supporting staff and its buildings and equipment are allocable (in principle) to the three functions.

Not only are the three functions of education, research, and public service carried on jointly; they are often mutually supportive. Education may be enriched if it occurs in an environment of discovery, intellectual excitement, and contact with the real world and its problems. Similarly, research and public service may be enhanced when they are combined with instruction. This does not imply that every community college or liberal arts college should become a great research center. Nor does it deny that universities can overdo research and service to the neglect of instruction. It implies only that the spirit of inquiry and public service enriches academic enterprise and lends coherence and unity to the American system of higher education.[1]

Production in Higher Education

In performing its three functions of education, research, and public service, higher education is engaged in the *production* of learning. The production of any good or service—for example,

---

[1] Several other formulations of the functions of higher education are of interest. Kaysen (1969, pp. 5-8) cites the following functions: (1) creation of new knowledge; (2) transmission of knowledge to the new generation; (3) application of knowledge to the solution of practical problems in the wider society; and (4) socialization of late adolescents and young adults. Ladd and Lipset (1975, pp. 10-11) suggest these functions: (1) socialization in the sense of the transmission of traditional values; (2) innovation and scholarship; and (3) community service. Johnson (in Lumsden, 1974, pp. 21-23) refers to: (1) a symbol and repository of civilization; (2) a home for research; (3) a place of information storage; and (4) a center for the teaching of young adults.

bread, gasoline, or medical care—requires valuable resources, consisting partly of various kinds of labor, capital, and land, and partly of goods and services purchased from other industries. Like all other producing entities, colleges and universities have management groups that decide on the types and amounts of production, on the types and amounts of needed resources, and on the way these resources are to be organized. Learning emerges from this productive process, to be available for consumption (or for use in production elsewhere).

The productive process may be regarded as the *transformation* of resources into goods and services, in this case, learning. The quantity and quality of the goods or service produced are determined by the amounts and kinds of resources used and by the way they are used. For convenience, the resources are often referred to as *inputs*, the goods or services produced as *outputs*, and the way they are used and organized as *technology*. The theory of production consists of the laws or principles determining the relationship between inputs and outputs as mediated by technology.

The production of a particular good or service (or family of similar goods and services) is seldom concentrated in a single firm. Rather, it is carried on in several or many firms referred to collectively as an industry. The separate decisions of the firms determine the organization of an industry as to size, number, and location of productive units. In reaching its decisions, each firm is influenced by the cost of available resources, by the known technological options, and by the prospective prices and sales potential for the outputs, taking into account the competition of other firms. As a result of all these decisions within any industry, particular resources are employed in given amounts and particular products are produced in given amounts. These products may be uniform in type or quality, or they may be varied as to intrinsic characteristics, appearance, packaging, and so on. They may be produced at different costs, they may appeal to different consumers, and they may sell for different prices. They are, however, close substitutes.

Higher education produces only a small part of all human learning (Machlup, 1962). Learning is ubiquitous and incessant. Virtually all of the experiences of life result in some of it.

Indeed, it is hard to spend a single day without adding to our knowledge through current events, casual conversations, reading, watching TV, reflective thought, and so on. The family, the elementary and secondary school, the neighborhood, the workplace, the mass media of communications, the church, the armed services, the shopping center, the cocktail party, and the conference with one's lawyer or physician are all, in a sense, educational institutions. Although higher education is only one source of learning among many, it successfully competes for resources because it provides most of the personnel to the other educational media and much of the knowledge and ideas transmitted by them.

Each college or university employs resources in the form of labor, land, durable capital, and nondurable services and supplies purchased from other industries. The labor includes the services of paid faculty, administrative officers, and supporting personnel. It also includes the valuable but uncompensated time and energy of students and of volunteer workers (for example, trustees). The land and durable capital consists of campus, buildings, and equipment. The nondurable services and supplies include legal advice, auditing, artistic performances, fuel, stationery, books, chemicals, and so on. All of these resources are deployed within a unified organization to "produce" learning through instruction, research, and public service. In this way, higher education "transforms" resources into the desired product.

Each institution, as it evolves over time, adjusts to changing conditions in the markets for the resources it employs and in the markets for its products. The adjustments are sometimes initiated from within the institution and sometimes dictated from without. For whatever reason, choices must be made about the kind, quality, and quantity of products or outcomes to be produced, and about the technologies or methods of production to be employed.[2] These choices are made partly on the

---

[2] The technologies in higher education include administrative organization, admissions procedures and policies, curricula, degree requirements, methods of instruction and research, kinds of equipment in use, work loads, rules, general "atmosphere" of the campus, and so on.

basis of the labor, land, and capital it already employs and partly on the basis of conditions in the market for resources—the terms on which additional land and capital can be obtained, the expected rates of salaries and wages, and the expected prices of purchased supplies. And these choices are made partly on the basis of market conditions—the "market" including students and others who pay tuitions and fees, governmental agencies that contribute appropriations and grants, private donors who make current gifts, and the institution itself, insofar as it has endowments from which current income flows. Interestingly, students are both a part of the market (since they contribute funds for the support of higher education) and also part of the resources employed in the production of educational services (since their time is an essential ingredient of the productive process).

Each college or university competes for resources with other institutions of higher education and with all other industries as well. Each institution, therefore, seeks for itself a suitable niche in the higher educational industry. It strives to provide that particular range and quality of services and to serve that particular clientele for which it can obtain the necessary resources. In general, colleges and universities aspire to serve society, to attain prestige, and to achieve institutional stability and security. They try to position themselves accordingly. The striving of institutions for useful and secure places in the competitive arena determines their distribution by size, geographic location, clientele, and programs. From this competitive process emerges the collection of 3,000 varied institutions that we know as the higher educational system (Van den Haag, 1956).

Learning, the chief product of higher education, consists primarily of changes in people—changes in their knowledge, their characteristics, and their behavior. Production in higher education, then, is not the transformation of resources into tangible products; rather, it is the transformation of resources into desired intangible qualities of human beings. Another way to approach the definition of outcomes is to assume that the institution should provide only adequate faculties, facilities, programs, and services—a suitable environment—and that students should use this environment for the purpose of "getting an education." On this assumption, the environment represents the final output for the institution and an input for the students (along with their time). In this formulation, the institution provides opportunity; the students avail themselves of the opportunity. Though this way of looking at outcomes has advantages, we have chosen to relate the institutional environment to ultimate outcomes on the ground that the institution has the responsibility to lead and motivate students actively, not merely to offer passively an environment that students may take or leave.

A college or university achieves its production through creating an environment calculated to bring about desired change in people—what Bloom (1975, p. 18) refers to as "growth-inducing climates." The environment of a college or university consists of several closely interrelated parts. It is an aggregation of land, building, equipment, and supplies, and a population of students, faculty, staff, and governing groups. The physical plant and the people are what one sees on a visit to a campus. The unseen environment is a *culture*. This culture consists in part of the prevailing technologies (or ways of doing things), such as administrative organization, degree requirements, curricula, methods of instruction and research, work loads, rules, rewards and penalties, extracurricular opportunities, and so on. The culture also includes the common values, expectations, standards, assumptions, traditions, general "atmosphere," and behavior patterns of the people involved.

The people and the culture are related in complex ways. For example, each student brings to his college or university a unique set of interests and traits. He interacts with his fellow students, exerting influence upon them and they upon him. Through such interplay, a student subculture evolves that becomes an influential source of change for all the individuals who are inducted into it. Thus, paradoxically, students are not only the objects of the educational process but also an important part of the environment in which instruction takes place. Similarly, individual faculty and staff members bring to an institution their unique interests and traits. Individually and collectively they create a subculture that influences their own members and also their students. The sum of the various subcultures, including the interactions among them, becomes a total campus culture.

Culture formation within a college or university tends to be partly spontaneous or self-propelled—especially so because higher education by its very nature calls for considerable latitude in thought, expression, and behavior. The campus culture is seldom tightly under the control of administrative and governing bodies, though it may be guided through charismatic leadership, legislated rewards and penalties, and selection of students and faculty.

Similarly, the environment is designed to facilitate and encourage the intellectual and research activities of the faculty as they preserve and advance knowledge, cultivate the arts, and serve the public.

Through the three major functions of instruction, research, and public service, the institution hopes to influence students, faculty, and members of the public to help set these people on a course of continuing and desirable activity and, through them, to achieve broad social and cultural advancement of the entire society.

The outcomes of instruction are not likely to be the same for all students. Each student brings to the campus environment a particular background of biological, psychological, and emotional traits and needs, and a special set of experiences.[3] He is a unique personality. The effect of any given institutional environment may be quite different for students of differing entering personalities. Moreover, each institution is unique and has a special environmental "press" that is "found in the characteristic pressures, stresses, and conformity-demanding influences of the college culture" (Pace, 1957, p. 4). Thus, the outcomes for different students in the same institution may be different, and the outcomes for comparable students in different institutions also may be different. (On differences among institutions, see Chapter Eight.)

[3] Fägerlind (1975, pp. 33-39) refers to the transformation of early childhood resources into adult outcomes.

The environment may be regarded as a source of opportunities, not specific objectives forced upon people but rather options that people may freely accept and respond to in different ways. Though colleges are often justly criticized for being conformist, ideally—and to a considerable degree in practice—they are places of stirring, catalysts to help people find their unique ways, not rigidly patterned communities designed to produce programed outcomes. The purpose of college is not to cast all persons in an identical mold, but to give each the chance to work out his or her destiny within an environment that encourages certain broad general outcomes, or certain ranges of outcomes. As Keniston and Gerzon have said (1972, p. 52), "there are as many kinds of higher education as there are student-institution pairs: 8,000,000 students times 2,500 institutions equals approximately 20 billion different potential educational experiences in America today."

The interaction between the environment and the student is affected by the practices through which institutions admit students and students choose institutions. Each institution selects those who will be admitted as students, those who will be allowed to remain, and those who will be given credits, degrees, and other credentials. Each institution also sets the terms on which instruction will be available by deciding on the programs to be offered, the academic schedule, the location at which instruction takes place, tuitions and other fees, and student aid. Institutions are often controlled or influenced in all of these matters by law, administrative rules of government, custom, and financial expediency. Decisions on these matters determine which persons will be excluded from the higher educational system altogether. In the selection of its students, most institutions encourage the enrollment of those whose traits will be compatible with the programs and purposes of the institution. Correspondingly, most students seek out the institutions that offer programs and opportunities compatible with their backgrounds and interests. Through this double selection process, at least some congruity is achieved between the characteristics of institutions and the characteristics of their students. The tendency toward compatibility, present in all institutions to some degree, leads to stratification of institutions according

to social class and academic ability. It facilitates mutual adjustment and the avoidance of sharp incompatibilities. Some studies
suggest that higher congruity contributes to a positive influence
on students. Others conclude that institutional impact is
favored by the shock of incongruity. Perhaps both are true in
different situations and for different people.

As in the case of instruction, the outcomes of research and
public service are determined primarily by the interaction of the
institutional environment with the characteristics of faculty.
Each faculty member brings to the environment a particular
background of traits, interests, and experience. Each institution
provides particular values, facilities, incentives, and expectations.
This interaction generates outputs of research, scholarship, criticism, artistic creativeness, and services to the public. The outputs are not wholly programmed but flow partly from the activities of unique people operating within a particular environment.
The role of institutional leadership lies in selecting faculty and
influencing the character of the values, incentives, and facilities
present in the environment.

The chief products of higher education, learning in all its
manifestations, consists primarily of changes in people—changes
in their knowledge, their characteristics, and their behavior.
These changes are generated in the first instance by instruction,
research, and public service. But learning may set in motion a
dynamic process leading to further changes in people and also
to broad social changes. For example, it may lead to lifelong
personal development of college alumni, it may affect the lives
of the descendants of alumni, it may induce broad social and
cultural change affecting all people (including those who have
never been in direct contact with higher education), and it may
generate such by-products as choice of career and direct satisfactions and enjoyment during the college years and later. And
these in turn generate still further individual and social changes.
Higher education is part of a dynamic process that may extend
far into the future, bringing about consequences that no one
can predict. Table 1 presents a schematic outline tracing the
productive process in higher education from resources to environment to immediate outcomes to future effects on society to
further changes generated by these future outcomes. (For other

Table 1. Schematic description of the productive process
in higher education

RESOURCES
(Labor, Land, Capital, Purchased Services, and Supplies)
↓
are transformed into
↓
ACADEMIC ENVIRONMENTS
(Physical, Human, Cultural)
↓
which produce
↓

(a) IMMEDIATE AND INDUCED FUTURE CHANGES IN STUDENTS
(Cognitive Learning, Emotional and Moral Development, Practical
Competence)

(b) BY-PRODUCTS FOR STUDENTS
(Career Placement, Direct Satisfactions, Lifetime Satisfactions)

(c) SECONDARY BENEFITS AND SATISFACTIONS ACCRUING TO
RELATIVES, ASSOCIATES, AND OFFSPRING OF STUDENTS

(d) IMMEDIATE AND INDUCED FUTURE CHANGES IN KNOWL-
EDGE AND THE ARTS

(e) DIRECT SERVICES TO THE PUBLIC
↓
which produce
↓

CHANGES IN SOCIETY
(Improved Performance of Government, the Economy, and other
Social Institutions, Human Equality and Freedom, Amelioration of
Social Problems, Improved General Quality of Life)
↓
which in turn give rise to
↓

FURTHER CHANGES IN INDIVIDUALS
(including those of Future Generations)
AND SOCIETY

"models" of production in higher education, see Astin, in Bowen,
1974a, pp. 23-33; Clark and others, 1972, p. 14; Micek and Wallhaus, 1973, pp. 5-22; Walsh, 1973; Weisbrod, 1966, p. 268.)

Efficiency

In asking whether American higher education is worth what it costs, we are really asking: Has the American higher educational system become a ponderous, bloated, wasteful enterprise, expanded out of all proportion to the genuine returns it yields, or is it an undernourished enterprise that produces outcomes of far greater value than the resources it uses? These are questions about the *efficiency* of the higher educational system, so it may be worthwhile to consider briefly the concept of efficiency.

The degree of efficiency in any activity is commonly measured, or judged, by comparing the resources used and the outcomes or benefits achieved. The greater the benefits with given resources, or the fewer the resources with given benefits, the greater the efficiency. Such comparisons are commonly expressed as ratios, using pairs of words like *resource-outcomes, input-output, cost-revenue, cost-effectiveness,* or *cost-benefit.* Regardless of the terminology, the underlying concept is that the use of resources involves a *cost* and that the results should be at least commensurate with that cost. The cost is in the form of sacrificed alternatives. When resources are committed to any given end, the cost consists of the sacrifice of the best alternative end to which the resources might have been committed. Comparisons between different uses of the same resources are aptly expressed by the common word *trade-off*, which implies that before committing resources to any one end, the possible benefits of applying the same resources to one or more alternative ends must be considered. Thus, for higher education the degree of efficiency is judged by comparing the outcomes (at the margin) with the outcomes that might have been realized if the same resources had been employed for other purposes, such as personal consumption, health services, or national defense. To decide whether the higher educational system should be maintained, expanded, or contracted, one must judge whether greater outcomes could be attained by transferring resources into higher education or out of it.

The idea of efficiency may be illustrated by a homely example. If the object is to heat a house, one part of the efficiency problem is to decide on *quantity*—in this case, the temperature to be maintained and possibly the number of rooms to be heated. A temperature of 80° throughout the house will require more fuel and therefore more money cost than 65° throughout the house or 80° in part of the house. The lower the temperature or the fewer the rooms heated, the more income the householder will have left over for food, clothing, recreation, and other ends. The higher the temperature or the more rooms heated, the less income will be available for other purposes. To make his income go as far as possible, the householder will set the temperature and number of rooms heated at a level such that the last dollar spent on heating will yield as much benefit as the last dollar spent on food, clothing, or recreation. He also may be interested in the *quality* of the heating, for example, stability of temperature, desirable humidity, freedom from drafts, and quietness. Again, he will make expenditures for quality up to the point that the last dollar spent for this purpose will yield as much benefit as the final dollars for other purposes. When the householder has decided on quantity and quality, efficiency will require that these goals be attained at the least possible cost. He will then be led to consider the design and orientation of his house, insulation, type of fuel, and type of heating system. Moreover, if he succeeds in heating his house with high efficiency and low cost, he may decide he can afford to raise the temperature, to heat more rooms, or to improve quality. He finally achieves maximum efficiency when the ends (temperature, number of rooms heated, and quality) and the means (heating system and house design) are so adjusted that the last dollar he spends for heating yields as much benefit as the last dollar spent for other purposes. Relative benefits from alternative uses of resources are estimated through the householder's best judgment. There are no ready-made formulas to guide him in making these judgments.

The idea of efficiency for the American system of higher education is not so different from that for heating a house. In both cases, the problem is one of deciding to what extent and at what quality a benefit shall be achieved and how resources shall be deployed to attain that benefit. However, higher education is a social good with consequences for the larger social "household." The benefits may be available to millions of persons but not necessarily on equal terms to all. The benefits may be valued differently by different persons, and the costs may be financed to some extent through involuntary taxation. Under these conditions, the decision making takes on a political dimension and inevitably involves compromises among individuals.

Aside from the necessity of compromise, another problem in considering efficiency in higher education is that neither the costs nor the outcomes can be measured precisely in dollars. The costs for capital, labor, and purchased supplies and services can be so measured, but the time of students, the various inconveniences borne by students and their families, and the time of volunteer workers can only be roughly estimated. The benefits to society in the form of learning derived from education, research, and public service could conceivably be sold in the market and measured in dollars. But higher education is almost universally dispensed at prices set arbitrarily and far below cost; these prices do not reflect the value of the resources employed. Under these circumstances, the efficiency problem becomes one of judgmental comparisons of costs and outcomes rather than precise comparisons of easily measurable dollar amounts.

The idea of efficiency, however, is not confined to values that are measured in money or traded in a market. It applies wherever ends are sought, whether these ends be mundane consumer goods such as bread and gasoline, broad social goals such as national defense or crime abatement, or lofty individual goals such as personal serenity, artistic appreciation, or humane learning. As Fritz Machlup has said (in Solmon and Taubman, 1973, p. 361), "Choices must be made among all sorts of alternatives, and the gratification of cultural desires—music and art, beauty and truth, peace and justice—is not outside economic considerations. We cannot measure such benefits, but we cannot help evaluating them as long as they do not fall like manna from heaven."

In popular discussions of efficiency in higher education, two fallacies frequently recur. The critics of higher education often judge efficiency only in relation to cost, by assuming that lower cost is preferable to higher cost; for example, an institution that can educate a student for $2,000 a year is adjudged more efficient than one that expends $3,000 per student. Clearly, the question of efficiency can be answered only when something is known about the outcomes. The second error, common to educators, is to judge efficiency only in relation to outcomes by assuming that improved outcomes are desirable regardless of cost. Both of these approaches fail to recognize that efficiency is a relationship between two variables, cost and outcome. On the one hand, to cut costs would not be efficient if the outcomes sacrificed were more valuable than the product of the saved resources in another use. On the other hand, to add to cost could not be efficient if the outcomes added were less valuable than the benefits the added resources would yield in another use. Higher education has no claim on resources for minor gains in outcomes at the expense of major sacrifices of other goods. In assessing the efficiency of higher education (or any other purposeful activity), one must consider both cost and result.

Are the Outcomes of Higher Education Ascertainable?

In this chapter we have pointed out that American higher education is a huge industry that annually costs an amount equal to about 5 percent of the GNP. We have outlined the functions of higher education, the productive process that goes on in our colleges and universities, and the nature of the final products or outcomes. We have considered the concept of efficiency in higher education as a relationship between the resources employed and the outcomes. And we have explored the idea of accountability, which relates to the responsibility of higher education to conduct its operations efficiently and to disclose both its costs and its outcomes. All of this was by way of background for the rest of the book, which is concerned almost solely with the outcomes. But before embarking upon the exploration of the actual outcomes of American higher education, it will be well to consider some of the difficulties and limitations connected with the study of outcomes.

The demand for efficiency and accountability is legitimate.

Higher education has a clear responsibility to operate efficiently and to report its costs and results to the American people in ways that transcend the tired rhetoric of commencement speeches and slick brochures. But the call for accountability cannot be satisfied if all the results of higher education must be reduced to neat quantitative terms, preferably with dollar signs attached. Higher education is concerned with matters of intellect, personality, and value that simply cannot be rigorously quantified or aggregated by adding up dollar amounts or computing rates of return. To evaluate the diverse outcomes of American higher education presents enormous conceptual and methodological difficulties. The outcomes are numerous, complexly interrelated, often subtle, sometimes unintended, unstable over time, difficult to substantiate, sometimes negative, and judged differently by different observers. Just as education itself is an art, so also is the evaluation of education. There is little chance that in this century a simple accounting scheme will be devised for the direct and reliable comparison of costs and outcomes, in the manner of a commercial profit and loss statement.[4]

That the problem cannot be reduced to a simple pecuniary calculus does not mean that it is insoluble or that human beings are incapable of dealing with it. In such matters of political and personal import as foreign policy, military strategy, taxation, investments, art, religion, marriage, medical practice, and even poker, human beings must reach decisions with incomplete and unreliable information. When we are prudent, we arrive at decisions by acquiring as much information or evidence as possible and then rely on informed judgment—a combination of sensitivity, insight, logical inference, and common sense. Perry (1970, p. x), in facing the methodological problems relating to his theory of human development, wrote: " . . . the scheme . . .

---

[4]For further discussion of the methodological issues see: Sanford, 1962, pp. 811-816; Feldman and Newcomb, 1973, Vol. 1, Chapter 3; Feldman, 1970; Hartnett, 1971; Withey, 1971, pp. 4-12; Bachman, 1972, p. 33; Astin, 1973, pp. 120-121; Astin, in Bowen, 1974a, pp. 23-46; Hyman and others, 1975, pp. 1-39; Trow, 1975, pp. 118-119; Powers, 1976, pp. 11-38.

may carry its own plausibility. Indeed, its essentials may on occasion seem to reveal only the inevitability of the obvious, in the sense of 'How could life be otherwise?' These feelings of recognition and plausibility must be honored; in most of life they are all one has to go on. But these feelings can be seductive of belief; they require the check of explicit limit and the balance of generous skepticism."

The styles of thought of our time, dominated as they are by natural sciences and technology, stress *measurement*. There is a tendency to rely on whatever quantitative data may be available—and to ignore or discredit other evidence, however pertinent it may be (H. Howe, 1975). Public officials, critics of education, and the general public fall easily into these habits of mind. So also do some economists and other social scientists. For example, in commenting on two papers on the social benefits of higher education, Freeman remarked (in Solmon and Taubman, 1973, p. 324), "alleged social benefits appear in various places in the two papers. . . . most sound plausible. In the absence of quantification, however, it is impossible to evaluate their potential significance or to determine whether they exceed or fall short of costs, on the margin. . . . the listing of possibly valid, possibly mythical benefits rapidly becomes sterile. For persons who believe that such benefits are important—or that on the margin they justify current or additional expenditures—it is incumbent to provide numerical estimates of what they amount to."

Admittedly it would be good to have complete and reliable quantitative data as a basis for decision making in all fields of human endeavor. Unfortunately the world is not so constituted, nor is it likely to be. Meanwhile decisions must be reached and accountability must be achieved on the basis of such evidence as can be mustered using reasonable judgment. As Aristotle said (*Nicomachean Ethics*, Book I, quoted in Ulich, 1968, p. 71), "It is the mark of an educated mind to expect that amount of exactness in each kind which the nature of the particular subject admits." Or, as Pace has said, "There is only so much one can learn by looking at an IBM card " (1972, p. 95).

The demand for quantitative information leads to exclusive concentration on such outcomes as monetary earnings of college graduates, changes in test scores on standardized tests, or, simply, number of students in attendance. The following introductory passage of an article on "Cost Functions for University Teaching" (Verry and Layard, 1975, p. 57) supplies a vivid example of the emptying out of content in the search for measurability:

> A fundamental problem involved in the estimation of university cost functions is the definition and measurement of output. Even though we concentrate on teaching and research outputs, ignoring universities' more intangible functions of preserving knowledge (rather than extending it), of providing a source of independent social comment and so on, we are forced to adopt second-best definitions. With regard to the teaching output, there are many characteristics of a graduate that are relevant. Some, such as cognitive skills and attitudes to change, mainly affect his capacities as a producer, while others mainly affect his capacities for enjoyable consumption. However, although we experimented with more ambitious measures we end up using the number of undergraduate and postgraduate student years (U, P) as proxies for undergraduate and postgraduate teaching outputs.

Information on enrollments, earning of graduates, test scores, and so on are surely part of the evidence on which the outcomes of higher education may be judged. A considerable amount of reliable quantitative information is available, and ongoing research constantly produces more of it. Nevertheless, we are a long way from adequate quantitative data expressing marginal benefits in dollars, as demanded by Freeman. Meanwhile, we must rely on our best judgment, disciplined by such evidence as we have. Learning—like liberty, equality, love, friendship, charity, and spirituality—carries qualitative connotations that defy numerical measurement. As Keniston and Gerzon (1972, p. 52) have observed:

To place primary emphasis on the monetary benefits of higher education does violence to the motives and hopes with which most students enter college, to the central effects of higher education, and to its most important benefits to the individual and society. . . . Discussions based on the technist conception ultimately strive for complex equations in which factors that cannot be quantified are deemed unreal, "subjective," and irrelevant—or simply ignored. The broader concept of rationality, in contrast, emphasizes those individual and social characteristics that do not readily lend themselves to quantification: human values, feelings, desires, loyalties, and motives; social cohesion, cooperation, and morale; political pluralism, tolerance, democracy, and diversity; and so on. Seen from this perspective, a calculus limited to dollars or to quantified social indicators is not rationality at all, but a constricted analysis which achieves rigor at the expense of truth.

Difficulty of quantification is by no means the only methodological pitfall inherent in the study of higher educational outcomes. A major problem is that higher education is only one of myriad influences upon the development of human beings. Each individual is shaped in part by his or her genetic endowment, socioeconomic background, elementary and secondary schooling, religious background, contact with the mass media, the normal process of maturation, and a multitude of life experiences. For example, it has been said that "most individuals will spend at least three times as much of their lives in contact with the mass media as in school " (Withey, 1971, p. 95). A book like this one could be written on the outcomes for human beings of any social institution or cluster of institutions, for example, the family, the school, the media, the church, the health care system, the arts, private business as employer, private business as marketer, the civil service, the military, and so on. These institutions have in common that they help shape human personality and influence human behavior patterns.

Higher education is just one species of a large and varied genus. To separate out the unique and specific effects of higher education with reliability borders on the impossible. Few if any studies achieve the control of extraneous variables necessary for definitive conclusions about the effects of higher education. As R. A. Fisher once wrote, "the authoritative assertion 'his controls are totally inadequate' must have temporarily discredited many a promising line of work." (Quoted in Hyman, Wright, and Reed, 1975, p. 24.) And in the words of Arnold Anderson, "Society consists of an intricate network of 0.5 correlations."

An egregious error in everyday appraisals of the outcomes of higher education is to assume that the characteristics and achievements of alumni are due solely or largely to their college experiences. It is not uncommon for colleges and universities blandly to take credit for the accomplishments of their graduates, whereas they can legitimately claim credit only for the *change* that occurred by reason of the college education. By far the most important determinant of the achievements of alumni is their characteristics when they were entering freshmen. Obscure colleges serving students of mediocre qualifications can, and some do, produce more change or value added than the most prestigious institutions with the most carefully selected student bodies (Upton, 1963).

Some of the effects of higher education inevitably occur only after a long time lag between cause and effect. For individuals, the outcomes of higher education are harvested over adult lifetimes averaging fifty to sixty years after graduation from college. For society the impacts may persist through centuries. Since the final outcomes cannot be known fully until many years have elapsed, the knowledge of outcomes at any given time is likely to refer to the state of higher education as it was a decade or a half-century ago and not as it is today. Further, higher education undoubtedly has a cumulative dynamic impact in the sense that the changes it brings about give rise to further changes. Changes in people wrought by education may influence the effects upon them of such later lifetime experiences as work, military service, family life, on-the-job training, or viewing television. Similarly, through its education and research, higher education may set in motion forces that produce cumulative dynamic social changes in the future. The impact of higher education may be relative to the social environment. The outcomes of a college education in the life and times of 2000 may be quite different from those in 1975 or 1925 or 1875. Conditions of life change by virtue of changes in technology, the labor market, social issues, values and morals, sex roles, race relations, personal interests, and life-styles. And these changes may alter both the individual and the social outcomes of higher education. Similarly, the impact of higher education may vary as colleges and universities change in response to changes in the social environment. Over time, existing institutions are modified with respect to the kinds of students admitted, overall size, curricula, teaching methods, characteristics of faculty, parietal rules, residential arrangements, and extracurricular life. Also, some of the new institutions that are established—community colleges, for example—differ markedly from traditional ones and probably alter subsequent outcomes (Withey, 1971; Clark and others, 1972).

Available studies on outcomes tend to be fragmentary, of uneven quality, and difficult to interpret. There are six principal kinds of studies: (1) investigations of changes in the achievements, personalities, attitudes, and behavior of students during the college years; (2) surveys of the views of students and alumni about their college experiences; (3) censuses, public opinion polls, and other explorations of attitudes, economic status, and behavior of adult respondents; (4) multiple regression studies for particular populations incorporating many variables and designed to sort out the separate impact of education on income, career choice, health, voting behavior, religion, and so on; (5) case histories of individuals; and (6) critical and analytical studies without empirical data. Though there are some remarkably well-conceived and ingenious studies, most suffer from defects. Some of the studies are out of date or limited to atypical single institutions. Some, for want of better data, use inappropriate statistics or rely on inadequate or biased samples. Some draw upon verbalizations of attitudes, opinions, and behavior that rely on uncertain memory and unreliable subjective

evaluations of respondents. Some use tests or survey instruments that are cruder than they purport to be. Some studies,
especially in the public opinion field, are inadequate because
the methods were chosen for purposes other than the study of
higher education. Finally, interpretations of results are questionable because the studies are not solidly based on widely
accepted theory about the causation of change during college.
For example, the theory of human development during late
adolescence and adulthood is not settled or well understood.
And the theory of the effect of various ingredients of the college experience (curricula, peer groups, residential arrangements, and so on) on outcomes is not well developed. Moreover,
the studies are influenced frequently by fashionable—and tran-
sient—personality theories. Thus, the findings of many studies
lack an established theoretical context that would impart coherent meaning to them (Trent and Medsker, 1968; Withey, 1971;
Clark and others, 1972).

The studies often concentrate on outcomes relating to the
accepted goals of higher education and may overlook side effects and unintended outcomes, some of which may be negative.

A final difficulty, to which we shall frequently allude in
this book (see Chapter Seven), is that most of the available
studies of change in students report their results in terms of
average change for large groups of students on particular dimensions of personality. For example, a study may show that, on
the average, students during college gained ten points on a scale
measuring intellectual interest, lost five points on a scale measuring religious interest, and made no change on a scale measuring political orientation. Each of the averages would conceal
wide variations among individual students. For example, some
students might have gained substantially, others might have lost
considerable ground, and some might have experienced little or
no change. Thus, enormously important changes might have
occurred in the lives of students as individuals, while the averages showed only mild impacts of college. A valid picture of the
effect of higher education calls for a consideration of what happens in the lives of whole individuals, not merely what happens

to average scores on particular dimensions of achievement or interest. Few studies are concerned with whole human beings; most are focused on averages relating to particular dimensions for large groups and thus obscure the true flux that is associated with the college experience.

A recital of these many difficulties hardly inspires confidence in any conclusions that may be reached in this book about outcomes of higher education. Indeed, a definitive treatment of the subject cannot be promised. Yet there is a wealth of evidence on the subject from many sources, and when this evidence is cumulated it leads to conclusions that can be advanced with considerable confidence. To assemble, criticize, interpret, and augment what is known or believed about outcomes is a useful undertaking. This is what we hope to do.

Our point of view, however, will be that of skeptic. We have no delusions of certainty. The substance of this section resembles the warning on a package of cigarettes. It implies that most studies on the outcomes of higher education, including this one, should be taken with caution. In the chapters ahead, we shall be careful to make no claims that cannot be substantiated and to separate evidence from opinion and to distinguish the known from the unknown. Our purpose is not to provide another vague rhetorical apologia for higher education, or to invent some magic formula for the measurement of outcomes, but to discover what can be said about actual results. In carrying out this purpose, we shall try to avoid the mistake of counting only those outcomes that can be measured. To meet the demand for accountability by trying to relate the numerically quantified worth of higher education to its dollar cost would be an impossible and largely irrelevant task. As Sar Levitan has said, "Statistics are no substitute for judgment."

Boundaries

To keep this inquiry within manageable bounds, some limitations have been adopted.

The study is concerned only with conventional not-for-profit four-year and two-year colleges and universities operated under public or private auspices. A large amount of higher (or postsecondary) education takes place outside conventional colleges and universities in proprietary schools, libraries, the armed services, business, labor unions, and independent study. These nontraditional types of education have much to be said for them. They are likely to grow in the future. Nevertheless, conventional colleges and universities are likely to remain the dominant centers of higher education—especially because the other parts of the "knowledge industry" depend heavily on colleges and universities for their personnel, ideas, books, and other educational materials.

Though most available knowledge of outcomes is related to undergraduate education, this study includes graduate and advanced professional instruction, research, and public service. All of these, produced jointly with undergraduate instruction, are obviously of great importance to the nation.

We do not deal with the question of how the costs of higher education should be financed. The funds are derived mostly from tuitions and fees, philanthropic gifts, endowment income, state and local taxes, and federal taxes. The attitudes of different persons about the relation between outcomes and costs will be affected by the amount of cost each is called upon to bear. For this reason, the way the costs are distributed will affect the judgment of the public and their representatives as to whether the outcomes justify the cost. In this study, we sidestep the matter of financing higher education by assuming that the cost will be distributed in a socially equitable manner. Our primary objective is to identify and evaluate the overall outcomes, to discover to the degree possible whether these outcomes taken as a whole are worth the cost, and to point out the broad implications for higher educational policy.

2

Goals:
The Intended Outcomes
of Higher Education

*Marx sought to change the world through
changing social institutions,
Jesus through changing the hearts of men.
Higher education tries to do both.*[1]

What do educators *hope* will be the results of their efforts? These hopes, though often inconsistent or unrealistic, are the intended outcomes; they are sufficiently esteemed and thought to be sufficiently achievable to qualify as goals (Rivlin, 1973). They are presumably guides to educational decision making and criteria by which actual outcomes can be judged. They are a useful starting point in a study of outcomes because they may be regarded as hypotheses about the consequences of higher education and they give guidance as to what to look for by way of actual outcomes. This starting point also has the advantage of

[1] This is an adaptation of a quotation for which we are unable to provide the source. It should be noted that Marx's third thesis on Feuerbach reads, "The materialist doctrine that men are products of circumstances and upbringing, and that, therefore, changed men are products of other circumstances and changed upbringing, forgets that it is men that change circumstances and that the educator himself needs educating."

permitting us to begin on familiar terrain. Though surprisingly little is known about outcomes, the goals of higher education have been considered since the time of Plato by philosophers, psychologists, sociologists, literary figures, social critics, and educators. Indeed, if the goals of higher education are defined as a list of desirable objectives, without priorities among them, there is even considerable agreement. As one reviews the literature of educational philosophy, the same goals appear time after time. It is sometimes asserted that higher education is virtually without coherent goals and can be described as "organized anarchy" (Breneman, 1974, pp. 5-6; Coleman in Kaysen, 1973, pp. 368-374; Cohen and March, 1974). In our view this position greatly overstates the case. Higher education does lack hierarchical organization and its goals are not as simple or unidimensional as profit maximization, but it nevertheless operates with a quite definite set of goals that command widespread assent.

The literature on the goals of higher education is vast. Some of it is in the great classics, some in the treatises of scholars, some in the writings of critics, and some in fugitive publications such as speeches, tracts, essays, college catalogues, institutional self-studies, and government documents. If, from this literature, a catalogue of widely accepted goals were compiled, it would be a kind of check list for use in the study of actual outcomes. Such a list would doubtless contain some goals that are not in fact achieved, and it might omit some unintended ones— especially negative outcomes. At the very least, however, the list would be a starting point in discovering the outcomes.

This chapter represents a systematic effort to identify widely accepted goals of higher education. Based on a sampling of the extensive literature on goals, it provides general discussion of some of the broader aims of higher education and concludes with a detailed catalogue of specific goals. This catalogue provides a useful taxonomy for considering the possible outcomes of higher education.

The goals included describe the final outputs of higher education, not intermediate or enabling objectives. For example, such objectives as increasing the financial support of higher education, raising the faculty-student ratios, modernizing buildings and equipment, improving curricula—objectives that loom large in the plans of educators—are regarded here not as final outputs but as means (Gross and Grambsch, 1974, pp. 43-74). The goals are related to the three main functions of higher education: education, research, and public service.

Goals for Individual Students Through Education

Education, or the teaching-learning function, is defined to embrace not only the formal academic curricula, classes, and laboratories but also all those influences upon students flowing from association with peers and faculty members and from the many and varied experiences of campus life. As we have observed, colleges and universities may be seen as environments exerting influence in many ways and not merely as formal academic programs having only intellectual goals. As Cardinal Newman (1958, p. 123) said: "When a multitude of young persons, keen, open-hearted, sympathetic, and observant, as young persons are, come together and freely mix with each other, they are sure to learn from one another, even if there be no one to teach them; the conversation of all is a series of lectures to each, and they gain for themselves new ideas and views, fresh matters of thought, and distinct principles for judging and acting, day by day."

Woodrow Wilson expressed the same idea when he was trying to change the campus life of Princeton (quoted in Trow, 1975, p. 270): "The real intellectual life of a body of undergraduates, if there be any, manifests itself not in the classroom, but in what they do and talk of and set before themselves as their favorite objects between classes and lectures." The detailed goals for education may be considered in the context of several widely accepted principles.

The whole person. Education should be directed toward the growth of the whole person through the cultivation not only of the intellect and of practical competence but also of the affective dispositions, including the moral, religious, emotional, social, and esthetic aspects of the personality. No theme runs more consistently through the goal literature. Plato (1974, p.

130) quoted Socrates, "And we shall begin by educating mind and character, shall we not?" Aristotle, however (Ulich, 1968, p. 65), was less positive on the matter. He said, "There are differences of opinion as to the proper tasks to be set; for all peoples do not agree as to the things that the young ought to learn, either with a view to virtue or with a view to the best life, nor is it clear whether their studies should be regulated more with regard to intellect or with regard to character . . . and it is not at all clear whether the pupils should practise pursuits that are practically useful, or morally edifying, or higher accomplishments." However, Aristotle went on to advocate attention to the intellect, the character, and practical competence.

In his essay "Literature and Science" (1927, p. 62), Matthew Arnold observed that "when we set ourselves to enumerate the powers which go to the building up of human life, and say that they are the power of conduct, the power of intellect and knowledge, the power of beauty, and the power of social life and manners, [we] can hardly deny that this scheme, though drawn in rough and plain lines enough, and not pretending to scientific exactness, does yet give a fairly true representation of the matter. Human nature is built up by these powers; we have the need for them all. When we have rightly met and adjusted the claims of them all, we shall then be in a fair way for getting soberness and righteousness, with wisdom." Nevitt Sanford (1969, p. 76) offers a contemporary restatement of Arnold's theme: "Our goal is to expand both the intellect and the area of motive and feeling, and to bring the two together in a larger whole."

Similarly, Donald Michael (1968, p. 109) argued that: "We must educate for empathy, compassion, trust, non-exploitiveness, non-manipulativeness, for self-growth and self-esteem, for tolerance of ambiguity, for acknowledgment of error, for patience, for suffering." And Keniston and Gerzon (1972, p. 53) suggested that: "The critical component of education . . . attempts to expose students to multiple and conflicting perspectives on themselves and their society in order to test and challenge their previously unexamined assumptions. It strives to create conditions which stimulate students' intellectual, moral, and emotional growth, so that they may ground their skills in a more mature, humane framework of values. Critical education deliberately tries to stimulate the student to reformulate his goals, his cognitive map of the world, the *way* he thinks, and his view of his role in society. Thus the more successful critical education is, the more difficult that success is to measure, for its aim is the transformation of persons and of the purposes to which they devote their knowledge." This idea is also expressed in such ubiquitous phrases as "intellectual and emotional maturity," "education of the whole person," "full development of personal capabilities," "individual fulfillment," and "education appropriate to the whole of man's nature" (Trent and Medsker, 1968, p. 14). Almost every commentator emphasizes that the goals of instruction transcend intellectual development, though many refer to a close interrelation between the affective side of human personality and academic learning. For example, Spaeth and Greeley (1970, pp. 174-175) concluded: "The cognitive dimension of the personality cannot face critical issues of life in a state of aloof disinterest . . . cognitive development is, in fact, a personality need. . . . the late adolescent developmental process can be helpful in facilitating intellectual development of the student." Similarly, Sanford and Katz stated (1966, p. 400), "We view as one of the chief goals of undergraduate education the application of rationality to the conduct of life. Mere exercise of cognitive skills is not enough." (See also McDaniel, 1976.)

A note of caution about "totalism" in the approach of colleges to students was recently sounded by the Carnegie Commission on Higher Education (1973c). In this matter, the commission struck an almost solitary dissenting chord in a chorus of advocacy for campus concern and responsibility for the "whole person." They wrote (pp. 16-17): "the campus cannot and should not try to take direct responsibility for the 'total' development of the student. That responsibility belongs primarily to the individual student by the time he goes to college . . . the college should particularly devote its attention to what it can do best and to what students cannot so well obtain anywhere else. The campus is, above all, a place where students can enrich their minds by study. 'Totalism' in the campus approach to students, we believe, is neither wise nor possible." However, the commission softened its stand by declaring (p. 16) that: "the college years are an important developmental period, and cognitive and affective activities are closely related to each other . . . the college does provide an important environment [for nonintellective personal development] ."

Spaeth and Greeley (1970, pp. 172-173) sounded a similar note of caution. They found that the American people "make rather stringent demands on the higher educational enterprise— parent, priest, psychiatrist, master craftsman, confidant, charismatic leader, prophet, social reformer—the college is expected to be all these. It is supposed to *do* something to the people who attend it. . . . It seems to us that it would be very desirable if a national consensus could be established that would not make as many demands of the college experience. We are not in agreement with those who argue that all we may expect of higher education is custody and screening, but neither are we willing to agree with those who think that it has failed if it does not produce lots of people with a degree of personal nobility never before seen on a mass basis. Somewhere between screening and ennobling, we suspect, can be found a series of goals for higher education that are both feasible and challenging."

Despite these demurrers, the overwhelming sentiment on the responsibility of higher education in the cognitive and affective domains was summarized by Alexander Heard (1973, p. 15): "Our first concern is the human intellect, but our ultimate concern is the human being. . . . The concern for personal development results from the need to be able to cope with those conditions of a technological society that led to the decline in the authority of other institutions. Involved are the development of standards of value, a sense of civic responsibility, the capacity for religious reconciliation, skills, understanding, a sense of purpose, and all the rest required to be a well-integrated person. The institution that can help its student become a better-integrated person, with a sense of command over his own destiny and a sense of how he fits into his complicated and mercurial social environment, will have achieved the most demanding and significant educational objective of our time."

Individuality. A second widely held principle is that education should take into account the uniqueness of individuals. It should help each person develop according to his particular characteristics and potentialities. It should be responsive to the reality that individuals vary in background, abilities, talents, aspirations, and age of readiness, and that a wide range of opportunities and options must be available if all are to be served well. As Cardinal Newman so eloquently remarked (1958, p. 122): "A university is, according to the usual designation, an Alma Mater, knowing her children one by one, not a foundry, or a mint, or a treadmill." A corollary to this principle is that higher education should seek out, develop, and certify talent that is sorely needed in a complex society of vast organizations, advanced technology, and sophisticated culture. Much remains to be learned, however, about the nature of talent.

Accessibility. A third principle is that higher education should be readily and widely accessible to persons of a broad range of abilities, circumstances, and ages. This represents a fairly recent extension of the older idea of equality of opportunity, which was usually based on a somewhat narrow conception of the content and purpose of higher education and on the assumption that only a limited number of persons could benefit from it. Today, most people agree that there should be not only easy access but positive encouragement to attendance through new kinds of institutions, new programs, substantial financial aid, guidance, special compensatory instruction, and so on. Husén (1974b, p. 143) has described this concept as the "quest for greater equality of life chances, coping power, and participation." Recently, even openness and equality of access have been declared by some to be obsolete, and demands are heard for equality of *results*, though it is usually acknowledged that equality of results and equality of opportunity are inherently incompatible.

    Given basic and perhaps ineradicable individual differences, equality of results appears to be an impossible goal, though disparities in results might be substantially narrowed. John Dewey, who emphasized the implications of education for democracy, proposed equality of *concern* as a practicable solution to the equality problem. He used the analogy of a family in which the children are loved and valued equally despite their quite different capacities and interests. The parents in such a family should be equally concerned for all of the children. But for the best development of each child, the family would not necessarily provide identical or even equal opportunities, and certainly would not expect the results to be equal. As Dewey put it (quoted in Hook, 1973, p. 75), "Moral equality means incommensurability, and inapplicability of common and quantitative standards. It means intrinsic qualities which require *unique* opportunities and differential manifestation." And again Dewey (1974, p. 295) wrote: "What the best and wisest parent wants for his own child, that must the community want for all of its children. Any other ideal for our schools is narrow and unlovely; acted upon, it destroys our democracy." More recently, Nevitt Sanford (1969, pp. 189-190) expressed a similar concept: "As we approach the challenge of universal higher education, we need to keep in mind that the poor, the culturally deprived, even the stupid are our own. In the absence of effective institutions for helping them, a society that cares for its own has no alternative to creating new institutions in which the child or young person who has low intelligence or is 'unmotivated' can be educated up to the level of his potential, which now is usually unknown."

Despite the ascendency of the principle of wide access, some educators express concern that higher education may be expanded only at the cost of educational and cultural excellence (Berman, 1975, pp. 3-11; Craig, 1974, pp. 143-147; Shils, 1975, pp. 1-37). Others, equally concerned, seek ways to reconcile access and excellence (Gardner, 1961; Husén, 1974b). There is a relatively new element in the discussion—the recognition that human talents are relative to social values and are more widely distributed than once had been believed (Cross, 1975; Taubman and Wales, 1972; Levitas, 1974). These matters will be discussed further in later chapters.

The basic principles concerning access were eloquently summarized in the influential report of the 1947 President's Commission on Higher Education (1947, p. 9): "The first goal in education for democracy is the full, rounded, and continuing development of the person. . . . [T]o liberate and perfect the intrinsic powers of every citizen is the central purpose of democracy, and its furtherance of individual self-realization is its greatest glory."

Specific goals of education. From these basic principles the specific goals for the education function are derived. This function, which embraces both the formal academic program and the extracurricular life of an academic community, is intended to help students develop as persons in three respects: *cognitive learning*, by expanding their knowledge and intellectual powers; *affective development*, by enhancing their moral, religious, and emotional interests and sensibilities; and *practical competence*, by improving their performance in citizenship, work, family life, consumer choice, health, and other practical affairs.

Insofar as these three goals are achieved, they are the ingredients for the flowering of the total personality. In varying combinations—reflecting individual differences and uniqueness of persons—they define the ideal personalities to which many educators aspire for their students.

Cognitive and affective vs. practical goals. Distinctions among the cognitive, affective, and practical goals are blurred, and there is much overlap among them. Moreover, we do not imply that the cognitive and practical outcomes would be derived solely from formal curricula, or that the affective outcomes would be produced solely through extracurricular academic life. All three types of goals may be achieved in part from both formal instruction and extracurricular experience.

The goals relating to the cognitive and affective dimensions of the human personality are of wide applicability. They should enhance the individual's life in all his experiences and endeavors, including his practical activities. The goals relating to practical affairs, on the other hand, tend to be more specific. They are expected to assist the individual in the several practical roles that he will be called upon to fill. Recent literature on goals contains many references not only to careers but also to the importance of preparing individuals to cope with the ordinary affairs of life: preparing for changes in the life cycle as one progresses from adolescence to old age; dealing with interpersonal problems within the family; using the health care system; getting proper legal advice; coping with bureaucracy; managing investments, insurance, and taxes; buying and selling real estate; and so on (Organization for Economic Cooperation and Development, 1973b; Bailey, 1976).

Observers differ sharply about the relative importance of instruction for practical affairs and instruction to develop desirable cognitive and affective personal characteristics. At the one extreme are those who regard higher education primarily as training for practical affairs, particularly work and citizenship, and consider liberal education as secondary or fitted only for an elite. At the other extreme are those who hold that the main task of higher education is to produce good and competent people who possess the desired general cognitive and affective qualities. On this view, liberally educated persons will be able to cope with the practical affairs of life without much special training. John Stuart Mill expressed this second view in a famous passage in his inaugural address as Rector of the University of St. Andrews (1875, pp. 334-335):

> Universities are not intended to teach knowledge required to fit men for some special mode of making their livelihood. Their object is not to make skillful lawyers, or physicians, or engineers, but capable and cultivated human beings. It is very right that there should be public facilities for the study of professions. It is well that there should be Schools of Law and of Medicine. . . . But these things are no part of what every generation owes to the next, as that on which its civilization and worth will principally depend. . . . Men are men before they are lawyers, or physicians, or merchants, or manufacturers; and if you make them capable and sensible men, they will make themselves capable and sensible lawyers or physicians. What professional men should carry away

with them from a University is not professional knowledge, but that which should direct the use of their professional knowledge, and bring the light of a general culture to illuminate the technicalities of a special pursuit. Men may be competent lawyers without general education, but it depends on general education to make them philosophic lawyers—who demand, and are capable of apprehending principles, instead of merely cramming their memory with details.

Most contemporary opinion lies between the extremes (Martin, 1968; Cheit, 1975). Thoughtful people acknowledge that liberal education designed for development of a whole person is a basic responsibility. They believe that such knowledge and skills as reading, writing, mathematics, science, history, economics, and so on—all associated with liberal education—facilitate the conduct of practical affairs. They also recognize that practical education in such fields as medicine, law, nursing, architecture, and administration carries with it content of intellectual, moral, and esthetic value and contributes toward development of the whole person. The relative emphasis on liberal and practical education fluctuates. At the moment, the balance seems to be swinging toward the practical side. Yet a preponderance of authority over the centuries gives higher priority to general human development than to practical training and warns against the persistent tendency to neglect broad human development in favor of training for practical pursuits (compare Bisconti and Solmon, 1976).

Dispositions vs. behaviors. The goals of education are usually expressed as characteristics, skills, abilities, competencies, dispositions, motivations, sensibilities, orientations, commitments, understandings, and so on. To the extent that students achieve these personal qualities by the time of their graduation, it may be assumed that they are headed toward desirable lifetime behavior patterns. But *behavior patterns* are the ultimate goals. The basic purpose of instruction is to change lifetime behavior and thus to change lives, not merely to produce abstract dis-

positions or tendencies toward change that may never mate-
rialize.

Each of the specific goals for higher education implies a
future behavior pattern. For example, the goal of verbal skill, a
subgoal under cognitive learning, implies effective verbal communication as a desired behavior of later life. Similarly, the subgoal of esthetic sensibility implies consistent and sympathetic
attention to the arts and to natural beauty. The goals of instruction are, in the first instance, to change students with respect to
their dispositions and tendencies. But these immediate outcomes reach fruition only as they produce changes in lifetime
behavior.

By-products of education as goals. We have referred to the three
primary goals of education as the personal development of students with respect to their cognitive abilities, their affective
characteristics, and their practical competence. In addition,
three additional goals are achieved largely as by-products of
instruction: personal self-discovery, career choice and placement, and direct satisfactions and enjoyments.

Personal self-discovery. Closely related to the aim of helping
students attain personal development is the goal of helping
them discover themselves—their aptitudes, interests, values,
commitments, and aspirations. Personal self-discovery is in a
sense a by-product of the instructional process, but it is nevertheless one of the most far-reaching purposes of higher education. Colleges and universities are designed to offer students a
wide variety of experiences, to introduce them to a broad range
of ideas, to put them into contact with peers and role models,
to acquaint them with the multiple possibilities that life affords,
to allow them to try themselves out in a variety of fields and
tasks, to help them discover their limitations, and to motivate
them to achieve their ultimate potential as human beings. The
goal of self-discovery justifies and makes intelligible the floundering that is characteristic of many college students who are
trying to choose courses, major fields, careers, philosophies of
life, and even marriage partners.

Career choice and placement. The goal of facilitating appropriate career choice and placement of students is closely related to the goal of personal self-discovery. Both goals together reflect the process by which students will achieve their self-identity and work out their career objectives and style of life.

Colleges and universities assist in career choice and placement through guidance, brokerage, and credentialing. Guidance often occurs through formal counseling and also through the informal influence of peers and professors. Brokerage occurs when colleges and universities serve as middlemen between students or alumni and prospective employers—often through placement offices. Credentialing refers to the issuance of grades, transcripts, honors and recognitions, letters of recommendation, recommendations by word of mouth, certificates, and degrees signifying academic achievements.

Historically, the practice of credentialing originated as part of the academic incentive system. Grades, degrees, certificates, and so on were designed to motivate students to do good work and encourage them to complete coherent courses of study. While continuing to serve as motivators, they evolved into effective sorting devices for placement in the labor market. In recent years, credentialing has become a subject of sharp controversy. Critics argue that career placement is dominated by paper credentials rather than genuine competency, that educational requirements for many jobs have become excessive, that many competent people without the required paper credentials are unfairly discriminated against, and that the premium earnings received by the college-educated are due largely to their credentials rather than to their superior productivity. On the other hand, the advocates of credentialing argue that it provides a reliable incentive system without which academic standards could not be maintained, that the granting of credentials helps people to find congenial and suitable jobs where they will be productive, that credentialing provides the community with reliable information that would otherwise have to be provided in more costly and less efficient ways, and that credentialing in many cases provides protection for consumers.

Credentialing provides a system of "signals" that alerts

prospective employers to worker characteristics that are not easy to observe through ordinary screening for employment. This signal system helps in achieving appropriate placement and avoids costly errors for both employer and employee (Madden, 1975, pp. 15-16). A degree and other credentials indicate with some reliability that the individual can "speak and write clearly, understand what he reads, reason about matters of some complexity, recognize historical and cultural reference points, feel somewhat at home amidst philosophical and generally abstract ideas" (Harris, 1975, p. 222). A degree or other credential also indicates its holders have "demonstrated the discipline necessary to attend classes, prepare for examinations, [and] bring their minds to bear at least minimally on a certain amount of initially uninteresting material, and an ability to survive in a world focused on intellectual concerns" (Harris, 1975, p. 222).

For the present, we concede that credentialing has both positive and negative results but assert that on balance it is a legitimate and perhaps necessary function of higher education. The granting of credentials motivates students effectively and facilitates efficient allocation of the labor force by taking into account both the interests and competencies of workers and the needs of the economy. We shall have more to say on this subject under the topic, "grading and labeling." (See Chapter Five.)

Direct satisfactions and enjoyments. Many—probably most—students gain pleasure from learning and enjoy being part of an academic community where they may experience the stimulus of interesting people and ideas, sociability, recreation, and agreeable surroundings. Because people spend much of their time in formal education—in some cases as much as a third of their whole lives, and seldom less than a sixth—personal satisfaction and enjoyment is by no means a frivolous goal. And it becomes even more important when one considers that enjoyment of education undoubtedly enhances its effectiveness. Indeed, Jencks (1972, pp. 256-257) has made the radical suggestion (with reference to schools) that, since educators have meager knowledge of the relation between the forms and methods of education and its outcomes, one of the main criteria for deciding on educational method might be the degree of direct satisfaction obtained by students and teachers.

The families and friends of college students also may obtain satisfaction from the college experience. This satisfaction takes many forms: it may be simply vicarious enjoyment from contemplating a rich opportunity available to a loved one; it may be a sense of pleasure in helping open up opportunity to a family member; it may be the introduction of a new source of interest and ideas into a family circle; or it may be sheer relief on the part of parents who are able to shift part of the responsibility for guiding and developing their sons and daughters to an institution. On this point, Adam Smith observed that, in the absence of worthy universities in his time, many families sent their sons abroad for several years. By so doing, he said, "a father delivers himself at least for some time, from so disagreeable an object as that of a son unemployed, neglected, and going to ruin before his eyes." Smith also noted that for a young man of seventeen or eighteen "it is very difficult not to improve a good deal in three or four years" (Smith, 1937). At any rate, anyone who has observed the pride of parents and spouses of graduates on commencement day can hardly deny that the satisfactions to family members are real.

Social Goals of Higher Education

As higher education brings about changes in individuals through its educational function, as it contributes toward the advancement of knowledge and the arts, and as it renders various public services, its work is bound to have broad social consequences. Therefore, goals for society, as well as for individuals, must be considered.

Individualism vs. collectivism. There are two opposing extremes on the continuum of educational philosophies in the world today: the individualistic, emphasizing the development of persons as the final end, and the collectivistic, emphasizing the advancement of society as the final end (Emmerij, 1974, pp. 147-151, 170-171, 191-200).

The assumptions underlying the extreme individualistic

point of view are (1) that education should be designed to produce autonomous individuals who are civilized and effective in practical affairs; (2) that a society of such individuals will spontaneously work out a desirable social destiny through the democratic process as a result of their separate and collective decisions and actions; (3) that research and related intellectual and artistic activities of the academic community should be designed to foster learning for its own sake; and (4) that such learning will spontaneously turn out to be useful for both cultural development and practical affairs.

The assumptions underlying the extreme collectivistic point of view are (1) that "society" has goals that may be distinguishable from the interactive summation of individual goals; (2) that education should be designed to shape individuals to serve the purposes of the nation—usually set forth by the government or by a party leadership; and (3) that research and related intellectual and artistic activities should be directed toward the achievement of national goals, including the solution of social problems. This point of view was recently described by Jan Szczepanski, a leading Polish sociologist and educator. He defined higher education (1974, p. 7) as: ". . . a process of intentional formation of the personality according to an established personality idea. . . ." He then outlined the goals of higher education as follows (1974, pp. 10-11):

> First is the education of the desired personality type required by the relations of production—to use the Marxian terminology—or, in other words, the type of personality required by the structure of the economy and this type of socialized society.
>
> Next, the most important goal is the vocational and professional education of graduates required by the present state for the expected future development of the economy. . . .
>
> The third goal is preparation for participation in social and cultural life—the development of the cultural values to keep up the cultural identity of the nation. . . .

The final goal is to assure the optimal development of human individuality, to provide the individual with the chance for self-orientation and self-edu-
cation. This goal is to prepare him fully to function in
all contexts of social life, not only in the economic
sphere. This is, I might say, an echo of the Humboldt-
ian idea of the fully developed creative personality.

Szczepanski added (1974, pp. 18-19):

Within every institution of higher education the party
organization has to watch that the political line is
being respected. . . . One of the most important problems is the harmonization of the state and governmental goals and societal goals with the personal goals
of the families who send their children to an institution of higher education, and students who want to
achieve personal life goals. The traditional images of
the role and function of higher education still influence the expectations of students and their families.
But the traditional images are irrelevant to contemporary reality.

Each nation must find its place on the continuum between
the individualistic and the collectivistic extremes of educational
philosophy. American opinion has leaned toward the individualistic view and the concepts of education and democracy have
been linked closely, for example, by Thomas Jefferson, Horace
Mann, and John Dewey. Education has been regarded as a
means of preparing individuals capable of choosing sound goals
for society and effective in achieving these goals through the
democratic process. Jefferson expressed this idea in his *Notes
on the State of Virginia*, recommending a basic law for universal
education (1955, p. 148):

But of all the views of this law none is more important, none more legitimate, than that of rendering the
people the safe, as they are the ultimate, guardians of

their own liberty. For this purpose the reading in the first stage, where *they* will receive their whole education, is proposed, as has been said, to be chiefly historical. History by apprising them of the past will enable them to judge of the future; it will avail them of the experience of other times and other nations; it will qualify them as judges of the actions and designs of men; it will enable them to know ambition under every disguise it may assume; and knowing it, to defeat its views. In every government on earth is some trace of human weakness, some germ of corruption and degeneracy, which cunning will discover, and wickedness insensibly open, cultivate, and improve. Every government degenerates when trusted to the rulers of the people alone. The people themselves therefore are its only safe depositories. And to render even them safe their minds must be improved to a certain degree. This indeed is not all that is necessary, though it be essentially necessary. An amendment of our constitution must here come in aid of the public education.

American thought and practice, however, have never wholly rejected the idea that education should serve national goals. A striking illustration of this idea is found in the title of the first important federal legislation on education after World War II, The National Defense Education Act. Moreover, the American literature on goals is replete with references to the social objectives of higher education. The contemporary American position is that priorities for education, research, and public service may properly be influenced by broad social goals but not at the cost of unduly warping the personal development of individuals as whole and autonomous persons or of preventing intellectual freedom in the preservation and advancement of knowledge. Americans have traditionally leaned toward the individualistic position and have looked upon the collectivistic position with some suspicion as threatening to basic democratic principles.

Social change vs. social stability. A related issue concerns the seemingly inconsistent functions of higher education as, simultaneously an agent of social change and an agent of social stability. A widely acknowledged goal of higher education is to equip students to view their own society with some detachment, to compare it with other societies, to discover discrepancies between its aspirations and its realities, to gain perspective on its social problems and shortcomings, and to acquire the will as well as the political and technical skills needed to work for change. Similarly, a widely accepted goal of research and related intellectual and artistic activities is to induce change through exploring new values and discovering new technologies. Indeed, it is frequently argued that the college or university itself, as a community of learners and researchers, should serve society in the capacity of social critic—as a center from which ideas basic to social change would radiate. The obverse of this theory is that higher education should equip students to understand and appreciate the cultural heritage, to value social continuity, to discover what is right in society as well as what is wrong, to distinguish between the possible and impossible in social reform, and to work toward the preservation of that which is worth preserving. The dual roles of higher education as agent of change and agent of stability, though seemingly incompatible, may not be in conflict. The true goal may be men and women with free minds who can form balanced judgments about change and stability and who can work toward orderly and progressive social development, drawing on both old and new (see Ottoway, 1962; Clark and others, 1972; Ladd and Lipset, 1975).

Conclusions. Regardless of one's views on individualism versus collectivism or on change versus stability as outcomes of higher education, one cannot reasonably avoid the conclusion that higher education has consequences for society. The immediate outcomes of higher education consist primarily of changes in people and changes in ideas. These changes may be in conservative or radical directions, but in either case they inevitably influence the character of social organization, social institutions, and broad social values and attitudes. When millions of college-educated people are inducted into a society, they are bound to affect that society. Similarly, when the ideas derived from the intellectual-artistic pursuits of the academy make their way into a society, these ideas are bound to influence the course of social development. Higher education thus sets in motion a dynamic process leading to changes in society, which in turn will lead to further changes in both individuals and society. This process may extend far into the future and bring about consequences of the most far-reaching import. Though it would be difficult to trace these long-run dynamic influences, it is hard to believe they do not exist (Organization for Economic Cooperation and Development, 1973a, pp. 21, 91-102).

Negative Outcomes

Educators direct their efforts toward outcomes they believe to be beneficial. Despite good intentions, however, actual outcomes may be harmful or may be judged harmful by some observers. Because it is a potent force, higher education may open up possibilities for bad as well as good outcomes. If it were otherwise and the results always good, higher education would be so unlike real life as to have no practical utility.

In its effect on students, higher education may produce some liars, cheats, and con men; it may foster tendencies toward exploitation of other people; it may enhance the capacity of people to employ intellectual jargon for purposes of rationalization and deceit; it may foster indolence in some people; it may cause contempt for the Puritan virtues of thrift and hard work; it may deaden rather than quicken the love of learning; it may offer a shelter that retards maturation; it may produce unfortunate personality traits such as arrogance or superciliousness; it may encourage drug abuse and excessive use of tobacco and alcohol; it may demoralize students who fail or who achieve low social or academic ranking. By enlarging the opportunity and raising the social status of those who are college-educated, college education may correspondingly restrict the opportunity and social status of the less-educated (Solmon and Taubman, 1973).

Some of the results of higher education may be controversial to the extent that some people regard them favorably and others view them adversely. As Hodgkinson (1972, p. 39), speaking to a group of state legislators and other officials, remarked, "Your constituents may not like it if, as a consequence of this greater significance [of higher education] students become aware of the wide range of ways of life, or governmental and economic structures, and more aware and critical of how our society is using its human and natural resources. Is it a benefit to society if the young are exposed to material that will make some of them more critical of that society?"

Higher education may produce religious dissent, political liberalism, or radicalism; conversely, it may harden conservative views. It may lead to espousal of exotic or fundamentalist religion. It may bring about alienation from families. It may widen the generation gap. It may produce pacifist attitudes and thus weaken national military power. It may encourage qualities of independence and autonomy when what is wanted in some jobs is conformity, dependence, and loyalty (Trent and Medsker, 1968). Further, the direct satisfactions and enjoyments from higher education may be offset wholly or in part by boredom or academic pressure, and some of the most creative students may find college regimentation intolerable and drop out (Parnes, 1971). Similarly, in its research and scholarly activities, higher education may discover new forms of nerve gas; it may develop philosophies alien to traditional politics or religion; it may discover psychological techniques for manipulating people (Heard, 1974).

Many controversial outcomes are beset with semantic confusion. For example, if an outcome of higher education is described as helping to induct students into cosmopolitan culture and to emancipate them from provincialism, the result may be considered beneficial; if the same result is described as alienating young people from their families and from the traditions of their local communities or ethnic groups, it may be considered harmful. Moreover, some outcomes are viewed differently at different times according to the social context. For example, in a time of peace and pacifistic sentiments, the discovery of a new biological weapon may be viewed widely as an outrage; in the midst of a desperate war, the same outcome could be regarded as a justifiable expedient.

Because of such differences of opinion, determination of the operative goals of higher education becomes a major social issue. In the American experience, the goals of higher education have been shaped partly within higher education through the influence of faculties and administrators and partly through external societal influences exerted by governing boards, legislators, donors, students, parents, and others. Though external social control has been ever-present, internal institutional influence on goals has been real in both the public and private sectors. Evolving within a framework of decentralized authority, the goals have been strongly influenced by professional considerations as well as by social dictate. Potential conflict over goals is softened by a dual recognition by many leading members of the public, who believe that it is in the long-run social interest for the academy to maintain substantial control over its own destiny, and by many members of the academy, who believe that their institutions are ultimately responsible to serve society (see Peterson, 1975). Thus, when we speak of the goals of American higher education, we refer to goals that have evolved through professional discussion and professional practice as tempered by outside influences. The degree of consensus about goals is perhaps greater among the professionals than among members of the general public. Nevertheless, differences of judgment and opinion are real and higher education undoubtedly produces some outcomes that are looked upon by many with askance.

Obviously, differences of opinion about goals complicates the matter of accountability. A report by the Organization for Economic Cooperation and Development (OECD), *Indicators of Performance of Educational Systems* (1973a, p. 31), refers to the multitude of goals for education and the inherent difficulty of translating them into some aggregate criterion of the overall performance of an educational system: "With regard to the multidimensional nature of the goals for the educational system, the weights will be determined by the political decision-making process. There is therefore no such thing as *the produc-*

tivity of a specific educational system as long as the idea that education is a multigoal activity is accepted. Different people will give different weights to the different sub-goals, and for a given set of inputs there might be as many productivity measures as there are people." The uncertainties and differences of opinion about goals and outcomes foster that diversity in the higher educational system that it needs serve its varied clienteles, protect it from the colossal errors of monolithic systems that can operate by rigid formulae, and promote a healthy spirit of experimentation and innovation.

A Catalogue of Goals

The goals of higher education are hypotheses about desirable outcomes that can be achieved—or at least approximated—in practice. A useful taxonomy for the study of outcomes, therefore, is a catalogue of widely accepted goals. The catalogue presented in this section forms the outline for all that follows. In subsequent chapters, we try to discover whether and to what extent each goal is actually achieved. The items in the catalogue are meant to be the ingredients of a well-ordered educational system. Taken together, they constitute the model that many educators adopt when setting educational policy, and they provide the criteria by which educators and others ideally try to judge the performance of higher education.

We compiled the catalogue by combing through an extensive literature that includes the writings of noted educational philosophers and critics of the past and present, reports of public commissions and faculty committees, and statements of leading educators in speeches, articles, and institutional reports. In going over this literature, we assembled and classified more than 1,500 goal statements from widely varied sources, historical and contemporary. (The sources that were of particular value are marked with an asterisk in the references at the end of this book.)

We reviewed a large sampling of the literature to identify goals that important authorities had frequently mentioned. The selection process was simplified by the remarkable agreement among the authorities. It was not, however, a mere polling of the authorities. In the end, the authors' judgment influenced the final selection.

Each of the goals is, to a degree, considered an important responsibility of higher education. But this does not mean that every institution pursues every one of the goals or gives the same emphasis to all of them. There is room for variety among institutions in their goal patterns.

Not all the goals are achieved in practice, and some of them may not even be achievable. Still others may function as ideals—ever to be approached but never to be achieved fully. The catalogue has a utopian quality about it: It appears as a compendium of all possible human virtues and hopes. Higher education has limitations, and educators should not claim so much as to lose credibility. Many are shared goals pursued jointly with the family, the school, the church, the media, governmental agencies, and the workplace (Spaeth and Greeley, 1970). In recent decades, with the weakening of some of these other institutions, more of the load has been shifted to education. The result may be an overloading of the entire educational system, including higher education. In any event, there is need for educators to sort out priorities among the goals, to recognize that there are trade-offs among them, and to be realistic about what can and cannot be achieved with the resources that are likely to be available. Since each goal in the catalogue is widely accepted as a desirable objective, however, it is hard to avoid the conclusion that the purpose of higher education is to seek all of them to the degree that time, resources, and human improvability permit.

The goals of higher education are concerned with the development of the full potentialities of human beings and of society. The goals correspond closely to the goals of human life. As Alexander Heard (1973, p. 16) has remarked: "Our largest common goal in higher education, indeed in all education, is to create and stimulate the kind of learning that breeds strength and humor and hope within a person, and that helps build a society outside him that stirs his pride and commands his affection." The catalogue of goals for higher education follows.

I. Goals for Individual Students

A. Cognitive Learning

(1) *Verbal skills.* Ability to comprehend through reading and listening. Ability to speak and write clearly, correctly, and gracefully. Effectiveness in the organization and presentation of ideas in writing and in discussion. Possibly some acquaintance with a second language.

(2) *Quantitative skills.* Ability to understand elementary concepts of mathematics and to handle simple statistical data and statistical reasoning. Possibly some understanding of the rudiments of accounting and the uses of computers.

(3) *Substantive knowledge.* Acquaintance with the cultural heritage of the West and some knowledge of other traditions. Awareness of the contemporary world of philosophy, natural science, art, literature, social change, and social issues. Command of vocabulary, facts, and principles in one or more selected fields of knowledge.

(4) *Rationality.* Ability and disposition to think logically on the basis of useful assumptions. Capacity to see facts and events objectively—distinguishing the normative, ideological, and emotive from the positive and factual. Disposition to weigh evidence, evaluate facts and ideas critically, and to think independently. Ability to analyze and synthesize.

(5) *Intellectual tolerance.* Freedom of the mind. Openness to new ideas. Willingness to question orthodoxy. Intellectual curiosity. Ability to deal with complexity and ambiguity. Appreciation of intellectual and cultural diversity. Historical perspective and cosmopolitan outlook.[2] Understanding of the limitations of knowledge and thought.

---

[2] Appreciation of the local, provincial, and parochial is commendable. Values such as cosmopolitanism are not undesirable but perhaps they are most valuable when they occur in tension with their opposites, when the person achieves an appreciation of both the cosmopolitan and the provincial and a critical capacity to stress the merits and deficiencies of both.

(6) *Esthetic sensibility.*[3] Knowledge of, interest in, and responsiveness to literature, the fine arts, and natural beauty.

(7) *Creativeness.* Imagination and originality in formulating new hypotheses and ideas and in producing new works of art.

(8) *Intellectual integrity.* Understanding of the idea of "truth" and of its contingent nature. Disposition to seek and speak the truth. Conscientiousness of inquiry and accuracy in reporting results.

(9) *Wisdom.* Balanced perspective, judgment, and prudence.

(10) *Lifelong learning.* Love of learning. Sustained intellectual interests. Learning how to learn.

B. Emotional and Moral Development

(1) *Personal self-discovery.* Knowledge of one's own talents, interests, values, aspirations, and weaknesses. Discovery of unique personal identity.

(2) *Psychological well-being.* Progress toward the ability to "understand and confront with integrity the nature of the human condition" (Perry, 1970, p. 201). Sensitivity to deeper feelings and emotions combined with emotional stability. Ability to express emotions constructively. Appropriate self-assertiveness, sense of security, self-confidence, self-reliance, decisiveness, spontaneity. Acceptance of self and others.

(3) *Human understanding.* Humane outlook. Capacity for empathy, thoughtfulness, compassion, respect, tolerance, and cooperation toward others, including persons of different backgrounds. Democratic and nonauthoritarian disposition. Skill in communication with others.

(4) *Values and morals.* A valid and internalized but not dogmatic set of values and moral principles. Moral sensitivity and courage. Sense of social consciousness and social responsibility.

[3] Esthetic sensibility is often classified under affective development rather than cognitive learning. It contains elements of both.

(5) *Religious interest.* Serious and thoughtful exploration of purpose, value, and meaning.

(6) *Refinement of taste, conduct, and manner.*

C. Practical Competence

(1) *Traits of value in practical affairs generally.* Virtually all of the goals included under cognitive learning and emotional and moral development apply to practical affairs. In addition, the following traits, which are more specifically related to achievement in practical affairs, may be mentioned:

   (a) *Need for achievement.* Motivation toward accomplishment. Initiative, energy, drive, persistence, self-discipline.

   (b) *Future orientation.* Ability to plan ahead and to be prudent in risk-taking. A realistic outlook toward the future.

   (c) *Adaptability.* Tolerance of new ideas or practices. Willingness to accept change. Versatility and resourcefulness in coping with problems and crises. Capacity to learn from experience. Willingness to negotiate, compromise, and keep options open.

   (d) *Leadership.* Capacity to win the confidence of others, willingness to assume responsibility, organizational ability, decisiveness, disposition to take counsel.

(2) *Citizenship.* Understanding of and commitment to democracy. Knowledge of governmental institutions and procedures. Awareness of major social issues. Ability to evaluate propaganda and political argumentation. Disposition and ability to participate actively in civic, political, economic, professional, educational, and other voluntary organizations. Orientation toward international understanding and world community. Ability to deal with bureaucracies. Disposition toward law observance.

(3) *Economic productivity.* Knowledge and skills needed for first job and for growth in productivity through experience and on-the-job training. Adaptability and mobility. Sound career decisions. Capacity to bring humanistic

values to the workplace and to derive meaning from work.

(4) *Sound family life.* Personal qualities making for stable families. Knowledge and skill relating to child development.

(5) *Consumer efficiency.* Sound choice of values relating to style of life. Skill in stretching consumer dollars. Ability to cope with taxes, credit, insurance, investments, legal issues, and so on. Ability to recognize deceptive sales practices and to withstand high-pressure sales tactics.

(6) *Fruitful leisure.* Wisdom in allocation of time among work, leisure, and other pursuits. Development of tastes and skills in literature, the arts, nature, sports, hobbies, and community participation. Lifelong education, formal and informal, as a productive use of leisure. Resourcefulness in overcoming boredom, finding renewal, and discovering satisfying and rewarding uses of leisure time.

(7) *Health.* Understanding of the basic principles for cultivating physical and mental health. Knowledge of how and when to use the professional health care system.

D. Direct Satisfactions and Enjoyments from College Education.

(1) During the college years.

(2) In later life.

E. Avoidance of negative outcomes for individual students.

II. Goals for Society

(Note: These goals may be achieved through education, through research and related activities, or through public services.)

A. Advancement of Knowledge

(1) Preservation and dissemination of the cultural heritage.

(2) Discovery and dissemination of new knowledge and advancement of philosophical and religious thought, literature, and the fine arts—all regarded as valuable in their own right without reference to ulterior ends.

(3) Direct satisfactions and enjoyments received by the population from living in a world of advancing knowledge, technology, ideas, and arts.

B. Discovery and Encouragement of Talent.
C. Advancement of Social Welfare.
    (1) Economic efficiency and growth.
    (2) Enhancement of national prestige and power.
    (3) Progress toward the identification and solution of social problems.
    (4) "Improvement" in the motives, values, aspirations, attitudes, and behavior of members of the general population.
    (5) Over long periods of time, exerting a significant and favorable influence on the course of history as reflected in the evolution of the basic culture and of the fundamental social institutions. Progress in human equality, freedom, justice, security, order, religion, health, and so on.
D. Avoidance of Negative Outcomes for Society.

Part Two

Consequences
for Individuals

The chapters in this section of the book are concerned with the impacts of higher education on its students as *individuals*. These impacts are achieved not only through formal academic teaching but also through the many extracurricular influences of colleges and universities. The opening chapter reviews knowledge about the cognitive or intellectual development of students. Chapter Four concerns their emotional and moral development or "affective" growth. Chapters Five and Six review their growth in practical competence—the development of valuable traits for citizenship, economic productivity, family life, consumer behavior, leisure, and health. Chapter Seven surveys the impact of higher education on students regarded as whole persons, and it includes the views of students and alumni about the worth of their education. Chapter Eight considers the range of differences among colleges and universities in their impact on students.

3

Cognitive Learning

*Education must be contributing to the skills,
the ability to understand, the interest in
serious information, and the habit of seeking
it. Education . . . must be outlining a cognitive
map which the individual spends the rest of
his life filling out and, to some extent,
revising. Education must be arousing a
curiosity that lasts after the school years.*

Wilbur Schramm (1967, p. 120)

The goals of higher education described in the previous chapter
are potential outcomes. To learn about actual outcomes, we
shall marshall evidence about the degree to which each of the
goals is attained, beginning with an exploration of the effects of
college on students as individuals. We shall be trying to find out
how persons who attend college differ from comparable persons
who do not. This question will be approached from two points
of view: differences observable during the college years and differences manifest in later life. The present chapter focuses on
cognitive learning; subsequent chapters deal with affective development and preparation for practical living.

Throughout these chapters we shall be plagued with the
methodological problems described at the end of Chapter One.

The available evidence on outcomes is scattered and of uneven reliability. It refers mostly to the past and may not be valid in the present or future. Controls for such variables as intelligence and socioeconomic background are sometimes absent and often inadequate. Much of the available evidence is based on verbal opinion rather than actual behavior. We are keenly conscious of these limitations. Nevertheless, the evidence, when taken as a whole, does convey significant information from which some useful and general inferences may be drawn. We make no apologies for the data we present, because they are the best and only data available. Nor do we expect to make a detailed methodological criticism of each study or each bank of data cited. There is great need for additional research on higher education outcomes.

One of the anomalies of studies conducted on outcomes is that less attention has been devoted to cognitive learning than to affective development (Withey, 1971; Ellison and Simon in Solmon and Taubman, 1973; Lenning and others, 1974). As Bloom and Webster observed (1960, p. 323), "That students possess more information and greater facility in attacking cognitive problems at the end of a course or curriculum than they had at the beginning has been so well demonstrated that this fact perhaps explains the recent paucity of research in this direction." Sanford (1962, p. 806) added, "There is no doubt that students gain in skill and information . . . yet there does not seem to be a single study in which alumni have been compared with seniors in terms of achievement test scores. It is as if there were a conspiracy of silence on this point, as if educators well knew what interviews with young alumni in fact reveal— that very little of the content of college courses is retained three or four years after graduation." There is, of course, no conspiracy to withhold information on cognitive learning. Everyone knows that the halflife of memorized details from academic learning is short unless the information is used frequently. What we do not know, and should investigate, is the residue left over from academic learning when the details have been lost. The residue may take the form of verbal facility, broad general principles, ways of looking at the world, and improvement in the ability to learn, instead of retained knowledge and information. But there is little satisfactory documentation of the learning that people actually carry over from college into later life.

Two apparent reasons may account for this sad state of ignorance. First, there are few occasions in adult life to examine or retest people on knowledge they may have acquired in college. Second, the diverse academic and career experiences of students virtually rule out standardized tests. These reasons are not wholly persuasive, however. Skill and knowledge are "the easiest of all personal characteristics to measure" (Sanford, 1962, p. 806), and the logistics of examining or testing small *samples* of alumni would not be prohibitive. It would not be totally out of the question to devise tests covering skills, ideas, and information that should be common to educated persons, among them, the ability to read, write, and speak, and knowledge of certain basic concepts and reference points.[1]

Despite the relative neglect of cognitive outcomes, ignorance of the subject is not total. What has been learned will be summarized in the remainder of this chapter under these headings: Verbal and Quantitative Skills, Substantive Knowledge, Rationality, Intellectual Tolerance, Esthetic Sensibility, Creativeness, Intellectual Integrity, Wisdom, Intellectual and Cultural Pursuits of Students, and Lifelong Learning.

Verbal and Quantitative Skills

Verbal and quantitative skills are especially significant outcomes of higher education, not only because they are valuable in their own right but also because they facilitate learning of all kinds in college and throughout life (Duncan, 1968). Available data indicate that students do make significant gains during the college years in verbal and quantitative skills (though comparable data for persons not attending college are scarce). We found no substantial evidence to the contrary. One series of studies, conducted from 1934 to 1951, measured gains on the Psychological

[1] I am indebted to Dr. Leo A. Munday of American College Testing Program for helpful comments on the problem of identifying cognitive outcomes.

Examination of the American Council on Education, an instrument designed to measure linguistic and quantitative ability at the college level. In general, the gains between the beginning of the freshman year and the end of the senior year averaged just under one standard deviation[2] (Powers, 1976, pp. 40-43). Another series of studies from 1930 to 1964, showing changes in scores on various scholastic aptitude tests, showed gains on the average of about half a standard deviation during the college years. These studies, however, showed losses on the quantitative test for those students not taking mathematics or related subjects during college (Powers, 1976, pp. 40-43). Using the Carnegie General Culture Test, Learned and Wood (1938, p. 28) compared sophomore and senior scores on spelling, grammar, punctuation, vocabulary, and mathematics for 2,830 college students during the years 1930 and 1932. They reported gains of the order of one fourth of a standard deviation for all of these subjects except mathematics. In this field, the average remained virtually unchanged, reflecting the fact that those students who do not take mathematics or mathematically related subjects in college tend to lose ground in that field.

Lannholm (1952) conducted a study using the *Tests of General Education* (part of the Graduate Record Examination of the Educational Testing Service). These tests were designed to measure achievement in general education and included sections on mathematics, effectiveness of expression, and vocabulary. Lannholm compared individual scores for 1,012 students who took the test as sophomores in 1946 and as seniors in 1948. The results were as shown in Table 2.

Lenning and others (1968) compared English and mathematics scores for an identical sample of students during their senior year in high school and at the end of their sophomore year in college. They used the ACT college admissions tests. They found mixed results but generally small gains of one tenth to one fifth of a standard deviation.

More recently, two studies reported on the opinion of

---

[2] For a discussion of the meaning of differences expressed in standard deviation units, see the Appendix at the end of this chapter.

Table 2. Scores on achievement in general education,
sophomores vs. seniors

	Sophomore Mean Score		Senior Mean Score		
	Mean	Standard Deviation	Mean	Standard Deviation	Gain in Mean Score
Mathematics	466	94	497	102	31
Effectiveness of Expression	482	94	517	97	35
Vocabulary	449	90	477	91	27

Source: Lannholm (1952, p. 647).

upperclassmen and alumni as to the effectiveness of their colleges in the area of verbal communication. In one study from a large sample of college alumni, 98 percent reported that "my college should have developed my abilities to think and express myself." Of the same group, 41 percent stated that college actually developed their abilities "greatly" and another 46 percent said that it developed their abilities "somewhat" (Spaeth and Greeley, 1970, p. 40). Another recent study based on a large sample found that 63 percent of the alumni of the class of 1950 reported that they had benefited "very much" or "quite a bit" from college in ability to write and speak clearly, correctly, and effectively; 49 percent of the persons who were upperclassmen in 1969 reported similar benefit (Pace, 1974a, pp. 52-53, 56-57).

Though distressingly meager, the evidence about the effectiveness of college in imparting verbal and quantitative skills points mostly to positive results. These results square with the common-sense conclusion that four years of reading, writing, speaking, and conversing in an academic setting can hardly impair the verbal skills of students and might be expected to improve them. Also, it is likely that many students learn something in college about gathering and processing information, especially through the use of libraries and computers. Regarding quantitative skills, the sparse data are not conclusive. Some suggest positive change; others tend to support the assumption that those students who do not take courses in mathematics or do not use mathematics in their studies show little progress in quantitative skills.

The studies cited relate mostly to the fairly distant past. A disquieting factor of the present is that verbal and quantitative skills may be deteriorating, on the average. The steady fall in average scores on the Scholastic Aptitude Tests for college admission suggest that these skills as measured at the end of high school are declining for the entire population of college-bound students. Colleges cannot be held directly responsible for changes occurring in high school. However, the rising chorus of complaints of college professors (Bowen and Minter, 1976) and of employers about the apparent decline in the ability of college students and graduates to read and write raises questions about the effectiveness of colleges in imparting skill in verbal communication. The alleged deterioration is sometimes attributed to technological change related to radio, television, telephone, and aviation, which favor oral over written communication; it is also sometimes attributed to the increasing diversity of background of college students. In the absence of adequate knowledge, one can only conclude that there is little ground for complacency among educators with respect to verbal communication. However, popular complaints about the alleged inability of college graduates to speak and write effectively and correctly are not new. They have been frequently voiced over many decades.[3]

Substantive Knowledge

The overwhelming weight of evidence is that, on the average, students make gains in substantive knowledge during the college years. Using the Carnegie General Culture Test, Learned and Wood (1938) compared sophomores and seniors on literature, foreign literature, fine arts, history and social sciences, and

---

[3]This is documented in the writings of Richard Ohmann and Wallace Douglas (see, for example, Ohmann, 1976). We are indebted to Professor Richard Lloyd-Jones of the University of Iowa for a helpful letter on the subject.

general science. They reported average increases in scores for these subjects of the order of .6 of a standard deviation. Had freshmen been included in the study, the change would have been considerably larger.

Lannholm (1952) and Lannholm and Pitcher (1956, 1957, 1959) made a series of studies of scores of the Area Tests of the Graduate Record Examination for identical students as freshmen, sophomores, juniors, and seniors. The gains were substantial, considerably exceeding the standard deviations in the freshman year (Table 3). A side effect of the Lannholm and Pitcher

Table 3. Scores for identical students as freshmen and seniors
on the area tests of the Graduate Record Examination

	Freshman Scores		Senior Scores		Gain in Mean Scores
	Mean	Standard Deviation	Mean	Standard Deviation	
Social Science Test					
Social Science majors	344	77	454	93	110
Humanities majors	352	80	444	98	92
Natural Science majors	399	84	491	90	92
Humanities Test					
Social Science majors	391	65	483	89	92
Humanities majors	411	79	519	97	108
Natural Science majors	400	62	499	91	99
Natural Science Test					
Social Science majors	390	60	446	62	56
Humanities majors	392	59	454	76	62
Natural Science majors	465	84	578	87	113

Source: Lannholm and Pitcher (1959, p. 4). The data relate to 460 students in three "typical" liberal arts colleges.

studies was to show that gains occurred on the average in each year of college, though the average gains from the freshman to the sophomore year exceeded those in the later years of college.

Lenning and others (1968) compared scores on the ACT college admission tests in social studies and natural science for a sample of identical students in the senior year of high school and at the end of the sophomore year in college. They found that the gains in the first two years of college were generally in the range of one fifth to one half a standard deviation. Several other studies relating to particular colleges tend to confirm these results (Heston, 1950; Silvey, 1951; Beecher and others, 1966; Harris and Hurst, 1972. See also Bloom 1964, especially pages 95-131).

A different evaluation of substantive learning in college was reached by Koon (1974, p. 136). Approaching the impact of college on students from the standpoint of total personality development, he concluded, "Because of many lost potentials, the net impact of the *formal* college experience has been very modest, involving growth and change for many, but inertia and even regression for many others. . . . most students appear to have gathered a smattering of knowledge and some skills, but only a little understanding. A formal education has often involved little more than adjustment to the norms of a profession or discipline, with boundaries of learning sharply delimited according to standards acceptable to the professional and/or societal status quo." This judgment is of course reached by criteria different from those implied in standardized tests—criteria that should not necessarily be rejected.

Another approach to the question of outcomes in the form of substantive knowledge is to ask students and alumni to assess the impact of college upon them. The responses to such questions are, of course, highly subjective. Reporting on the responses of 1,475 students in nine diverse institutions on the extent of the cognitive change they had experienced, Gaff (1973, pp. 9-10) concluded that: "Virtually all students reported making at least some progress toward acquiring knowledge of specifics and knowledge of universals and abstractions in their major field of study, toward developing the ability to comprehend or interpret ideas, to evaluate materials and methods, to apply principles in particular situations, and toward understanding scientific methods. However, there was considerable variability between those who reported only moderate progress and those who reported much progress." Similarly,

Pace (1974a), in a study covering seventy-nine varied institutions, asked upperclassmen and alumni to indicate how much, if any, benefit they had received from various aspects of their college experience. The responses, relating to substantive knowledge expressed as percentage of respondents indicating they had received "very much" or "quite a bit" of benefit, were as shown in Table 4. Bisconti and Solmon (1976, p. 10), in a survey of a

Table 4. Benefits received from college as reported by
upperclassmen and alumni

	Upperclassmen	Alumni
Background and specialization for further education in some professional, scientific, or scholarly field	71%	64%
Awareness of different philosophies, cultures, and ways of life	69%	64%
Vocabulary, terminology, and facts in various fields of knowledge	69%	79%
Broadened literary acquaintance and appreciation	57%	62%
Science and technology—understanding and appreciation	43%	54%

Source: Pace (1974a, pp. 52-53, 56-57).

large sample of alumni, found that virtually all respondents had found college useful in imparting general knowledge and that 73 percent said it had been "very useful."

Rationality

Rationality is here defined as the ability and disposition to think logically on the basis of useful assumptions; see facts and events objectively—distinguishing the normative, ideological, and emotive from the positive and factual; weigh evidence and evaluate facts and ideas critically; think independently; analyze and synthesize.

In the research on higher education outcomes, these characteristics are included in such descriptive terms as "thinking introversion and complexity," "critical thinking," "intellectual orientation and disposition," and "theoretical orientation."

One series of studies conducted over the period from 1938 to 1968 measured changes in the value system of students during the college years, using tests devised by Allport and Vernon or by Allport, Vernon, and Lindzey (Feldman and Newcomb, 1969, Vol. II, pp. 2-9). "Theoretical value," one element measured in these studies, was defined as interest in discovery of truth, in ordering and systematizing knowledge, and in empirical, critical, and rational thought (Vol. I, p. 7). The studies produced mixed and seemingly discouraging results: Among sixteen studies, gains were found in seven, losses in five, and no change in four. Most of the cases of loss or no change, however, occurred in institutions attracting exceptionally gifted students, students who undoubtedly were high in intellectuality on admission to college and whose gains were therefore limited by a "ceiling effect." But the one study relating to community college students also showed a loss in intellectuality over two years. This series of studies appears to be inconclusive on the effect of college on "theoretical value."

Another series of studies, covering the years 1959 to 1972, measured changes during college in intellectual orientation and disposition (Feldman and Newcomb, 1969, Vol. II, pp. 37-48). Some of these studies were longitudinal, comparing the scores of individual students as they progressed through college; others were cross-sectional, comparing students of different classes at given moments in time. Many of these studies (but not all) used the Omnibus Personality Inventory developed at the Center for Research and Development in Higher Education of the University of California, Berkeley (Heist and Yonge, 1968). The Inventory includes two dimensions related to rationality: (1) Thinking Introversion, defined as interest in academic activities, abstract reflective thought, and the broad range of ideas typically expressed in literature, art, and philosophy; (2) Theoretical Orientation, defined as an interest in scientific, logical, and critical thinking. Most of these studies reported that gains in thinking introversion and theoretical orientation do occur in college. In general, however, the gains were small—usually of the order of

.10 to .40 of a standard deviation—and a substantial number of studies reported losses in intellectual orientation and disposition.

Stern (1966), using an intellectual interest scale, found varying results at fifteen institutions. Men scored higher as seniors than as freshmen at two liberal arts colleges and eight engineering schools and lower at three business administration schools; senior women scored lower than freshmen at three liberal arts colleges. Other scattered studies also showed decreases in intellectual disposition at particular institutions (Powers, 1976). In some very selective institutions this may have been due to a ceiling effect.

Lehmann and Dressel (1962, 1963) measured change in "critical thinking" from the freshman to the senior year in college for large samples of students who were in college from 1958 to 1962. The measurements were based on a Test of Critical Thinking developed under the auspices of the American Council on Education. The test related to five abilities: (1) defining a problem, (2) recognizing stated and unstated assumptions, (3) selecting pertinent information, (4) formulating and selecting relevant hypotheses, and (5) drawing valid conclusions. This test was supplemented by other tests, inventories, and background information. Lehmann and Dressel found that critical thinking ability increased substantially over the four years, the gain being greater in the first two years of college than in the last two years. The mean scores are presented in Table 5.

Schuman and Harding (1964, p. 371) concluded that "extended college experience radically increases the amount of

Table 5. Increase in critical thinking ability, freshmen vs. seniors

	Freshmen		Seniors		Gain Expressed in Standard Deviation Units
	Mean Score	Standard Deviation	Mean Score	Gain in Mean Score	
Men	32.82	6.75	39.72	6.90	1.02
Women	33.07	6.88	39.45	6.38	.92

Source: Lehmann and Dressel (1962, 1963).

rationality" but also noted that certain irrational biases remain.

Trent and Medsker (1969), using short-form scales of the Omnibus Personality Inventory, other instruments, and personal interviews, measured change over four years in a large sample of high school graduates, including those who went to two-year and four-year colleges and those who did not attend college.[4] The special importance of this study lies in the large sample, the longitudinal data, and the valid comparisons between those who attended college and those who did not.

The results of the Trent and Medsker studies, as they relate to the effect of college on rationality, are presented in Table 6, which shows average scores on "Thinking Introversion" (defined as interest in academic activities, abstract reflective thought, and the broad range of ideas typically expressed in literature, art, and philosophy). Generally, those who attended college made greater gains in thinking introversion than those who were employed or became homemakers. Homemaking apparently had a strongly negative impact upon the thinking introversion of young women. The gains for men were greater for those of low ability and low socioeconomic status than for those of high ability and high socioeconomic status. The opposite was true for women. A surprising (or, perhaps, anomalous) result was that male college dropouts showed a slightly greater gain than those who persisted in college for four years. As Trent and Medsker pointed out (p. 176), the change in thinking introversion for college students as compared with other high school graduates was not striking. The net gains (gains of the college group minus the gains of the noncollege group) were less than one point for men (about .10 of the standard deviation) and about four points for women (or about .40 of the standard devi-

---

[4]Their initial base data, gathered in 1959, included 10,755 high school graduates representing 37 high schools in fifteen communities in Pennsylvania, the Midwest, and California. The same students were surveyed annually over the period beginning in the Spring of 1959 and ending in the spring of 1963. Responses were received from 4,673 persons in the 1963 survey, and a later follow-up survey of those who had gone to college was made in the fall of 1964 (pp. 17-37).

Table 6. Average standard scores on thinking introversion of high school graduates of the class of 1959, by sex, college attendance, employment, and socioeconomic status, 1959 and 1963

	Men			Women		
	1959	*1963*	*Gain*	*1959*	*1963*	*Gain*
Attended college 4 years	48.62	51.76	3.14	50.24	53.74	3.50
Employed: did not attend college	41.31	43.57	2.26	43.57	42.88	−0.69
Homemaker: did not attend college	—	—	—	44.41	41.91	−2.50
Attended college 4 years	48.61	51.76	3.15	50.24	53.74	3.50
Attended college 1 to 3 years	45.06	48.87	3.81	46.41	47.07	0.66
Students of high ability						
Attended college 4 years	49.79	53.03	3.24	51.87	55.54	3.67
Employed: did not attend college	41.68	44.51	2.83	44.68	44.32	−0.36
Students of low ability						
Attended college 4 years	45.96	50.61	4.65	48.13	49.55	1.42
Employed: did not attend college	40.70	41.87	1.17	42.72	41.41	−1.31
Students of high socioeconomic status						
Attended college 4 years	50.28	53.45	3.17	51.28	54.97	3.69
Employed: did not attend college	41.71	44.06	2.35	47.39	47.80	0.41
Students of low socioeconomic status						
Attended college 4 years	47.78	52.06	4.28	48.02	50.52	2.50
Employed: did not attend college	41.55	42.78	1.23	42.31	41.68	−0.63

Source: Trent and Medsker (1968, pp. 133, 137, 140, 301-304).

ation). (The results shown in the table are in the form of standard scores where the normative mean was 50 and the standard deviation 10.)

Clark and others (1972, p. 109) measured change in intellectual disposition for students enrolled in eight varied colleges —Antioch, Reed, St. Olaf, San Francisco State, Swarthmore, University of California at Berkeley, University of the Pacific, and University of Portland. They used an index of intellectual disposition (a composite measure found in the Omnibus Personality Inventory manual). The index was designed to measure for individual students "gradations in degree of interest and potential involvement in intellectual activity. The categories extend from an orientation of broad, intense intellectual and esthetic interests . . . to one characterized by a very limited intellectual or even antiintellectual orientation." The index, which contained some elements that lie outside our definition of rationality, was based primarily on four scales of the Omnibus Personality Inventory: Thinking Introversion, Theoretical Orientation, Estheticism, and Complexity.

Using this index, Clark and others classified the freshmen and the seniors four years later into three groups and then showed the change in proportions of students falling within each group. The results are shown in Table 7. In each of the

Table 7. Comparison of freshmen and seniors in ranking on index of intellectual disposition

Ranking on Index of Intellectual Disposition	*Freshmen 1958-59 or 1959-60*	*Seniors 1962-63 or 1963-64*
Below average	49%	33%
Average	35	40
Above average	16	27
	100%	100%

Source: Clark and others (1972, p. 150).

institutions studied, the percentage in the below-average group declined and, in all but one, the percentage in the above-average group increased. The one exception was Reed College, where the intellectual disposition of students at admission was so high that a ceiling effect was operative.

Clark and others also provided separate data on change during college in scores on the Thinking Introversion and Theoretical Orientation parts of the Omnibus Personality Inventory (pp. 165, 169). These data suggest that the gain in intellectuality or rationality during college was of the order of .10 or .30 of a standard deviation, a significant but scarcely dramatic change.

In interpreting these figures, it should be noted that, because some students score very high on intellectuality upon admission to college, the ceiling effect can block significant further change. It may be argued that many students with very high scores on any single personality trait probably need no further development in that trait but instead broadening of the personality by cultivating other traits. Thus, a few colleges that admit large numbers of freshmen with high disposition toward intellectual development show a decline in Thinking Introversion or Theoretical Orientation (Clark and others, pp. 165, 169).

A different approach to the effects of college on rationality is to obtain self-assessments from students and alumni. Of the several studies that provide such information, almost all indicate that an overwhelming majority of students and alumni believe they achieved considerable progress in intellectual interests and rationality during college. These studies suffer from the subjectivity inherent in the method, but they provide evidence to reinforce other data. Lehmann and Dressel found that 73 percent of male students and 84 percent of female students reported an increase in their "interest in intellectual and cultural matters" (1962, p. 62). In a survey of alumni, Spaeth and Greeley found that 87 percent thought college had "greatly" or "somewhat" developed their "ability to think and express" themselves (1970, p. 40). Pace (1974a, pp. 52-53, 55-56) found that 72 percent of both alumni and upperclassmen thought college had benefited them "very much" or "quite a bit" in critical thinking ability. Gaff (1973, pp. 9, 10) indicated that "79 percent said they had developed more intellectual interests." Bisconti and Solmon (1976, p. 10), in a large survey of alumni, found that 96 percent reported that college had been useful in developing the ability to think clearly—43 percent that it had been "very useful" and 53 percent that it had been "somewhat useful." One possible dissenting note was sounded by Katz and Associates (1968, p. 23). Using a different means of assessment, in a study conducted at Stanford and Berkeley, they judged that "the current academic-intellectual program of the college has a strong intrinsic interest for no more than a quarter of the students."

A review of the data relating directly or indirectly to
change in rationality suggests that on the average students do
make gains but that the amount of these gains is modest.

Intellectual Tolerance

Intellectual tolerance refers to freedom of the mind. It includes
such personal qualities as openness to new ideas, willingness to
question orthodoxy, intellectual curiosity, ability to deal with
complexity and ambiguity, appreciation of intellectual and cultural diversity, historical perspective, and cosmopolitan outlook. These qualities probably are closely related to tolerance in
human relations, but we focus here on tolerance in the realm of
ideas.

Change in students' intellectual tolerance during the college
years has been studied frequently, with the use of various tests
designed to measure such negative qualities as rigidity, authoritarianism, dogmatism, and ethnocentrism and such positive ones
as complexity, autonomy, and social maturity. Some of these
tests measure interpersonal tolerance as well, but most do not.

Feldman and Newcomb (1969, Vol. II, pp. 49-56) summarized the results of many studies of change in intellectual
tolerance during college. The findings were so clear and striking
that they require very little explanation or interpretation. Almost every study revealed substantial increases in intellectual
tolerance among college students from the freshman to the
senior year. In the vast majority of the studies—for various
types of institutions and for various types of students and over
a period from 1938 to 1967—average increases ranged from one
third to one standard deviation unit.

We shall cite three examples of studies bearing on intellectual tolerance. In their work with students at Michigan State
University, Lehmann and Dressel (1962, 1963) used a dogmatism scale, developed by Rokeach, in which a high score signified a high degree of dogmatism. The results, as represented in
Table 8, show a substantial decline in dogmatism. Using scales
that are part of the Omnibus Personality Inventory, Clark and
others (1972, pp. 175-185) found gains of about a third of a
standard deviation on the Complexity Scale and gains of about

Table 8. Comparison of freshmen and seniors on a scale
measuring dogmatism

| | Freshmen | | Seniors | | Gain Expressed in Standard Deviation Units |
	Mean Score	Standard Deviation	Mean Score	Gain in Mean Score	
Men	166.85	25.61	153.98	−12.81	−.50
Women	162.87	25.14	146.69	−16.18	−.64

Source: Lehmann and Dressel (1962, 1963).

four fifths of a standard deviation on the Autonomy Scale. Trent and Medsker (1968, pp. 128-166, 291-313), who also worked with the Omnibus Personality Inventory, were able to provide comparative Complexity, Nonauthoritarianism, and Social Maturity for a large sample of high school graduates, some of whom went to college for four years, some of whom attended college one to three years, and some of whom went to work or became housewives. (See Table 9.)

In interpreting these results, a description of the tests will be useful (Heist and Yonge, 1968; Trent and Medsker, 1968; Clark and others, 1972). The Complexity Scale measures intellectual adventurousness: "High scorers are experimentally oriented rather than fixed in their way of viewing and organizing phenomena. They are tolerant of ambiguities and uncertainties, fond of novel situations and ideas, and frequently aware of subtle variations in the environment. Most persons high on this dimension prefer to deal with complexity, as opposed to simplicity, and are disposed to seek out and to enjoy diversity and ambiguity." The Autonomy Scale measures "nonauthoritarian thinking and a need for independence. High scorers are sufficiently independent of authority, as traditionally imposed through social institutions, that they oppose infringements on the rights of individuals. They are nonjudgmental, realistic, and intellectually liberal." The Social Maturity Scale is related to nonauthoritarianism and flexibility in thought: "High scorers tend to be uncompulsive, nonpunitive, independent, and not subject to feelings of victimization. They also possess genuine

Table 9. Average scores on complexity, nonauthoritarianism, and
social maturity, high school graduates of the class of 1959, by sex,
college attendance, and employment, 1959 and 1963

	Men			Women		
	1959	*1963*	*Gain*	*1959*	*1963*	*Gain*
Complexity						
Attended college four years	50.69	51.28	0.59	48.79	50.61	1.82
Attended college one to three years	52.28	50.67	−1.61	49.20	46.42	−2.78
Consistently employed: did not attend college	50.95	48.03	−2.92	46.44	44.43	−2.01
Homemaker: did not attend college				49.57	44.79	−4.78
Nonauthoritarianism						
Attended college four years	46.26	52.28	6.02	44.52	52.60	8.08
Attended college one to three years	45.23	47.08	1.85	43.84	47.47	3.63
Consistently employed: did not attend college	43.02	42.03	−0.99	40.78	40.46	−0.32
Social Maturity						
Attended college four years	53.34	62.50	9.16	52.85	63.37	10.52
Attended college one to three years	53.78	58.72	4.94	52.68	58.32	5.64
Consistently employed: did not attend college	50.00	53.76	3.76	47.82	51.16	3.34

Source: Trent and Medsker (1968, pp. 133, 137, 140, 151, 153). The normal standard deviation for all these data was 10.

curiosity and interest in intellectual and esthetic matters. Low scorers tend to be more judgmental, intolerant, and conventional in their thinking." The Nonauthoritarianism Scale, a derivative of the Social Maturity Scale, is designed to provide "a broad assessment of the subject's openness, objectivity, and flexibility of thinking."

Table 9, based on the work of Trent and Medsker, shows substantial gains during college in Complexity, Nonauthoritarianism, and Social Maturity. More significantly, it shows the dramatic differences in gains for those who attended college four years as compared with those who dropped out of college, worked, or became housewives. These findings remained valid when controls for student ability levels and socioeconomic status were introduced (Trent and Medsker, 1968, pp. 301-308). Feldman and Newcomb (1969) also summarized numerous studies showing differences in the degree of change in intellectual tolerance by academic fields. These results showed that gains in tolerance are greater among students of the arts and sciences than among those in such professional fields as business and engineering.

In the matter of change in the intellectual tolerance of students during the college years, seniors tend to be less authoritarian, less dogmatic, and less prejudiced than freshmen and more open to new ideas, and more able to deal with complexity and ambiguity. Numerous studies amply confirm this conclusion and reveal relatively large degrees of change.

As Keniston and Gerzon (1972, pp. 64-65) suggest, the liberalizing effect of college may have been on the increase over the past several decades.

Empirical data show that, other things equal, older college graduates tend to be less liberal than younger college graduates in almost every area measured. This lesser liberalism seems not to be the simple result of aging or true generational difference, but at least partly of different kinds of education received by college students in the past. . . . William Perry's work suggests one reason for the apparent increases in the liberalizing effects of college. Perry argues (*Forms of Intellectual and Ethical Development,* 1970, pp. 3-7) that a prime catalyst for the development of a relativistic and postrelativistic orientation is confrontation with multiple perspectives on truth and morality. He examined Harvard College examination questions in the years between 1900 and 1960, rating them according to whether or not an adequate answer required the consideration of two or more frames of reference. He found that a perspectival outlook was required by less than 10 percent of all examinations in 1900, but by about 50 percent of examinations in the same departments in 1950-60. Taking into account shifting patterns of course enrollment and curriculum, Perry estimates an overall jump from 10 percent to 75-80 percent in questions demanding a relativistic outlook from 1900 to 1960.

Esthetic Sensibility

One of the most frequently mentioned goals of higher education is to foster knowledge and interest in and responsiveness to the fine arts, literature, and natural beauty. There is evidence of moderate success in the attainment of this goal, at least for many students.

Feldman and Newcomb (1969, Vol. II) cite numerous studies. One series (pp. 2-9) shows without exception that seniors, on the average, score substantially higher than freshmen on a scale assessing esthetic values as measured by the Allport-Vernon (or Allport-Vernon-Lindzey) Study of Value or by similar instruments. The gains were mostly in the range of a quarter to a half of a standard deviation. Other studies produced comparable results, using the Estheticism Scale of the Omnibus Personality Inventory or similar instruments (see Lenning and others, 1974, pp. 371-398). Using the Estheticism Scale for 1,287 students in eight varied institutions, Clark and others (1972) reported the findings presented in Table 10. Trent and Medsker (1968) reported the mean score on the Estheticism

Table 10. Comparison of freshmen and seniors on an
estheticism scale

| | Mean Raw Scores | | Gain | Standard Deviation |
	Freshmen	Seniors	Gain	Standard Deviation
Men	11.0	12.1	1.1	5.1
Women	13.4	14.9	1.5	4.6

Source: Clark and others (1972, p. 172).

Scale of a large sample of persons four years out of high school, comparing those who had attended college four years with those who had been employed consistently. (See Table 11.) The

Table 11. Comparison of college-educated and employed youth on an estheticism scale

| | Mean Standard Scores | | |
	College	Employed	Difference
Men	47.9	41.3	6.6
Women	55.4	44.8	10.6

Source: Trent and Medsker (1968, p. 142).

magnitude of these latter differences can be judged in relation to the normal standard deviation, which is 10.0. The authors point out that the differences can be explained only partially by differences in ability levels or socioeconomic status. As would be expected, the above figures show that scores on estheticism tend to be higher for women than for men and that the gains in college are greater for women than for men—probably because more women than men take courses in the arts.

In his survey of upperclassmen in 1969, Pace found the following percentage of respondents reporting that they had benefited "very much" or "quite a bit" in "broadened literary acquaintance and appreciation" and "esthetic sensitivity—appreciation and enjoyment of art, music, drama" (1974a, pp. 56-57): in literature, 57 percent; in art, music, and drama, 53 percent.

From the many studies reviewed, we may conclude that college does, on the average, raise perception or appreciation of the fine arts and literature. We found no evidence on the effect of college on appreciation of natural beauty.

Creativeness

Educators aim, or hope, to enhance the creativeness of their students—to encourage imagination and originality in formulating new ideas and in producing new works of art. Though critics of higher education often allege that conventional techniques of instruction, such as textbooks, lectures, and examinations over assigned content, tend to suppress rather than encourage creativeness, there is little direct evidence on the matter one way or the other. Change during college with respect to creativeness has not been fully revealed in any studies because this complex phenomenon cannot be addressed by use of any single scale. (See Heist, 1968, Appendix.)

The Omnibus Personality Inventory includes two scales related to creativeness, the Originality Scale and the Complexity Scale. We have already explored changes in students during the college years as measured by the Complexity Scale and found that college is favorable to the maintenance, if not development, of ability to deal with complexity. Feldman and Newcomb (1969, Vol. II, p. 38) refer to three studies, by Flacks, by Chickering, and by Stewart, using the Originality Scale. These studies, relating to three atypical institutions (Bennington College, Goddard College, and University of California at Berkeley), showed modest gains. Nichols, in a study of a sample of National Merit Finalists, found that seniors were slightly more imaginative than freshmen (Feldman and Newcomb, p. 39). However, neither the Complexity Scale nor the Originality Scale was intended by the authors of the Omnibus Personality Inventory to be used singly to address creativeness, and so the meaning of these results is not clear.

Feldman and Newcomb (pp. 16-18) also cite numerous studies of the attributes that students value in future jobs. These studies reveal that "opportunity to be original and creative" is valued more highly by seniors than by freshmen. However, Heist (1968, p. 54), in a study of seven quite dissimilar institutions, found that in five of them the dropout rates were higher for students identified as creative than for students not so identified.

The evidence on creativeness is so scanty and so nebulous that educators should be cautious in making claims about the effect of college in enhancing this quality in its students. In extenuation, it should be added that the sources and conditions of true creativeness are so little understood that its appearance—often in unexpected circumstances—appears more as an act of

God than as an outcome of educational technique. (For discussions of the relationship between creativeness and education, see Heist, 1967; Kagan, 1967; Lytton, 1971; Lenning and others, 1974.)

Intellectual Integrity

Intellectual integrity, as we define it, refers to an understanding of the idea of truth, a disposition to seek and speak the truth, conscientiousness of inquiry, and accuracy in reporting results. Though intellectual integrity is part of the basic creed of the academic world that educators seek to impart to students, we have been able to find no evidence or even opinion about the success of higher education in this area. One would suppose that through four years of study involving constant contact with the results of research and scholarship in a variety of academic fields, a student scarcely could avoid acquiring some sense of the academic commitment to truth, of the necessity to maintain high standards of research and scholarship, of the importance of veracity in reporting results, of the role of criticism, and of the incompleteness and contingency of the truth as it is understood at any time. But to what extent this happens is unknown. One disquieting recent development is the apparent increase in cheating and plagiarism in the academic work of students and the collapse of many of the traditional honor systems.

Wisdom

Though there is almost no evidence that higher education helps students to develop into *wise* men and women, the higher educational experience can hardly fail to acquaint them with some of the benefits of foresight and restraint. We may presume that it contributes to the balanced perspective and ability to manage uncertainties that we associate with wisdom. One bit of evidence relates to that aspect of wisdom called judgment or prudence. Comparisons of college-educated persons with others, as shown in the discussion of practical competence (Chapters Five and Six), suggest that the college-educated may be somewhat more prudent than others in their savings and investments, consumer choices, mobility, practices relating to health, and so on. These data are suggestive but no more conclusive than the many definitions of wisdom itself.

Intellectual and Cultural Pursuits of Students

Some indirect and quite limited evidence on the effect of college on the cognitive development of students is derived from studies of their participation in intellectual and cultural activities during the college years.

Trent and Medsker (1968, p. 143) found substantial differences in cultural activities between high school graduates who had attended college four years and those who had been employed consistently for four years. The college group was more likely to browse in a bookstore and attend dramatic performances, concerts, public lectures, and art exhibits. Even after control for ability and socioeconomic status, the differences were marked. However, these results were undoubtedly influenced by the greater accessibility of bookstores and cultural events to college students than to working young people. Regarding reading preferences, Trent and Medsker found that the college group had shifted their interest slightly toward cultural magazines and significantly toward news magazines but that "as manifested by their reading habits, the college students did not appear to have increased markedly in intellectual interests more than employed youth" (p. 144). Regarding interest in classical music, the findings of Trent and Medsker were more positive. (See Table 12.)

Table 12. Percentage of 1959 high school graduates reporting "a great liking for classical music"

	College	Employed
Men		
1959	31%	16%
1963	37	14
Women		
1959	50	26
1963	50	13

Source: Trent and Medsker (1968, pp. 144-145).

Feldman and Newcomb (1969, Vol. II, pp. 47-48) mention several studies at various colleges indicating that college seniors are more likely than freshmen to engage in "self-propelled intellectual activities. . . . to attend university-sponsored film showings and lectures, to make extensive use of the library, to be more regular readers of newspapers, news magazines, and literary periodicals . . . to own a large number of books, to read poetry for enjoyment, to like classical music . . . to withdraw unassigned books and journals from the library and to read unassigned materials in their major fields." Clark and others (1972, pp. 219-223) found, in a study of eight varied institutions, that the percentage of students with personal libraries of at least modest size increased during the college years; that the percentage of students who said they liked classical and serious music increased and the percentage who said they liked popular music declined; that magazine preferences shifted from popular general magazines "toward more serious and demanding mass circulation magazines of comment, in part toward 'highbrow' magazines, and in part toward professional and scientific journals." The authors commented further (p. 223) that the college graduates who have acquired a taste for serious reading will make up ". . . the 'attentive audience' for serious political and cultural discussion, the large and growing audience of educated men. This is not the least important effect of mass higher education: not that it creates an educated cultural elite (which other more selective systems of higher education perhaps do more effectively), but that it raises the standard of mass entertainment and information by creating an audience for more serious popular journals and magazines."

Pace (1974a, pp. 66-67) reported on the responses of a large sample of upperclassmen regarding their participation in civic and cultural affairs. He found substantial participation. For each of nine political, artistic, and religious activities, a third to a half of all the respondents had taken part to a significant degree. Similarly, Katz (1968, p. 31) reported comparable data for students at Berkeley and Stanford. Both of these studies showed considerable participation in a wide range of activities.

Using data from the Undergraduate Survey of the Carnegie Commission on Higher Education, Bradshaw (in Trow, 1975) compared the responses of identical students at the time they entered college during the period 1966-1969 and in December 1969. In the 1969 survey, he found a sharp decline in the percentages for those who reported frequent or occasional visits to art galleries or museums and for those who reported frequent or occasional unassigned reading for courses. He also found in the follow-up that only about 20 to 30 percent of the respondents reported that they had attended a play or listened to classical music (p. 283). These results are not consistent with those from other studies.

The available information on the intellectual and cultural pursuits of students indicates that college has some impact, but how significant or lasting is hard to say.

Lifelong Learning

The literature on the goals of higher education is filled with the ardent hope that students will be prepared and motivated to go on learning throughout their lives. The evidence relating to this goal is found largely in surveys of the attitudes and behavior of alumni.

The residue of a college education. So far we have considered only cognitive gains that are revealed during the college years. The evidence would seem to support the conclusion that students learn something during their college years. But people tend to forget unused knowledge. Most studies show that 50 to 80 percent of what is learned in courses is lost within one year. However, one must be leery of easy generalization about the residue of education in college: No one remembers everything— or forgets everything. As Hodgkinson (1972) has pointed out, some courses may go into oblivion almost at the moment after the final examination, whereas others may set in motion forces that lead to continuing learning over a lifetime. And while exact chemical formulas and equations, the details of political life in the era of Charlemagne, the conjugation of Latin verbs, or the kinky demand curve as understood by economists may be retained by some, they tend to slip away if not used in later life. As Robert Benchley pointed out in an amusing essay, "What College Did To Me" (quoted in Howe, 1976, pp. 9-10), the residue is vague and miscellaneous. It is, therefore, unreasonable to judge the results of higher education on the basis of retained data; it is inevitable that much of the detail will vanish or prove useless.

However, the important *substantive* aims of higher education do lie in the realm of residues. These are likely to be broad general principles and concepts, such as the laws of thermodynamics; the basic differences between socialism and capitalism; the ideas of Freud; the concepts of natural selection and ecological succession; the concept of culture; the major episodes in history, such as the fall of Rome, the Renaissance and Reformation, the colonization of America, the American Civil War. The residues also consist of the skills and perspectives that enable students in later life to learn or relearn detailed knowledge in a variety of fields as occasion demands and to fit this knowledge into a framework of larger principles and concepts. "Information once possessed but not now available is not necessarily useless—it may function as a background, coloring one's attitudes and affecting . . . the assimilation of kindred ideas" (Hartmann and Barrick, 1934, pp. 256-257). The residues include the general knowledge and perspectives that enable students to participate in the general culture, for example, to read significant literature, to understand and appreciate the arts, to converse with educated people about matters of importance, to comprehend the news in historical, geographic, and social perspective, to have some basic understanding of science and technology, and to be at home with religious and philosophical issues. Perhaps most important of all, the residues may include the tendencies, triggered by college, that encourage future exploration and learning.

If the residues are the true and ultimate aims, and if precise memory of the details must be written off, then ought higher education to convey so much detail? (See Ellison and Simon in Solmon and Taubman, 1973, p. 56.) This is a matter of educational technique. The answer depends on whether

attention to detail produces more or better residues than instruction devoted to broad general principles and concepts.
Doubtless, it is less than productive to teach each subject as
though the student were on the way to becoming a specialist in
that field; on the other hand, it is probably not productive to
concentrate on broad principles at high levels of abstraction and
to skim over the content to which these principles apply. It may
be that general principles cannot be well understood without
reference to the details to which they apply; concern for detail
may provide experience in coping with complexity and may
give weight to the insubstantial world of abstractions; experience in coping with details may be necessary when students
confront new problems in later life. Moreover, there may be a
useful discipline derived from a degree of mastery over subjects
of study. The overwhelming opinion of faculty members, judging from their behavior, is that instruction involving considerable detail helps to produce desirable residues. It must be
acknowledged, however, that very little is known about the nature or extent of the residues from college learning. That is the
subject to which we now turn.

The cognitive abilities of alumni. A considerable body of literature about the attitudes, knowledge, and behavior of alumni
casts some light—albeit rather subdued—on the carry-over of cognitive learning to the years after college. The testimony of
alumni as to what college meant to them is one source of information.

Pace (1974a) asked a large sample of alumni of the class of
1950 about the benefit from various aspects of their college
education. The percentages reporting "very much" or "quite a
bit" are shown in Table 13. Though these data do not speak
decisively to the question of carry-over of college learning, they
do suggest that roughly two thirds of alumni feel that they received lasting benefits from it.

An ingenious study on "Measuring the Obsolescence of
Knowledge" by Rosen (in Juster, 1975, pp. 199-232) revealed
that college graduates are either "more efficient users of prior
knowledge in acquiring more knowledge" than high school

Table 13. Percentage of alumni reporting "very much" or
"quite a bit" of benefit from college education

Background and specialization for further education in some professional, scientific, or scholarly field	64%
Broadened literary acquaintance and appreciation	62%
Awareness of different philosophies, culture, and ways of life	64%
Understanding and appreciation of science and technology	54%
Vocabulary, terminology, and facts in various fields of knowledge	79%

Source: Pace (1974a, pp. 52-53).

graduates or, alternatively, that high school graduates "are subject to greater rates of depreciation-obsolescence" of knowledge than college graduates (p. 229). Though unable to distinguish clearly between these two possibilities, Rosen concluded (p. 231) that "college graduates are more efficient learners *relative* to their depreciation-obsolescence rates than high school graduates."

The many public opinion polls that have tested the information or knowledge of the U.S. population as stratified by level of education provide another source of evidence. This mass of material has been skillfully assembled and analyzed by Hyman, Wright, and Reed (1975).[5] Their data are derived from samples of the entire population and measure the ability: (1) to identify correctly prominent public figures and major public events; (2) to respond correctly to questions on vocabulary, humanities, history, civics and government, geography and science, and so on; and (3) to respond correctly to miscellaneous questions on popular culture and sports. On virtually all questions in these three areas, correct responses are closely correlated with level of education, the differences between college graduates and the high school graduates being substantial. Table 14 illustrates the results. It presents data for the thirty-seven-to-

[5] An earlier important study along the same line is recorded in Schramm and others (1967). They found that education is the dominant factor in people's knowledge of science, health, and public affairs.

Table 14. Mean percentages of persons of ages 37 to 48 responding correctly to questions in public opinion polls on information and knowledge, by level of education

	Number of Tests	1 Elementary School Only	2 High School Graduates	3 College Graduates	Difference 3 minus 2
From Surveys in the Early 1950s					
Domestic public figures	14	29%	52%	62%	10%
Domestic events	20	36	60	78	18
Foreign public figures	7	29	57	81	24
Foreign events	14	36	56	68	12
History	4	36	70	90	20
Humanities	13	13	46	78	32
Geography	5	33	53	77	24
Civics	9	38	67	82	15
Other academic items	2	85	94	99	5
Prominent figures from the world of popular culture and sports	11	42	57	61	4
From Surveys in the Late 1960s					
Domestic public figures	15	39	60	70	10
Domestic events	7	29	45	65	20
Foreign public figures	3	41	77	84	7
Foreign events	6	57	77	95	18
Civics	3	31	41	75	34
Vocabulary	6	36	64	77	13
Tools used by metal caster	3	41	54	53	– 1
Tools used by boilermaker	3	60	57	61	4
Duties of newspaper proofreader	3	45	79	89	10
Duties of personnel director	3	32	61	82	21

Source: Hyman, Wright, and Reed (1975, pp. 132, 134, 141, 143, 146).

forty-eight age group from surveys made in the early 1950s and late 1960s. The recorded differences between the college and high school groups are, of course, dependent on the nature of the questions and on their difficulty. However, it is evident that the college group consistently outperformed the high school group.

Hyman, Wright, and Reed were able to buttress their conclusions on the cognitive effects of education by introducing a variety of statistical controls. The effect of race was eliminated because their data refer only to the white population. Their basic data compared college graduates with high school graduates, but they also collected some information on high school and college dropouts. The introduction of controls for sex, religion, ethnicity, and geographic origin appeared to have little effect on the impact of college upon information and knowledge. Similarly, the controls for age and socioeconomic origin produced only slight overall change in the results (p. 69). Differences between the college and high school groups persisted into the oldest age bracket (p. 47) though they were somewhat smaller for this group. The control by current social position did reveal modest differential effects of education. As the authors state (p. 74): "In the great majority of tests, the effects of education persist even when the opportunities provided by current class position are equated. However, . . . there is considerable evidence that education, although significantly effective no matter what the opportunities or life style available, functions differentially depending on the circumstances. The effects of education are frequently enhanced among those whose circumstances are advantaged and attenuated among those in the less-advantaged positions." Regarding the relative effects of education on high school and college dropouts as compared with graduates, the authors found (pp. 52-53) that, in general, the knowledge of college dropouts was superior to that of high school graduates but inferior to that of college graduates. "Knowledge tended to rise with each step up the educational ladder, including the steps up to *some* secondary education and *some* higher education" (p. 52).

Hyman, Wright, and Reed (1975, pp. 59-60) concluded:

"These many basic findings establish that the better educated have wider and deeper knowledge not only of bookish facts but also of many aspects of the contemporary world; that the differences override obstructions and endure despite aging, and characterize individuals who represent several generations and several historical periods. . . . The differences by educational level are hardy. They withstand the massive barrage of controls. Thus the conclusions seem safeguarded by strong, if not definitive, measures. Reasonable men, recognizing the impossibility of exercising complete control over every conceivable factor that may contribute to both knowledge and educational attainment . . . should find the evidence persuasive."

The remarkable body of evidence assembled by Hyman, Wright, and Reed is indeed persuasive, but it may not be as decisive as they assert. Knowledge that is measured in public opinion polls consists mostly of knowing the identity of famous people and contemporary or historical events. The small number of questions relate mostly to geographic places, definitions of words, structural details of government (for example, number of U.S. senators), science (planet nearest the sun), health (symptoms of cancer), and practical everyday affairs (number of feet in a mile). The questions refer to discrete facts rather than broad principles, and require no reasoning, analysis, synthesis, judgment, or critical thinking. They resemble questions suitable for quiz shows—questions that call for single correct answers—rather than tests of deeper learning. Further, since they may be related more closely to information acquired through the media of mass communications than to what is learned through education, they may merely reflect the tendency of education to encourage media use. To be assured that the results obtained from polls are valid as measures or proxies of educational outcomes, one would need to explore the association between the ability to answer pollsters' questions and true learning of the kind educators hope to achieve. Nevertheless, the suggestive data provided by Hyman, Wright, and Reed constitute one bit of useful evidence on the outcomes of college.

Studies on the use of the media of mass communications

provide additional evidence on the cognitive residues of college. There is abundant evidence that college alumni read more than high school graduates. They buy, own, and read more books. They are more likely to have library cards. They read more magazines of all types, particularly more magazines devoted to news (such as *Newsweek* or *Time*) and analytic commentary (such as *The New Yorker, The New York Times Magazine,* and *The National Observer*). And though they do not spend much more time with newspapers, they pay more attention to serious content such as national and international news and editorials (Withey, 1971, pp. 95-109; Spaeth and Greeley, 1970; Hyman and others, 1975; Powers, 1976). These differences in reading habits persist when the college and noncollege groups are stratified by income (Powers, 1976) and by social origins (Hyman and others, 1975). Moreover, college alumni are less addicted to television than other people. When television was first introduced they lagged behind the rest of the population in purchasing sets. Though acquiring them eventually, alumni now spend less time as viewers and their viewing is weighted more heavily toward news, documentaries, and programs of educational stations (Withey, 1971; Roper, 1975). The percentage of college-educated people attending motion pictures is higher than that for the rest of the population (Withey, 1971). College-educated people are more likely than others to be engaged in adult education courses or self-study (see also Morgan, Sirageldin, and Baerwaldt, 1966, p. 155; Withey, 1971, p. 100).

The magnitude of the differences in media use between the college educated and the rest of the population may be judged by the figures in Table 15. These data are reassuring to a degree. Though one would wish that these data were controlled to screen out the effects of income, socioeconomic background, intelligence, and so on, nevertheless the differences between the college and noncollege groups are substantial, and it is scarcely credible that they do not in some degree reflect direct effects of college education.

To round out this assessment of the cognitive effects of college, we must attend to the artistic and cultural activities of college alumni. Though data on this subject are sparse, a few

Table 15. Percentage of population reporting use of various media of mass communications, by levels of education

	Noncollege			College	
	Elementary School Only	High School Graduates	All Noncollege (including High School Graduates)	Graduates	All College (including College Graduates)
Read newspapers daily (1961-67)[1]	65%	90%		92%	
Read about election campaigns in newspaper (1952-68)[1]	19	43		62	
Follow public affairs daily in newspapers (1960-70)[1]	24	48		67	
Read magazines (1955-67)[1]	45	78		93	
Follow public affairs in magazines weekly (1960-70)[1]	7	25		42	
Read news magazines regularly (1970)[2]			30%		54%
Read about election campaigns in magazines (1952-68)[1]	2	9		29	
Reading a book now or read one during past year (1952-63)[1]	32	63		91	
Read a book all the way through during last six months (1971)[2]			46		79
Have a library card (1973)[2]			28		64
Attended a movie within past six months or past year (1955-63)[1]	41	65		89	
View television daily[1]	77	79		71	
Watch election campaigns on television[1]	36	44		47	
Listen to radio daily[1]	61	60		55	
Listen to election campaigns on radio[1]	12	14		21	
Follow public affairs daily on radio or television (1960-70)[1]	41	54		58	
Taken adult education course in past year[1]	5	17		46	
Tried self-study[1]	24	39		61	

Sources:

[1]Hyman, Wright, and Reed (1975), pp. 164-183. The data refer to averages of several surveys made during the indicated period. They refer to persons of ages 37 to 48 or 36 to 50. Data for other age groups are available from the same source.

[2]Powers (1976, pp. 63-66).

pertinent public opinion polls show that substantial percentages of alumni take an interest in the arts. They engage in such activities as listening to classical music, reading poetry, attending concerts and plays, visiting museums, playing musical instruments, and painting. The participation of college-educated people is significantly higher than that for the rest of the population, and this conclusion holds when controls for income are introduced (Powers, 1976).

Pace (1974a, pp. 60-61) gathered data on participation in civic and cultural affairs as reported by a large sample of alumni of the class of 1950, representing varied institutions. He made no comparisons with noncollege groups, but he found that 40 to 50 percent of responding college graduates do take part to a marked degree in each of eleven political, artistic, religious, educational, and cultural activities.

All this evidence on alumni behavior as it relates to the goal of "desire and ability for lifelong cognitive development" resists definitive appraisal. Unfortunately, most of the data do not provide adequate controls to allow isolation of the effects of college from many other effects. Our judgment is that the goal is attained to a moderate degree.

Conclusions

We find the evidence about the cognitive outcomes of college education to be spotty, partly obscure, and incomplete. It is as though we have made an automobile tour on a day of patchy fog and clouds. Though much of the landscape was hidden, we have been afforded momentary glimpses from which we can try to reconstruct the whole landscape in our mind's eye. Virtually all of the evidence encountered suggests that college does, on the average, have a substantial cognitive impact—whether outcomes are measured by comparing freshmen with seniors, college students with comparable persons not attending college, or alumni with comparable noncollege people.

While there are some isolated studies that show no gains and a few that show losses in cognitive development, yet from the accumulation of evidence one can scarcely avoid the conclusion that college has a strongly positive impact on cognitive learning. The evidence points to the conclusion that, on the average, higher education significantly raises the level of knowledge, the intellectual disposition, and the cognitive powers of its students. We offer judgments about the cognitive effects of higher education as summarized in Table 16.[6]

Table 16. Summary of estimated average changes in cognitive learning resulting from college education

	Descriptive Term	Estimated Overall Change Expressed in Standard Deviation Units
Verbal skills	Moderate increase	.50
Mathematical skills	Small increase	.20
Substantive knowledge	Large increase	1.00
Rationality	Small increase	.35
Intellectual tolerance	Moderate increase	.60
Esthetic sensibility	Moderate increase	.60
Creativeness	Small increase	.20
Intellectual integrity	Not ascertainable	
Wisdom	Not ascertainable	
Lifelong learning	Moderate increase	.40

Evaluations of these cognitive impacts will vary, depending upon ideals held for college education and upon concepts of the possible. For those whose ideals and concept of the possible are very high, the performance may seem disappointing. On the other hand, for those willing to settle for less than perfection, the record is good. In interpreting these results we must recognize that there are several types of outcomes from college, the cognitive outcomes being only one. College serves diverse students with different talents and goals. Some students may receive their benefits from college largely in the form of affective development or practical skills. As Clark and others have

[6]See Appendix to this chapter for a description of the procedure by which these judgments were reached.

pointed out (1972, p. 148), "One of the strengths of American higher education is that it is diverse enough to accommodate the students who enroll for reasons other than the pursuit of scholarly interests." Not every academic purist will agree with this sentiment; if carried to an extreme, it would rationalize inferior academic performance. However, a realist will recognize that since the actual development of college students occurs unevenly along several dimensions, students whose development is primarily in noncognitive areas will tend to pull down average gains in the cognitive areas. As discussed at length in Chapter Seven, the impact of college must finally be judged by its effect on the whole person—not solely by its influence on the development of particular aspects of personality.

In ending this discussion of the cognitive outcomes of college, it may be useful to refer to the conclusions reached in some of the most distinguished studies of the subject. Feldman and Newcomb (1969, Vol. I, pp. 28-29) reached this cautious conclusion:

> Generally speaking, seniors, as compared to freshmen, have more liking for reflective thought, are more intraceptive (referring to an inner, subjective life), show more independence of thought, are more creative, and are more critical and analytic. Further, seniors are more interested in natural science, social science, and the humanities; they show more interest in artistic matters and activities. They are somewhat more likely to engage in self-propelled intellectual activities, such as attending lectures and cultural events, reading unassigned books, listening to classical music, and the like. Not all increases in intellectual orientation, however, are large enough to be statistically significant. This, together with the fact that some samples do not show any increases on some of the "intellectuality" scales, will not be altogether encouraging to those who feel that the primary goal of a college education is to make young men and women more intellectually disposed. . . . Other studies have

shown that on the average college students increase in
intellectual aptitudes (as measured by intelligence
tests)—including the ability to think critically—as
they progress through college, and that they show
gains in factual knowledge in various content areas, as
measured by achievement tests.

Trent and Medsker concluded (1968, p. 176): "Degree of measured intellectual orientation distinguished the groups [college
and noncollege], but while many of the differences were statistically significant, they were by no means great, particularly
when level of ability and socioeconomic status were held constant. Likewise, although a number of reported activities and
interests, such as viewing art exhibits and preference for classical music, distinguished the groups, many activities did not distinguish them to the extent that might have been expected. . . .
What distinguished [the two groups] was the development of
autonomy. Definitely there was a strong relationship between
entrance to and length of stay in college and the growth of
open-minded, flexible, and autonomous disposition." The conclusions of Hyman, Wright, and Reed are more definite and
optimistic (1975, p. 21): "The better educated do have wider
and deeper knowledge not merely of bookish facts but also of
the contemporary world, and . . . they are more likely to seek
out knowledge and be attuned to sources of information. The
differences will be found to be substantial in magnitude."

Appendix: The Estimation of Differences

A problem in interpreting such scattered data as those presented
in this chapter is to judge the *amounts* of change resulting from
college education. It is one thing to show that seniors differ
from freshmen or that college alumni differ from other comparable persons; it is another thing to describe meaningfully the
degree of change.

   One possible way to describe change quantitatively would
be to show percentage differences in average scores on various
standardized tests. This method would be acceptable if the various scales in use were expressed in dollars or some other univer-

sal measure. However, the scales are likely to reflect only ordinal, not cardinal, differences. A rather cumbersome, but widely used, method of solving the problem of measuring differences is to express them in standard deviation units.

The standard deviation is the geometric average of deviations from the mean. A geometric average allows both positive and negative deviations to be appropriately included in the average. In a normal distribution (see Figure 1): (1) about 68 per-

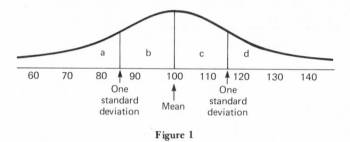

Figure 1

cent of the cases will fall within one standard deviation from the mean (areas b and c) and 32 percent will lie beyond one standard deviation (areas a and d); (2) if the distribution is divided into two equal halves (one including scores that are lower than the mean and the other scores higher than the mean), at each end of the distribution about 16 percent of the cases will lie beyond one standard deviation from the mean (areas a and d).

Suppose, on a test of verbal skills, the average score for a group of freshmen is 100 and the standard deviation is 15. Then suppose the same students, when tested as seniors, show an average score of 115. The gain is equal to one standard deviation unit. This tells us that the mean for seniors has reached a point that had been exceeded by only about 16 percent of the same students when they were freshmen. Had the senior scores been 130, that would have represented a change equal to two standard deviation units and would have signified that the mean score of seniors had been exceeded by only about 2.3 percent of the same students as freshmen. The same principles would apply, for example, in the comparison of scores for alumni with scores for noncollege persons.

The meaning of differences expressed in standard deviation units is illustrated by the data in Table 17. The percentages in

Table 17. Illustration of the degrees of difference as expressed in standard deviation units

If the difference between the mean score for seniors and the mean score for freshmen (in standard deviation units) is:	The senior mean will have been exceeded by the indicated percentage of freshmen:
.00	50%
.10	46
.20	42
.30	38
.40	34
.50	31
.60	27
.70	24
.80	21
.90	18
1.00	16

this table are applicable to the comparison of any two or more distributions measuring the same dimension, and so they provide a kind of universal measure of degree of difference among frequency distributions. They are strictly accurate, however, only in the case of normal distributions.

In judging the degree of impact of college on individual students or alumni with respect to various personality dimensions, our method is to review available evidence, make judgments about overall differences as expressed in standard deviation units, and then convert these judgments into descriptive terms as shown in Table 18. In making these judgments, the weights attached to various studies vary according to our

Table 18. Comparison of change expressed in standard deviation units
and change expressed in descriptive terms

If the overall change (in standard deviation units) is judged to be:	*Descriptive term to characterize degree of change:*
less than −.10	negative
−.09 to +.09	no change
.10 to .39	small increase
.40 to .69	moderate increase
.70 to .99	large increase
1.00 and over	very large increase
not ascertainable	not ascertainable

estimates of reliability of the data, adequacy of controls, and relevance to the personality dimension in question.

4

Emotional and
Moral Development

*The term, "aspects of personality," suggests
that there are many ways of looking at the
student. The meaning or significance of any
one of these aspects must ultimately be
understood in terms of the whole of which
it is a manifestation.*

from Burton R. Clark and
others (1972, p. 191)

We turn now to the impact of college on the *affective* development of students. The distinction between the cognitive and
affective dimensions of human personality is arbitrary. The two
domains are closely interrelated. Cognitive learning affects the
emotional and moral make-up of people, and affective development influences cognitive learning, especially through its impact
on motivation and purpose. Moreover, the available criteria and
measures of cognitive and affective development tend to overlap. Nevertheless, the distinction between the two is useful in
considering educational outcomes. This chapter deals with the
emotional and moral development of students, including such
elements as values and aspirations, personal self-discovery,
psychological well-being, human sympathy, morality, religious
interest, and refinement of taste, manner, and conduct.

At the outset we need to sound a note of caution. Withey (1971) warns against inflated expectations about the extent of affective change that is possible through college education. And Bidwell (1975, p. 1) expresses deep skepticism: "Despite a very great deal of research . . . the evidence is preponderantly of weak associations between college attendance and fairly trivial varieties of nonintellective change in students. It has not been shown persuasively . . . that the 'effects' observed are indeed attributable to college influence; more important, the processes by which they may occur have not been specified." Despite these caveats, we find considerable evidence that college not only can influence significantly the affective traits of students but actually does. Before launching into the subject, however, some preliminary comments on human development are in order.

The traditional way of looking at human development is that personality is formed largely in early childhood and that later education and life experience do not matter much for basic personality structure. In the past decade or two, however, a number of scholars have suggested that substantial human development and learning go on not only through early childhood and adolescence but throughout life even into old age (Freedman, in Sanford, 1962; Erikson, 1963; Singer, 1967; Kohlberg and Turiel, 1971; Hodgkinson, 1974; Adelson, 1975; DePalma and Foley, 1975; Cross, 1976). Though still in a formative and tentative stage, this viewpoint could have an important bearing on actual and potential outcomes of higher education—not only for students in the eighteen-to-twenty-two age group but for older adult learners as well. At any rate, many authorities (but not all) look upon the traditional college years as a period of significant personality change and regard the college or university as a favorable environment for achieving desirable personality development. Erikson (1963, pp. 262-263) spoke of the adolescent mind as "essentially a mind of the moratorium, a psychosocial stage between childhood and adulthood, and between the morality learned by the child, and the ethics to be developed by the adult." Freedman (in Sanford, 1962, pp. 864-865) suggested that "juniors and seniors should be regarded as belonging to a phase of development closer to that of the young alumnae than to that of freshmen and sophomores. Perhaps we should think of a developmental phase of late adolescence, beginning at some point in high school . . . and terminating around the end of the sophomore year in college; followed by a *developmental phase of young adulthood* that begins around the junior year and carries over to a yet undetermined extent into the alumnae years." Trent and Medsker (1968, p. 1) referred to "a growing emphasis on the view that although the effect of early environment is critical, there is potential for change, growth, and personality development at all stages of life, and particularly in adolescence and early adulthood." Similarly, Heath (1976, p. 185), in an intensive study of sixty-eight male college graduates in their thirties, concluded that after college the subjects had "become more mature on every single general measure of maturity used in the study," and he found "hundreds of specific examples in their interviews of how they had continued to mature."

Perry (1970, pp. 9-10) fashioned these ideas into a theory of personality evolution occurring during the college years in a series of distinguishable stages:

A. Main Line of Development

Position 1: The student sees the world in polar terms of we-right-good vs. other-wrong-bad. Right answers for everything exist in the Absolute, known to Authority, whose role is to mediate (teach) them. Knowledge and goodness are perceived accretions of discrete rightnesses to be collected by hard work and obedience (Paradigm: a spelling test).

Position 2: The student perceives diversity of opinion, and uncertainty, and accounts for them as unwarranted confusion in poorly qualified Authorities or as mere exercises set by Authority "so we can learn to find The Answer for ourselves."

Position 3: The student accepts diversity and uncertainty as legitimate but still temporary in areas where Authority "hasn't found The Answer yet." He supposes Authority grades him in these areas on "good expression" but remains puzzled as to standards.

Position 4: (a) The student perceives legitimate uncertainty (and therefore diversity of opinion) to be extensive and raises it to the status of an unstructured epistemological realm of its own in which "anyone has a right to his own opinion," a realm which he sets over against Authority's realm where right-wrong still prevails, or (b) the student discovers qualitative contextual relativistic reasoning as a special case of "what They want" within Authority's realm.

Position 5: The student perceives all knowledge and values (including authority's) as contextual and relativistic and subordinates dualistic right-wrong functions to the status of a special case, in context.

Position 6: The student apprehends the necessity of orienting himself in a relativistic world through some form of personal Commitment (as distinct from unquestioned or unconsidered commitment to simple belief in certainty).

Position 7: The student makes an initial Commitment in some area.

Position 8: The student experiences the implications of Commitment, and explores the subjective and stylistic issues of responsibility.

Position 9: The student experiences the affirmation of identity among multiple responsibilities and realizes Commitment as an ongoing, unfolding activity through which he expresses his life-style.

B. Conditions of Delay, Deflection, and Regression

Temporizing: The student delays in some Position for a year, exploring its implications or explicitly hesitating to take the next step.

Escape: The student exploits the opportunity for detachment offered by the structures of Positions 4 and 5 to deny responsibility through passive or opportunistic alienation.

Retreat: The student entrenches in the dualistic, absolutistic structures of Positions 2 or 3.

Kohlberg (1971) and others have constructed comparable patterns of human development. The purpose here is not to delve into the extensive literature or the subtleties of the theories but to suggest as a reasonable hypothesis that important affective change may occur in the lives of people while they are students in college. In the remainder of this chapter these changes will be considered under these following headings: Change in Values and Aspirations, Personal Self-Discovery, Psychological Well-Being, Human Understanding, Values and Morals, Religious Interest, Refinement of Taste, Conduct, and Manners, and Changes in Masculinity and Femininity.

Change in Values and Aspirations

There is some evidence of change in the broad general values and aspirations of students during the college years. The All-port-Vernon (or the modified Allport-Vernon-Lindzey) study of values purports to measure changes in the *relative* importance of six values: theoretical (cognitive learning); economic (practical affairs); esthetic (beauty); social (interpersonal relationships); political (power and influence); and religious (spiritual experience and theology). The many studies using this approach (Feldman and Newcomb, 1969) generally show that, on the average, the relative emphasis on esthetic values increases and the relative emphasis on religious values decreases. The results on the other four dimensions are less clear. However, most of the studies report small relative increases in social value and small relative decreases in economic and political value. These results pertain to relative emphasis on the several values, and say nothing about absolute changes. It would be possible for an individual's interest in all these values to grow (or decline) without any change in the relative emphasis on the several values. These studies tell us only that student values change during college, so that some values (especially esthetic) grow and that others (especially religious) decline, relative to one another. Another approach to the study of changes in values during college is through student attitudes toward the purposes of a college education, desirable attributes of a job or career, and lifetime plans and aspirations.

Regarding the purposes of a college education, all studies show that seniors place substantially greater emphasis on general or liberal education and less emphasis on vocational education than do freshmen (Feldman and Newcomb, 1969; Clark and others, 1972; Trent and Medsker, 1968; Lehmann and Dressel, 1962). Similarly, in considering the goals of higher education, alumni tend to give substantially greater emphasis to general education than to vocations (Spaeth and Greeley, 1970; Pace, 1974a; Beaton, in Juster, 1975).[1]

Regarding the desirable attributes of a job or career, seniors place less emphasis than freshmen on money, material possessions, and security and more emphasis on intrinsic rewards, such as opportunity to be creative, to use special talents, to be helpful to others, and to enjoy some independence (Withey, 1971; Clark and others, 1972; Feldman and Newcomb, 1969; Davis, 1965; Chickering, 1970; Bayer, Royer, and Webb, 1973). Some studies of alumni also show that college-educated people on the average are more concerned than other people about the importance, intrinsic interest, and opportunity for advancement in their jobs, and less preoccupied with income and security—as shown in the illustrative data in Table 19 (see also Withey, 1971). However, some studies suggest caution in accepting this conclusion. For example, Pace (1974a, pp. 72-73) reported that only a quarter of the upperclassmen of the class of 1970 and alumni of the class of 1950 approve of current social trends toward "less value on success and achievement." Similarly, a recent public opinion poll reveals little difference between freshmen and seniors in their personal aspirations for income (Gallup, 1975).

College apparently tends to raise the educational aspira-

---

[1] Clark and others (1972, pp. 216-217) found in a study of eight varied institutions (over half of them very selective) that seniors place much less emphasis than freshmen on grades. Dressel and Lehmann (1965), however, found the opposite result at Michigan State.

Table 19. Preferences for lifetime goals and job characteristics,
by level of education

	Education of Family Head			
	0-11 Grades	*High School Graduate*	*College No Degree*	*College Graduate*
Percentage of respondents giving first rank to following life goals:				
Prosperous life	40%	30%	30%	16%
Secure life	46	55	51	31
Important life	8	10	8	30
Exciting life	6	5	11	22
	100%	100%	100%	100%
Percentage of respondents giving first rank to following job characteristics:				
Income steady	39%	39%	24%	8%
Income high	24	10	16	8
No danger of being fired	19	9	11	1
Hours short	1	1	1	1
Advancement good	7	17	23	18
Work important	10	23	25	63
	100%	100%	100%	100%

Source: Strumpel (1976, pp. 34, 35). Based on a 1971 random sample of 574 male heads of family, most of whom were under 40 years of age.

tions of students. The percentage reporting plans to attend graduate or professional schools is greater among seniors than among freshmen—and the extent of change is greatest in institutions with a small proportion of freshmen who planned to go on (Clark and others, 1972; Feldman and Newcomb, 1969; Spaeth and Greeley, 1970). In recent years, however, with rapid changes in the labor market and in the larger culture, the effect of college on educational plans may have changed.

Several scholars (Jacob, 1957; Feldman and Newcomb, 1969; Bachman, 1972) point out that college has the effect of accentuating trends in personality development that were evident at the time the student entered. As Feldman and Newcomb (1969, p. 333) have written: "Whatever the characteristics of an individual that selectively propel him toward particular educational settings—going to college, selecting a particular one, choosing a certain academic major, acquiring membership in a particular group of peers—those same characteristics are apt to be reinforced and extended by the experiences incurred in those selected settings." Clark and others (1972) modified this conclusion by distinguishing among the anchoring, accentuation, and conversion effects. The anchoring effect refers to the tendency of some colleges or subenvironments within colleges to sustain the conservative social attitudes and religious beliefs of their students. The accentuation effect refers to the various ways that tendencies present at admission are strengthened. And the conversion effect refers to significant changes in the trend of development, resulting in alteration of personality structure. They wrote (p. 306), "The conversion effect is witnessed in the student who makes the big leap in orientation and/or commitment, an alteration in mind and character that academics so often hope to impel. Just as 'conversion' is a dramatic change, it is also a rarity; even those who hope for significant impact from college experiences would not expect it to occur easily or frequently." Their studies indicated (p. 307) that, on the average, about 7 percent of the students undergo personality changes sufficient to be described by the word "conversion" and that colleges of various types differ considerably in their impact (see also Feldman and Newcomb, 1969).

Personal Self-Discovery

One of the most far-reaching functions of higher education is to help students consider their lifetime aspirations for careers and other pursuits, and to reach decisions—some short-term and some long-term—affecting the basic shape of their future. During the college years each student attempts to discover a way of life that suits his or her unique talents, interests, and values. The process of individual self-discovery is also important to society, because it helps to discover talent and to place people in those roles where they can be socially useful and productive as well as personally fulfilled.

College emancipates young people from their childhood environments and subjects them to new experiences, challenges, and influences. It presents new styles of life, new people in the form of student peers and faculty, new ideas and ways of thinking, new extracurricular activities, and new options. And it offers various forms of counseling and vocational placement. It allows each student to try out different fields of study, to take part in varied activities, to encounter people of diverse personalities and values, and to reach decisions on his own. It opens up aspects of the world of which the student had not been aware and thus presents new horizons and new possibilities. It motivates the student through grades, certificates, degrees, honors, letters of recommendation, and many less formal but effective evaluative devices. In many cases, all this happens without forcing the student into irrevocable commitments and without the constraint of heavy family and other responsibilities. As Withey (1971, p. 38) observed: "For many people college may represent the last significant self-confronting experience. It provides an opportunity for meeting people of varying backgrounds with different ideas, at a time of life when self-examination is maximized and in an institution that legitimizes the identity task of exploring and reevaluating one's values and ideologies."

There is an abundance of evidence about personal self-discovery during college and related changes in values, attitudes, and life choices. In the preceding section we have seen that interests and values evolve, that attitudes toward the purposes of college education are modified, that the likelihood of graduate or professional education is increased, that the desired attributes of careers are changed, and that aspirations are raised. Feldman and Newcomb (1969) cite many studies reporting changes on the part of college students in major field of study and in occupational choice. (See also Spaeth and Greeley, 1970; Davis, 1965; Astin and Panos, 1969.) These studies show generally that between one third and two thirds of all students significantly alter their choices of major fields or careers during the college years (Feldman and Newcomb, 1969, Vol. I, p. 37).

But personal self-discovery goes beyond the choice of a major field and of a career. It includes search for identity and discovery of interests, values, and aspirations in the nonvocational aspects of life. Monsour (1975, pp. 1-2) reports that "the interests uppermost in the minds of freshmen have to do with academic interests, choices of majors, and career directions whereas questions about personal values, personal identity, and personal growth preoccupy juniors and seniors. . . . In American society and culture at least, the time when these questions are first seriously considered coincides precisely with the college years." Gaff (1973, p. 10) found that 86 percent of the students in a group of varied institutions reported greater self-awareness as a result of their college experiences. Pace (1974a, pp. 52, 56) found that among the benefits of college, personal development—understanding one's abilities and limitations, interests, and standards of behavior—was ranked first by upperclassmen and third by alumni. Eighty-four percent of the upperclassmen and 66 percent of the alumni in his sample indicated that they had received "very much" or "quite a bit" of benefit from college in the form of "personal development." In the studies of Spaeth and Greeley (1970, p. 40), 64 percent of alumni reported that college had "helped me to formulate the values and goals of my life." In a longitudinal study of Haverford College alumni, Heath (1976, p. 178) concluded "that it is important for educators who wish to evaluate the effects of their programs to distinguish between short- and long-term effects. For example, the principal effects of the college on its undergraduates while in college were, in terms of the model of maturing, to increase the integration of their skills and knowledge; the symbolization of their self-concepts; and the integration, symbolization, and allocentric maturation of their personal relations. However, for the alumni, the effects of the college that persisted as the enduring ones were different; namely, the stabilization and integration of their self-concepts and values."

In conclusion, the evidence, though largely based on subjective reports, supports the view that a major outcome of higher education is to facilitate the search of each student for his identity—for discovery of his talents, interests, values, and aspirations. It may well be that this is one of the more important services that higher education can render for its students. Moreover, this outcome inevitably has a bearing on the "placement" of students, not only in their careers but also in their roles as participants in family life, religious organizations, political activities, recreation, and cultural pursuits.

Psychological Well-Being

The preceding chapter on cognitive outcomes of higher education considered changes in students during college in "intellectual tolerance," and reported on evidence drawn from tests purporting to measure nonauthoritarianism and social maturity. Because these dimensions of personality cover aspects of mental health beyond intellectual tolerance, they are pertinent to the present section. These tests, as reported in Table 9, showed pronounced gains during college in autonomy, nonauthoritarianism, and social maturity, and pronounced differences between those attending college and those not attending. However, additional evidence on the impacts of college on mental health should be reviewed.

Feldman and Newcomb (1969, Vol. II, pp. 57-60) summarized a large number of miscellaneous studies comparing freshmen and seniors on "dominance" and confidence, including such traits as social poise, self-assurance, imperturbability, self-sufficiency, and leadership. An overwhelming majority of these studies showed gains between the freshman and senior years. The degree of change, however, was not striking, ranging between one tenth and one third of a standard deviation.

Similarly, a review of many studies relating to "Readiness to Express Impulses" (Feldman and Newcomb, 1969) shows consistent increases during college. The meaning of these findings is somewhat ambiguous. When carried too far, impulse expression may be construed as irresponsibility, lack of self-control, or inability to defer gratification. But, when kept within reasonable bounds, it may be a sign of mental health that reflects spontaneity and freedom from the need to suppress inner needs, tendencies, and feelings. The degree of increase in the observed scores on Impulse Expression has been generally regarded as favorable. As Clark and others (1972, pp. 191-192) pointed out: "A mark of a mature person is a degree of openness not only to others and their viewpoints, but to oneself, to one's own sometimes socially undesirable fantasies, wishes, and desires as expressed in a certain degree of spontaneous, impulsive behavior or at least a recognition that one has these thoughts, wishes, and tendencies. A denial of one's tendencies and feelings, when he has them, will keep a person from fully coming to terms with himself and his environment. The measure of Impulse Expression assesses the degree to which a student is open to, and accepts, his own impulses and fantasies."

Coupled with the gain in Impulse Expression is a pronounced decline among college students, on the average, in Schizoid Functioning. This measure, focused on anxiety and alienation, represents the obverse of the spontaneity and freedom measured by Impulse Expression. Clark and others (1972, pp. 191-200) reported their findings on both these measures in their study of 1,287 students representing eight varied institutions. The degree of change on these two dimensions was of the order of half a standard deviation and suggests a substantial average gain in well-being during the college years. This finding is important in view of the reliability and rigor of the research techniques.

Other studies relating to psychological well-being have produced less definite returns, possibly because of the variety of attributes measured: emotional stability, guilt proneness, tension, mental health, adjustment, neurotic tendency, anxiety, depression, paranoia, and hysteria, among others. Some show gains, some losses, and some little or no change (Feldman and Newcomb, 1969). Feldman and Newcomb (Vol. 1, pp. 35-36) concluded: "Considering these scales as general indicators of psychological well-being, we find no uniform directional trend in these studies. . . . Even if the trends were clearer, their interpretation would in many cases be problematical." (See also Lenning and others, 1974.)

Public opinion research contributes some interesting and suggestive, though not definitive, evidence about the relation between college education and mental health. Gallup (1975, p. 59) shows that 95 percent of college students report that they are "very happy" or "fairly happy." However, freshman reported the same degree of happiness as seniors did. Another study covering the general adult population in 1974 (Powers, 1976) showed only a slight difference in favor of the college-educated over others in reported degree of happiness, especially when the data were stratified by income. A 1960 study produced similar results (Withey, 1971). A study relating to sense of self-esteem (Cobern and others, 1973) showed only a slight difference between high school graduates and those with education beyond high school. Several studies relating to sense of control over one's destiny do show modest differences in favor of the college-educated. In one study, 53 percent of those with a high school education reported that their "sense of personal effectiveness" was high, as compared with 61 percent of those who had attended college (Lansing and Mueller, 1967, p. 180; see Strumpel, 1976). In another study, 73 percent of the non-college group and 85 percent of the college group reported a sense of significant control over their personal destiny (Powers, 1976, p. 98). In a study of the general evaluation of life, 60 percent of the noncollege group and 41 percent of the college group said that life was routine or dull (Powers, 1976, p. 97). Finally, a study of the extent of worry showed that 61 percent of the college group and 54 percent of the high school group indicated that they have few worries (Withey, 1971, p. 87). All of these results give a slight edge to the college experience.

Perhaps the most important study relating education to psychological well-being was conducted by Gurin, Veroff, and Feld (1960, pp. 210-211). Basing their investigation on an in-depth survey of a representative sample of 2,460 persons over the age of 21, the authors reached these conclusions regarding the impact of education:

> First, people with more education seem to be more introspective about themselves, more concerned about the personal and interpersonal aspects of their lives. Secondly, more educated people seem to have,

coupled with this introspectiveness, a greater sense of well-being and satisfaction.

Their introspectiveness is reflected in the greater prevalence among the more educated respondents of (1) feelings of inadequacy both as a parent and as a husband or wife, (2) reports of *both* short-comings and strong points in the self, and (3) more of the psychological immobilization symptoms.

In addition to these indications of introspectiveness, the context within which these more highly educated respondents evaluate their adjustment reflects a greater awareness of the potential for gratification or frustration of emotional needs in various aspects of their life functioning. . . . The more highly educated respondents . . . seem to be more aware of *both* the positive and the negative aspects of their lives. They are happier—in their overall evaluation of their current happiness, in their marriages, and in their jobs— and are more optimistic about the future than the less educated respondents.

These two themes which appear so clearly in our data seem to point to education as broadening one's perspective and raising one's aspiration level—which leads to both an increased realization of problems and unfulfilled expectations, and a greater awareness of life satisfactions. . . . these educational differences are maintained even when . . . income level is held constant. . . . Thus, the findings on the greater satisfactions associated with higher education cannot be viewed merely as a reflection of the greater material advantages that also tend to come with higher education.

The idea expressed by Gurin and his colleagues, that happiness is a function not only of people's objective conditions but also of their subjective standards and interests, has been developed in some detail in a report for the Organization for Economic Cooperation and Development (OECD), *Subjective*

Elements of Well-being (Strumpel, 1974) and in Campbell, Converse, and Rogers, *The Quality of American Life* (1976). (See Chapter Nine.)

Data on admission to public mental hospitals show sharply lower rates of admission for college-educated people than for others (Cobern, Salem, and Mushkin, 1972). But the data on admission to public and private outpatient psychiatric services are less clear. For younger age groups, the admission rate for college-educated people is greater than that for high school graduates, whereas for older age groups the reverse is true (Coburn, Salem, and Mushkin, 1972, p. 53). These data are doubtless affected by the greater awareness of and accessibility to psychiatric services on the part of college-educated people. Berelson and Steiner (1964) concluded that the higher the social class and level of education, the better the chances that people will finish and benefit from psychotherapy.

Another bit of evidence on mental health, based on a 1970 study of Dupuy and others, is summarized by Withey (1971, p. 84): "Looking particularly at symptoms of psychological distress, such as headaches, dizziness, and nervousness, a definite trend of higher symptom rates occurred for the less-educated compared with the more-educated groups. The symptoms showed the greatest number of statistically significant variations with education. But only nervousness showed a counter pattern in that the less-educated had lower rates for nervousness than the more educated. But the incidence of nervous breakdown was always lower for the better educated, for each sex, at all age levels." Moreover, several psychologists have expressed the view that college provides needed emotional support for students who are passing through several critical stages of development on their way from adolescence to maturity (Bloom, 1975; Perry, 1970).

College education in its current state of development may contribute slightly to psychological well-being and is probably, on the average, not harmful to mental health. Although nothing in life offers a sure road to serenity, happiness, or psychological adjustment, the higher education experience does seem to provide a range of resources from which the individual can build a sound psychological base.

Human Understanding

The evidence quite clearly suggests that college increases the capacity of people to tolerate, to understand, and to communicate with others. Indeed, education is the most significant predictor of tolerance. As we have already seen, college reduces authoritarianism, dogmatism, ethnocentricism, and prejudice in the intellectual sphere. College achieves the same result in the area of interpersonal relations (Feldman and Newcomb, 1969; Withey, 1971; Lehmann and Dressel, 1962; Lenning and others, 1974). These two effects are closely linked. Most studies find that college-educated people are more tolerant and less prejudiced toward different races, nationalities, and religions, and also toward women's liberation. Moreover, the majority of alumni and upperclassmen report that college helped them to become more tolerant and understanding of others and more skilled in interpersonal relations (Spaeth and Greeley, 1970; Pace, 1974a). Indeed, most students and alumni report that getting along with people is one of the most significant results of their college education.

On the other hand, college apparently does not have a marked impact on Social Value, as measured by the Allport-Vernon and Allport-Vernon-Lindzey instruments (Feldman and Newcomb, 1969). *Social value* refers to interest in other persons in terms of love, altruism, kindness, sympathy, and unselfishness. Most, but not all, studies reveal a modest gain in social value during the college years. Though the amount of gain varies from study to study, in most cases it is less than one fifth of a standard deviation. In another set of studies, which measure sociability and friendliness (Feldman and Newcomb, 1969, Vol. II, pp. 71-74) on the Social Introversion scale of the Omnibus Personality Inventory or other instruments, seniors appeared to be "less sociable," "less socially adventurous," "less socially integrated," "less friendly," and "more aggressive." They also appeared to have less need for affiliation and less need to be nurturant to others. Comparative attitudes of freshmen and seniors toward developing "ability to get along with different kinds of people" supply another bit of evidence on the matter of sociability. In a series of studies, relatively fewer seniors than freshmen rated interpersonal skills as an important goal (Feldman and Newcomb, 1969). These various results may well be a manifestation of the increasing leadership ability, confidence, self-sufficiency, independence, and autonomy that characterize seniors as compared with freshmen.

The conclusions regarding the effect of higher education on human understanding are mixed. On the one hand, college appears to reduce authoritarianism, dogmatism, ethnocentrism, and prejudice. This is a notable achievement and may be one of its most important outcomes. On the other hand, college seemingly does not have a marked impact on attitudes of altruism and philanthropy leading to kindness, sympathy, unselfishness, sociability, or friendliness toward other individuals. These results may mean that college reduces prejudice toward groups of people on the basis of their race or sex or nationality without greatly affecting their one-to-one human relationships.

Values and Morals

In 1957, Philip Jacob shocked the world of higher education with his book, *Changing Values in College*. On the basis of evidence then available, he concluded that American college students of the mid-fifties were "gloriously contented," "self-centered," aspiring to "material gratifications for themselves and their families," "conformists," "vocationally oriented," and "easily tolerant of diversity" (pp. 3-5). He commented (p. 6):

> The main overall effect of higher education upon student values is to bring about general acceptance of a body of standards and attitudes characteristic of college-bred men and women in the American community. There is more homogeneity and greater consistency of values among students at the end of their four years than when they begin. Fewer seniors espouse beliefs which deviate from the going standards than do freshmen. The student has ironed out serious conflicts of values or at least achieved a workable compromise. Throughout, no sharp break seems to occur in the continuity of the main patterns of value which the students bring with them to college.

Changes are rarely drastic or sudden, and they tend to emerge on the periphery of the student's character, affecting his application of values, rather than the core of values themselves. To call this process a *liberalization* of student values is a misnomer. The impact of the college experience is rather to *socialize* the individual, to refine, polish or "shape up" his values so that he can fit comfortably into the ranks of American college alumni.

Since the appearance of the Jacob study, much has happened: the student outbursts of the 1960s, the revolution in campus parietal rules and behavior patterns, the enormous growth of enrollments, the introduction of millions of "new students" to college campuses, and the proliferation of research on the effects of college. More recent appraisals of college impact on values have differed from Jacob's. For example, Feldman and Newcomb commented (1969, Vol. I, p. 4): "Our conclusions are more optimistic than Jacob's. There are conditions under which colleges have had (and, we assume, will continue to have) impacts upon their students, and not least upon student values. Moreover, the consequences of these impacts often persist after the college years."

Some authorities have postulated that the effect of college may be not only to change the specific content of values but also to bring about a total integration of the personality as the matrix for formation of specific values. For example, Perry (1970, p. 202) has suggested that one of the hoped-for stages of personal development among young men and women is the "ultimate welding of epistemological and moral issues in the act of commitment." Through detailed interviews with students at Harvard, he concluded that many students reach the stage at which they experience "the affirmation of identity among multiple responsibilities" and realize "commitment as an ongoing, unfolding activity" (p. 10). Similarly, in a study of small colleges, Chickering (1972) has suggested that college may be a significant vehicle for the achievement of integrity. He wrote (p. 123): "Development of integrity is closely related to establishing identity and clarifying purposes. A personally valid set of beliefs and values that have internal consistency and that provide at least a tentative guide to behavior, affect, and are affected by, conceptions of the kind of person one is and would become, and by dominant interests, occupational plans, and life-style considerations. . . . Values are the standard by which behavior is evaluated." Along with many others, Chickering found that the values students bring to college change slowly, but he added (pp. 126-127), "The bases on which values rest, the ways in which they are held, and the force with which they operate in daily life, may be of more importance—within limits—than the particular values held."

Another approach to the matter of values is through a series of studies in which students were asked to express their views about the purposes of a college education. These studies found virtually no difference between seniors and freshmen in responses to the question of whether college should help develop their "moral capacities, ethical standards, and values" (Feldman and Newcomb, 1969, Vol. II, pp. 10-15). Similarly, in his study at Berkeley and Stanford, Katz (1968) has shown that freshman and senior value rankings are very similar, signifying little or no change during the college years. Another obvious warning against too easy acceptance of college influence as favorable to the development of sound values is that academic cheating, shoplifting, and vandalism have been on the increase on most campuses in the past decade. Moreover, the revelations about misconduct in the higher reaches of business and government—where virtually all of the persons involved are college-educated—surely implies that the spread of college education has not brought on a great moral renaissance (Halberstam, 1973). Some observers who are concerned about the allegedly slack moral condition of American society hold college and university educators primarily responsible (Benson and Engeman, 1975).

Insights into the effects of college on certain aspects of morality may be derived from surveys of attitudes toward specific kinds of personal behavior. These surveys suggest strongly that higher education has, at least in recent years, tended to impart greater flexibility, tolerance, permissiveness, and individual choice in matters of personal behavior (see Katz, 1968; Chickering, 1972). Higher education appears to have been near the vanguard in the decline of Puritan values in our society. This appears to be true whether one compares seniors with freshmen, college students with other young people of comparable age groups, college alumni with noncollege adults, or trends over time in the attitudes of college students. As Yankelovich (1974b) has shown, noncollege youth have been following college students—with a lag of only a few years—in the espousal of new attitudes that place an emphasis on individual freedom and choice in personal behavior and that deny conventional values. Yankelovich (p. 9) provided this account of "cultural diffusion."

> Social change is often initiated by small extremist groups. The mass of the public react initially by rejecting the new ideas, and then begin to consider them with tempered selectivity. The proposals of the extremist groups become, in effect, a vast smorgasbord from which people of more moderate temperament pick and choose those ideas that fit best with their own traditional life styles. The process may be maddening to the purists, but a remarkable amount of social change is eventually effected.
>
> In the mid-1960s we identified a subgroup of college students as "Forerunners." This group—never a majority of the college population—struggled to live by a new set of post-affluent values. We were struck by two motivations that seemed to enjoy exceptional strength among the so-called Forerunner students: one was private, directed toward personal self-fulfillment; the other was public, directed toward a vision of what a just and harmonious society might be.

The experience of the late 1960s, when student unrest was at its height, may also shed some light on the question of values. This episode was a sudden mobilization of values long latent in the college population, against such acute social problems as racial and sexual injustice, deterioration of the environment, rampant population growth, paternalism on campus, and, in particular, the Vietnam War and the draft. The student movement, built around humanistic conceptions, sought an egalitarian and person-centered society and opposed material values, bureaucratic organizations, nationalism, militarism, and individual conformity. The implicit values were akin to those often prized within the academic community and which in one form or another are part of the teachings of liberal education. At least one possible interpretation of the experience of the turbulent 1960s may be construed to mean that college transmits values to some of its students, that these values may be latent much of the time, and that under certain stimuli they can erupt into overt social action. One of the embarrassments to educators in dealing with the student protests was that on the whole they were sympathetic to some of the demands of students and to the value premises on which these demands were based, while being shocked and revolted by the tactics employed. (The events of the 1960s will be discussed further in Chapter Nine.)

From the potpourri of data, analysis, and conjecture on higher education and morality, only one definite conclusion emerges: the situation is fluid. In the last two decades, as our society has been undergoing a revolution in values and moral standards, higher education has had different effects at different stages. If Jacob was right in his emphasis on socialization in the 1950s, those who see forceful expression of the latent values of college students in the 1960s are also right, for that era. Yankelovich's theory of the Forerunners appears to be correct for the early 1970s. Finally, current critics of higher education seem to hit the mark by stressing a breakdown of conventional standards of personal morality on the campus. It is clear that in the late 1970s colleges and universities are far from being bulwarks of *conventional* morality, though some would argue that the new campus morality has more depth and less hypocrisy than the traditional brand.[2]

[2]For an extensive bibliography, see Lenning and others, 1974, pp. 399-476.

Two threads run through all this change. The first, which probably antedates the 1950s, is this: the influences of higher education that make students intellectually more flexible and tolerant, as well as less authoritarian and dogmatic, also operate to make students more flexible, permissive, and relativistic in their personal and social value judgments. Second, higher education probably has been more effective in promulgating social values as *ideas* about war and peace, international affairs, human rights, human equality, and the environment than it has in strengthening individual value systems of *personal* morality. College seems to be more influential in its effect on the attitudes of students toward groups of people in the abstract than toward particular individuals in the flesh. In the matter of personal morals, however, many would argue that in recent years college promoted greater candor, openness, and honesty—a new kind of morality rather than a stronger enforcement of conventional forms.

Religious Interest

The effect of college on religious attitudes and religious observance has been investigated in great detail. The results of the many studies can be discussed conveniently under three headings: changes in religious attitudes and beliefs during college; changes in religious observance during college; and comparisons of the religious attitudes and observances of college alumni with those of other members of the adult population.

Changes in religious attitudes and beliefs during college. As measured by the Allport-Vernon and Allport-Vernon-Lindzey scales, the relative strength of religious values declines during college. Virtually all studies using this scale have reached this conclusion (Feldman and Newcomb, 1969). The degree of change ranges mostly from .10 to .70 of a standard deviation.

Another set of studies on religious orientation, mostly conducted from 1929 through the 1960s (Feldman and Newcomb, 1969, Vol. II, pp. 25-36), yield somewhat more specific conclusions. With few exceptions, they indicate that students become less favorable toward the church, less convinced of the reality of God, less favorable toward observance of the Sabbath, less accepting of religious dogma, less fundamentalistic, less conservative, less orthodox, and more religiously liberal. The degree of change varies among different institutions. It is generally between .10 and .60 of a standard deviation. Moreover, the degree of change varies with the major fields of students, the greatest change occurring for those in the liberal arts, and the least for those in professional fields (1969, Vol. II, pp. 115-116).

In a study of 1,287 students at eight varied institutions, Clark and others (1972, p. 185) found that college students on the average gained nearly half a standard deviation in religious liberalism from the freshman to the senior year. Gains of these general magnitudes occurred for both sexes and at all eight colleges (except at one where there was no change for men).

Webster, Freedman, and Heist (in Sanford, 1962) reported on the responses of National Merit Scholarship winners to the question: "Do you personally feel that you need to believe in some sort of religious faith?" The percentages of affirmative responses were as shown in Table 20.

Table 20. Responses of National Merit Scholarship winners
on the need to believe in religious faith

	Men	*Women*
At time of entrance to college	88%	91%
At end of freshman year	70	76
At end of sophomore year	61	74
At end of junior year	51	69

Source: Webster, Freedman, and Heist (in Sanford, 1962, p. 826).

Trent and Medsker (1968) found that, of a large sample of young people four years out of high school, college graduates had substantially higher scores on religious liberalism than those who had been employed. The difference was especially marked for women. Trent and Medsker also asked the members of the sample whether they valued religion more or less than they did in high school. They responded as shown in Table 21. These results are of special interest. Though they show that the num-

Table 21. Percentages of college-educated and employed youth
reporting that they value religion

	Percentage Who Valued Religion		
	More	Same	Less
Men			
College group	47%	26%	26%
Employed group	43	43	12
Women			
College group	50	24	24
Employed group	59	33	7

Source: Trent and Medsker (1968, pp. 172-175).

ber of defectors from religion is greater among college youth than among working youth, they also show that half of the college group values religion more, and only a fourth of them report a decline in interest.

Lehmann and Dressel (1962, pp. 267-268) found that most students "feel they have become less attached rather than more attached to a religion that they believe in and can defend." Yet many of these same students continue to believe in the value of religion as the foundation of a mature life. A 1975 survey of the Carnegie Council found that 53 percent of undergraduate college students "believe there is a God who judges men" and that another 23 percent have the same belief "with reservations." Moreover, 15 percent considered themselves "deeply religious" and another 56 percent considered themselves "moderately religious." (Trow, 1977, tables 6, 8.) A 1960 study by Ferman compared the theological views of freshmen and juniors at Cornell University (Feldman and Newcomb, 1969) and reported remarkable stability in the percentage distributions of those holding various beliefs about God. A public opinion poll (Gallup, 1975) reflecting changes in religious beliefs during college also suggested that the changes may be of modest proportions. In this study, however, the direction of change was clearly toward less orthodoxy and less affiliation with formal religious organization. In another poll, Yankelovich

(1974b, p. 90) reported that 23 percent of college students responded affirmatively to the question of whether religion is a very important value, as compared to 42 percent of noncollege youth. Pace (1974a, pp. 56-57) found that among the many "benefits" upperclassmen reported they had received from college, "appreciation of religion" was at the bottom of the list. Only 35 percent indicated that they had received "very much" or "quite a bit" of benefit in the area of religion. This response may suggest the weak interest of students in religion, the ineffectiveness of the college environment in this area, or both.

Changes in religious observance during college. Formal religious observance as measured by church attendance drops off during the college years. Clark and others (1972) disclosed a substantial decline in frequency of church attendance in seven of the eight institutions they studied. Similarly, Gallup (1975) reported a significant though not dramatic decline in church attendance for a national sample of college students. Bradshaw (1974, p. 73), using data from the Carnegie Commission student survey, found a sharp drop-off in "frequent" church attendance from 64 percent of the students at time of entry to 30 percent among seniors. He also found a somewhat smaller decline in the percentage of students reporting "frequent" informal religious discussion from 35 percent among entering freshmen to 20 percent among juniors.

Church attendance is not the only vehicle that college offers for formal religious expression. Another is the formal study of philosophy and religion. The number of courses offered and the enrollments in them has increased greatly over the past two decades. These courses may be taking the place of the more traditional activities associated with the college chapel. Departments of religion now exist in many public as well as private institutions, and enrollments have been growing steadily. For example, the number of students enrolled for advanced degrees in religion (not counting those seeking professional degrees in theology) increased from 5,314 in 1960 to 15,431 in 1974 (American Council on Education, *Fact Book on Higher Education*, Second Issue 1976, p. 118). The number of undergraduate enrollments in religion is also known to have increased (Hoge, 1974). Along the same line, a recent poll of college students inquiring about the subjects of study that had most changed their outlook on life revealed that philosophy and religion were among the leading fields, along with psychology and sociology (Gallup, 1975). Perhaps more important, most of the available data on the religious outcomes of college antedate the current resurgence of evangelical or fundamentalist religious thought and practice, both on and off the campus, and the more publicized (though less widespread) vogue for various Far Eastern forms of religious thought and expression. The relatively rapid growth of private colleges affiliated with conservative or fundamentalist sects is also worth noting. In view of these crosscurrents, we should be wary of concluding that the higher education experience as a whole lessens lifelong interest in religious thought and practice or discourages the quest for the meaning of human existence.

Religious attitudes and observance of college alumni. The evidence about religious attitudes and observance of college alumni leaves the impression that higher education is less than a potent stimulus to lifelong interest in religion and to religious observances. From a public opinion study conducted by Roper in 1968, one would infer that, though most college alumni are interested in religious issues, many are skeptical of orthodox views and also of organized religion. Comparing the religious views of alumni with those of college students (Ferman, 1960; Gallup, 1975; Roper, 1968, quoted in Powers, 1976), one might conclude that interest in traditional religion declines after college. On the other hand, church attendance appears to be greater among alumni than among college seniors (National Opinion Research Center, 1974, quoted in Powers, 1976; Gallup, 1975). Also, most studies of church attendance report that college alumni attend in relatively greater numbers than noncollege persons (Morgan, Sirageldin, and Baerwaldt, 1966; Withey, 1971). A recent survey, however, reports no difference between the college and noncollege population in church attendance (National Opinion Research Center, 1974, quoted in

Powers, 1976). Finally, Pace (1974a) found that the percentage of alumni who mentioned religion as one of the important benefits from college was smaller than the percentage mentioning any other of a long list of benefits.

Conclusions on religious interest. Though data about religion abound, interpretations are difficult. The data clearly show a decline during college in relative emphasis on religious values. They also indicate that students on the average become less loyal to the church, less faithful in religious observance, less convinced of the reality of God, less accepting of orthodox religious dogma, and more religiously liberal. The decline in religious interest is of the order of a third of a standard deviation and the increase in religious liberalism is around half a standard deviation. Studies of the religious attitudes and observance of college alumni as compared with the noncollege adult population do not lend much support to the hypothesis that college arouses religious interest. But alumni, though evidently religiously more liberal than other people, probably attend church in about the same relative numbers.[3]

Most of the data on which the above conclusions rest refer to the recent past and do not take account of the current revival of religious evangelism and fundamentalism and the growing interest in Far Eastern religious thought. Also, they do not take account of the growth of formal courses in religion, in number of courses offered, and enrollments. For these reasons, it may be wise to reserve judgment on the effect of higher education in the area of religion. As Robert Bellah observed (in Hoge, 1974, pp. 8-9), "The categories of empirical social science seem much more oriented to traditional social forms and beliefs whose decline they accurately describe than to the newer social forms, commitments, and beliefs that may be taking their place. . . . New modes of social organization and belief may be emerging that our traditional concepts and indices are not picking up, modes that may reverse long-term apparent trends by initiating

[3]For a detailed bibliography of literature on college and religion, see Lenning and others, 1974, pp. 399-476.

entirely new tendencies. . . . Interest in religion among young people, as measured by class enrollment in religion courses, has not declined in the last twenty years and may have increased, even though orthodoxy has declined sharply. Does this not indicate a reservoir of support for new religious crystallizations?"

Refinement of Taste, Conduct, and Manners

Though the cultivation of good taste, good conduct, and good manners has been a traditional goal of higher education, no evidence exists as to the degree of its actual attainment. The change in student values and mores associated with the unrest of the 1960s, the rise of egalitarian values, and the rejection by most students of campus paternalism has led colleges and universities to play down their emphasis on taste, conduct, and manners. Nevertheless, college undoubtedly helps many students—especially those from limited family backgrounds—to acquire the kind of behavior patterns and manners needed for successful participation in both practical affairs and polite society.

Changes in Masculinity and Femininity

An unintended effect of college of special interest at a time of growing feminism is the bringing about of some convergence of interests and attitudes on the part of men and women. On the average, male students apparently move some distance from the stereotypic interests and attitudes of men, and women move some distance in the opposite direction. This subject will be considered further in connection with the discussion of family life (see Chapter Six).

Conclusions

The assembled evidence on the affective results of college education is far from definitive. The following outcomes, however, appear to be reasonable hypotheses if not settled conclusions:

1. Human personality development probably does not stop in early childhood but may persist at least

through adolescence and early adulthood and probably throughout life, even into old age.

2. The structure of values, that is, the relative strength of different values, appears to shift during college, with substantial increases in theoretical and esthetic values, substantial decreases in religious values, minor increases in social values, and minor decreases in economic and political values.

3. Several other indices of changes in values are: (a) college seniors and alumni assign a higher value to liberal education (as compared with vocational education) than do freshmen; (b) college seniors and alumni place more emphasis on intrinsic rewards from work (such rewards as opportunity for creativeness, use of special talents, independence, importance) and possibly less emphasis on money and security than do freshmen or persons without college education; (c) college tends to raise the educational and career aspirations of its students.

4. Colleges and universities appear to be effective in helping students to achieve personal identity—that is, to discover their talents, interests, values, and aspirations —and to assist them in making lifetime choices congruent with personal identity.

5. To the extent that college affects the personality of students, it is more likely to reinforce already present tendencies than to bring about a marked change or "conversion," though conversion occurs for a small percentage of students.

6. In its impact on the psychological well-being of students, college appears to strengthen autonomy, non-authoritarianism, and social maturity; to increase self-assurance and confidence; to enhance spontaneity and freedom; to lessen anxiety and alienation; and to increase the sense of self-esteem and control over one's destiny. These are significant achievements. However, other measures of psychological well-being yield variable and ambiguous conclusions. Nevertheless, on bal-

ance the evidence may justify the tentative conclusion that college fosters psychological well-being.

7. In its effect on human understanding, college quite clearly reduces prejudice, authoritarianism, dogmatism, and ethnocentrism. These are significant accomplishments, but they refer primarily to attitudes about other people in the abstract. In personal relationships, college apparently has little if any impact on such qualities as altruism, kindness, generosity, friendliness, and helpfulness.

8. The effect of college on the social and personal morality of students is uncertain. Some authorities hold that college assists in the integration of personality and thus provides the needed framework or foundation for coherent moral choice throughout life. Also, some point to the student uprisings of the 1960s as evidence of the success of college in the moral domain—however fleeting that moment of success may have been. Others ascribe the alleged moral weaknesses of our society to failures of college educators. At any rate, in the realm of personal behavior, the campus clearly has been in the vanguard of recent tendencies toward flexibility, relativity, tolerance, permissiveness, and individual choice.

9. Regarding religious belief and observance, college is associated with increasing liberalism of religious thought. It is also associated with decreasing interest among students in formal religious expression and observance, though church attendance among alumni is at least as great as among those without college education. The growth of enrollments in college courses on philosophy and religion and the rise of evangelical and Far Eastern religious thought and practice among college students and college-educated people suggest that religious expression may be changing in form rather than declining in amount. However, the evidence does not justify the conclusion that higher education enhances religious interest.

10. There is no evidence on the effect of college upon re-
    finement of taste, conduct, and manners. Common
    observation suggests that college does help students to
    acquire personal refinement—sometimes more than
    they are willing to exhibit.
11. College produces some convergence of interests and
    attitudes between men and women and thus narrows
    personality differences between the sexes.

The evidence in this chapter about the influence of higher
education on affective characteristics may be summarized in
Table 22. (See appendix to Chapter Three for a description of
the procedures by which these judgments were reached.)

Table 22. Summary of estimated average changes in emotional and
moral development resulting from college education

	Descriptive Term	*Rough Estimates of Overall Change Expressed in Standard Deviation Units*
Values and aspirations	Small increase	.20
Personal self-discovery	Large increase	.90
Psychological well-being	Moderate increase	.40
Human sympathy		
Toward groups in the abstract	Moderate increase	.60
Toward individuals	No change	0
Morality	Not ascertainable	—
Religious interest	Moderate decrease	−.50
Refinement of taste, conduct, and manners	Small increase	.20

Though impressive, these conclusions do not add up to a
resounding affirmation of the positive impact of college upon
the emotional and moral development of its students. (See
Heath, 1976.) The evidence on which they are based is weak
and partly contradictory. Some of the evidence consists of ques-

tionnaires and opinion polls, which at worst are superficial and unreliable and at best do not penetrate very deeply into the personalities of individuals. Some of the evidence is dated and may not be relevant to the present or the future. For example, studies of attitudes on religion, personal morality, or lifetime aspirations done in the quiescent 1950s will not necessarily produce the same results as studies done in the turbulent 1960s or in the more tranquil 1970s. Finally, the outcomes revealed by the data—especially in the area of personal morals—will be judged differently by persons holding different philosophies and values. One of the main impacts in the affective domain appears to be in the direction of reduced prejudice and greater tolerance and liberalism toward particular groups, religion, and personal morality. This is a result that probably will be regarded by most people as favorable, but by some as deplorable.

The chief reservation about these conclusions is that they deal mostly with particular aspects of personality, one at a time. Because they are expressed in averages that obscure wide variability among persons, they do not make contact with whole human beings. One has the sense that it would be possible to go on and on, adding new statistics of this kind and refining the old, without ever knowing what really happens to *people* who go to college. In Chapter Seven of this book, we shall consider further the questions of changes in whole personalities.

The state of knowledge on affective development in college has been summarized usefully by Trow (1974a, p. 16):

> There really is no doubt that the experience of higher education has effects on students, both in their attitudes and behaviors. . . . It is true that most of the indicators of change . . . leave us dissatisfied: They are not adequate measures of things we are really interested in, such as growth and refinement of a student's sensibilities, the development of independence of mind, personal integrity, and moral autonomy. We know that these qualities are extremely difficult to study systematically: We don't know how to measure them; their appearance in action is often delayed

until long after the college years; they are the product
of a person's whole life experience, so that it is difficult to disentangle the independent effects of the college experience upon them. Nevertheless, to infer
from the difficulty of measurement that these effects
don't occur . . . is to make the most serious error to
which we members of the research community are
prone, the error of believing that if a phenomenon
can't be measured, it doesn't exist.

5

Practical Competence
for Citizenship and
Economic Productivity

*The outsiders want the students trained for
that first job out of college, and the academics
inside the system want the student educated
for 50 years of self-fulfillment. The trouble is,
the [students] want both. The ancient
collision between each student's short-term
and long-term goals, between "training"
and "education," between "vocational" and
"general," between honing the mind and
nourishing the soul, divides the professional
educators, divides the outside critics and
supporters and divides the students too.*

Harlan Cleveland (1975, p. 6)

To prepare people for competence in the practical affairs of life
is a major goal of higher education. The strident call for "relevance," so prominent in educational discourse during the past
decade, has been a demand for increasing attention to preparation for practical affairs—whether vocational or societal. Similarly, the frequent references to the need to help people cope
with the problems and complexities of modern life restate the

same demand. Educators hope and intend that college shall impart to students traits and skills that will help them function effectively as citizens, workers, family members, and consumers and that will assist them also to enrich their leisure and enhance their health. Opinions may differ as to the relative emphasis that should be devoted to liberal education and to vocational education, or as to the efficacy of liberal education in practical affairs, but no one disputes that practical competence is a significant outcome of both. This chapter and the following one assemble evidence on the effects of higher education on practical competence.

General Traits of Value in Practical Affairs

Almost all of the cognitive and affective outcomes of college described in the preceding two chapters are useful in everyday life. In addition, students may develop certain other personal qualities or traits that are equally helpful in their lives. We shall consider four of these: need for achievement; future orientation; adaptability; and leadership.

Need for achievement. This includes such qualities as motivation toward accomplishment, persistence, energy, and drive. McClelland (1961 and 1971) has strongly emphasized this factor as a basic element in the accomplishments both of individuals and of nations. He has found interesting correlations between measures of "need for achievement" and the rise and fall of civilizations, the characteristics of statesmen, and the performance of individuals. McClelland has suggested that "need for achievement" is correlated with education (1971, pp. 7-13), but the direction of causation is not clear. Feldman and Newcomb (1969) have summarized studies relating to the attitudes of college students about the desirable attributes of a future job or career. These studies generally show that seniors value more than freshmen an opportunity for leadership, creativeness, and independence. These attributes may be vaguely associated with need for achievement. In another series of studies on "achievement, persistence, and vigor" summarized by Feldman and Newcomb (1969, Vol. I, pp. 68-70), the results were mixed, most of the studies reporting less need for achievement among seniors than freshmen. (See also Lenning and others, 1974.) It has even been observed that "educational attainment also appears to be associated with level of serum uric acid, which is associated with achievement drives" (Withey, 1971, p. 9). All of this evidence can only be described as inconclusive.

Future orientation. A valuable trait for practical affairs is the propensity to plan ahead and to be prudent in risk-taking. People with this trait are likely to be able to defer immediate gratification in favor of larger future benefits, to avoid mistakes and emergencies, and to be generally more circumspect than those who live only for the present.

Morgan, Siragelden, and Baerwaldt (1966, pp. 234-237) constructed an "index of planning and time horizon" based on planning behavior in such family decisions as vacations, retirement, and children's education. They found that the index was moderately higher for families in which the head had some college education than in other families. Their conclusion (pp. 248-249) was that: "It has been known for some time that the length of a man's time horizon and his willingness to plan ahead were related to his formal education and social class." Another bit of evidence on the question of the planning horizon comes from a survey which elicited responses of college alumni and others on "Living for Today." The survey suggested that relatively more alumni are attuned to planning for the future than are people without college education (Withey, 1971; National Opinion Research Center, 1974).

Another kind of evidence on future orientation comes from data on propensity to save. A careful study of saving behavior by level of education—with controls for important variables such as income, age, family size, and value of consumer durables—was made by Solmon (1975; see also Powers, 1976). He found that both the average and marginal propensity of families to save shows a strong association with educational attainment of the head of the household.

Still another aspect of future orientation is willingness to assume reasonable risk. Partial evidence on this subject comes

from the studies of desirable attributes of a job or career reviewed in Chapter Five. These studies indicate that substantially
fewer seniors than freshmen regard job security or stability as
an important factor in choice of vocation and also that college-
educated adults are less interested in job security than other
persons.

Another approach to future orientation is to consider differences among people by level of education in the degree of
prudence they exercise in practical affairs. Morgan, Sirageldin,
and Baerwaldt (1966) constructed an index of caution and risk
avoidance based on use of seat belts, willingness to try new
products, use of polio vaccine, medical and hospital insurance
coverage, amount of liquid financial reserves relative to income,
and use of family planning. They found that the index was
closely correlated with education: the more education, the
greater the prudence or risk aversion. This held true when controls for income, age, and other factors were introduced (see
Withey, 1971). This finding is not necessarily inconsistent with
the findings about risk assumption related to job preferences.
College-educated people may prefer challenging and meaningful
jobs to safe ones and yet may follow prudential behavior with
respect to seat belts, family planning, and so on. These miscellaneous bits of evidence suggest that college-educated people
tend to have a stronger future orientation than others.

Adaptability. Adaptability is a trait that is widely applicable to
practical affairs. It includes such dispositions or abilities as tolerance of new ideas or practices, adjustment to change, versatility and resourcefulness, willingness to negotiate and compromise, and generally keeping options open. As Trow has
remarked (1974c, p. 36), one of the main functions of higher
education is "to educate a whole society to be adaptable to
rapid social and economic change."

We have already seen that college clearly tends to raise the
level of openness and tolerance of its students. This is an important ingredient to adaptability, which thrives on open minds.
College also has pronounced effects on other aspects of adaptability. College-educated people are more disposed to change

jobs, more willing to move geographically, more open to new products, more attracted to scientific developments, and more concerned with "progress" and receptive to it (Morgan, Siragel-din, and Baerwaldt, 1966; Lansing and Mueller, 1967; Spaeth and Greeley, 1970). These findings remain valid when controls are introduced for income, age, and other factors.

Morgan, Sirageldin, and Baerwaldt (1966) constructed an index of receptivity to change based on job changes, use of new products, and interest in such new developments in applied science as fluoridation of water, use of polio vaccine, and space exploration. The resulting index was positively and strongly correlated with education. An interesting example of the strength of the correlations between education and receptivity toward the new is found in studies of the addition of fluoride to water, the introduction of the electric frying pan, and the use of seat belts, when these products were new (Morgan and others, 1966, pp. 229, 231). Still another example is provided by the relationship between geographic mobility and education (Lansing and Mueller, 1967).

Morgan, Siragelden, and Baerwaldt (1966, pp. 344-351) also constructed a general index related to adaptability which they called "Concern with Progress." Included in the index were the following items: ambition and aspiration (8 items); planning and time horizon (6 items); achievement orientation (9 items); and receptivity to change, including use of new products (6 items); attraction to new scientific developments (3 items); attitude toward new products (2 items); and attitude toward making changes on the job (1 item). The average scores on this index for persons under 55 years of age ranged from 14 for persons with grade school education to 22 for college graduates (p. 351).

Finally, regarding adaptability, education has the effect of keeping lifetime options open. If a person stops his education short of college, he may cut off his access to further education, to many jobs, and to other lifetime opportunities and satisfactions. It is true that he may compensate by self-study, by profiting from experience, or by returning to school or college as an adult learner. Yet, in practice, it is difficult to make up for ground lost in youth, and the options tend to be narrowed. Even if students attend postsecondary vocational education, options may be restricted by the high degree of specialization involved. For example, if one prepares to be a medical technologist, the chance of ever becoming a physician is greatly lessened. It can be justly argued that some of the loss of adaptability from dropping out is due to the requirement of meaningless credentials for entry into advanced education and into many jobs. But the restricted options are by no means entirely due to arbitrary credentialing.

To conclude, education is strongly and positively associated with adaptability. College-educated people tend to be relatively open-minded, tolerant, receptive to new ideas, geographically mobile, and willing to change jobs. Also, merely by virtue of their higher education, they keep more options open (including further education) than those who did not attend college. It should be added, however, that adaptability is not necessarily an unmixed blessing. It may help to hasten obsolescence of old products and create a ready market for new ones. It may open people to useless or wasteful change. It may expose people to untried and unsafe new products. It may contribute to restlessness and the instability of communities. A case can be made for critical skepticism toward new products, new jobs, new ideas, and new ways of life.

Leadership. Though leadership has long been held up as a major goal, we were able to find little information on the effect of higher education on its cultivation. In a survey of alumni, Bisconti and Solmon (1976, p. 10) asked about the usefulness of college in developing leadership: 22 percent of the respondents reported that it had been "very useful," 58 percent "somewhat useful," and 20 percent "not at all useful." Roskens (1958) found substantial correlations between leadership and participation during the college years and in later life. Most of the leaders of our society in virtually all walks of life are college-educated, and it may be presumed that the cognitive and affective traits developed or strengthened in college would be useful to them; yet it is apparently not known whether higher education helps people to combine these traits in ways that produce the quality we call leadership. It may be safely asserted that higher education does provide abundant opportunities and incentives for students to develop their leadership potential, but the information to back up this assertion is lacking.

Citizenship

An enduring feature of the American dream is that education is an essential foundation for citizenship in a democracy. In this section, we assemble evidence about the effects of higher education on attitudes toward public policy issues, on interest and participation in community and governmental affairs, and on knowledge of public affairs.

Attitudes. Scattered studies of the social, political, and economic attitudes of college students have been made over a period of fifty years or more, one of the earliest being Murphy and Likert (1938). Most of these studies indicate that, during the college years, students veer toward liberal, as distinct from conservative, views. A large number of such studies were summarized by Feldman and Newcomb (1969). Without exception, these studies showed that the attitudes of seniors—generally or on specific social or political issues, were more liberal than those of freshmen. Powers (1976) summarized several recent studies with similar results. Withey (1971), Clark and others (1972), Pace (1974a), Yankelovich (1974b), and Gallup (1975) have also contributed greatly to the knowledge of student attitudes.

On specific issues, most studies find that seniors are more likely than freshmen:

1. to favor civil liberties, individual autonomy, and freedom of choice in personal conduct;
2. to oppose discrimination on grounds of race, age, sex, religion, and national origin, and to favor racial integration;
3. to oppose economic growth and growth of population;

4. to favor conservation of natural resources and environmental protection;
5. to be concerned about foreign affairs, to favor international understanding and world government, and to lean toward pacifist views;
6. to have opposed the Vietnam War;
7. to have a low regard for conventional patriotism;
8. to be tolerant of activism and disorderly political activity;
9. to hold somewhat tolerant views toward Communism, foreign and domestic;
10. to hold mildly unfavorable views toward business and labor unions;
11. to be suspicious of the political establishment and big government.

Observers will, of course, differ in their evaluation of these results. Some of the studies on which they are based were made in the late 1960s and early 1970s, and it is not certain that they reflect present or future attitudes. However, the great bulk of evidence through 1977 suggests that seniors are generally more liberal in political attitudes than freshmen.

Some of the attitudinal differences between freshmen and seniors were illustrated in an exceptionally revealing recent study by Gallup (1975) based on interviews with a national sample of 904 college students enrolled in 57 institutions. The most striking finding of the Gallup study was that seniors tend to hold less favorable views about American institutions and the "establishment" than freshmen. In one series of questions, students were asked how they would rate the honesty and ethical standards of people in different professional or business fields. For ten of the eleven fields included, the senior rating was lower than the freshman rating, the one exception being "journalists." Similar questions were asked about attitudes toward nineteen major public leaders of the recent past and present and toward ten major social institutions. Most of the public leaders of all shades of political position were regarded less highly by seniors than by freshmen, the only exceptions being two foreign communist leaders (Mao and Castro) and three liberal American public figures (William Douglas, Morris Udall, Eugene McCarthy). Also, all but one of the social institutions were rated less highly by seniors than by freshmen, the exception being labor unions. Moreover, when students were asked whether they thought that almost everyone in American today could get ahead if he wanted to, 67 percent of the freshmen and 47 percent of the seniors responded "yes" (p. 6). On the other hand, attitudes of seniors toward governmental regulation of business were not very different from those of freshmen. When students were asked if they would like to settle in some other country, "if they were free to do so," there were no significant differences between the responses of freshmen and seniors. Similarly, the views of seniors and freshmen did not differ on the proposal that every young person spend one year in some form of service to the nation (p. 58).

College students appear to hold more liberal attitudes than comparable noncollege youth, though on many issues the differences are quite small (Yankelovich, 1974b). Bachman (1972), in a longitudinal study of high school youth covering four years after the ninth grade, found that those who attended college became more opposed to the Vietnam War, less trustful of government, more conscious of racial discrimination, and more politically aware than those who entered the military, went to work, or were employed.

In his 1975 survey of college students, Gallup assessed student perceptions of the effects of college on their political attitudes. The data suggest the importance that students assign to the study of man (psychology, sociology, philosophy and religion). They also suggest that the overt impact of teachers on political views is more balanced with respect to liberal and conservative viewpoints than is often alleged.

A comparison of college freshmen, college seniors, graduate students, college alumni, and noncollege adults in their political leanings is instructive. As shown in Table 23, college seniors and graduate students are considerably to the left of college freshmen, and college alumni are to the right of college seniors, but college alumni are to the left of other adults. Lipset

Table 23. Percentages of respondents placing themselves on a
conservative-liberal scale

	College Freshmen 1975[1]	College Seniors 1975[1]	Graduate Students 1962[2]	College Alumni 1971[3]	Noncollege Adults 1971[3]
Far right; very conservative	4%	3%	3%	5%	8%
Right of center; moderately conservative	20	17	23	38	34
Center; middle of the road	44	24	27	23	30
Left of center; moderately liberal	24	42	40	27	16
Far left; very liberal	6	11	7	5	4
Don't know; no answer	2	3		2	8
Total	100%	100%	100%	100%	100%

Sources:

[1] Gallup (1974, p. 16) and Yankelovich (1974b, p. 121) report that 21 percent of college students are conservative, 21 percent are middle-of-the-road, 53 percent are "one or another shade of liberal," and 5 percent are radical.

[2] Fay and Weintraub (1973, p. 6).

[3] Roper organization (1971). Quoted in Powers (1976, p. 115).

and Ladd (1971) explain the differences described here. They point out that (1) the trend of American society has been toward greater liberalism; (2) each generation of college students has been more liberal than the preceding one; (3) though alumni may be as liberal as they were in college, they are less liberal than their successors in college.

An interesting feature of Table 23 is that it shows college seniors and graduate students to be more decisive than college freshmen, in that more of them see themselves on the right or left and fewer in the middle. Similarly, the percentage of college alumni found in the center is smaller than that for noncollege adults. These data suggest that college influences some people not only to move leftward but also to become less bland or centrist in their political outlook (see Withey, 1971).

Ladd and Lipset (1975, pp. 37-38) have advanced the hypothesis that college students and alumni tend to be more ideological in their thinking than their noncollege opposite numbers. They describe ideology in this way: "Anyone viewing the flow of public life encounters a diverse array of issues. These he may respond to 'one at a time' or may order by imposing some integrative conceptual dimension. To the extent that he perceives an interconnection among issues and organizes his responses in terms of a larger 'package' or system of policy preferences, his thinking manifests constraint. An ideology is a constrained set of political positions prescribing the 'appropriate' responses to matters of government and public policy." Ladd and Lipset go on to point out that though most Americans are not strongly ideological, "It is also commonly acknowledged that there is a strong link between exposure to formal higher education and an inclination to evaluate politics in terms of systematic issue concerns." Ladd and Lipset then quote Lester Milbraith (1965, pp. 39-40), who observed that persons who have experienced higher education are less likely to shut out political stimuli and that "exposure to stimuli about politics increases the quantity and sharpness of political knowledge, stimulates interest, contributes to the decisiveness of political choices." Then Ladd and Lipset (p. 38) argue that "If education promotes an ideological construction of political life, faculty should manifest unusually ideological politics." And they show that faculty do indeed exhibit clear signs of ideological thinking, as measured by high correlations among opinions across a broad array of issues. This does not, however, refer exclusively to left-wing opinions, because there can be ideologies of the right and the center as well as of the left, and some of the sharp divisions within faculties may be due to the ideological mode of thought among those of the right, center, and left. In interpreting the Ladd and Lipset hypothesis, one may distinguish ideology as coherent thinking about a range of political and social issues from ideology as the total acceptance of ready-made doctrines about such issues. It is ideology as coherent thinking, rather than blind acceptance of ready-made doctrines, that characterizes most college-educated people.

Ladd and Lipset (1975) also compared the political views of juniors and seniors with those of freshmen and sophomores, by actual or intended fields of study. They discovered wide differences among the several academic fields and also a strikingly high positive correlation between the views of those intending to major in particular fields and of those who were actually studying in the same fields. The inference is that differences among fields of study in the political views of students are explained primarily by the political views the students bring with them, not by the impact of the field of study.

The relationship of education to political attitudes of adults is revealed by data on expressed preferences relating to public expenditures. Curtin and Cowan (in Strumpel and others, 1975, pp. 57-74) asked a national sample of adult respondents to indicate their preferences for public expenditures for these nine different purposes:

Group 1. Relating to "Social Environment":
—education
—mass transit
—pollution abatement
Group 2. Relating to "National Concerns":
—defense
—highways
—agriculture
Group 3. Relating to enhancement of well-being through transfers that are "responsive to individual need":
—public assistance (welfare)
—housing for low-income families
—medical care

They computed mean preference scores for all nine items combined, indicating attitudes toward public spending generally. They also computed mean preference scores for each of the three groups of items, indicating preferences for particular types of public programs. They then investigated the relation of education to public expenditure preferences with controls for age, income, and other factors. As shown in Table 24, mean preferences for all three groups combined are positively corre-

Table 24. Preferences for public expenditures, by level of education

	Adjusted[a] Mean Preference Scores			
Years of Education	*Nine Items of Public Expenditures Combined*	*Group 1: Expenditures for education, mass transit, pollution abatement*	*Group 2: Expenditures for defense, high- ways, agriculture*	*Group 3: Expenditures for welfare, low- income housing, medical care*
0-8	.119	−.160	.112	.014
9-11	.102	−.049	.047	−.042
12	.118	.038	.032	−.026
13-15	.125	.087	−.052	.026
16	.138	.234	−.267	.131
17 or more	.184	.228	−.310	.404

[a]Adjusted to control for income, age, urbanism.

Source: Curtin and Cowan in Strumpel and others, 1975, pp. 71, 74.

lated with education, and the same is true for expenditures in group 1 and group 3. However, for group 2 (relating to defense, highways, and agriculture) the correlation was negative. The implication is that the more-educated are more likely to favor expenditures for humane and environmental purposes and less likely to support expenditures for national defense, highways, and agriculture than are the less-educated.

Other studies reveal that college alumni tend to hold some-what more liberal views than other people on such matters as civil liberties, individual freedom, discrimination, political activism, taxes, public expenditures, and other issues (Spaeth and Greeley, 1970; Withey, 1971; Beaton, in Juster, 1975; Roper, 1975; Powers, 1976; Advisory Commission on Intergovern-mental Relations, 1976). One study of particular interest was that of Hyman and Sheetsley (1964, pp. 16-23), which showed that in both 1956 and 1963, very early in the struggle over racial integration, "the better-educated groups, both North and South, were more favorable to integration of schools and public transportation than people of less education were." The percentages favoring integration are as shown in Table 25.

Consequences for Individuals

Table 25. Percentage of people favoring integration,
by level of education

	North		South	
	1956	*1963*	*1956*	*1963*
Grade school	50%	60%	5%	20%
High school	63	75	15	32
College	75	86	28	48

Source: Hyman and Sheetsley (1964, pp. 16-23).

To conclude, the data we have assembled on sociopolitical attitudes suggest that college probably exerts a moderate influence toward liberal viewpoints and toward skepticism about the virtues of American society. These generalizations appear to be true when seniors are compared with freshmen, when college students are compared with comparable noncollege youth, and when alumni are compared with other adults. However, alumni tend to be to the right of college seniors in their political views —perhaps simply because they are older. The data suggest that higher education is conducive to ideological thinking on political matters in the sense that views on various political and social issues tend to be integrated into a more or less coherent system —and this may be interpreted as a positive result. Undergraduate college students are, on the whole, moderate in their political views. Massive surveys in 1969 and 1975 both showed that only 6 or 7 percent of students may be categorized as strongly left or strongly conservative. The overwhelming majority are liberal, middle-of-the-road, or moderately conservative (Trow, 1977, table 9).

Interest and involvement in political affairs. Studies relating to the political interest and involvement of college students have yielded ambiguous results. Some studies of change during college in students' interest in politics or their valuation of political activity gave no clear indication that college stimulates increasing interest in political affairs (Feldman and Newcomb, 1969). These surprising results can probably be explained by the fact that many of the studies cited were conducted a decade or more ago. However, Powers (1976), in reviewing several recent studies, found evidence that students become more socially conscious and more interested in politics during the college years. Yankelovich, 1974a, p. 38) reported that 23 percent of college students are actively interested and involved in political matters, whereas 12 percent of noncollege youth are so involved. Fay and Weintraub (1973, p. 11) found that graduate students reported various degrees of interest in national politics: extremely interested (43 percent); moderately interested (40 percent); only slightly interested (9 percent); and not interested at all (9 percent). Pace (1974a, pp. 66-67) found that 39 percent of upperclassmen said they were involved in at least five of a list of ten activities relating to national and state politics. One may reasonably conclude that in recent college generations, higher education has had a perceptible impact on political interest of students.

Turning to college alumni, the evidence overwhelmingly indicates that they are more interested and involved than noncollege people (Withey, 1971). Perhaps the most thorough study of the subject was that of Campbell and others (1960). In extensive surveys, they gathered the results on political interest and participation as shown in Table 26.

Table 26. Political interest and participation by educational level

	Grade School	High School	College
Voting in a presidential election	69%	82%	92%
Attempts to influence others in a presidential election	20	29	45
High degree of involvement in political affairs	23	32	48
High sense of political efficacy	21	43	75
High sense of citizen duty	33	54	64

Source: Campbell and others (1960, pp. 477-481). Data refer to sections of the country other than the South.

In a detailed study of factors affecting participation in community and political affairs, Verba and Nie (1972) found that participation is strongly correlated with education. They found that college-educated people were disproportionately represented among persons who were deeply involved in the affairs of their communities, among those who actively campaigned in political and civic causes, and among those who were members of organizations.

Hyman, Wright, and Reed (1975, pp. 176-179) found a high correlation between education and interest in politics from studies covering the period 1952 through 1971. For example, of those from thirty-seven to forty-eight years of age, 71 percent of college graduates professed strong interest in politics, as compared with 41 percent for high school graduates, and 27 percent for those whose education ended at elementary school. Moreover, the authors discovered a strong correlation between education and the extent to which respondents follow public affairs through the media and discussion. Pace (1974a, pp. 60-61) found that 40 percent of college alumni reported that they were involved in at least eight of fourteen activities relating to national and state politics. Berelson and Steiner (1964, p. 423) summed up the matter on the basis of evidence available to them: "The higher a person's socio-economic and educational level—especially the latter—the higher his political interest, participation, and voting turnout."

Information on public affairs. Hyman, Wright, and Reed (1975, pp. 89-93) gathered a mass of data about media usage and information concerning public affairs by levels of education, and concluded: "Education is clearly related to adult interest in politics. . . . The more formal schooling the members of any age cohort had, the more likely they were to follow news about public affairs regularly. . . . Adult attention to public affairs . . . is directly related to the amount of formal schooling obtained . . . earlier in life. . . . Adults who start out with more formal schooling are more likely to exploit the communications opportunities in their society that will keep them informed about significant social, political, personal, and academic matters of concern to them." They added that the conclusion about the impact of education is affected only negligibly by controls for socioeconomic status and ethnicity. Mandell and others (1973) also found that the college-educated are more in touch with economic news than other people.

Party affiliation. In recent years, great changes have been occurring in the party affiliation—or nonaffiliation—of American citizens generally. To disentangle the impact of college from these broad trends is difficult. A study by Gallup (1975, p. 15) indicated that seniors are less likely than freshmen to call themselves Republicans and more likely to call themselves Democrats. The differences, however, were slight. A more important finding of the study was that 50 percent of all college students regarded themselves as independents. This percentage is far higher than that for the population generally and raises the possibility that the spread of higher education may be a factor in the pronounced trend in the general population toward independent status. On the other hand, two studies on the comparative political party preferences of college and noncollege youth showed that the differences were slight and that the influence of college appeared to be small (Trent and Medsker, 1968; Yankelovich, 1974). The attitudes of students toward political parties appears to have become jaundiced in recent years; 61 percent of college students reported that they believe "political parties need reform or elimination" (Yankelovich, 1974b, p. 122) although the attitude of college students did not differ significantly from that of noncollege youth. Seven percent of students expressed a "highly favorable" attitude toward the Republican party, and 13 percent were "highly favorable" to the Democratic party; fewer seniors than freshmen were "highly favorable" to either party (Gallup, 1975, p. 32).

Among college graduates, Republicans have consistently outnumbered Democrats, but by a small margin; among those with some college, the membership of the two parties has varied but on the average has been about equal; in the noncollege group, the Democrats have been heavy favorites. However, because these data are not controlled for income, age, and other pertinent variables, one cannot conclude that these differences in party affiliation are due to the effects of college education.

In conclusion, college is probably not very influential in affecting the ratio between Democrats and Republicans, but it may be significant in determining whether people belong to any party or become independents.

Voting. College-educated people are more likely to vote than other persons. A recent tabulation of voting in 1972 among those of ages eighteen to twenty and twenty-one to twenty-four showed that the percentage voting among those enrolled in school (including high schools, colleges and universities, and other educational institutions) was strikingly greater than among those not in school (data provided by American Association of State Colleges and Universities). The difference was consistent when the data were classified by sex and race. Gallup (1975, p. 14) found that 72 percent of college students reported that they were registered, and 62 percent said that they had voted in a local election and 56 percent in a national election. Yankelovich (1974b) reported the political status of college and noncollege youth as shown in Table 27.

Table 27. Voting activity and party affiliation among noncollege and college-educated

	Noncollege	*College*
Registered	62%	86%
Voted	48	74
Voted for Nixon	23	31
Voted for McGovern	23	40
Other	2	3
Party identification		
Democratic	45	49
Republican	21	24
Other	7	5
None	27	22
Active in 1972 Campaign	14	35

Source: Yankelovich (1974, pp. 120-121).

When college alumni are compared with other adults, higher voting rates of alumni are clearly evident. This holds true with controls for income, sex, and race (U.S. Department of Health, Education, and Welfare, National Center for Education Statistics, *The Condition of Education,* 1976).

Community participation. College education appears to favor community participation and the cultivation of a disposition toward community activities. Pace (1974a, pp. 56-57) found that slightly more than a third of upperclassmen reported that they had received "very much" or "quite a bit" of benefit from college in preparation for citizenship. Citizenship was defined as "understanding and interest in the style and quality of civic and political life." One third is a significant proportion; however, as it turned out, citizenship stood near the bottom in a long list of benefits from college. The only item lower on the list was religion. Pace also discovered (pp. 66-67) that slightly more than a third of upperclassmen participated in at least three of a list of seven "community affairs" and in at least five of a list of ten activities related to "national and state politics." Again, participation in these activities was low compared with that in art, music, drama, and even religion. Bidwell and Vreeland in their study of Harvard students during the early 1960s found "an increasingly skeptical and jaundiced view of political participation" (Bidwell, 1975, p. 5). But a 1974 survey about the plans and aspirations of college seniors (*The Graduate Magazine,* 1974) indicated that 78 percent of the respondents mentioned at least one form of community activity to which they aspired.

An information exploration of community participation during adult life was made by Morgan, Sirageldin, and Baerwaldt (1966). They approached the subject from the point of view of *volunteer work,* which they defined as "voluntary contributions of time, serving people and organizations outside the family unit" (pp. 139-140). They found that in 1964 American families spent an average of 87 hours of their time annually in volunteer work. They then explored the factors influencing the amount of such work by individual families. Among the most important factors was education of the head of the family, which was found to be related to volunteer work even when other factors such as income and age were controlled. In explaining the relationships of income and education, the authors wrote (p. 144): "Income and education are correlated, but we have reason to believe that education is more basic since, aside from its correlation with income and tax considerations, it affects both people's basic motives to do volunteer work, and the demand for their volunteer services."

More recently, Solmon (1973b, p. 29) made some experimental studies of the relationship between education and the extent and intensity of participation in service work—that is, hours of volunteer effort devoted to youth activities, veterans' affairs, politics, PTA, churches, community and social action groups, volunteer work, and helping friends and relatives. After controlling for age, IQ, father's occupation, income, health, religion, marital status, number of children, and geographic region, he found the number of years of college to be a highly significant determinant of social service activities: "The typical member of our sample spends 11 hours per month in social service activities; an additional year of schooling increases this participation by almost one half-hour." He found also that increased education raises the intensity of participation. Berelson and Steiner (1964, p. 379) concluded on the basis of available evidence that "participation in voluntary associations in the United States is greater among people of more education and high socio-economic status." Another bit of evidence on community participation is that college alumni are more likely than other adults to belong to political clubs, service clubs, PTAs and other school organizations, and church-affiliated groups (Powers, 1976). Also Pace (1974a, pp. 60-61) found that 44 percent of alumni reported participation in at least eight out of a list of twelve community affairs, and 40 percent in at least eight out of a list of fourteen activities related to national and state politics—though he presented no comparative data for noncollege people. To summarize, higher education appears to exert a minor influence toward community participation during the college years but seems to be a significant influence in adult life.

Crime. It is often asserted that higher education reduces the propensity toward criminal activity (Benson and Hodgkinson,

1974). The evidence on this matter is cloudy because of the difficulty of defining crime and of separating the effects of education from other influences. Crime as usually defined is clearly less prevalent among college students than among other youth, but the causal connections are not apparent. Levin (1972, p. 44) estimated that the annual cost of crime attributable to inadequate education is of the order of $2 to $4 billion. Cobern and others (1973, pp. 57-58) assembled data showing that the prison population contains disproportionately few persons who have completed high school or attended college. In 1960, college graduates represented 8.4 percent of the total U.S. population but only 1.1 percent of inmates of correctional institutions; in 1966, only 3.7 percent of prisoners had completed high school. Ehrlich (in Juster, 1975, pp. 313-338) conducted a sophisticated economic analysis suggesting, among other things, that the economic incentives to crime are greater among the uneducated than among the educated and that equality of education and training, if it produces equality of earnings, might reduce crime (pp. 335-336).

Antisocial and illegal behavior is not unknown in the most educated and affluent circles. This has been well documented—for example, by Sutherland in *White Collar Crime* (1949), by Clinard in *The Black Market* (1952) and *Sociology of Deviant Behavior* (1963, pp. 160-165, 261-270, 598-600), and by Benson and Engeman in *Amoral America* (1975). Recent revelations about bribery of foreign officials, illegal campaign contributions, misleading advertising, marketing of unsafe products, murder of labor union leaders, transgression of antitrust laws, and Mafia intrusions into legitimate business suggest that white-collar crime easily crosses class lines.

The evidence scarcely justifies the assertion that higher education discourages antisocial or illegal behavior. It is plausible, however, to conclude that, to the extent that education at both the high school and college levels produces *jobs*, it could inhibit the kind of violent crime that flourishes in conditions of economic desperation.

Economic Productivity

That higher education has favorable effects upon the economic productivity of its students is widely acknowledged—though opinions differ on the degree and specific causes of these effects. Usually, studies in this area compare the monetary earnings of college-educated people with those of other persons. Frequently the results are expressed as rates of return in the form of incremental lifetime earnings resulting from investments in higher education. These studies usually concentrate on the results and do not explore the causal connection between higher education and increased earning. As Taubman (in Solmon and Taubman, 1973, p. 3) has observed, "No good explanation of what in particular education does to make a person more productive is available." Similarly, Hansen and Witmer (1972, p. 26) have written: "Neither economists nor educators pretend to have any well-developed theories that explain exactly how and why increased schooling facilitates occupational entry, enhances worker productivity, increases earnings, and ultimately helps to account for a more rapid rate of economic growth. The vast gaps in our knowledge also dictate caution about relying heavily on the magnitude of *economic* benefits of education or of higher education as a major rationale for public financial support." Welch (1975, p. 69) has added to the chorus by observing: "It seems that a full description of individual differences in earnings capacity would answer these questions: (1) Within a market, what is the nature of the various human skills that affect earnings? (2) What determines variations in the level of remuneration for given skills between markets? (3) What factors determine the distribution of skills among individuals? Given our ignorance on these questions, I do not think we can be very sanguine about the accomplishments of labor economics in general or of human capital economics in particular. Human capital approaches have highlighted schooling and all that it conceals as 'the' skill of interest. At the expense of this myopia in regard to the first question on the above list we remain largely ignorant of answers to the second and third."

These warnings are appropriate. The linkages between education and economic productivity are not precisely known and they are subject to controversy. Nevertheless, there is evidence on the matter and it is obvious that some of the known effects of higher education on its students do contribute to their productive powers.

The productivity of individuals as workers may be increased by education in at least six ways.

1. *Quantity of Product.* Workers may be enabled to produce more of given goods and services per unit of time. This would happen, for example, if skill or dexterity were enhanced, or if individuals attained greater drive and energy as a result of higher aspirations and better health.

2. *Quality of Product.* Workers may be enabled to produce given goods and services of higher quality. Quality might include technically "better" products or services; it might also include greater skill or sensitivity in human relations or a more pleasant environment surrounding the production and delivery of products or services.

3. *Product Mix.* Workers may be enabled to produce goods and services that are more highly valued by society than those which could be produced with less education. Thus, if through education they can produce automobiles, whereas without it they can produce only horse-drawn vehicles, the value of the social product may increase. Or if through education people are trained who would otherwise be mechanics and clerks to be designers and administrators, the value of their contributions to society may be enhanced. However, the market is not an infallible guide to social values. For example, the services of teachers who need higher education are not necessarily less valuable from the societal point of view than those of mechanics who do not need higher education—even though the latter may earn more money.

4. *Participation in the Labor Force.* Workers may become more inclined to be in the labor force, less susceptible to lost time from unemployment and illness, and willing to work longer hours. Labor-force participation, however, is not necessarily more *productive* than nonlabor-force activities such as unpaid social service activities, child care, and hobbies.

5. *Allocative Ability.* Workers may be helped to assess their talents, may be more selective in choice of jobs, achieve greater communication skills, and become more receptive to new technologies, new products, and new ideas. They may, therefore, be more able to adjust appropriately and promptly to changing conditions underlying demand and supply and thus to bring

about more efficient resource allocation. Heilbroner (1976) points out, however, that education may bring about a decrease in the ability of persons to perform work outside their trained speciality. He suggests that people were more versatile in earlier times.

6. *Job Satisfaction.* Workers may be placed in jobs that yield greater personal satisfaction. The return for work is partly in the form of money income and partly in the form of personal experiences, which may range from irksome or degrading to satisfying or even exalting. One part of the national product (not counted in the statistics) is the psychic income from job satisfaction.

Higher education clearly has some relation to each of these six ways of increasing the economic productivity of workers.

Quantity, quality, and product mix. Through its impact on the aspirations of its students, on their technical knowledge or skill, and possibly on their health, self-discipline, and drive, higher education may enable them to be more productive in the sense of producing more of particular goods and services. Through the effect of higher education on their knowledge, ingenuity, skill, taste, and personal attributes, they become more productive in the sense of producing goods and services of higher quality. For example, physical goods may have better design or be more serviceable; services such as medical care and legal advice may be more reliable or may be delivered with more understanding of the clients and regard for their welfare; the environment in which transactions occur or services are rendered may be more humane or agreeable. Similarly, through the growth of higher education, the number of persons able to produce goods and services of high social value (health care, teaching, engineering) may be enlarged and the number of persons obliged by necessity to produce goods of low value (domestic service, clerical work, unskilled farm labor) may be reduced. As a result, the value of the national product may increase. On the other hand, higher education may guide students away from careers (especially blue-collar careers) in which the value of the product and the job satisfactions may be high.

The impact of higher education on productivity is due partly to broad, general traits that it helps its students to acquire,[1] and it is due partly to specific skills or knowledge—some derived from general education and some from professional or vocational education. The results from vocational training should not, however, be exaggerated. The theory that workers acquire their skills through formal education and then bring these skills to the labor market is only partially valid. As Thurow (1975, p. 78) has pointed out, "Most cognitive job skills, general or specific, are acquired either formally or informally through on-the-job training after a worker finds an entry job and the associated promotion ladder. . . . Even among college graduates, over two thirds reported that they had acquired cognitive skills through informal, casual processes on the job." In the same vein, Solmon (1976) found that only about half of college graduates reported a close relationship between their major fields of study in college and their later jobs. Bisconti and Solmon (1976, p. 5) found that most alumni had not selected their careers during the college years: 17 percent of the men and 31 percent of the women had chosen their professions before entering college and two thirds of the men and half the women had made their career choices afterward. These findings are of course not surprising. Many students deliberately pursue nonvocational studies with the intention of acquiring their work skills through on-the-job training and experience, and many jobs do not require specific prior training but are learned on the job. Solmon found that the great majority of those who were holding jobs unrelated to their college majors were doing so voluntarily, that most of this group were satisfied with their jobs, and that the difference in job satisfaction between those with jobs related to their college major and others was slight. These find-

---

[1]Solmon, in personal conversation with the author, indicated that in studies currently in progress he is finding that many traits and skills derived from the general college experience are useful on the job, among them, getting along with people, perseverance and hard work, general knowledge, critical thinking, and learning how to learn. He pointed out that a common lack of congruence between college majors and jobs does not mean that college is without significant vocational effects.

ings are consistent with a study conducted in the U.S. Bureau of Labor Statistics (Young, 1974).

Pace (1974a, pp. 52-53, 56-57) found that only 43 percent of a large sample of 1950 alumni and 40 percent of a sample of 1969 upperclassmen thought that college had given them "vocational training—skills and techniques directly applicable to a job," but that 64 percent of the alumni and 71 percent of upperclassmen thought that college had benefited them "very much" or "quite a bit" in helping them to acquire "background and specialization for further education in some professional, scientific, or scholarly field." Spaeth and Greeley (1970, p. 40) discovered that 66 percent of recent college alumni reported that college prepared them "greatly" or "somewhat" to get ahead in the world and 67 percent reported that college trained them for their present jobs. Similarly, Bisconti and Solmon (1976), in a large survey of college graduates who had entered college in 1961, found that college education had been useful to the respondents in many ways in which specific job skills were of secondary importance. The responses are shown in Table 28.

Another well-established effect of college education is that it increases the capacity of individuals to benefit from on-the-job training, other adult education, and experience. It also conditions individuals to take advantage of adult learning opportunities (Mincer, 1974; Knapp, 1977; Klemp, 1977).

In conclusion, many students receive education and training in college or university that is directly applicable to their work and these must be counted among the outcomes of higher education affecting economic productivity (Lenning and others, 1974). Machlup (1970, pp. 7-8) summarized the effects of education upon increases in productivity as follows:

> It is with regard to . . . improvements in the quality of labor, that education can play a really significant role. Positive effects may be expected on five scores: (a) better working habits and discipline, increased labor efforts, and greater reliability; (b) better health through more wholesome and sanitary ways of living; (c) improved skills, better comprehension of working

Table 28. Usefulness of college education in vocation

	Very Useful	Somewhat Useful	Not at All Useful
College increased my general knowledge	73%	27%	
It increased my chances of finding a good job	69	27	5%
My bachelor's degree was a factor in my being hired by my current employer	60	21	19
It increased my ability to think clearly	43	53	4
It taught me a skill that enabled me to get my first job	42	29	29
It gave me knowledge and skills that I use in my current job	38	50	12
It increased my leadership ability	22	58	20
It helped me choose my life goals	21	49	29
The contacts I made in college with professors or friends helped me get my current job	5	11	84

Source: Bisconti and Solmon (1976, p. 10).

requirements, and increased efficiency; (d) prompter adaptability to momentary changes, especially in jobs which require quick evaluation of new information and, in general, fast reactions; and (e) increased capability to move into more productive occupations when opportunities arise. All levels of education may contribute to improving the quality of labor.

To the use of better machines, education can contribute in at least two ways: (a) by making people more interested in improved equipment, more alert to its availability, and more capable of using it; and (b) by training people in science and technology and expanding their capacity for the research and development work needed to invent, develop, adapt, and install new machines.

Machlup referred also to the effect of education upon technical progress that is embodied in trained people rather than machines—for example, improved organization and management. And he concluded (p. 15): "The theory of the productive contribution of education remains plausible even if the attempts to measure the contribution have not had convincing results."

One may concede that some individuals achieve positions of high productivity without great amounts of formal education and that some people with much formal education do not acquire characteristics conducive to high productivity. One may also concede that the placement of some educated people in professional-technical-managerial jobs may be due to sorting and credentialing, to discrimination based on race, sex, and religion, to differences in socioeconomic background, and to differences in underlying ability or aptitude (Lebergott, 1968). Allowing for these possibilities, however, does not alter the high probability that higher education contributes to the economic productivity of many of its students.

Labor force participation, unemployment, and working hours. Participation in the labor force refers to the percentage of persons of any classification who are working or seeking work. In the official definition, a person is considered a labor-force participant if: (a) he or she did any gainful work during the week when a survey was made, or (b) if unemployed, sought work within the four weeks preceding the survey. This definition generally excludes persons who are in school full-time, who are retired, or who are not working and choose for any reason not to seek or engage in gainful employment. (Some of those who choose not to work are "unemployable" or have ceased to seek work because they have been discouraged in quest of a job.)

There is a well-established correlation of educational level with labor-force participation rates, the relationship being more pronounced for women than for men. (See Table 29.) Since most men are in the labor force between the age of leaving school and the age of retirement, level of education is a weak influence on participation (row 4 of Table 29). The participation rate varies from 90 to 99 percent from the lowest to the highest educational level, and only from 97 to 99 percent from

Table 29. Labor force participation rates by age and education, 1960, 1971

	Educational Attainment in Years							
	0-4	5-7	8	9-11	12	13-15	16	17 or more
1. Men,[1] 1960								
2. Age 55-64, urban	75%	80%	85%	88%	88%	92%	93%	100%
3. Age 65-74, urban	26	32	41	44	47	52	58	66
4. All men	90	94	96	97	97	98	99	99
5. Married women,[1] 1960								
6. Age 14-54; no children under six	27	38	39	43	50	55	63	78
7. Age 14-54; with children under six	11	15	17	17	20	21	24	32
8. Age 14-54; black	41	46	45	45	49	43	83	—
9. All married women	19	28	29	33	38	41	47	61
10. Single women,[1] 1960								
11. Age 55-64	45	58	60	63	69	73	73	—
12. Age 65-74	14	22	25	26	29	32	37	—
13. Black	78	77	82	80	90	—	—	—
14. Never married	74	84	90	94	96	94	97	97
15. All single women	78	74	84	85	90	89	93	94
16. All women, 1971[2]	17	26	30	40	50	49	57	69
17. All women, age 25-54, 1974[3]	—	—	41*	49	54	57	68**	

The data are adjusted for age, marital status, race, and income from sources other than work.

Cobern, Salem, and Mushkin, 1973, p. 61. Data are unadjusted.

McEaddy, 1975, p. 67. Data are adjusted.

*8 grades or less

**16 grades or more

Source: W. Bowen and Finegan, 1969, pp. 55, 116, 255, 297.

high school graduate to college graduate. These rates are not much influenced by changing economic conditions and are quite stable over time (W. Bowen and Finegan, 1969, pp. 60-62). For older men, however, level of education appears to be a potent influence (rows 2 and 3 of Table 29). Similarly, the recent data in Table 30 on labor force participation of men by age and education (McEaddy, 1975) show clearly that educa-

Table 30. Labor force participation by men, by age and education

Education in Years	25-54	55-64	65 and Over
0-8	87.3%	70.6%	16.7%
9-11	94.2	78.1	23.2
12	96.2	83.1	25.5
13-15	94.7	84.6	30.8
16 and over	97.5	87.1	40.8

Source: McEaddy (1975, p. 67).

tion has the effect of delaying retirement. The relations between education and labor force participation of older men may be explained in part by the dropping out of those with less education for reasons of health, low earnings, unattractiveness of available jobs, and inability to find work. Best (1976) found that the preference for early retirement among those now working was considerably weaker for more-educated people than for less-educated people. On the other hand, Barfield and Morgan (1969) found no systematic relationship between education and retirement *plans*. Plans are, of course, different from either preferences or actual decisions.

For women, labor force participation is strongly and positively affected by level of education (rows 6 through 17 of Table 29.)[2] The relationship in the case of women is stronger than for men because the American culture allows more choice, at least for married women, in the matter of labor force participation. Men are "expected" to work if they are able; married women may choose at various times of their lives to work or to drop out of the labor market. However, the percentage of women in the labor force is steadily rising over time, and the effect of edu-

[2] See also Mincer, 1962b; Katona, Strumpel, and Zahn, 1971a; Mandell, Katona, Morgan, and Schmiedeskamp, 1973; Metropolitan Life, *Statistical Bulletin*, January 1976.

cational attainment on participation may be expected to diminish and eventually to approximate that for men. Labor force participation of women is influenced not only by education but also by age, marital status, presence of young children in the home, attitude of husband, income of husband, and other factors. Education nevertheless remains an important determinant, even after these other factors are controlled (Morgan, Sirageldin, and Baerwaldt, 1966; Withey, 1971; Leibowitz in Juster, 1975).

Attitudes toward wives' working are also influenced by education. As shown in a 1974 survey of the National Opinion Research Center, college alumni are considerably more favorable than other adults to wives' working and much less favorable to the proposition that "women should take care of running the home and leave running the country up to men." This difference in attitude holds when the data are classified by income.

The evidence is overwhelming that for both men and women unemployment varies inversely with the level of education (Morgan and others, 1966; Perella, 1973; Cobern and others, 1973; Executive Office of the President, 1973; A. Katz, 1974). This has long been true and continues to hold today, despite the widespread (but erroneous) belief that the rate of unemployment is higher among college-educated people than among other groups. Even among young people, unemployment rates for college students and college graduates are far below those for groups of less education. On this matter, Young (1975a) reported unemployment rates in 1974 as shown in Table 31. Gilroy (1975, p. 20) has shown that the higher unemployment among blacks as compared with whites is partly due to differences in formal education—both in quantity and quality. He found "that education factors alone accounted for between three fifths and three quarters of the excess black male and female unemployment in both 1960 and 1970." (See also Masters, 1975.)

The relative stability of employment for educated people is undoubtedly due in part to the widespread practice in our economy of providing stable career jobs for white-collar work-

Table 31. Unemployment rates among young persons, 1974,
by level of education

	All Persons Age 16-24		High School Graduates and High School Dropouts
High school dropouts	19.1%	High school dropouts 1973-74	28.3%
High school graduates	9.8		
Attended college 1 to 3 years	7.1	1974 high school graduates not enrolled in college	17.0
College graduates	5.0	1974 high school graduates enrolled in college	13.6

Source: Young (1975a, pp. 33-36).

ers and of allowing the employment of other workers to fluc-
tuate with changing economic conditions. However, even in
boom times, unemployment rates are lower among college-educated workers than among other members of the labor force.
The explanation may be partly that college-educated people are
on the average more healthy, more versatile, better able to learn
on the job, more mobile, more enterprising in finding jobs,
more disciplined, and more effective in their work. Also it may
be that the economy as we have known it has provided a
stronger demand for persons with specific educational qualifications than for other workers.

Education appears to encourage longer working hours.
Finegan, in an important study (1962, p. 460), found a strong
positive relationship between education and average weekly
hours of work. Each additional year of education added about
one hour to the average weekly working time. Also, Blank and
Stigler (1957, Chapter 7) have shown that the relatively high
earnings associated with professional and managerial occupations are explained in part by the relatively long hours of work.
The explanation may be that successful work in technical, professional, and managerial occupations requires long hours; that
their high rates of compensation reward them for long hours;

that people in these occupations enjoy their work; that education conditions people to work long hours; that educated people have exceptional energy; or that people who are destined to work long hours are the very ones who choose to become well educated.

Morgan, Sirageldin, and Baerwaldt (1966, p. 94) gathered data on preferences of family heads as to hours of work. They asked the respondents to indicate whether they would prefer to work more hours with more pay, to work fewer hours with less pay, or to maintain the status quo. Those with more education tended to favor fewer hours; those with less education tended to favor more hours. This result might be explained by the fact that many well-educated people are already working long hours and would welcome relief (see Best, 1976).

From the data on labor force participation, unemployment, and hours of work it may be concluded that the proportion of their lives people spend at work is positively correlated with their level of education. One cannot blithely assume that this result is due solely to education. Other factors are doubtless responsible in part, among them socioeconomic background, income, job satisfaction, labor market conditions, and others. Yet, it appears that education exerts a consistent influence in the direction of higher productivity as measured by time spent in the production of goods or services sold in the market. It does not necessarily follow that this is the best use of time, but long hours and years spent at work do add to economic productivity as conventionally measured.

Allocative ability. The productivity of individuals or of the economy is increased when people adjust appropriately and rapidly to changes in consumer demand, in technology, and in resource supplies. Allocative ability may be defined as the propensity to adjust to changing conditions of demand and supply. Education almost certainly contributes to allocative ability that involves versatility, mobility, capacity to gather and interpret information, and astuteness in appraising options. In an important paper on the subject, Schultz (1975, pp. 827, 835) wrote:

No matter what part of a modern economy is being investigated, we observe that many people are consciously reallocating their resources in response to changes in economic conditions. How efficient they are in their responses is in no small part determined by their "allocative ability." The ability to reallocate is not restricted to entrepreneurs who are engaged in business. People who supply labor services for hire or who are self-employed are reallocating their services in response to changes in the value of the work they do. So are housewives in devoting their time in combination with purchased goods and services in household production. Students likewise are reallocating their own time along with the educational services they purchase as they respond to changes in expected earnings along with changes in the value of the personal satisfactions they expect to derive from their education. Consumption opportunities are also changing, and inasmuch as pure consumption entails time, here too people are reallocating their own time in response to changing opportunities. . . .

The effects of education in this connection can be tested empirically, and it is proving to be a strong explanatory variable.

Schultz cited numerous studies in which education (as well as experience) has been shown to facilitate the reallocation of resources, with resulting increases in productivity. These studies refer to the adoption of new technologies by business, agriculture, and households; to adjustment to changes in consumer demands and in resource supplies; and to personal choices relating to marriage, family planning, and education. He concluded (p. 843): "The ability to deal successfully with economic disequilibria is enhanced by education and . . . this ability is one of the major benefits of education." It could be added that the low unemployment rate among educated people may be partially attributable to their allocative ability—one aspect of which is simply the ability to find a job.

Mobility is an aspect of allocative ability on which there is abundant evidence. College-educated people on the average are considerably more willing than other persons to change geographic location (Lansing and Mueller, 1967). They are more disposed to change careers, jobs, and houses not involving significant geographic movement and they are more willing to move their families to get ahead (Katona, Strumpel, and Zahn, 1971; Strumpel, 1976). Mobility is, of course, only one species of a large genus of actions or traits that make up what Schultz called allocative ability. These include versatility, alertness, ability to process information (Welch, 1970), and capacity to appraise options (Madden, 1975). All of these are undoubtedly enhanced through higher education.

In a careful study, "The Market for College-Trained Manpower," Freeman (1971, p. xxvi) concluded that "The market operates ... with an informed group of suppliers responding rapidly to economic incentives and salaries determined, albeit with a lag, by supply and demand. . . . The contrast between these findings and those from studies of 'blue-collar' markets suggests that the trend toward an increasingly professional, college-trained work force will produce a more 'classical' labor market." Similarly, Juster (1975, p. 31), commenting on allocative ability, wrote: "Differences in educational level have a major impact on the ability of individuals to adjust to changing circumstances, whether the question includes managing their economic affairs in the labor market, managing their own private financial affairs as consumers and investors, or planning the number and spacing of their children. And in a world where information flows are growing exponentially and where optimal decision-making requires the efficient processing of increasingly large amounts of new information, the ability to adapt effectively to changes is likely to be of major importance." Trow (1974, p. 40) generalized on the matter as follows:

> Whatever its nominal goals or content, higher education tends to erode narrow ethnic, regional, national and group identifications, that is to say, all kinds of nonrational loyalties that are incompatible with rapid

social and geographical mobility and change. Modern higher education is a universal solvent; it generates, in the people exposed to it, a skepticism toward all received values and allegiances. It is heavily oriented toward the future, rather than toward tradition or place. It places a high premium on the capacity to learn how to learn, on an infinite adaptability to new situations—organizational, technological, or social. In these institutions, and in the society for which they prepare, it matters less what one knows if one can only *learn* rapidly. Indeed, it is almost a virtue not to know too much in too much detail for fear of having acquired what Veblen called "a trained incapacity" to learn something new.

Vocational choice: grading and labeling. One fact of "allocative ability" is wisdom in choice of vocations and in finding jobs within chosen fields. We have observed that one of the major outcomes of higher education is "personal self-discovery," or the finding of personal identity (see Chapter Four). When higher education helps students to discover themselves, it also helps them to discover their vocations (defined literally as "callings"). Thus, out of the college experience many students are led toward new career decisions (or to the confirmation of old ones) that mesh their talents with their occupations. In this way, their productivity is enhanced and the national product is increased.

The career decisions reached in college are not necessarily final and irrevocable. The search for identity does not necessarily stop with graduation and new opportunities unfold in later years. Nevertheless, the college years are critical in the career decisions of many students and higher education exerts a strong influence on the supply side of the labor market in helping to match people to jobs. Increasing numbers of colleges have formalized the function of vocational counseling and placement by establishing special offices—though the impact of college on career placement is by no means confined to these designated offices.

College education is important in helping its graduates acquire accurate labor market information, which in turn is needed to bring about efficient allocation of the labor force to different occupations and geographic areas. Parnes and Kohen (1975, p. 54) found that occupational information is strongly correlated with education. They concluded: "The higher earnings associated with additional years of education have generally been attributed to the contribution that education makes to productivity via work skills and knowledge. However, the correlation . . . between extent of occupational information, on the one hand, and both years of schooling and hourly wage rate on the other, suggests that part of the return to additional education may be a reflection of education's contribution to *labor market* skills and know-how as distinguished from purely *vocational* skills and know-how."

College also plays a significant role in the labor market by "grading and labeling" its students. It does this in many ways. It provides various formal credentials, such as transcripts, certificates, and degrees. It confers various honors and awards, such as prizes, membership in honor societies, and graduation with various degrees of distinction, and it provides prospective employers with letters of recommendation and dossiers on students. The grading-and-labeling function of colleges has been much discussed in recent years, the terms commonly used being *screening, sorting, filtering, signaling, credentialing,* or *licensing.*

Two criticisms of the role of higher education in the career placement of its students have been frequently expressed. The first criticism is that higher education is oriented unduly toward supplying the manpower needs of the economy and maintaining the class structure of the society, rather than toward the optimal development of its students as persons. One formulation of this criticism is that higher education is a tool of the "military-industrial complex." It is argued that American people have overemphasized the relation of college education to careers and that colleges and universities have been too ready to adjust their goals and programs toward vocationalism—possibly at the expense of the broad education and personal development of their students. This criticism has some substance, but it should not be pressed too far. American higher education maintains a substantial and widespread program in liberal learning. Except in a few fields (the most notable being medicine), it has not rationed places in various fields of study but has permitted students to choose freely among many major fields. It has not deliberately indoctrinated students with prevailing ideologies but instead has probably made them more questioning and critical of established institutions. It has encouraged students in many ways to select fields of study and vocations involving service to others at the sacrifice of pecuniary gain—for example, teaching, the ministry, and nursing. Indeed, higher education in America, as compared to that in other countries, may be the least specialized, the least oriented toward vocations, the least inclined to ration places in various fields of study, and therefore the least subservient to the economy. In any event, it is no crime to prepare young people for careers so long as that single objective is not allowed to overwhelm other important goals relating to personal development and to preparation for nonvocational aspects of life. Nor is it a disservice to the society or to young people to help them locate jobs within their chosen vocations (Bowen, 1973; Bowen, 1974c).

The second criticism of the role of higher education in career placement is that the above-mentioned grading and labeling of students as practiced by colleges and universities leads employers to select workers on the basis of paper credentials rather than on the basis of actual qualifications. The higher earnings of college-educated people as compared with those of less education are alleged to be due largely to grading and labeling rather than to differences in actual productivity.[3] This criticism also has some substance. Employers probably find it easier and cheaper to select employees on the basis of college credentials, which are essentially costless to them, than to screen all candidates and develop their own credentials for employment

[3]A substantial literature on credentialing, screening, and sorting has appeared in recent years, perhaps triggered by Berg (1970). Other authors having varying points of view include Mincer (1970); Chiswick (1973); Arrow (1973); Taubman and Wales (in Juster, 1975); Stiglitz (1975); and Bowles and Gintis (1976).

decisions. College-educated people have an employment advantage in that they can instantly present informative credentials, whereas other applicants must assume the burden of proof in explaining why they did not attend college or why they did not graduate or why they are qualified for the particular job despite limited education. The advantage to college-educated people of grading and labeling is reinforced when practice in most professions is contingent upon licenses based in part on college education. In such cases, persons without the requisite education are ruled out regardless of qualifications. The situation becomes even more rigid when, as sometimes happens, the requisite education exceeds the amount necessary for successful professional practice (Greenberg and Greenberg, 1976). Sometimes, people in professions even push for higher educational qualifications for new entrants as a way of restricting entry and raising the status and income of the profession. In this effort they are sometimes abetted by educators who covet the additional enrollments generated by the higher requirements.

It must be conceded that grading and labeling may give college-educated people an advantage in the labor market that is not always based on superior productivity. It may endow college people to some extent with a partial monopoly position. However, the amount of the advantage can easily be exaggerated. For many reasons it must be small. First, the assumption that college-educated people are blindly chosen to the exclusion of others underrates the acumen of employers. If it were true that college-educated people were being employed in preference to more promising other candidates, alert employers would soon realize that they could assemble a better staff for less money by doing their own screening and employing noncollege-educated people. Indeed, the net saving in cost to employers through college credentials must be quite small. Even when ready-made college credentials are available, employers nevertheless carry on substantial screening activities by giving tests and interviewing candidates (Chiswick, in Solmon and Taubman, 1973, pp. 151-158; Layard and Psacharopoulos, 1974).

Second, some research findings on employment of the college-educated are not consistent with the grading and labeling hypothesis. For example, the differentials between the earnings of college-educated and other workers are greater for older workers than for younger workers (Layard and Psacharopoulos, 1974); rates of return to college education are as high for workers who did not complete their courses as for those who did (Layard and Psacharopoulos, 1974); and persons who expect to be self-employed and who cannot benefit from grading and labeling are nevertheless motivated toward education (Welch, 1975).

Third, grading and labeling have a reverse effect in some cases, because it shuts college-educated people out of jobs on the ground that they are "overqualified" and would be neither productive nor satisfied in these jobs.

Fourth, the argument that the earnings of the college-educated are being raised by unrealistic and unnecessary increases in educational requirements imposed by licensing agencies must be interpreted with some caution. In a society where the educational level of the entire population is increasing and where the technical complexities of everyday activities are multiplying, rising educational requirements for various professional and semiprofessional positions are not necessarily inappropriate. For example, the tasks of a policeman, secretary, garage mechanic, bank clerk, beauty-shop operator, or salesman all involve dealing with an educated public and coping with technical complexities that did not exist fifty years ago. Similarly, the growing size and complexity of organizations increases the number of interactions, communications, conflicts, and negotiations that occur daily and require educated people with technical knowledge and interpersonal skills. The upgrading of vocational requirements may also have some spin-off in broad human development that can be justified for its own sake. Thus, in judging the rise in educational requirements connected with licensing, sweeping generalities are dangerous and each situation must be considered on its own merits.

Fifth, legal obstacles are being raised against discrimination in employment based on educational qualifications unrelated to the requirements of jobs. Finally, sixth, enrollment growth in higher education has greatly increased the supply of college-educated people in virtually all fields, with the result that premium salaries for the college-educated are declining. Stiglitz (1975, p. 299), in a perceptive analysis, concluded: "That attempts to curtail educational screening may simply shift the focus of screening (for example, to on-the-job screening), with the possibility of a lowering of net national output without any commensurate gain in equality."

In the matter of "grading and labeling," the criticism has been directed toward colleges or universities. The unstated implication has been that they should desist from these activities. It would seem more constructive to direct the criticism to the inadequacy of our institutions for grading and labeling people who have *not* been to college. There should be more comprehensible and more widely recognized ways of establishing their qualifications so that they may compete without disadvantage. In fact, the higher education community has been taking positive steps to improve the situation through such programs as expanded financial aid to students, open admissions, recognition of experiential learning, external degrees, cooperative work-study, and various forms of independent study. These may not be adequate, as they are tied too closely to the formal higher educational system, but they are a beginning.

There is a kernel of truth in the criticisms that grading and labeling by higher education produces inequities in the labor market, but the problem has been exaggerated. Indeed, one of the most important and socially valuable outcomes of higher education is to help students find their identity and to facilitate their placement in vocations where they can be productive and happy. As long as this is done in an atmosphere of freedom—such that individuals are not influenced to become something alien to their natures and may choose their courses of study and their vocations—then the effect on individuals and on society is clearly beneficial. The real problem is to provide comparable facilities to help noncollege people find their identity and to assist them in selecting appropriate careers and finding jobs.

Grading and labeling does not stop with college. It goes on throughout life, as people accumulate credentials through employment, financial dealings, community activities, family life, the criminal courts, and so on. Indeed, credentialing goes on from the cradle to the grave. But the grading and labeling that occurs in college is of special significance because it is done just prior to entry into adult life, when careers and ways of life are being established. Moreover, self-discovery in college can also help students find their roles in family life, political activities, religion, and recreation, as well as in work. Colleges and universities have a responsibility to facilitate appropriate placement of students in these areas as well as in the economy.

Job satisfaction. A large part of human life is spent in work; what happens to people on their jobs is one of the major ingredients of human welfare. Work yields not only extrinsic goods and services to be converted into income but also intrinsic experiences and meanings, which may be either richly satisfying or irksome and degrading. Does higher education contribute to job satisfaction?

If one looks at the matter historically and from a broad social point of view, it is almost certain that higher education has had a favorable influence on the intrinsic rewards from work. Education has been an important element in technological progress, which has brought about the elimination of millions of dirty, menial, back-breaking jobs and widespread improvement of working conditions. Education has also had a part in the major shift of the labor force from the production of physical goods to the rendering of services. This trend has progressed to the point that the majority of American workers are in white-collar work. But when the job satisfaction of college-educated people is compared with that of other workers,[4] the evidence is mixed. College-educated people gain more satisfaction from their work than others, but the difference is small, partly because job satisfaction is high among all groups. Mueller and others (1969) found a weak relationship between education and job satisfaction. The responses they received from a nationwide sample are presented in Table 32. Beaton (in Juster, 1975)

[4] A national survey revealed that workers evaluate their jobs along five dimensions: comfort, challenge, earnings, relations with coworkers, and resources to get the job done (Quinn and Baldi de Mandilovitch, 1975).

Table 32. Job satisfaction by level of education

Job is:	0-11 Grades	12 Grades	College No Degree	College Degree
Enjoyable	70%	78%	82%	89%
All right	22	16	14	8
Drudgery	7	4	3	2
Not ascertained	1	2	1	1
	100%	100%	100%	100%

Source: Mueller and others (1969).

similarly found that education is a weak predictor of job satisfaction—much weaker than income. Solmon (1976) found that though 60 percent of his respondents (all college graduates) were "very satisfied" with their jobs, only 32 percent thought their skills were being fully utilized. At the same time, he reported (p. 2) that "neither income nor job satisfaction seems to be much affected by the extent to which college education is used on the job" (see Bisconti and Solmon, 1976). Quinn and Baldi de Mandilovitch (1975, p. 23), after reviewing nine studies on the relationship of education to job satisfaction, concluded that there was "little or no relationship between education level and job satisfaction up to the 'some college' level." But they discovered a sizeable increase in satisfaction from the "some college" group to the college-graduate group. They concluded that a "credentials effect" was at work in favor of college graduates and that there was no payoff in the form of job satisfaction for those who attended college but did not stay on to get a degree.

Stern (1975) attempted to place a dollar value on differences in six nonpecuniary benefits of jobs held by college graduates and of jobs held by other workers.[5] He found that college graduates received more nonpecuniary benefits than noncollege workers, the difference being worth 49¢ per hour on the aver-

---

[5] The benefits were: making less physical effort, making more of own decisions, being more creative, having less repetition, having more say, and making more friends.

age. He concluded (p. 13) that the value of these benefits, as part of real earnings, would increase the spread between the real earnings of college alumni and noncollege workers by about 25 percent—a significant result.

We conclude, then, that the objective conditions of work for the whole society have been improved over the decades as a result of education, and that the subjective satisfactions from work are probably somewhat higher for college-educated people than for others.

Rates of return and national economic growth. Economists have devoted an enormous amount of effort to exploring the outcomes of higher education. Literally hundreds of studies have been made, especially during the past two decades, on the "rates of return" to "investments" in higher education, and other studies have been made on the effect of higher education on economic growth. On the whole, economists have not tried to discover the particular aspects of education that produce investment returns or economic growth but have been content to learn about the effects. Also, they have confined their studies mainly to effects that can be measured in dollars and, in most cases, have not been concerned with nonpecuniary outcomes—though most economists freely admit that monetary returns are only part of the outcomes. In Chapter Twelve, we present a detailed account of the economic studies of higher educational outcomes and of their findings. We present here only a concise summary of the findings.

The concept of the rate of return to investments in higher education is based on an analogy with investments in physical capital. For example, if a young person should go into business by buying a filling station for $40,000, or should buy securities with the money, he would expect to achieve a return on his investment in the form of a stream of future income (over and above expenses and depreciation). If, instead, the same person invested $40,000 (including his expenses and his time) in a college education, the expected return on his investment might also be in the form of a stream of future additions to his income. In either case, if the addition to his income, after allow-

ance for expenses and depreciation, were $4,000 a year, the rate
of return would be 10 percent. To estimate the return from
higher education, it is necessary to separate the effects of education from such factors as ability or aptitude, motivation, and
socioeconomic background. In most studies, these extraneous
factors are isolated through the method of multiple regression,
though the success in achieving this isolation is uneven.

A distinction is made between private and social rates of
return. The private rate of return relates to investments made
by the individual student and his family in connection with a
college education and the future returns reaped by that same
student. The investments include out-of-pocket expenses and
earnings lost during college attendance; the returns are in the
form of augmented future earnings after taxes. The social rate
of return adds to the investment the amount of subsidy supplied by government and philanthropists and considers the return as augmented future earnings before taxes.

The many studies on rates of return from higher education
do not produce a simple and clear-cut conclusion about the
effects of higher education on future income. However, virtually all studies report positive private and social returns on
investments in higher education, usually in the range of 8 to 15
percent—though some studies show lower returns. The results
vary greatly among groups as classified by race, sex, and level of
education, and they may well vary at different historic periods,
depending on the market demand for and supply of educated
people. The question of what is a "satisfactory" rate of return is
also unsettled. From the point of view of students and their
families, the alternative investments (savings accounts, stocks,
bonds, and houses) yield from 5 to 8 percent. Business investments in capital equipment, on the other hand, may yield
from 10 to 15 or even 20 percent, depending on the risk involved. Moreover, from the broadest social point of view, a high
rate of return suggests that a dollar today of benefit to the present generation is more valuable than a dollar in the future of
benefit to our descendants, a conclusion that seems morally
questionable to those who are deeply concerned about their
obligations to posterity. Thus, even if we could learn with preci-

sion what the rate of return to investments in education would be, we would be unsure whether or not the investment was paying off in comparison with other investments. Moreover, the "rate of return" analysis is subject to much criticism on technical grounds relating to the uneven quality of the data employed and to imperfections in the controls for extraneous variables.

Despite these problems and uncertainties, which plague all efforts to learn about the outcomes of higher education, the evidence from the rate-of-return studies is surely worthy of consideration in a broad-based review of the outcomes of higher education. Though the studies vary in reliability and plausibility, most have been executed with care and ingenuity and have been subjected to rigorous criticism. They cannot properly be brushed aside. They show overwhelmingly that higher educational investments produce substantial and positive returns. Since they concentrate only on monetary returns and admittedly leave out of account the many valuable returns that are not reflected in augmented money income, the rates of return estimated by economists (at roughly 8 to 15 percent) may be regarded as a kind of lower boundary to the range of possible "true" rates of return that would fully reflect all costs of higher education and all benefits, including nonmonetary benefits.

Another approach to the economic effects of higher education is to relate higher education to long-term economic growth of the nation as reflected in the rising trend of GNP. Studies of the sources of economic growth usually recognize five potential factors increasing the national income: the use of more labor; the use of more physical capital; improvement in the productivity of labor; improvement in physical capital; and more effective organization of these resources in production. Thus growth in the capacity to produce requires either additions to the supply of productive resources or more effective methods of utilizing given resources. Educational outlays clearly are most directly related to the third of these possible sources—improvement in labor productivity—but there are indirect links between education and most of the five sources. Education may raise labor quality by imparting greater discipline and reliability, better health, increased efficiency, prompter reactions to new information, and heightened mobility. Education also may influence the amount of available labor by altering the age of entry and exit from the labor force, the labor force participation rate, and the pattern of workdays and vacations, among other factors. It may alter the amount of available physical capital as well, by boosting the rates of saving and investment. Then, too, it may improve the quality of physical capital by creating a population better attuned to the needs and uses of machinery and equipment and better capable, through research and development efforts, of designing, adapting, installing, and using new equipment. Finally, educated people are essential to the tasks of improving the organization and management of production.

Most empirical studies of the sources of economic growth have begun by trying to isolate the influence of greater supplies of labor and capital on growth of national income over a period of time. This technique results in an amount of residual national income at the end of the period that cannot be explained by incremental growth of labor and capital. Since the residual presumably includes various influences of education operating through improvements in the quality of labor and capital and in the organization of production, scholars who have wished to trace the influence of education on the behavior of national income have tried to dissect it. The outstanding study in this genre was that of Denison (1974). He found that for the period 1929-1969, the accumulation of education per worker accounted for 14.1 percent of total growth. For a variety of reasons, this percentage can be taken as minimal. Assuming (after Psacharopoulos, 1973) that one fourth of the economic growth due to education at all levels was due to *higher* education, then perhaps 3.5 percent of total growth might be traced to *higher* education. The growth in annual national income over this period was $438.2 billion (in 1958 dollars); thus, in 1969, 3.5 percent, or $15.3 billion per year, would be directly attributable to higher education (excluding academic research and public service). This is an exceedingly rough and probably low estimate, but it may give some idea of the magnitude involved.

Sociological research related to earnings and status.[6] In recent
years sociologists have been conducting important quantitative
studies of factors determining earnings and occupational status
of the members of the population. The leading studies in this
genre are Blau and Duncan, 1967, Duncan, Featherman, and
Duncan, 1972, Sewell and Hauser, 1975, and Fägerlind, 1975.
These studies include useful reviews of the literature. Their procedures have been: (1) to construct theoretical models of the
factors that directly or indirectly determine earnings and occupational status; (2) to discover or gather data to test their
models; and (3) through the method of path analysis, which is a
variant of regression analysis, to estimate the relationships
among the principal variables and thus to "explain" individual
earnings and occupational status.

Our interest in these studies is to learn what they tell us
about the effect of higher education on earnings and occupational status. Earnings and occupational status are highly,
though of course not perfectly, correlated. Most of these studies
treat them separately because they provide somewhat different
information about status, which is the sociologist's main concern. Occupational status is measured by means of classifications based on opinion studies in the general population on relative statuses of various occupations. Earnings are usually measured by annual income.

Earnings and occupational status may differ according to
the time in the life cycle when they are measured. The results of
any study will depend on the age or ages at which earnings and
occupational status are observed. The observation can be in
early years of careers, at middle age, or over a period covering
all or part of a lifetime. These studies suggest that the effects of
higher education on earnings and occupational status increase
on the average over individuals' lifetimes.

In explaining earnings and occupational status, some of the
independent variables have direct effects, some indirect effects
—in that they are mediated by, or operate through, other variables—and some have both direct and indirect effects. The

[6]We were assisted in preparing this section by Suzanne Estler.

intention of the investigators is to separate out the direct and indirect effects and the paths by which the effects are exerted, and to measure the relative total effect of each variable upon earnings and occupational status. Because neither data nor computers are ever adequate to include all potentially significant variables and because many variables appear insignificant upon empirical testing, investigators generally concentrate on a few variables and streamline their theoretical models in accordance with the range of useful data available and the importance of different variables. They have also concentrated primarily on the study of the white male population, for whom data are more complete than for other groups. The models are usually similar to that shown in Figure 2.

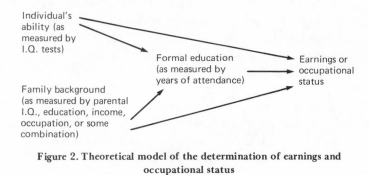

Figure 2. Theoretical model of the determination of earnings and occupational status

Over the past decade or two, the studies have become more sophisticated and possibly more reliable in the sense of explaining an increasing amount of the variance in earnings and occupational status. Generally, the studies are more successful in explaining occupational status than earnings. Among American studies, however, none has succeeded in explaining more than about half the variance in occupational status or one fifth of the variance in earnings. One Swedish study based on an exceptionally rich data source has explained about half the variance in earnings (Fägerlind, 1975).

Several tentative conclusions may be drawn from this line of investigation:

1. Ability and family background exert both direct and indirect influence on earnings and occupational status. The indirect influence of these variables, however, tends to be considerably greater than the direct.
2. The indirect influence of ability and family background is transmitted mainly via education. Education, then, serves as a mediator or conduit by which the resources of the individual in the form of ability and family background are converted into earnings and occupational status. Thus, education is an important link between ability and family background on the one hand and earnings and occupational status on the other.
3. Education not only serves as a conduit for ability and family background but also exerts the strongest direct influence of these three classes of variables upon occupational status. Occupational status, in turn, exerts the strongest direct influence on earnings.
4. These conclusions are in accord with the studies of economists—most of which reveal a positive and substantial rate of return to investments in education when ability and family background are controlled.
5. Encouragement of peers, parents, and teachers has a direct effect on achievement in higher education and thus an indirect effect on earnings and occupational status.
6. The unexplained portion of the variance suggests that there are important factors that have not, or cannot, be included in the models. Those left out may be such hard-to-measure factors as educational quality or intensity, personal motivation, creativeness, attitudes and values, and work-related input, such as time spent at work and on-the-job training.

In summary, studies of this kind are relatively new and future studies are likely to offer more complete models of the status attainment process. However, the available studies clearly indicate the critical role of higher education in converting innate and familial resources into lifetime occupations and financial achievements, and they also show its function as a direct influence on earnings and occupational status.

Conclusions

In this chapter, we have considered the effects of higher education on practical competence with reference to general traits of value in practical affairs and also with reference to citizenship and economic productivity. In the next chapter, we shall continue our study of education and practical competence as related to family life, consumer behavior, leisure, and health.

We found that college contributes significantly to such practical and useful general traits as future orientation and adaptability, but we have found little or no evidence, one way or the other, on the effect of higher education on the traits referred to as need for achievement and leadership.

In the area of citizenship, college has pronounced effects. It produces moderate shifts toward liberal views and ideological thinking, toward greater interest, information, and involvement in political and public affairs, and toward greater inclination to vote. Also, college-educated people are more active than others in community affairs. Regarding crime, educated people are less prone than others to ordinary criminal activity, but the effect of higher education on "white-collar crime" or other antisocial behavior is unclear.

In many ways, higher education undoubtedly contributes to economic productivity. It improves the labor force with respect to traits generally useful in production as well as skills needed for particular jobs. It tends to increase the numbers in the labor force and hours of work and to reduce unemployment. It helps people develop the flexibility, mobility, and knowledge that are associated with that important economic trait, "allocative ability." It assists people in discovering their interests and talents and finding suitable vocations, though it may achieve this result in part through grading and labeling its students in ways that do not necessarily add to their productivity. It probably contributes modestly to job satisfaction. The studies of both economists and sociologists strongly suggest, without specifying the reasons, that higher education contributes significantly to the earnings of individuals and to the economic growth of the nation. Also, as we shall see in the next chapter, education is favorable to health and thus probably enhances productivity of college-educated people.

6

Practical Competence for Family Life, Consumer Behavior, Leisure, and Health

There is only one subject-matter for education,
and that is Life in all its manifestations.

Alfred North Whitehead (1949, p. 18)

In the preceding chapter, we considered the effects of education on general traits that are widely useful in everyday life, citizenship, and economic productivity. In this chapter we continue the discussion of practical affairs by considering the effects of higher education on family life, consumer behavior, leisure, and health.

The Family

Among the most definitive and important outcomes of higher education are its many influences on the family. College appears to have profound effects upon traditional sex roles, marital relationships, divorce, family planning, rearing of children, and other family relationships. Curiously, the literature on the outcomes of higher education has tended to minimize or even overlook these effects. In the many studies in which students or alumni have been asked to rank the various goals of college education, the rank order given to preparation for marriage and the family has been uniformly low (Feldman and Newcomb, 1969; Spaeth and Greeley, 1970). Faculty and administrative leaders also seem to ignore the importance of college education for the family—at least judging by their rhetoric. It could be that one of the most important outcomes of higher education is attained without the participants being aware that it is happening.

Traditional sex roles. College education is associated with a perceptible narrowing of traditional differences between the sexes in interests, attitudes, and behavior patterns. This effect is shown in several studies of college students summarized by Feldman and Newcomb (1969) and Powers (1976). Some of these studies were based on the masculinity-femininity scales of the Omnibus Personality Inventory, some on scales measuring vocational interest, and some on opinion surveys.

Yankelovich (1974b) found that college women are less inclined than noncollege young women to demand or expect traditionally "masculine" behavior of men. A Gallup survey of college students of both sexes (1975) reported that seniors are somewhat more favorable to women's liberation than freshmen.

Studies directed to the entire adult population also reveal differences between college alumni and others in attitudes toward sex roles. We have already observed in the preceding chapter that college-educated women are more likely to be in the labor force than other women. Moreover, college alumni are more likely than others to approve of women working and participating in public affairs. College-educated men are somewhat more likely to share with their wives in housework, care of children, and companionship with children than are noncollege men (Leibowitz in Juster, 1975). Higher education is associated with a preference on the part of both men and women for role-sharing in marriage, that is, for husband and wife roles that are not strongly differentiated (Brigante, 1972).

Marriage. College education affects attitudes and behavior toward marriage in several ways. It has a significant influence on choice of marriage partners. College-educated people are likely to marry persons of similar educational levels (Havemann and West, 1952). For example, in one survey of high school graduates, 70 percent of the fathers who were college graduates were married to women who had achieved education beyond high school (Fetters, 1975, p. 70). Indeed, one study of alumni found that a quarter of the respondents had attended the same college as their wives or husbands (Spaeth and Greeley, 1970, p. 4). Johnson (in Lumsden, 1974, pp. 23-24) suggests—perhaps with tongue in cheek—that influence on choice of marriage partners "might well be the main contribution of a modern university . . . that is, universities facilitate marriages among the intelligent, so breeding higher intelligence."

College-educated people marry at a somewhat older age than other persons (Berelson and Steiner, 1964). The median age of marriage for all persons in the United States is twenty-one for women and twenty-two for men (Statistical Abstract of the United States, 1975, p. 67). Though the average age of college students—men and women combined—is about twenty-two (U.S. Department of Health, Education, and Welfare, *Digest of Education Statistics,* 1975, p. 87), only 29 percent of male college students and 19 percent of female college students are married.[1]

Some older studies have suggested that marital happiness is greater among college-educated people than among other groups (Berelson and Steiner, 1964). A 1960 study by Gurin, Veroff, and Feld indicated that education is positively and strongly associated with marital happiness but that college-educated people reported somewhat more adjustment problems than less-educated people. Kinsey (1948), it may be noted, reported a somewhat lower frequency of sexual intercourse among college-educated men than among other men. Trent and Medsker (1968, p. 168) showed modest differences between college youth and employed youth in assessment of the factors leading

[1]U.S. Bureau of the Census, *Current Population Reports,* Series P-23, No. 44. Also, a 1974 survey of recent B.A. recipients indicated that only 17 percent were already married. More than half said they did not expect to marry within the next two years (*Graduate Magazine,* 1974, p. 7).

to a happy marriage, the noncollege-educated young people being more inclined to emphasize "sex life." Recent surveys by the National Opinion Research Center have conveyed the good news that previous differences in degree of marital happiness between the two groups have been narrowed and also that both groups are experiencing greater marital happiness than had been indicated in a comparable study made in 1960 (Powers, 1976).

Divorce. Divorce rates probably vary somewhat among persons of different educational levels. Unfortunately the data on this subject are sketchy and difficult to interpret. One bit of relevant information is that, in each of the eight states that keep appropriate records, the level of education of persons being married was (in 1960) slightly higher than that for persons being divorced, despite the fact that those being divorced may have acquired education between marriage and divorce. (U.S. Department of HEW, 1969.) These data suggest that the divorce rate was lower among the more-educated than among the less-educated. The results are not very impressive, however, in that the difference in median years of education was only about a third to a half a year. Another approach to the problem is to compare the educational levels of divorced persons with those of the entire population twenty to fifty-four years old. This comparison suggests that the divorce rate is slightly lower among college-educated people than among the majority of persons with a high school education. For different reasons, the divorce rate is also low among those with only an elementary school education.

Family planning. Education has historically been inversely related to the number of children in a family (Freedman, in Sanford, 1962; Berelson and Steiner, 1964; Morgan, Sirageldin, and Baerwaldt, 1966; Whelpton, Campbell, and Patterson, 1966; Machlup, 1970; Ryder and Westhoff, 1971; Withey, 1971; U.S. Bureau of the Census, 1975). However, such radical changes in the birth rate have occurred in recent years among persons of all levels of education that generalizations from the past may not hold in the present or future.

Mitchell (1973) in his survey of fertility preferences found that, on the average, young husbands who are college students prefer more spacing between children than husbands who are not students. This generalization held when he controlled for socioeconomic status as measured by fathers' occupations. Gallup (1975, p. 42) compared the preferences of college freshmen and seniors for various numbers of children and found that seniors favor somewhat smaller families than freshmen. The average number of children preferred by seniors was 2.3 and by freshmen 2.7. Also, other recent surveys of the general population have found that college-educated people favored slightly smaller families than persons with less education. All available evidence, however, suggests that there is little support for childlessness or even for families with only one child. A 1970 survey of unwanted fertility by the U.S. Commission on Population Growth and the American Future (*Statistical Abstract of the United States,* 1974) indicated that unplanned, unwanted, and actual births are all inversely related to education.

Robert Michael, in a study of the relation of education to human fertility (in Juster, 1975) found several interesting effects of education. First, there was a weak positive correlation between family income and number of children but a negative relationship between the actual or potential earning power of wives and number of children. Since education affects both family income and the earning power of wives, it has an indirect effect on family size. Second, education is associated with the use of contraceptive measures and with the effectiveness of these measures. Michael stated (p. 355) that "education favorably affects the proficiency with which couples control their fertility. . . . Furthermore, the education effects remain strong whenever a cross-classification by age and income is made." Third, in one study of suburban families, Michael found a clear negative relationship between the education of wives and number of children. He concluded (p. 361): "Controlling for the age of the wife, the negative effect persists when variables measuring the husband's education, wage rate, and age-adjusted income are held constant. It is not suggested that these regressions represent a well-specified, completed fertility demand equation, but rather that they indicate, with yet another data set, the persistent negative effect of education on fertility." Fourth, one explanation of the effect of education on fertility is that educated people expect to make relatively large investments in each of their children in the form of time and money—investments larger than those planned by the less-educated. The more-educated are thus led to have fewer children and are, in a sense, trading quality for quantity in their total outlays for children. Another way of putting this matter is that college-educated parents have higher aspirations for their children than do other parents (see Berelson and Steiner, 1964, p. 599).

Easterlin (1975, p. 179) has shown not only that fertility rates are inversely correlated with education but that the reduction in birth rate among young women from 1960 to 1970 was much more pronounced among college-educated women than among less-educated women.

In conclusion, most available evidence suggests that education is directly correlated with family planning and inversely correlated with family size. However, because of rapid changes in fertility and family size, affecting both college-educated and other persons, the validity of these conclusions in the future must be regarded with some reservation.

The rearing of children. College education of parents is highly favorable to the careful rearing of children. It encourages the parents' expenditure of thought, time, and money on behalf of their children, with the effect of improving the children's characteristics and achievements.

College-educated parents devote more time to their children than other parents (Hill and Stafford, 1974; Morgan, 1974; Leibowitz, in Juster, 1975). Morgan and others (1974, Vol. II, p. 341) have concluded that "differences in both religious preference and educational attainment of the parents lead to dramatic differentials in the allocation of time to children." Leibowitz (in Juster, 1975, pp. 187-194) found that college-educated wives devote about 25 percent more time than other women to child care, and also that the husbands of college-educated women spend about 30 to 40 percent more time in child care

than other husbands. In addition, Leibowitz reported that although college-educated women are more likely to be in the
labor force than other women, they are less likely to be working
when there are children of preschool or school age in the
family.

College-educated parents also spend relatively more of
their money in ways that foster personal development of their
children than do other parents. For example, college graduates
spend a substantially higher proportion of their incomes for
education (not all of it for children) than do persons of less education, and this holds at every income level. They also spend
more for books, magazines, and other reading materials
(Cobern, Salem, and Mushkin, 1972; Fetters, 1975; U.S. Bureau
of Labor Statistics, 1966).

Studies of Gurin, Veroff, and Feld (1960, p. 135) provide
interesting information about the relationships of college-educated people to their children. They found that most parents of
all levels of education face "problems" in rearing their children.
However, the problems faced by parents of lower educational
attainment are more likely to be economic, whereas those of
parents with higher educational status are more likely to be related to affiliation and behavior. College-educated parents are
more likely than others to have a sense of inadequacy in dealing
with these problems. The interpretation of these findings is not
obvious. On the one hand, they could mean simply that college-
educated parents have more difficulty than other parents in
rearing their children; on the other hand, they could mean that
college-educated parents are more sensitive and more concerned
about the psychological and behavioral development of their
children. The latter interpretation seems more reasonable, because college-educated parents are less subject to economic
limitations than other groups. Clark and others (1972, pp.
58-62) found that educated parents tend to discourage involvement of children in "pop culture" and to encourage their interest in books, serious reading, classical music, and so on (see
Table 33). Regarding popular culture, Clark and others stated
(p. 61) that "income and education work in opposite directions. . . . Education counteracts addiction to popular culture,

Table 33. Percentage of freshmen exhibiting various characteristics,
by cultural sophistication of their families

| Freshman Characteristics | Cultural Sophistication of Family [1] | | | | |
	Very High	High	Medium	Low	Very Low
Motivation to attend and complete college					
College regarded as very important	80%	71%	66%	63%	63%
Believe I am extremely likely to graduate	73	59	54	44	36
Readiness for college					
High index of cultural sophistication[2]	65	49	44	31	27
Combined verbal and mathematical SAT Scores over 1000	82	76	69	61	49
Low interest in popular magazines and popular music	63	52	47	41	45
Educational goals					
Want a liberal education	53	40	35	30	25
Plan to major in a liberal arts field	66	57	49	43	41
Plan to continue education after B.A.	73	65	57	52	51
Occupational goals					
Medicine, Law, Ministry, Professor, Researcher	51	41	38	31	32
Engineering, school teaching	25	34	43	51	53
Religiosity					
Attend religious services once a week	40	45	51	58	60
Political liberalism					
High score on index of support for civil liberties	50	38	34	25	21
Strongly disapprove methods of Senator Joseph McCarthy	53	38	28	16	15
Believe there is too much conformity among students	55	50	43	39	36

[1]Measured by an index based on number of books in the home, father's education, and grandfather's education.

[2]Measured by an index based on book ownership, enjoyment of poetry and classical music, serious reading apart from class assignments.

Source: Clark and others (1972, p. 60).

while income enhances it. At every level of family income, greater educational sophistication means less reading of popular magazines and less listening to popular music, while at every level of family educational sophistication, higher family income means that more of the young score high on addiction to popular culture." Withey (1971, pp. 85-86) suggests on the basis of several studies that college-educated parents "tend to hold developmental, future-oriented, long-range views concerning their children. They prefer that their children be curious and eager to learn, cooperative, confiding in them, and that they be happy, healthy, ambitious, and independent (some of these may be in conflict), as opposed to parents with conservative, traditional views that stress neatness, cleanliness, obedience, respect, and normative behaviours." These various bits of evidence suggest that college-educated parents give more (or different) guidance, support, and encouragement to their children. Table 33 summarizes the relationships between "family sophistication," which is closely related to education, and the various motives, attitudes, values, and aspirations of children.

An abundance of evidence based on major national studies with huge samples indicates a very strong and positive relationship between the education of parents and the measured intelligence, academic achievement, and extracurricular participation of children in school or college (Fetters, 1975; U.S. Department of Health, Education, and Welfare, *Digest of Educational Statistics*, 1974; Cobern, Salem, and Mushkin, 1973). Education of parents is strongly and positively correlated with childrens' attendance at nursery school (Cobern and others, 1972) and at college (Trent and Medsker, 1968; Withey, 1971; Anderson, Bowman, and Tinto, 1972). Clark and others (1972) found that the educational level of fathers is closely related to the importance children attach to college education, that the education of parents is a better predictor of college attendance than parental income.

Trent and Medsker (1968, pp. 25-26) found "a strong association between a senior's decision to go to college and his parents' educational level." In their study, which compared high school graduates who attended college with those who did not, they found that mothers' education as a factor related to college attendance was as important as fathers' occupation. They found also that serious reading by parents was associated with college attendance of children. In another study based on high school seniors of the class of 1972, fathers' education was found to be related to educational and career decisions of sons and daughters (Fetters, 1975). Nerlove (in Schultz, 1972) gives great emphasis to mothers' education as a determinant of the academic and economic success of children, and for this reason he suggests that the special subsidization of women's education might be appropriate.

Not all of the studies linking parents' education with children's characteristics and achievements have controlled adequately for other variables, especially income. However, because the relationship is strong and well documented and because it appears to hold up in those cases where controls are adequate, the conclusion is almost certain that one of the most important outcomes of higher education is the favorable effect of parents' education on the intelligence and achievement of children. This effect, moreover, may be transmitted on through many generations—though probably with declining impact on each successive generation. Indeed, this intergenerational effect may be the most important single consequence of higher education. When higher education adds to the ability and motivation of parents, it enhances the life chances of their children and through them influences the life chances of succeeding generations. The effect of education is thus multiplied as it is transmitted over the generations. The educational multiplier is comparable to the Keynesian multiplier familiar to economists, which governs the relationship between increases in investment and the national income. The Keynesian multiplier is equal to the reciprocal of the marginal propensity to save. The higher educational multiplier is equal to the reciprocal of the marginal loss in educational impact with each transmittal of an initial increment of education from one generation to the next. For example, if one half of the effect of parents' college education were passed on to children, and they in turn passed on to the third generation one half of the effect of the original parents' education, and so on down the generations, the multiplier would be two. This could mean that the initial impact of education upon the first generation would, over time, be doubled. This intergenerational transmission of higher education means that the effect on the generation receiving the education is augmented by its subsequent effect on later generations, and that estimates of the consequences for a single generation substantially understate the total impact of given increments of education.

The intergenerational consequences of higher education may also be considered in reverse. In most studies of educational outcomes, much attention is given to distinguishing the effects of the current generation's education from the effects of their socioeconomic background. But when socioeconomic background is seen as partly the effect of education received in the past by parents, grandparents, and even more distant ancestors, then some part of socioeconomic background must be ascribed to education. The abilities and achievements of the present generation are seen partly as a result of their own education and partly as a result of education received by their ancestors. When socioeconomic background is not properly taken into account, the error is not necessarily overstating the effect of education but rather failing to distinguish between education that occurred earlier and education that occurred later.

When considering the outcomes of education in the present, it is necessary to consider not only its effect on the present generation but on succeeding generations. This means that any outcomes for the present generation will be augmented over time by a multiplier as succeeding generations are affected by it. It also means that any estimate of outcomes that is limited to a single generation is bound to understate the total impact (Archibald in Lumsden, 1974). On the matter of the intergenerational effects, Henry Levin (1972, pp. 47-48), in a report to the Select Committee on Equal Educational Opportunity, United States Senate stated:

> The children of parents with inadequate education are themselves likely to suffer from inadequate education, low income, and low occupational status. This vicious circle of low attainment and poverty tends to repeat itself generation after generation unless there is a powerful social intervention. To the degree that we can raise the educational attainments of future par-

ents, we have also succeeded in raising the educational levels of their children. That is, the amount of schooling which children complete is heavily dependent upon their parents' education. Research has shown that not only is a child likely to attain more schooling the higher his parents' educational attainments, but he is also likely to show higher scores on standardized achievement tests at every level of schooling. Thus the alleviation of inadequate education in this generation will likely have a salient effect on reducing it in the next generation as well. Conversely the present burden of undereducation will likely translate into future costs for the society that our children inherit.

Other family relationships. We have seen that the college education of parents has a marked influence on children. It is likely also that the college education of children affects parents, spouses, and siblings as well. The evidence on these relationships is scant, but it is probable that the experiences of young people in college affect the opinions, attitudes, and behavior of other members of their families—and indeed of their friends and associates as well (Powers, 1976). It would be surprising if college students and graduates did not, through association and discussion, affect the opinions, attitudes, and possibly the behavior of relatives and friends.

It is sometimes asserted that college education alienates sons and daughters from their parents. Gallup (1975) presented some interesting evidence that casts doubt on this matter. He found that attitudes of college students toward their parents were overwhelmingly favorable and did not change over the four years of college. He also found that the attitudes of college students toward themselves was much less favorable than their attitudes toward their parents.

Conclusions. The effects of college education on the family are numerous and strong—so much so that these effects may be among the most significant outcomes of higher education. The impact of higher education on the family is revealed through a wide variety of data from many sources, including data controlled for age, income, socioeconomic background, and other variables. Among the familial impacts are the following:

1. Narrowing the traditional differences in attitudes and behavior between the two sexes.
2. Selection of college-educated persons as marriage partners.
3. Delay in age of marriage.
4. Slight reduction in the divorce rate.
5. Reduction in the birth rate.
6. More thought, time, energy, and money devoted to the rearing of children.
7. Increased achievement of children.
8. Influences on parents, spouses, and siblings of the college-educated.

Consumer Behavior

In modern industrial societies, our thinking about economic affairs tends to be concentrated on production. We tend to view economic efficiency and progress in terms of the amount of goods and services produced, as measured by indexes of industrial production and gross national product. We often overlook the possibility of achieving our goals more fully through greater efficiency in consumption—better values and better allocation of expenditures in achieving these values. Institutional economists have long pointed to the absurdity of our relative neglect of consumption as an instrument of economic and social progress. Thorstein Veblen in *The Theory of the Leisure Class* (1931) wrote a trenchant criticism of the prevailing patterns of consumption in an industrial society. Wesley Mitchell (1937) pointed out the enormous opportunity for societal betterment through improvement of consumer behavior and suggested that education is one way to combat the inefficiency in consumption that derives from misplaced values, ignorance of available options, and vulnerability to the persuasion of advertising and salesmanship. (Veblen, however (pp. 363-400), specifically identified "higher learning" as part of the apparatus that foisted on people values "traceable to the predilections of the leisure class or to the guidance of the canons of pecuniary merit" (p. 363).) In this section we shall consider the effects of higher education on the allocation of consumer expenditures and on savings and investment.

Allocation of consumer expenditures. The most significant information on the relation of education to consumption comes from data of the United States Department of Labor on allocation of family expenditures among various objects (U.S. Bureau of Labor Statistics, 1966; see also Linden, 1967). These data are classified by family income as well as level of education; they show, therefore, the effect of education on consumer behavior separately from the effect of income. These data show that college-educated people, as compared with other people of equal income, spend a considerably smaller percentage of their income on food, tobacco, alcoholic beverages, and automotive and other transportation. College-educated people also spend less on clothing and personal care, although they spend about the same percentage of their income on medical care and recreation; they also spend a considerably larger percentage on housing, reading, and education.

These results indicate that college-educated people pursue somewhat different values from those of other people having comparable incomes. Whether these values are superior is a matter for judgment. They do seem closer to the ideals of higher education than the values sought by less educated people.

Burkhard Strumpel (in Organization for Economic Cooperation and Development, 1974b), in considering the subjective elements of human welfare, has noted that there is an apparent tendency toward satiation with respect to consumption among the quarter of the population with the highest incomes. Whereas, as incomes increase, most of the population continues to seek more and still more consumer goods, in the top fourth the seeking for ever greater consumption seems to subside. Strumpel attributes this to the overrepresentation of professional persons in this group. He says (p. 89): "In our past research, professionals . . . were shown to exhibit a distinctive life-style. Professionals proved to be most attached to nonmaterial 'self-actualizing' values like 'important work' and 'exciting life.' They are most satisfied with their job, their education, their living standards. Their job involvement is the highest, they are most attached to its intrinsic rewards. They also harbor by far the strongest sense of fate control in its various facets. Although most of them are working as employees in organizations, their special skills and expert status provide them with a degree of autonomy. Their social position relieves them from some of the pressures felt by other segments to strive for status through increasing income and standard of living." (See Elgin and Mitchell, 1977.)

Strumpel is referring here to professional persons—not to all college-educated persons. Moreover, he is drawing conclusions about the impact of professional employment rather than about the impact of education per se. Yet it is possible that higher education does temper the struggle "to keep up with the Joneses" through what Veblen called "conspicuous consumption." It is possible also that the rejection of economic growth as a social goal and of material possessions as personal goals, exhibited in recent years by many college students and younger alumni, may be a sign that higher education has some influence on the values that are sought through consumption. These thoughts are, of course, speculative.

Another aspect of the relation between higher education and consumption is that consumption takes time. If one wishes to eat, sleep, work, commute, read, look at television, visit and converse with friends, give attention to children, travel, have two homes, operate and maintain myriad appliances, have a boat, attend the theatre, take part in community affairs, and so on and on, time pressure becomes intense (Linder, 1970). The educated person, since he is likely to have a wide range of interests and to feel this pressure keenly, may be forced to make choices that retard the expansion of his consumption. Thus, the values and opportunities afforded by higher education may tend to put a brake on the growth of consumption. This is especially so because higher education probably directs choices toward time-intensive consumption, for example, reading, the arts, care of children.

A significant study of the relation of education to consumption is that of Robert Michael (in Juster, 1975). His hypothesis (as summarized by Juster, p. 26) was that education enlarges the capacity of people "to process information, to evaluate new ideas and techniques, to make decisions in the face of imperfect information, to acquire new information in a relatively less costly manner, . . . households with more education should be able to get more outputs [in meaningful satisfactions] out of a given quantity of inputs." This hypothesis would be confirmed if the consumption patterns of more-educated persons differed from those of less-educated persons (when incomes were equal) in the same way that the consumption patterns of high-income persons differed from those with lower incomes (when level of education was equal). Additional education would then operate in the same way as additional income to achieve a higher standard of consumption.

Michael tested this hypothesis by correlating educational elasticities (that is, the effect of changes in education on the amount of particular goods or services consumed) with income elasticity (that is, the effect of changes in income on the amounts consumed). He found a positive association between the two elasticities, indicating that additional education leads to consumption patterns similar to those resulting from additional income. Michael's results relate to the efficiency of consumption with given values and say nothing about the effect of education on the kinds of values sought through consumption.

Savings and investment. Education appears to be related to the amount of family savings and to the manner in which these savings are managed and invested. The most conclusive evidence on the relation of education to family savings is found in a study by Solmon (in Juster, 1975). Solmon found, using two different definitions of savings,[2] that the percentage of family income

---

[2]The two definitions were (1) savings as conventionally defined to include change in financial assets and property other than housing minus change in

saved is strongly correlated with education when family income and other variables are held constant. Moreover, he found that the relationship held whether he considered average savings or marginal savings as percentages of income. Earlier, Kosobud and Morgan (1964) had also found a positive relationship between education and savings as a percentage of income—with controls for income and other factors.

Solmon also inquired into the motives of families for saving. After controlling for family size, age, income, and other variables, he still found a strong positive correlation between education and the desire to provide for children, as well as a negative correlation between education and saving to provide for emergencies. These findings support the proposition that college-educated people give relatively more attention than other people to the nurture and welfare of their children.

Regarding the investment behavior of families, Solmon found that the more-educated respondents were less likely than others to invest in fixed-income securities, such as savings accounts and savings bonds (see Mandell and others, 1973), and more likely to purchase equities, such as common stocks, real estate, and shares in mutual funds. He found that the educated families were more sensitive than others to potential capital gains, to tax effects on income from investments, and to potential effects of inflation on investment returns. These results were obtained when income and age were held constant. From these findings, Solmon concluded that the educated were more willing than others to accept risk, more informed and rational in their approach to investments, and more likely to plan ahead with a long-time horizon (see Withey, 1971).

Three related bits of information may be added. First, educated people are more likely than others to seek professional investment advice and to delegate management of their investments to asset managers (Barlow, Brazer, and Morgan, 1966). Second, educated people are more likely than others to use

debt not related to housing; and (2) "full savings," including net additions to business assets (in the case of proprietors and independent professionals), postschool investments in human capital, and the value of consumer durable goods purchased.

credit cards (Mandell, 1972, pp. 15, 18, 19, 35). For example, credit card use was 28 percent for those with a grade school education, 54 percent for those with a high school education, and 81 percent for those with a college degree. The relationship was still strong with controls for income (see also Katona, Stumpel, and Zahn, 1971). Third, college-educated people are more likely than others to use consumer credit in the form of retail charge accounts, personal loans, and automobile loans (Cobern, Salem, and Mushkin, 1973). The significance of this, however, is somewhat ambiguous, because the differences are not striking and the data are not controlled for income.

Ability to cope. College education probably helps people to deal with legal red tape and bureaucracies, to assert their rights, and to thread their way through compliated procedures. For example, an educated person is in a better position than an un-educated one to cope with the credit system and collection agencies, to enforce contracts, to avoid fraudulent investments, to see through misleading advertising and spurious guarantees, to prepare tax returns, to review property assessments and pro-test them if necessary, to achieve legal rights, or to petition pub-lic officials. There is little evidence on these matters, and one can only rely on the commonsense observation that higher education does help people cope with the complexities and the ambiguities of modern life. One bit of evidence is provided by Katz and others (1975), who have shown that college-educated people are considerably better informed about public agencies and their functions and express a greater sense of choice in deal-ing with these agencies than less-educated people (pp. 56, 94). However, before one is captivated by this finding, one should note a Duke University psychiatrist's report that "a person with a master's degree is twenty-eight times more likely to fall asleep behind the wheel of a car than a person with only a grade-school education."

Conclusions. The evidence strongly suggests that higher educa-tion tends to influence the values of consumers; that it orients these values toward the home, intellectual and cultural interests, and the nurture of children; and, with given values and tastes, that it tends to increase the efficiency of consumer choice. College-educated people save more than others relative to incomes, and this saving tends to be more largely directed toward the advancement and welfare of children than toward emergencies and provision for old age. Their investments tend toward equities rather than fixed-income securities; they seem to be more sophisticated in their investment and financial behavior than less educated people. Lastly, their ability to cope with life's daily problems is probably greater.

Leisure

Higher education influences leisure by influencing the amount of time available for leisure activities and the kinds of leisure activities pursued. The evidence on these matters is quite scattered, but the effects appear to be significant.

The concept of leisure time is somewhat ambiguous. It may be defined broadly as whatever time is not consumed in working; or it may be defined as that time left over for discretionary uses after allowance for work, personal care, sleep, household chores, child care, personal business affairs, and so on. The dividing line between working time and leisure time is indistinct, especially so for professional persons, executives, and housewives. And the division of nonworking time between nondiscretionary and discretionary personal and family activities is equally unclear. Nevertheless, one can say something about the effects of college education on the use of time.

One study of the effects of higher education on leisure activities during the college years suggests that the impact is less than impressive (Bradshaw, 1974). Between the freshman and senior years there is a moderate decline in visits with relatives, in religious activities, and in sports activities; little change in sociability and cultural activities; and a moderate increase in political activities and interests. Doubtless, the smallness of the changes during the college years is due to the stability of college life, which demands about the same responsibilities and affords about the same opportunities for both freshmen and seniors. Another study refers to "a strengthened preference for 'elite' leisure styles" among students of selective institutions (Bidwell, 1975, p. 5).

The impact of higher education on leisure is seen more clearly when college alumni are compared with persons of less education. The differences are in some cases substantial, even when the data are controlled for differences in income. We have seen that college-educated people spend more of their lives at work than do other people. They receive greater satisfaction from their work, they work longer hours, and they are inclined to retire later. Thus, they have less nonworking time than other people. In their use of discretionary nonworking time, they tend to be less addicted to television than others and more selective in the programs they watch; they are more inclined to read, engage in adult education, attend cultural events, and participate in the arts; they are more interested in the pursuit of hobbies and other interests; they are more likely to take part in community and civic affairs; and they are more likely to take vacations (Powers, 1976; Baumol and Bowen, 1966; Cobern, Salem, and Mushkin, 1973; Morgan, Sirageldin, and Baerwaldt, 1966; Strumpel, 1976; Withey, 1971).

One leisure activity that virtually every college or university explicitly encourages is physical education and sports. The encouragement extends not only to active participation but also to interest as spectators. The idea of a "sound mind in a sound body" has a long history. As far back as Plato physical education was considered important. In *The Republic* (Book III, sections 1 and 2), Plato attributes to Socrates and Glaucon the following words:

>   Socrates: . . . for the object of education is to
> teach us to love what is beautiful.
>   Glaucon: I agree.
>   Socrates: The next stage in the training of our
> young men will be physical education.
>   Glaucon: Of course.
>   Socrates: And here again they must be carefully
> trained from childhood onwards. My own opinion

about this is as follows: let me see if you agree. In my
view physical excellence does not of itself produce a
good mind and character: on the other hand, excellence of mind and character *will* make the best of the
physique it is given. What do you think?
  Glaucon: I agree.

The Duke of Wellington asserted that "The Battle of
Waterloo was won on the playing fields of Eton." There are
many references to character development, sportsmanship,
sense of fair play, self-discipline, courage, and health as hoped-
for outcomes of participation in physical education and sports.
And the spectator aspects of sports are often advocated on the
grounds that they help build school spirit, provide a wholesome
release for the pent-up energies of undergraduates, and help win
the financial support of alumni and the general public. Also,
colleges and universities train many athletes who take part in
professional sports. Indeed, the role of the academic community in the training of personnel for commercial athletics is not
unlike their function in the preparation of accountants, physicians, and other professional persons. Despite the long historical
association of education and sports, we have found little specific information about the effects of physical education on
character, on lifelong interest and participation in physical
activities, on physical fitness, or on general well-being. Perhaps
the most informative source is Paul Weiss' interesting and penetrating philosophical study of sport (1969). As shown in the
next section, college education does have an impact on health,
but it is not known whether or in what way campus activities in
physical education and sports are linked to this impact—though
exercise is widely believed to be favorable to health and well-
being. Our judgment is that physical education and sports can
best be rationalized as consumer goods, that is, as activities that
are agreeable and interesting in their own right as recreation,
and that their ulterior effects, if any, on personality, character,
and health are simply unknown. Studies of the various possible
effects of campus physical education and sports are urgently

needed. And these studies should not gloss over the possible adverse effects on character of the ambiguities and hypocrisies of intercollegiate athletics.

Health

Education exerts a positive influence on health. The causal connections are not wholly understood. Education may affect the use of health services, and it may be conducive toward a way of life favorable to good health. Whatever the causal connections, educated people are, on the average, more healthy than other people, and the connection appears to run from education to health.

Use of health services. Evidence from several sources indicates that the use of health services is positively correlated with education. Educated people visit physicians and dentists more frequently than others (Cobern, Salem, and Mushkin, 1973; Powers, 1976). This correlation holds even with controls for income (U.S. Bureau of Labor Statistics, 1966). It probably also holds with controls for age and relative incidence of illness, though there are no pertinent data. The older people who are the majority of the less-educated population are presumably subject to more illness than the better-educated young, yet they utilize health services less. The differential effect of education on the use of health services can, however, be reduced by liberalization of the availability and financing of services. For example, in 1953 there was a substantial difference between more- and less-educated women in the percentage of mothers who saw a doctor during the first three months of pregnancy. By 1963, when the program of prenatal care had been changed, this difference had disappeared (Morgan, Sirageldin, and Baerwaldt, 1966).

Way of life as related to health. The effects of education on way of life as it may affect health are not clearly established. It is possible that education leads to stressful activities that may detract from health; on the other hand, it may lead to behavior patterns conducive to health and to greater knowledge of health and hygiene. The limited evidence suggests that education is to some extent correlated with ways of life that are believed to be healthful.

One survey conducted in North Carolina suggests that quality of diet may be positively related to education (Cobern, Salem, and Mushkin, 1973). The smoking of tobacco may be somewhat less prevalent among educated people than among other persons. A 1961-1962 survey of consumer expenditures (U.S. Bureau of Labor Statistics, 1966) found that education is inversely related to dollar expenditures for tobacco when income is controlled.[3] The relationship is illustrated by average annual expenditures for tobacco of families by selected income and education groups, as shown in Table 34. A 1974 survey

Table 34. Average annual family expenditure for tobacco
by education and income level

	High School (9-12)	College (13-16)	Postgraduate (17 or more)
$ 3,000- 3,999	$ 81	$ 57	$ 36
5,000- 5,999	105	88	57
10,000-14,999	129	116	93
15,000 and over	192	142	103

Source: U.S. Bureau of Labor Statistics (1966).

based on the question: "Have you smoked any cigarettes in the past week?" revealed that 63 percent of the college-educated respondents and 58 percent of other respondents said "no" (Powers, 1976, p. 168). This small difference is hardly convincing evidence that education has a profound effect on cigarette smoking. The effect of education on expenditures for alcoholic beverages, when controlled by income classes, is inconclusive

[3]Exception: Those with only a grade school education spent less on tobacco than any other group. The low expenditure of the grade school group may have been due partly to their use of relatively less expensive forms of tobacco and partly to abstinence enforced by meager income.

(U.S. Bureau of Labor Statistics, 1966). In any case, expenditures are not necessarily a measure of alcoholic intake. It is more revealing that college-educated people are more likely than others to favor fluoridation of public water supplies, to use seat belts, and to be inoculated for polio (Morgan, Sirageldin, and Baerwaldt, 1966).

Hyman, Wright, and Reed (1975, p. 91) have shown that education is related to being informed on health through the media of communications and through seeking advice from practitioners. They conclude: "Persons with more formal education appear more likely than those with less to make the effort as adults to keep informed about health matters."

Most of the data on way of life as related to health suggest, but do not prove, that higher education is favorable to health. At least, no evidence was uncovered to the effect that college education is unfavorable to health.

Health status. The acid test of the relationship of education to health is actual health as measured by disability and mortality. Education is associated with good health apparently as an important causal factor. This conclusion is supported by a variety of data.

Hinkle and others (1968, p. 245), in a study of 270,000 men employed by the Bell Telephone system, found that "men who enter the organization with a college degree have a lower attack rate, death rate, and disability rate for coronary heart disease at every age, in every part of the country, and in all departments of the organization." They were careful not to claim that this difference was the result of the educational process itself, but the finding is strongly suggestive.

Kitagawa and Hauser (1973) carefully explored the relationship between mortality and education, with controls for both age and income, and found (p. 24) the following differences in adjusted mortality ratios for white men and women as presented in Table 35. In addition, they found a generally inverse correlation between education of parents and infant mortality rates (p. 28). Stockwell (1963) also found a strong negative relationship between education and mortality. Similarly,

Table 35. Average mortality ratios adjusted for age,
by sex and year of school completed

Years of School Completed	Men	Women
Grade school		
0-7	1.05	1.21
8	1.04	1.05
High school		
9-11	1.05	.93
12	.95	.90
College		
13 or more	.87	.89
All persons	1.00	1.00

Source: Kitagawa and Hauser (1973, pp. 11-33).

many studies show that persons of more education suffer less disability or enjoy better health than those of less education (Cobern, Salem, and Mushkin, 1973; Metropolitan Life Insurance Company, 1976). Moreover, relatively more of those persons who attended college report that they are in excellent health, and fewer that they are in poor health, than those who did not attend (National Opinion Research Center, 1974, in Powers, 1976). For example, 83 percent of the college group reported excellent or good health, as compared with 69 percent of the noncollege group. In Chapter Four, we have already reviewed the literature on mental health with the conclusion that education may be somewhat favorable to psychological well-being.

Perhaps the most persuasive study of the relation of education to health is that of Michael Grossman (1975). He used as a hypothesis that present health is determined by variables of the past, such as past health, education, parents' education, wife's education, intelligence, and scores on tests of various skills, and by variables of the present, such as income, body weight, and job satisfaction. Through multivariate analysis he found (p. 204), holding past health and other variables constant, that education has a "positive and statistically significant effect on current health" and that this result is "evidence in favor of a causal relationship that runs from schooling to current health." He also found that nearly 40 percent of the effect of education operates through wife's education, job satisfaction, and weight difference. One of his more striking conclusions is that a "one-year increase in schooling lowers the probability of death by .4 percentage points" (p. 202). Grossman's general conclusion is supported by other investigators who have found that education is perhaps the most important correlate of good health (Stockwell, 1973; Fuchs, 1974; Hinkle and others, 1968; Kitagawa and Hauser, 1973; Auster, Leveson, and Sarachek, 1969; Breslow and Klein, 1971; Lando, 1975; Orcutt and others, 1977; and Silver, 1972). Auster and others have suggested that to reduce mortality, investment in general education would be more effective than investment in improved medical care. Fuchs has pointed out (1974, pp. 34-35) that education has a strong influence on infant mortality. He states that "infants born to white mothers with eight years of schooling or less have almost double the mortality rate of those born to mothers with twelve or more years of scholing. (The correlation with length of father's schooling is also very strong)." Fuchs summed up the relation of education to health as follows (1975, pp. 46-47):

> One of the most striking findings of recent research on the socioeconomic determinants of health in the United States is the strong positive correlation between health and length of schooling. This result holds for several types of health indexes, ranging from mortality rates to self-evaluation of health status, and for comparisons of individuals or populations, such as cities or states. It also holds after allowing for the effects of such other variables as income, intelligence, and parents' schooling.
>
> This relationship *may* reflect a chain of causality that begins with good health and results in more schooling. In the most detailed investigation yet undertaken of this subject, however, Michael Gross-

man has shown that the reverse hypothesis—that more schooling leads to better health—stands up well under a number of critical tests. One of Grossman's most interesting findings concerns the relationship between schooling and premature death. Suppose you were studying, as he was, a group of white men in their thirties and you wanted to predict which ones would die in the next ten years. According to his results, educational attainment would have more predictive power than any other socioeconomic variable —including income and intelligence, two variables that are usually highly correlated with schooling.

Of course, neither Grossman nor anyone else is certain *why* or *how* schooling affects health. It may result in more sensible living habits; it may contribute to more effective use of medical care; or it may help people absorb new information about health and medical care more rapidly.

One possibility is that the completion of formal schooling increases self-confidence and thus reduces the stress associated with many social and work situations. Among business executives, for instance, it would not be surprising if those who work their way up from blue-collar positions are more prone to heart disease and ulcers than those who enter the executive suite via graduate schools of business. Another possibility is that both schooling and health are aspects of investment in human capital. Differences among individuals and their families in willingness and ability to make such investments may help explain the observed relationship.

Conclusions: College Education and Practical Competence

In this and the preceding chapter, available information and inferences about the impact of college education on practical competence have been assembled. The evidence is scattered and not all of it fully consistent; yet, when this mass of evidence is considered in its entirety, it leaves the distinct impression that higher education is closely linked with competence in the practical affairs of life and that the impact is, on the whole, favorable.

College education is influential in developing many general skills and traits that are useful in a wide range of practical affairs. Among these skills and traits are verbal and quantitative skills, substantive knowledge, rational approach to problems, intellectual tolerance, future orientation, and adaptability.

In the broad domain we have called "citizenship," college education leads toward somewhat more liberal political and social views, though it probably has minor influence in choice of party affiliation; it encourages ideological thinking in the sense of a consistent pattern of choices on various issues; it stimulates interest and active involvement in political affairs; it encourages acquisition of information on political matters; it is favorable to voting in political elections; it leads to community participation in the form of active membership in organizations and volunteer community work; and, finally, it is associated with low rates of ordinary crime, though not necessarily with low rates of unethical or illegal behavior.

In the realm of economic productivity, higher education has many profound effects. It contributes to general personal characteristics of value in work and provides specific vocational training for a wide range of professional and semiprofessional vocations. It is associated with increased participation in the labor force (especially for women and older men), with increased hours worked and with low unemployment. It enhances "allocative ability," that is, the capacity to make prompt and appropriate adjustments to economic changes in consumer demand, technology, and resource supplies. It assists students in the process of self-discovery and placement and thus helps them to achieve congruence between their talents and interest on the one hand and their vocations and other lifetime activities on the other. As part of the placement process, it provides a mechanism for "grading and labeling" students which, on the whole, facilitates their movement into appropriate jobs—but which may give them unfair competitive advantage over noncollege people in obtaining jobs. Finally, it is associated with good health, which also has economic implications.

The broad inference from these findings is that higher education substantially augments the economic productivity of its alumni. This inference is generally supported by economic studies of rates of return from investments in higher education, which usually show returns of the order of 8 to 15 percent, by studies that attribute part of national economic growth to education, and by sociological studies, which usually conclude that education has both direct and indirect effects upon earnings and occupational status.

The most important effect of higher education on practical affairs is its influence on family life. Higher education tends to bring about a narrowing of the differentiation between men and women in their roles in the family, especially with reference to breadwinning, child care, and household work. It affects the selection of marriage partners, college-educated people tending to marry partners with similar education. It tends to delay the age of marriage, to reduce slightly the divorce rate, and to reduce the birth rate. The most striking impact is that it leads to allocating more thought, time, energy, and money to the rearing of children. This in turn seems to lead to greater ability and achievement on the part of the children of college-educated people as compared with other children—even when income and other pertinent factors are taken into consideration. Finally, college education exerts indirect effects on the parents, siblings, and spouses of college-educated people.

College-educated people are relatively efficient consumers. On the average, they seem to get somewhat higher returns from given levels of income than other people. Their values and tastes are oriented relatively strongly toward the home, intellectual and cultural interests, and the nurture of children. They save more than others, relative to income, and this saving tends to be directed toward advancing the welfare of children. They probably have greater ability than others to cope with such complexities as taxes, the legal system, bureaucracies, the credit system, investments, and misleading advertising.

College-educated people engage in leisure-time activities that are somewhat different from those of other people. Their leisure time, while more limited, is used less for TV watching and somewhat more for intellectual and cultural pursuits, including adult education, hobbies, community and civic affairs, and vacations. Their tastes in television programs differ from those of other viewers.

Higher education is strongly associated with good health as measured by mortality, disability, self-evaluation of health status, and other indices. The causal connection appears to be from education to health, not the other way around.

The evidence assembled in this chapter is not suited to quantitative estimates of the influence of higher education on various aspects of practical competence. Yet, using the system described in the appendix to Chapter Three, we venture the estimates shown in Table 36, with descriptive terms rather than standard deviation units.

Table 36. Summary of estimated average changes in practical
competence resulting from higher education

Citizenship	Moderate qualitative gain
Economic productivity	Moderate increase
Family life	Large qualitative gain
Consumer behavior	Small qualitative gain
Leisure	Small qualitative gain
Health	Moderate improvement

7

The Whole Person

We hear reports of weak effects;
we know there are strong effects.
How do we reconcile the data of statistics
and the data of our judgment?

Kenneth Clark

In the preceding chapters of Part Two, we have reviewed a mass of evidence about changes in people associated with their attendance at college. These changes have been considered separately—one by one—for various dimensions of human personality or human achievement. For example, we have tried to judge how much difference college makes in particular areas of life, such as verbal skills, esthetic sensibility, religious interest, citizenship, economic productivity, or health, considered in isolation. Typically, the data for each area refer to large *groups* of people, and are expressed as average scores on test instruments or as percentages of respondents reporting or exhibiting various opinions, attitudes, or behaviors. The findings were clearly positive. In general and on the average, college produces favorable effects upon its students with respect to many dimensions of their personalities, and it has few if any negative effects. True, most of these outcomes, when considered individually, are not startling or dramatic. But the cumulation of many small effects adds up to a very impressive overall impact. No one can travel the road we have taken without concluding that college does indeed matter. Nevertheless, this fragmented approach tends to play down or obscure the more dramatic impacts of college because it makes virtually no contact with individual human beings as whole persons. The focus is always on particular aspects of personality, and on averages or aggregates for large groups of people, rather than on whole human lives. In this chapter, we shall consider the outcomes of college for its students considered as whole human beings.

A Review of Findings

It is not easy to measure the *amount* of change that occurs on the average along any given personality dimension. The basic data are of uneven quality, the results of various studies inconsistent, and the controls for extraneous variables inadequate or lacking; moreover, the very concept of *amount* of change or *amount* of difference resists simple definition. Nevertheless, using our best judgment and the method described in the appendix at the end of Chapter Three, we arrived at the appraisals shown in Table 37 for each of twenty-three personality dimensions.

As this tabulation shows, out of twenty-three dimensions considered, five were judged to be in the categories of "negative," "no change," or "nonascertainable" (which probably means little change), and seventeen were judged to be in the categories "small increase," "moderate increase," or "large increase."

It is worth noting that the dimensions for which the impact of college appears to be "negative change," "no change," and "not ascertainable" are precisely the dimensions usually associated with excellence of personal character: religious interest, human sympathy, intellectual integrity, morality, and wisdom. This finding perhaps explains the current widespread concern about values in higher education.

It is worth observing that only on the dimension of religious interest was the result a negative change, and even this change is subject to various interpretations. On all other dimen-

Table 37. Summary of estimated average changes in individuals
resulting from college education

Descriptive Term	Personality Dimension	Estimated Overall Change Expressed in Standard Deviation Units
Not ascertainable	Intellectual integrity, wisdom, morality.	
Negative change	Religious interest.	−.10 or less
No change	Human sympathy toward individuals.	−.09 to +.09
Small increase	Mathematical skills, rationality, creativeness, refinement of taste and conduct, consumer behavior, leisure.	.10 to .39
Moderate increase	Verbal skills, intellectual tolerance, esthetic sensibility, lifelong learning, psychological well-being, human sympathy toward groups, citizenship, economic productivity, health.	.40 to .69
Large increase	Substantive knowledge, personal self-discovery, family life.	.70 to .99
Very large increase	None.	1.00 or over

sions, the results were either "no change" (including "nonascertainable") or positive. The median score in the above tabulation lies just between "small increase" and "moderate increase."

It would be unreasonable to expect college to bring about dramatic changes in the average level on all twenty-three dimensions. Indeed, an overall improvement averaging, for example, between 5 percent and 15 percent over the whole population of college students would be an enormous achievement. One could then say that the intrinsic "value" of the entire population of college graduates had been enhanced by 5 percent to 15 percent as a result of college education. As will be shown in Chapter Fourteen, such a change, if it could be translated into dollars, would be worth many billions.

The Student as a Whole Human Being

By dropping the approach of considering each of the twenty-three personality dimensions separately and exploring what happens in college to individual human beings viewed as whole persons, quite different possibilities emerge. From this vantage point, we might find that college exerts a major impact on its students even when there are *no* changes in average results for particular dimensions. Every tabulation of scores on test instruments and other measuring devices shows wide disparities in what happens to people as individuals as they are influenced by college. On any given dimension, some students will gain ground, some will lose ground, and some will not change at all. Though aggregates and averages reflect the central tendency of all these wide variations, they conceal the substantial changes experienced by many individuals (Hartmann and Barrick, 1934; Lehmann and Dressel, 1962). "No change" in an average does not mean "no change" for the individuals making up the average (Withey, 1971, p. 26). For example, Feldman and Newcomb (1969, Vol. I, p. 9) cite a study in which a group of freshmen achieved an average score on religious value of 41.75 and the identical students scored 41.57 as seniors. But the individual students making up the group showed changes as follows: −19, −16, −14, −12, −2, +1, +3, +7, +11, +12, +16. A comparison of the two averages would lead to the conclusion that almost no change had occurred, yet the individual scores revealed enormous variability. Or, to offer another example, in this case hypothetical, suppose the level of esthetic interest increased substantially for half of a student population while it decreased for the other half. Suppose at the same time that intellectual interest declined for the half of the population that had become more interested in esthetics and that intellectual interest increased for the other half. The average scores on both estheticism and intellectuality might then remain constant, yet two profound changes in the individuals under study would have occurred (see Klitgaard, 1975).

The purpose of higher education is not necessarily to produce changes for all its students along every dimension of personality development. This clearly would be impossible and undesirable. Colleges accept individual differences among their students and encourage each student to develop along lines compatible with his or her unique interests and talents. Such development inevitably means substantial progress along some lines, no change along others, and regression along still others. Regression along some lines is not necessarily a sign of failure. For example, a student who had devoted much time in high school to music may discover interests in science in college. As a result, he may regress on estheticism and progress on intellectuality during college. Or, to take another example, a student may come to college with highly developed mathematical skills. He may discover new interests in social issues that result in a regression in mathematical skills but a progression in political interests. Such regressions are not necessarily negative outcomes; they may indicate constructive changes in personality configuration resulting from exposure to new opportunities.

It is unreasonable to expect any person to progress simultaneously along all possible lines of development. People differ in the distribution of their talents. Some individuals possess highly specialized talents and interests, whereas others may have more diversified ones. But few, if any, are so well-rounded (or dull) that they can be expected to make equal progress across all possible lines of personality development. The totally well-rounded individual who followed every conceivable interest surely would be a bland, innocuous, and mediocre person. Moreover, there is an economy of interests. The cultivation of any one interest takes time and energy. To pursue every interest equally would preclude significant achievement in any one area. To attain excellence in some will be at the cost of achievement in others. Excellence of personality involves choices based on a weighing of values in relation to interests and talents, not the equal pursuit of every imaginable value. There may be some values which should have high priority for all; for example, verbal skill, personal honor, consideration for others, and so on. But among the wide range of values that life presents, there must be trade-offs involving choices based on the unique characteristics of each individual. This being so, each individual must make special and unique use of the opportunities available in the college environment to develop his personality. In the process, every individual may change, but the average changes for all students with respect to each personality characteristic may be relatively small. As J. P. Guilford (1967, p. 475) wrote: "Should all children be educated so as to enhance all the abilities? In the extreme case, this would mean attempting to even up each child's status in all respects, as if the one ideal were to produce a 'well-rounded,' balanced individual. The other side of the issue is that such a goal is impossible to achieve and is even undesirable and that we should discover early where a child's strong points are and capitalize on them, for in these directions the individual is likely to make his greatest contributions to society. As usual, there is a middle ground. While seeing to it that no ability is allowed to remain below a minimum needed for ordinary living, we should also, in recognition of the specializing that prevails in the modern world, allow the individual to make the most of what he can do best and what gives him the greatest satisfaction."

To study the genuine outcomes of higher education in all their variability, then, it is necessary to observe the changes in individual students as whole persons rather than to look at average changes on particular personality dimensions. The problem calls for the study of people in some depth as well as the study of particular aspects of their personalities. The few studies that focus on whole persons yield results that come closer to the changes that every educator observes in his students, during and after college, than do typical studies based on average changes in particular dimensions of personality. Statistically, the changes should be measured as profiles or syndromes or gestalts, not as average changes on particular dimensions.

Future Research

Scholars have become increasingly aware that the next step in the study of higher educational outcomes should be the exploration of the lives of whole persons. For example, Sanford (1962, p. 809) wrote that "in order to understand the lasting effects of college we have to see the place of college within the whole life cycle—or at least within a developmental course extending from childhood to adult life. This permits us to see that the college experience is utilized in different ways by different people, and that it has different functions in different lives. The proper study of the effects of college, then, is the study of lives; and such study must in the present stage of our knowledge rely mainly upon intensive interviews." In the same vein, Martin Trow (1974a, pp. 29-30) expressed the view that the issues of moral development and higher education are not "most usefully studied through sample surveys. On the other hand, the anthropological research tradition of direct observation and qualitative interviewing is not strong in the community that does most of the research on higher education. There is, then, a gap between our research traditions and training, and the kinds of problems I have been discussing."

Referring to social psychology in its application to education and other fields, Deutsch (1976, p. 5) suggested that: "Despite its ancestry in individual psychology, social psychology has been too much a depersonalized psychology of homogeneous individuals. The individuality of people is frequently ignored in social psychological theorizing and research." Finally, in a recent report on the direction of research on higher education, McKeachie and Stephens (1976, p. 15) observed that "studies of abilities, values, and attitudes characterizing those who have been educated should be supplemented by studies of the lives of individuals. . . . It may be that one of the most important outcomes of education is a meaningful integration of personality. Typical cross-sectional studies of specific outcomes may miss unique interactions of educational experience, persons, and later environment."

Similar ideas have been expressed by Pace (1976) who, in a recent address, distinguished between the study of phenomena and the study of lives, and Brawer (1973, pp. 3-4), who called for greater attention to "total personality configurations." A considerable body of literature has appeared in recent years relating to the development of the whole person as a goal of higher education—some of it based on in-depth interviews with students and intensive case studies (Murphy and Raushenbush, 1960; R. Heath, 1964; White, 1966; D. H. Heath, 1968; Madison, 1969; Goethals and Klos, 1970; Perry, 1970; Kohlberg and Turiel, 1971; Kohlberg and Mayer, 1972; King, 1973; Cottle, 1973; Cross, 1976).

A suggestive study by Koon (1974, pp. 1-2) struck a

middle ground between case studies on individual students and studies of large groups focusing on particular dimensions of personality: "Because of the complexity and diversity among human beings, it seemed unrewarding to limit ourselves to the search for modest or weak generalizations uniformly applicable across either the entire group of interviewees or the larger sample. Indeed, traditional research, which has often taken a single-dimension, either/or approach to human reality, is likely to obscure the differences in the complex dynamics of interaction with the environment from one individual or group to the next. Unfortunately, the most human(e) solution to this problem, that is, treating each student individually, while essential in personalized settings, is usually too complex to be of much utility in research and invites one to obscure the many important but different socioculturally influenced patterns of regularity that do exist." Koon's method was to divide the student population under study into thirteen types, based on their scores on various personality dimensions, and then to study the impact of college on each type separately (see Clark and Trow, 1962). Although there is still need for both large group studies and case studies, Koon's compromise would seem to hold considerable promise in the future exploration of college impact. Along the same line, an effort is being made under the sponsorship of the National Institute of Education to computerize life history data. If this method should prove feasible, a new era in the study of lives would be opened up (Karweit, 1976).

Client Evaluation

Another approach to judging the impact of higher education on its students as whole persons is to explore the attitudes of its clients—students, alumni, and the general public—about its performance and its effects. Students are participants in the system of higher education. Alumni, who have been deeply affected by it, can reflect upon its meanings. And members of the public can see it as outsiders, observing its impact on their children and friends as well as on society in general. All three of these groups are in a position to offer independent and distinctive appraisals. The appraisals of students and alumni (and to some extent of others) will be influenced not only by the lasting effects of college but also by the *direct* satisfactions and benefits afforded by college life.

These immediate experiences are not a trivial part of the outcomes of higher education. Four college years make up 5 or 6 percent of an average lifetime; for some students, higher education may consume as much as 10 or 12 percent of a lifetime. What happens to people during these years surely is significant in itself, apart from any long-term benefits. We have been unable to find specific information on the direct satisfactions derived from college life. Investigation of this matter is needed. However, anyone who has himself been to college and anyone who spends his working life on the campus can hardly avoid the conclusion that for most students, most of the time, the college experience yields satisfaction, pleasure, and even joy. This is not to say that some students do not find college life boring, worrisome, anxiety-ridden, or lonely or that most students do not go through periods of frustration. But on the whole, the college experience is regarded as pleasant by most and as delightful by many.

Evaluation by Students

On the whole, surveys of student attitudes toward college, which have been made over many years, show that two thirds to three quarters of the students hold favorable attitudes. Feldman and Newcomb (1969, Vol. II, pp. 158-160) summarized several studies (conducted over the years 1931-1967) of student ratings of quality of instruction and student satisfaction with courses and teachers. Though the responses differed among the several studies depending on the form of the questions, about 75 percent of the students were favorable, about 4 percent were highly unfavorable, and the rest—about 20 percent—were either neutral or mildly dissatisfied.

In a survey of students in ten institutions, Jacob (1957, pp. 33-35) reported that 71 percent of the respondents agreed that "most of what I am learning in college is very worthwhile." Only 18 percent agreed that "college does not really equip you for life outside the campus." From 10 percent to 30 percent were critical of their colleges for inadequately emphasizing religious and patriotic values, for not achieving a reasonable balance between radical and conservative views, and for "production-line" teaching methods. Summarizing these results, Jacob observed (p. 34) that "on an overall appraisal, most college graduates cherish the education they have had, and if they had it to do over again would choose to repeat the course of study they took and at the same campus from which they graduated."

In its massive survey of college students in 1969, the Carnegie Commission on Higher Education gathered considerable data on student attitudes. The findings are in agreement with other studies: A substantial majority of students—roughly two thirds or more—are reasonably satisfied with their college experience, although there are specific complaints and a desire for improvement in some respect. In commenting on these data, which were collected at the height of the period of student unrest, the Carnegie Commission observed (1972, p. 16): "These opinions indicate that no revolutionary transformation in academic life need now be undertaken as a result of widespread general dissatisfaction by students. . . . We reject . . . calls for revolutionary changes. The whole system is not bankrupt." In a follow-up survey taken in 1975, the results were virtually identical (Trow, 1977, Tables 1 and 2). The disturbing fact remains that nearly a third of the students were either neutral in their evaluation of college (which is hardly a resounding endorsement) or were dissatisfied. Though it would be impossible to satisfy every student, one third may be an excessive proportion of students to have neutral or negative attitudes.

Pace (1974a, p. 57) found that a large majority of junior-senior student respondents reported that they were receiving "very much" or "quite a bit" of benefit from college in specific respects as follows:

Personal development	84%
Tolerance	78
Individuality	76
Social development	75
Friendships	74

Critical thinking	72%
Specialized skills	71
Philosophy, cultures	69
Vocabulary, facts	69

Pace (p. 32) also found that 68 percent of upperclassmen said that, if they were starting over, they definitely or probably would go to the same college again, whereas 11 percent said they would not.

A 1974 survey of a large sample of college seniors found that 66 percent considered themselves adequately prepared for a career and 29 percent ill-prepared. When asked, "If you had it to do over, would you go to college?" 97 percent said "yes," though a quarter of these said "yes, but not to the same college" (*The Graduate Magazine*, 1974, p. 9).

In a study involving 710 seniors from seven institutions, Koon (1974, p. 13) found that about 80 percent of the respondents were satisfied socially and about 77 percent were satisfied with their general college experience.

A 1975 longitudinal study of a large national sample of the high school class of 1972 found that of those who had received some postsecondary education, 82 percent were satisfied with intellectual growth, 76 percent were satisfied with development of work skills, and 73 percent were satisfied with the ability, knowledge, and personal qualities of most teachers (U.S. Department of Health, Education, and Welfare, National Center for Education Statistics, 1975b, p. 2).

An unusually interesting approach to the question of the evaluation of college by students is that of McMahon (1974). Using a sample of 2,766 nonfreshmen students, he obtained information on their expected rate of return to their investments in education, including not only monetary returns but also returns from job satisfaction, personal satisfactions, service to society, and serving the next generation by rearing children more competently. He discovered that students expected substantial returns from each of these types of benefits and that the combined expected return was almost double that for monetary returns alone (pp. 171-173). This evidence suggests that many students believe they are obtaining important and varied benefits from college—both monetary and nonmonetary.

Specifically, McMahon found that the expected rates of return for each type of benefit considered one by one were as follows:

Private monetary returns (male)	14.5%
Private monetary returns (female)	7.5
Job satisfaction	10.1
Personal satisfactions	10.0
Serving next generation by more competently rearing children	10.3
Service to society	11.0

When all these benefits—monetary and nonmonetary—were consolidated and converted into a social rate of return, he found the expected rate to be 22 percent.

Other studies reporting results consistent with those presented here are: Freedman in Sanford, 1962; J. A. Davis, 1965; Roper, 1968, quoted in Powers, 1976; Astin and Panos, 1969; Astin, 1972; Betz, Starr, and Menne, 1973; Gaff, 1974; Yankelovich, 1974b).

Evaluation by Alumni

As they reflect upon their college experience, a large majority of alumni also express positive attitudes that do not differ sharply from those of students. Pace (1949) conducted a survey of the attitudes of 1,600 University of Minnesota alumni of classes graduating in the period 1924 through 1929. He found that an overwhelming majority held a favorable opinion of the value of their college experience.

Havemann and West (1952) conducted a survey of 9,064 alumni from 1,037 colleges and universities. They found that 98 percent would choose to go to college if they were living their lives again; 84 percent said they would choose the same college; 70 percent said that college "helped a lot" in their work, and 28 percent said it "helped some." Only 2 percent reported that it did not help at all.

Spaeth and Greeley (1970, pp. 38-40) reported findings on the attitudes toward college of a large sample of alumni of the class of 1961. Their survey, made in 1968, reveals that these alumni held generally positive views of their college experience (see Keeton, 1971). About 86 percent of the respondents reported that they like their colleges or have a "very strong attachment" to them. Only 4 percent expressed negative reactions. Two thirds or more rated as "excellent or good" the classroom teaching, curricula and course offerings, knowledge and professional standing of the faculty, usefulness of college in preparation for careers, and other features of their college experience. There was a high correlation between their personal goals for college and the actual help college had given them. Finally, more than a half said they disagreed completely with such criticisms as "no sense of community or chance for students to participate," or "the rules were too restrictive," though two fifths or more of the respondents conceded at least some validity in them. From these data, one can only conclude that alumni on the whole place a high valuation on their college experience.

In a 1968 survey based on a small nationwide sample of alumni, the Roper Research Association (Powers, 1976, pp. 155-156) found that 89 percent expressed positive attitudes toward college and only 3 percent found it "very unsatisfactory." These evaluations, however, were subject to the reservation that improvements are needed. The opinions of alumni as reported in this survey were almost identical with those of a comparable Roper survey of students.

In a study with returns from about 8,300 alumni of the class of 1950 representing 74 institutions, Pace (1974a) found overwhelmingly positive attitudes about college. About 75 percent of the alumni indicated that they "definitely" or "probably" would attend the same college again if they were to live their lives over. Only 6 percent said they definitely would not select the same college again (p. 32). The percentages of alumni respondents reporting that they had received "very much" or "quite a bit" of benefit from college in various respects were as follows (p. 52):

Vocabulary, facts	79%
Critical thinking	72
Personal development	66
Specialized skills	64
Philosophy, cultures	64
Social and economic status	63
Communications skills	63
Literature	62
Social development	61
Individuality	61

A 1974 survey of college alumni who were freshmen in 1961 (Higher Education Research Institute, in Bisconti and Solmon, 1976, pp. 9-35) revealed these responses:

College education useful in finding jobs	69%
Content of undergraduate majors used frequently or sometimes	52
Content of undergraduate minors used frequently or sometimes	64
Jobs closely related or somewhat related to undergraduate majors	49

Evaluation by the General Public

The general public apparently attaches considerable importance to higher education and views it favorably, though in recent years their enthusiasm may have been diminished somewhat.

One group of surveys conducted during the decade 1958 to 1968 found that large majorities of the population placed high value on college as shown in Table 38.

A comparison of identical 1963 and 1972 surveys suggests that public attitudes have been turning against higher education. The data are presented in Table 39. Though nearly two thirds of the respondents still favored mass higher education, nearly a third thought that fewer students should be in college. And when the implications for taxes were raised, a majority opposed expansion of higher education.

Table 38. Responses in public opinion polls on the value of college
by college alumni and others

	College Alumni	Others
The president of the United States should be college-educated[1]	82%	86%
Every young man should try to get some college regardless of the type of work he is planning to do[2]	75	88
If a young woman plans to be a housewife, it's not too important that she have college training[3]		
Women	8	33
Men	29	40
Every capable person has a right to receive an education through college even if he cannot afford it[4]	87	85

Sources:

[1]American Institute of Public Opinion (1958). Based on a national sample of 232 college alumni and 1,185 others.

[2]The Minnesota Poll (1962). Based on a state sample of 113 alumni and 469 others.

[3]The Minnesota Poll (1962). Based on a state sample of 113-119 alumni and 256-470 others.

[4]National Opinion Research Center (1968). Based on a national sample of 323 alumni and 1,058 others.

A 1973 California poll indicating substantial public support for higher education suggested, nevertheless, that many people have reservations or mixed reactions. Whereas 70 percent of the respondents agreed that college is important for young persons who want to get ahead, and 75 percent viewed mass education as one of America's main hopes for the future, 79 percent conceded that there are other ways for young people to prepare themselves for life, and 72 percent thought colleges are admitting too many students. The net result of this survey, however, is that public attitudes toward higher education are quite positive (*Los Angeles Times*, July 3, 1973).

Finally, a 1975 national survey sponsored by Citicorp found that "80.2 percent of the 1,404 respondents in the poll

Table 39. Value of college in general public opinion

	1963	1972
This country spends more money on college education than any other country in the world. Do you think this is a good thing for our *country* to do, or would it be better not to have so many young people go to college?		
Good thing	88%	64%
Better not to have so many go to college	5	29
No opinion	7	7
If the people of your state were asked to pay a little more in taxes so that more young people could go on to college, do you think you would vote for this or against it?		
For	61%	35%
Against	33	53
No opinion	6	12

Source: Opinion Research Corporation (1972, pp. 2-4).

said college was important for their children. Moreover, almost 78 percent of the respondents with children currently in junior high or high school said there was a likelihood that the kids would go on to college."

Conclusions

Most studies of the effects of higher education on students provide data on average changes for large groups of students with respect to particular dimensions of personality. For example, they reveal average changes with respect to verbal skill or political liberalism or religious interest or esthetic sensibility. But students do not develop equally along all dimensions of personality, and so averages obscure what is happening to them as whole human beings.

The effects of higher education are almost surely greater than those revealed in the large group studies that present data as aggregates or averages. Further, there are effects of higher education—especially on total personality development—that cannot be captured at all by large group studies focusing on single personality dimensions. If the group studies show that college has some effect along each of many dimensions, as they do, then one can be reasonably sure that the true effects of college are different from, and far greater than, what these studies suggest. When the overall impact of college on the several personality dimensions lies between what we have defined as "small" and "moderate," then we would surely be justified in estimating that the overall impact of college on its students could be described as "moderate" or "large."

The effects of higher education on its students as whole human beings is revealed in evaluations made by its clients. Many studies made over several decades have shown that at least two thirds of students, alumni, and members of the public believe that higher education produces valuable outcomes for its students. The percentage of people who hold strongly negative opinions tends to be very small—of the order of 5 percent to 10 percent. Another quarter tend to be neutral or indifferent. On the part of the public, there has been some reduction in the percentage holding favorable views. Indeed, in light of recent publicity about the alleged shortage of jobs for college graduates, higher education may be in greater disfavor than the data indicate. But there is no evidence, either in survey data or in the behavior of families as revealed in college enrollment statistics, to suggest a major renunciation of higher education by the public at large. While speaking of college enrollments, it is perhaps germane to point out that the ratio of enrollment to population of ages eighteen to twenty-one has risen from .28 in 1955 to .51 in 1975, and the trend may be still upward (American Council on Education, *A Fact Book on Higher Education* Second Issue, 1976, p. 78). These statistics are the most persuasive evidence that higher education retains the confidence of the American people.

8

Similarities and Differences
Among Institutions

*Sometimes institutions are simply the sum of
the historical accidents that have happened to
them. Like the sand dunes on the desert, they
are shaped by influences but not by purposes.
. . . they are the unintended consequences
of millions of fragmented purposes.*

John Gardner (1965)

In our review of the evidence on the effects of higher education,
we have given little attention to possible differences among colleges and universities—on the assumption that the higher education establishment is a coherent *system* consisting of institutions that have much in common. In this chapter, we shall
explore the nature and extent of the similarities and differences
among institutions. Our purpose is twofold: to seek insights
about outcomes that may be revealed by examining differences
among institutions and to test our assumption that it is reasonable to investigate outcomes by considering the higher education system as a whole.

Though they have much in common, institutions of higher
education obviously differ from one another in many respects:
wealth, size, location, curricula, academic standards, teaching
methods, faculty characteristics, extracurricular life, educa-

tional philosophy, and traditions. These differences undoubtedly affect the precise impact of particular colleges and universities on their students. Institutions also differ from one another
in the characteristics of their graduates. The graduates of some
institutions are, on the average, more intellectual or more politically liberal or more religiously oriented or more disposed
toward community service or more sensitive esthetically or
more practical than the graduates of other institutions. The differences, however, may be explained only partly by differences
in institutional characteristics. To a larger degree, they are due
to differences among institutions in the characteristics of the
students they attract, recruit, and retain. For example, those
institutions with strong academic programs or with strong religious orientation will tend to attract students with well-developed intellectual or religious interests. The combination of program and student will probably produce intellectually disposed
or religiously oriented alumni. We need to know how much of
the differences among institutions in the characteristics of their
alumni result from the unique resources, programs, and environments of the institutions and how much from the kinds of students they attract. Feldman and Newcomb (1969, Vol. I, p.
328) expressed the view: "that those characteristics in which
freshman-to-senior change is distinctive for a given college will
also have been distinctive for its entering freshmen, initial distinctiveness being in the same direction as subsequent change.
. . . the kinds of college impacts that are massive enough to distinguish different colleges from one another are, in considerable
part, outcomes of the accentuation of initial distinctions." (See
Bachman, 1972.)

In contrast to the observed average differences among the
graduates of various colleges, an examination of the differences
in the *degree of change* in students occurring over the college
years reveals that differences among institutions in educational
impact are less than is commonly supposed. Graduates of Ober-
lin or Memphis State or of the University of California are what
they are partly because of what they were when they entered
college and only partly because of changes wrought by the particular colleges they attended. Sharp (1970, pp. 97-98), in a

study of employment experience of college graduates, concluded: "From the point of view of personality development and acquisition of a life style, the role of the specific college that a student attends for all or most of his undergraduate studies cannot be discounted (although the few systematic studies which have been conducted suggest that this role may be smaller than is generally assumed). But from the point of view of one's occupational and graduate school careers, the character and quality of the undergraduate institution attended seem to have a minimal impact. The early careers of graduates of the Class of 1958 seemed to reveal only minor inter-school differences."

That relatively small differences among colleges remain after allowances are made for variations in student characteristics should come as no surprise. The environments and programs of most institutions are quite similar. All provide courses with readings, laboratories, lectures, and discussion. All have faculties who have been educated in graduate schools with fairly similar programs and procedures. All use fairly similar textbooks and readings. Cultural, social, recreational, athletic, and student-government programs have much in common. All are influenced by the same accreditation standards and more or less common academic traditions. All try to offer incentives and encouragement for academic excellence (see Ben-David, 1972).

Of course, institutions differ on such matters as student-faculty ratio, distinction of faculty, elaborateness of facilities, relative stress on liberal and vocational education, religious emphasis, residential arrangements, and degree of cosmopolitanism. These differences are probably more important in determining the characteristics of the students attracted to each institution than in determining the change that takes place during the college years. Even after allowance for student characteristics, however, these differences do matter to some extent. We shall try to distinguish between those institutional outcomes which merely reflect the characteristics students bring with them to college and those which may be due to the special influence of particular institutions.

Cognitive Outcomes

The question of the cognitive "value added" by colleges having different characteristics has been explored in several studies. In an early investigation, Learned and Wood (1938, p. 384), using the Carnegie General Culture Test, compared the scores of sophomores and seniors at thirty liberal arts colleges and seven teachers colleges in Pennsylvania. They found considerable differences among institutions in the gain in mean scores from the sophomore to the senior year. For ten institutions the gain ranged from .75 to 1.25 of a standard deviation and for nine institutions it varied from .12 to .50 of a standard deviation. There was no correlation, however, between initial scores and amount of gain. Institutions with high initial scores showed both low and high gains and so did institutions with low initial scores. Heist and others (1961) found that high-ability students attending "quality" institutions (as measured by relative number of graduates going on to the Ph.D.) were more likely to acquire scholarly or intellectual traits than comparable students attending other institutions. In contrast, in a series of papers presented over the past decade (1968, 1969 with Panos; 1970, 1972, 1973b), Astin has suggested that differences among colleges in cognitive impact are likely to be small—after allowance for the initial ability of students as entering freshmen. He found that performance of graduating seniors on the Graduate Record Examination (presumably a measure of intellectual achievement) was not related closely to institutional "quality" when initial ability and socioeconomic background of the students were taken into account. Astin and Panos observe (1969, p. 145) that "the student's achievement (as measured by the three Area Tests of the Graduate Record Examination administered during his senior year in college) is neither improved nor impaired by the intellectual level of his classmates or by the level of academic competitiveness or the financial resources of his institution. Similarly, no evidence was obtained to support the common belief that the bright student benefits more than the less able student from exposure to these traditional features of 'high-quality' institutions. In general, differences among students in their achievement at the senior level are much more closely linked to variations in ability that existed prior to the student's entrance to college than to *any* characteristic of the undergraduate institutions."

Comparing initial ability as measured by the National Merit Scholarship Qualifying Test and achievement as measured by the Graduate Record Examination, Nichols (1964) found that differences in institutional characteristics exerted little effect on cognitive results. He wrote (pp. 52-53): "One might expect that the more a college has of things which are thought to promote student learning the greater would be its positive effect on both GRE-V and GRE-Q scores. This does not seem to be the case, since such variables as faculty-student ratio, library books per student, the average ability level of the student body, and the affluence of the college were all unrelated to residual GRE scores. . . . In short, the college influence is impressively less than might have been expected. To be sure there were no sow's ears in our sample, but the colleges did little more than rearrange the embroidery around the tops of the purses made from the very high quality silk supplied to them."

Rock, Centra, and Linn (1969) studied the relation between students' ability, as measured by Scholastic Aptitude Tests (SAT) at time of college entry, and cognitive achievement, as measured in the senior year by the Area Tests of the Graduate Record Examination (GRE). Their sample included 6,855 students in 95 colleges—mostly small private institutions. The institutions were classified according to resources, measured by library books, institutional revenues per student, percentage of faculty with doctorates, student-faculty ratio, type of control, etc. They found very high correlations of the order of .9 between SAT and GRE scores, indicating that a large part of the variance in cognitive achievement could be explained by initial ability. However, they learned that achievement relative to initial ability did differ among institutions according to their revenues per student and percentage of faculty with doctorates. They also found that, among the institutions with high revenues per student, those of smaller enrollment had relatively better performance than larger institutions. Size, however, had little bearing on performance among colleges of low revenue per student.

Heist and others (1961), in a study of National Merit Scholarship winners, concluded that students of high ability attending institutions that produced relatively large numbers of future scholars and scientists were more likely to exhibit serious intellectual tendencies than comparable students attending other institutions. Centra and Rock (1971) studied the effects on student achievement of personal interest of instructors in teaching and in their students, student freedom in choosing courses, and cultural facilities and programs. They found student achievement (relative to initial ability) to be higher in institutions where these factors were prominent than in other institutions.

Pace (1974a, pp. 56-57) approached the matter of differences among institutions in cognitive performance by asking end-of-year juniors and alumni of the class of 1950 about the benefits they received from college and classifying the responses by eight types of institutions. The percentage differences among the various types of institutions in reported cognitive benefits were, on the whole, modest but not negligible. The percentage of alumni reporting "very much" or "quite a bit" of benefit from the cognitive aspects of college education are shown in Table 40. When substantial differences in benefit were reported, they tended to reflect the curricular emphasis of the institutions rather than their fundamental cognitive impacts.

In a study of eight varied institutions, Clark and others (1972) discovered generally small *differences* among these institutions in gains on scores measuring intellectual and esthetic interests of students. This was true of scores on Thinking Introversion, Theoretical Orientation, Complexity, and Estheticism. Such differences as they did find resulted from a ceiling effect, which produced a negative correlation between the initial scores and the gains. For example, the gains were smaller for Reed College, which attracts freshmen with exceptionally high scores, and larger for San Francisco State, where initial scores were lower. In commenting on these findings, the authors (p. 179) concluded: "While these results offer some evidence for differ-

Table 40. Cognitive benefits reported by alumni, by type of institution

	Critical Thinking	Vocabu- lary, Facts	Litera- ture	Science, Technol- ogy	Background for Further Specializa- tion
Comprehensive universities					
Selective	74%	81%	62%	53%	63%
Less selective	71	80	56	54	62
State colleges and less com- prehensive universities	68	78	57	59	59
Liberal arts colleges					
Highly selective	77	84	83	45	64
Strongly denominational	69	78	71	46	60
Other	72	77	71	37	65
Teachers colleges	64	76	68	41	70
Colleges of Engineering & Science	81	79	31	94	70

Source: Pace (1974a, pp. 52-53).

ential change across schools, the findings are not particularly striking. Could it be that the relatively weak evidence for dif-ferential change in intellectual interests stems from the fact that change in this domain is one of the specific aims of most faculty, and that one must look to the domains of liberal atti-tudes and personal adjustment for clearer evidence of institu-tional impact or differential change?"

Another relevant bit of information comes from the re-markable study of Dubin and Taveggia (1968), in which they compared the results from various methods of teaching particu-lar subjects, including lecture, discussion, use of television, large classes, small classes, and so on. Their conclusion was (p. 35): "In the foregoing paragraphs we have reported the results of a reanalysis of the data from 91 comparative studies of college teaching technologies conducted between 1924 and 1965. These data demonstrate clearly and unequivocally that there is no measurable difference among truly distinctive methods of college instruction when evaluated by student performance on final examinations." This conclusion does not directly address the question of differences among institutions, but it does suggest that, if there are no differences in results from varied methods of instruction, there might be no difference among institutions whose distinctive characteristics relate to methods of instruction.

The tentative conclusion from these studies is that colleges differ in their cognitive performance when differences in initial student characteristics are taken into account but that the differences are neither marked nor systematic. This in no sense implies that college education in general makes little or no contribution to cognitive learning. Nor does it imply necessarily that many colleges do not uniquely affect the cognitive development of particular individuals. It only suggests that colleges produce similar results in their *average* contribution to cognitive learning. If valid, this finding is of great practical import. Like most conclusions about higher education, however, it rests on sparse and to some degree conflicting data. More research is needed.

Noncognitive Outcomes

The differences among colleges in noncognitive outcomes probably are greater than those relating to cognitive outcomes. This may be so because the most pronounced differences among institutions lie in such noncurricular features as size, residential arrangements, religious emphasis, cultural programs, and extracurricular activities. In assessing the noncognitive impact of colleges, it is necessary to compare students as entering freshmen and as graduating seniors. Changes in students over the college years—not merely their characteristics as they leave—provide the interesting measure of noncognitive outcomes. Though data describing the changes are scarce and of uneven quality, there is an evidential base for tentative conclusions.

Trent and Medsker (1968, pp. 159-160) compared scores on Nonauthoritarianism and Social Maturity for entering freshmen in 1959 and for identical students in 1963 who had persisted in college. Their data were classified by sex and by category of institution: College—public, church-related, or private nonsectarian; University—public, church-related, or private non-sectarian. The measured change on the two scales suggested that, for most types of institutions, the impacts were roughly similar for these two aspects of personality. The authors concluded (p. 177): "College students changed to about the same degree regardless of the type of college they entered." On the nonauthoritarian scale for men attending private nonsectarian institutions, however, the gain was relatively small, an exception that may be explained by their high initial scores on this scale and the character of such institutions. The other exception was the relatively small gain on both scales for men and women attending church-related universities. Apparently, these institutions produced smaller changes in the measured attributes than other types of institutions.

Clark and others (1972, pp. 180-204) compared scores of freshmen and seniors at eight varied institutions on several measures of liberalism and personal adjustment. These comparisons suggest that the institutions do vary somewhat in the degree to which their students change. And these variations cannot be explained entirely by differences in the initial scores. For example, for Autonomy, the amount of gain is negatively correlated with initial scores, but in the case of Religious Liberalism, Impulse Expression, and Schizoid Functioning, it is positively correlated with initial scores. In interpreting these results, the authors observe (pp. 191, 204):

> Evidence has been presented for a general gain in liberal attitudes, and also for differential change in liberal, nonauthoritarian attitudes among the institutions. Even so, the general rank order of schools based on senior average scores was essentially the same as the rank order based on freshman average scores. . . . In essence, the characteristics of the students at entry served as a major determinant of their relative attitudes as seniors. Students at the eight institutions were different enough from one another at the freshman level to make it possible for differential change to take place (it did) without significantly altering the

ranking of the schools on a given measure. . . . on three aspects of personality it seems evident that students changed to different degrees at different institutions. Although it cannot be specifically concluded that the institutions effected these results—since the characteristics of students who attend an institution in part define what it offers—the data do contribute to the issue of institutional impact on student values by establishing that there is a relationship between institution attended and changes in attitudes, values, and interests over four years.

Clark and others also gathered data on change during college in plans to attend graduate or professional school, relative valuation of liberal and vocational education, relative valuation of intrinsic and extrinsic rewards from occupations, intellectual and cultural interests as reflected in patterns of reading and music listening, religious observance, and attitudes on civil liberties (pp. 206-227). They found perceptible differences among the eight institutions on most of these criteria. They concluded by distinguishing among three overall impacts of college: the *anchoring effect,* which provides support for students in holding to their personal, political, and religious values; the *accentuation effect,* which leads to the reinforcement and strengthening of tendencies already present when students entered college; and the *conversion effect,* which involves (p. 306) a "virtual transformation of students' initial values, intellectual dispositions, and attitudes." They found in the eight colleges studied that about 7 percent of the students had changed "from the lower to the top intellectual disposition categories," indicating a conversion effect in the intellectual domain (p. 307). They discovered substantial differences among the institutions in the percentage of students who had experienced conversion. They suggested, however, that the conversion effect is adventitious in the sense that it tends to occur "in settings of high campus potency, in those students who had initially misperceived the institution or otherwise allowed themselves to be attracted to a place where they do not 'fit' the culture of the student body."

The authors go on to say that "conversion is least likely to occur in large colleges and universities. . . . In these settings students may not be confronted by a unified and embracing contrary point of view. They can 'hide' from those who would challenge them in the heterogeneity of the campus, the interstices of a loose and bulky formal structure, or the passive safety and segmentation of student (and perhaps faculty) subcultures" (p. 307).

In a study of change in students at twelve small and varied colleges, Chickering (1970, 1971) compared an identical set of students as freshmen in 1965 and as seniors in 1969. He found that changes in the students were surprisingly similar—though not precisely the same—at all twelve institutions. The similarities prevailed regardless of "dramatic differences" in the characteristics of the colleges, which ranged from poor to rich, from obscure to famous, from religious to secular, and from structured to free. He reported that "these changes occurred among very liberal students and very conservative ones, among 'authoritarians' and 'non-authoritarians,' among the activists and the alienated as well as among the silent majority and the apathetic" (1970, p. 2). But Chickering by no means suggested that there were *no* differences among institutions in impact or that institutions cannot increase their impact by conscious action. Indeed, his book *Education and Identity* (1969) is devoted exclusively to ways of improving higher education and is based on the assumption (p. 157) that "differences in institutional objectives and internal consistency, size, curriculum, teaching and evaluation, residences, faculty and administration, friends and student culture, make a difference to student development." Chickering also recognizes that college may have a conversion effect on some students, whom he calls misfits, who may not be fully adjusted to the prevailing culture of the institution (1971).

In his study based on the responses of upperclassmen of the class of 1970 and of alumni of the class of 1950, Pace (1974a) recorded the percentage of respondents who had indicated that they received "very much" or "quite a bit" of benefit in the form of noncognitive outcomes from their college experience. Though responses from persons who attended various types of institutions were similar on the whole, there were notable differences—especially in the esthetic and religious domains—among the liberal arts colleges, the colleges of engineering and science, and other institutions. In another study relating to small liberal arts colleges, Pace (1972) found significant differences in political and social views among upperclassmen and alumni of colleges classified as independent, mainline Protestant, and evangelical. Alumni and upperclassmen of the evangelical colleges veered toward conservative and puritanical views, whereas those of the independent colleges moved in the direction of liberalism. The differences, however, were not dramatic and probably could be explained more adequately by variations in the characteristics of students originally recruited to the several types of institutions than to differential educational effects (see Astin and Lee, 1972).

Keniston and Lerner (1971, p. 51) reported that, despite much opinion to the contrary, there was little difference among institutions in tendency toward campus unrest during the late 1960s. They concluded (p. 51) "Once we control for the kind of freshmen admitted, campus characteristics have a negligible effect on student involvement in protest."

Differences among institutions in their noncognitive impacts appear to be somewhat greater than differences in their cognitive impacts. Of course, the differences among institutions in the characteristics of graduates are very great, but they appear to be determined largely by initial differences in the students who chose to attend, who were admitted, and who persisted to graduation and less by differences in institutional programs and environments.

Institutional Characteristics as Related to Outcomes

We have seen that institutions of various types have much in common. Such differences as exist presumably are due to variations in the programs they offer and the environments they create—differences in such features as institution size, residential arrangements, curricular emphasis, student-faculty relationships, and religious orientation. Some insight into the differences among institutions may be achieved by briefly reviewing studies

on the relation between specific college characteristics and outcomes.

Institutional size. A considerable body of opinion and some
documented research supports the proposition that small institutions, other things being equal, produce more desirable
change in students than large institutions. Because most small
colleges specialize in liberal education, however, it is difficult to
sort out the separate effects of small size and dedication to liberal learning. Nevertheless, many researchers have found evidence that smallness is associated with educational advantage
(Chickering, 1965; Rock, Centra, and Linn, 1969; Withey,
1971; Clark and others, 1972; Astin, 1972; Chickering, 1972;
Feldman and Newcomb, 1969; Pace, 1974a; Bayer, 1975).

Residential arrangements. Another widely held view, also but-
tressed by research support, is that different modes of residential living affect the learning and personal development of students. Devoting an entire book to this matter, Chickering
(1974, pp. 84-85) concluded:

> Whatever the institution, whatever the group, what-
> ever the data, whatever the methods of analyses, the
> findings are the same. Students who live at home with
> their parents fall short of the kinds of learning and
> personal development typically desired by the institu-
> tions they attend and which might reasonably be ex-
> pected when their special backgrounds are taken into
> account. Students who live in college dormitories
> exceed the learning and personal development that
> are predicted when their advantages in ability, in
> prior educational and extracurricular activities, and in
> community and family backgrounds are taken into
> account. During the freshman year and during all four
> years for several different large samples, examined
> through simple retest comparisons and through com-
> plex multivariate analyses, the findings remain con-
> sistent.

> Students who live at home, in comparison with those who live in college dormitories, are less fully involved in academic activities, in extracurricular activities, and in social activities with other students. Their degree aspirations diminish and they become less committed to a variety of long-range goals. They enter educationally and developmentally useful experiences and activities less frequently. They report a shrinking range of competence. Their self-ratings for a diverse array of abilities and desirable personal characteristics drop. Their satisfaction with college decreases, and they become less likely to return.

Other evidence leading to similar but less positive conclusions on residential living has been supplied by Astin (1973a), Feldman and Newcomb (1969), Harrington (1972), and Bradshaw (1974). Bradshaw's data, however, suggest that campus residential living is not necessarily preferable to off-campus living separately from parents in apartments or rooms. His data suggest that in some respects off-campus living is associated with higher gains from the freshman to senior year than living in dormitories or in fraternities and sororities.

Curricular emphasis. A considerable body of research suggests that various student characteristics—attitudes, values, dispositions, and abilities—differ systematically among students pursuing different major fields of study. Feldman and Newcomb summarized much of this research (1969) and provided a useful commentary on it. The differences in student characteristics associated with the various major fields are largely due, of course, to self-selection on the part of the students who choose these fields—but not wholly. As Feldman and Newcomb concluded (Vol. I, p. 193), "The evidence is clear . . . that differential experiences in the several major fields do have impacts beyond those attributable to initial selection into those fields. Perhaps the most convincing evidence of this is the prevalence of the accentuation of initial major-field differences. It has been shown that preexisting differences in characteristics typical of students initially choosing different curricula tend to become more pronounced following experience in those major fields." Feldman and Newcomb also pointed out that the impact of field of study is greater in large than in small institutions (see Sharp, 1970).

A Carnegie Commission survey of a large sample of students suggested that student differences by field of study were less than most earlier studies had indicated (*Reform on Campus,* 1972, Appendix A). The questions and responses were concerned with student attitudes toward their institutions and toward their college experiences. The data did reveal some differences. For example, students of science and engineering were less keen than others about proposals to increase the number of elective courses, to abolish grades, or to require a year of youth community service. Students in the sciences and the professions were also less enthusiastic about liberal education than students in the social studies and humanities. Aside from these fairly obvious differences, however, field of study seemed not to be a major determinant of attitudes. The remarkable feature of the data was the similarity of responses among students in different fields of study on subjects such as these: overall evaluation of college, need for more relevance of course work to contemporary life, need for greater attention to emotional growth of students, and greater relative emphasis on teaching as compared with research as criteria for the promotion of faculty. Most evidence, however, supports the view that students differ by field of study in their basic values, their sociopolitical attitudes, religious conventionality, intellectual interests, and other personal characteristics. It would be expected then that institutions with different curricular emphases—music conservatories, colleges of engineering and science, liberal arts colleges, land-grant institutions—would vary in the kinds of changes brought about in their students.

Student-faculty relationships. Institutions apparently differ considerably in the nature and closeness of student-faculty contacts (Feldman and Newcomb, 1969). Though little is known about the impact of close relationships between students and faculty, the belief is widespread that the influence of faculty, as exemplars and as caring persons, can be substantial. For example, Gaff (1973), in a study of college impact in eight varied institutions, found that the involvement of college teachers with students significantly affected educational outcomes as perceived by both teachers and students. He wrote (pp. 8-9, 16) that: "Influential teachers are heavily interested in undergraduate teaching, and this interest probably motivates them to make their courses interesting, to talk with students about issues which are important to them, and to extend their conversations and interactions with students beyond the classroom. This high degree of involvement with students and student concerns allows them to make an impact on students and to perceive that they are effective. It also leads them to be regarded as effective by their students and colleagues, which probably reinforces their original interest in teaching. ... The implication is that conditions which increase the amount, closeness, breadth, and duration of student-faculty relationships would enhance the educational impact on the lives of students."

Religious orientation. Institutions clearly vary in intended religious emphasis. In particular, colleges closely affiliated with denominational groups hope to guide or reinforce the religious orientation of students and in some cases to restrain tendencies toward religious liberalism.

In comparing the impacts of eight quite different institutions, Clark and others (1972) found considerable difference in the degree of change on a scale measuring "religious liberalism" —the differences for men being greater than those for women. The findings are shown in Table 41. The low percentage change in the case of Reed women was doubtless due to a "ceiling effect," that is, the initial scores were so high that little space was left for change. The low percentage change for University of Portland men and women probably indicates that the institution is successful in sustaining the religious values of its students. The changes for the other institutions were varied, though of roughly the same order of magnitude.

Pace (1974a) gathered data from alumni and from juniors

Table 41. Average scores on religious liberalism at selected institutions

	Freshman Men / Women	Senior Men / Women	Gain Men / Women	Percentage Change Men / Women
Antioch College	17.5 / 17.3	20.2 / 21.8	2.7 / 4.5	15% / 26%
Reed College	19.2 / 20.5	22.3 / 21.9	3.1 / 1.4	16 / 7
Swarthmore College	17.0 /. 17.2	21.0 / 21.0	4.0 / 3.8	24 / 22
San Francisco State	13.7 / 11.1	18.7 / 13.8	5.0 / 2.7	36 / 24
University of California, Berkeley	15.8 / 14.1	19.0 / 17.5	3.2 / 3.4	20 / 24
University of the Pacific (Methodist)	13.5 / 10.5	15.9 / 14.0	2.4 / 3.5	18 / 33
St. Olaf College (Lutheran)	8.1 / 7.3	11.0 / 9.9	2.9 / 2.6	35 / 36
University of Portland (Catholic)	8.6 / 5.3	8.6 / 6.3	0 / 1.0	0 / 19

Source: Clark and others (1972, p. 185).

and seniors about their perceived benefits from college in the form of "religious appreciation." The percentages of respondents reporting "very much" or "quite a bit" of benefit are shown in Table 42. Although there are differences throughout, the notable cases are the "other liberal arts colleges," for which the percentages are very high, and the "colleges of engineering and science," for which the percentages are very low. From these data, one might infer that the differences among institutions in their impact on religious orientation are greater than their differences in most other respects.

Institutional environment and institutional quality. Some studies bearing on differences among institutions relate the total institutional environment to the outcomes for students. In some cases, the environment is more or less equated with general institutional "quality." For example, Astin (1968, p. 667) reported that institutional characteristics were not visibly related to student outcomes. He wrote: "Our analysis failed to confirm the hypothesis that the student's achievement in social science,

Table 42. Percentages of alumni and upperclassmen reporting benefits from college in religious appreciation, by type of institution

	Alumni	Juniors and Seniors
Comprehensive universities		
Selective	19%	24%
Less selective	23	26
State colleges and less comprehensive universities	23	38
Liberal arts colleges		
Highly selective	36	34
Strongly denominational	35	38
Other	74	62
Teachers colleges	35	41
Colleges of engineering and science	10	21

Source: Pace (1974a, pp. 52-53, 56-57).

humanities, or natural science is facilitated either by the intellectual level of his classmates or by the level of academic competitiveness or financial resources of his institution. Similarly, the evidence did not support the contention that the bright student benefits more than does the average student from exposure to these assumed indices of institutional quality." He presented similar conclusions in a later paper (1970).

In a detailed and rigorous exploration of the effect of college on student choices of fields of study and careers, Astin and Panos (1969) found that in all colleges an enormous amount of change occurs in major fields and in career plans. In exploring institutional differences in student choices, they found that the characteristics students brought with them to college far outweighed the impact of the institutional environment. They concluded (pp. 130-132) that "most student outputs for a given institution can be predicted with considerable accuracy from a knowledge of its student input characteristics ... a knowledge of the institution's environmental characteristics ... increases the accuracy of these predictions only slightly. ... In several instances, however, differences in outputs that were not solely attributable to differential student inputs showed substantial relationships to the environmental character-istics of the institutions."

Walizer and Herriott (1971) found somewhat greater ef-fects of college environment. They explored the relationship between the social structure of institutions and mean scores on the Social Maturity Scale of the Omnibus Personality Inventory. By *social structure* they referred to such features of the college or university as size, organization, governance, academic qual-ity, size of city in which located, and degree of collegiality. They concluded that Social Maturity is significantly affected by institutional social structure. They found (p. 27) that 15 per-cent of the variation in change in Social Maturity among college students "can be explained by a model containing only college structure variables," and that 26 percent of the variation can be explained by a model containing variables relating both to pre-collegiate socialization and college structure.

Astin (in Solmon and Taubman, 1973) found that students of selective institutions are less likely to drop out than students of nonselective institutions. Trent and Medsker (1968, pp. 109-110) also found that dropout rates vary among institutions of different types. They were cautious, however, in interpreting this finding: "at this point little can be said about the direct influence of the type of college on the persistence of its stu-dents, since traits leading to persistence may have been deter-mined before students entered college."

Bradshaw (1974) investigated the relationship between quality of institutions and participation of students in various leisure-time activities. Defining leisure-time activities to include not only recreation but also cultural, political, familial, and reli-gious pursuits, he attributed considerable influence to college in these areas—an influence due partly to student peer groups. Be-cause of differences among institutions in the kinds of students recruited and in the peer groups formed, he reasoned that insti-tutions would differ in leisure outcomes. Though he learned that different types of institutions do indeed vary somewhat in leisure styles, his findings suggest that institutional differences really are surprisingly small, both in the leisure patterns fol-lowed and in the degree of change.

In a series of papers, Solmon (in Solmon and Taubman, 1973a, 1975, 1976) found that "the quality of institutions of higher education has an important impact on lifetime earnings of those who attend" (1976, p. 3). To define "quality," he used the Gourman Index (an overall judgmental evaluation of institutions), Scholastic Aptitude Test Scores of entering freshmen, and faculty salaries. Solmon concluded: (a) that college quality is positively related to lifetime income, even allowing for certain exceptional occupational choices, individual ability, and socioeconomic background; (b) that college quality affects earnings for students dropping out as well as for those persisting to degrees; and (c) that college quality has less effect on earnings in the first job than on later earnings. Solmon was unable to explain the connection between institutional quality and greater lifetime earnings. Education in a "superior" institution may lead to greater self-confidence and higher aspirations; or identification with high-quality institutions may produce a grading-and-labeling effect that eases access to opportunities not equally available to others; or high-quality colleges may produce a superior education that leads to greater economic productivity. We surmise that all three of these factors may be at work. Regarding the possible grading-and-labeling effect, Solmon found that the financial advantage to alumni of high-quality colleges accrues to them in later life, not on their first jobs. Seemingly, grading and labeling would have its greatest potency soon after graduation, and actual performance on the job would be decisive in determining compensation in later life. The issue of grading and labeling is discussed in greater detail in Chapter Five.

Other studies of college quality as related to earnings also showed a positive relationship (Hunt, 1963; Weisbrod and Karpoff, 1968; Morgan and Sirageldin, 1968; Daniere and Mechling, 1970; Wolfle in Solmon and Taubman, 1973; Akin and Garfinkel, 1974; Sewell and Hauser, 1975; Wachtel, 1976 and in Juster, 1975). Daniere and Mechling (1970) found that the lifetime earnings of those attending "high-quality" colleges was on the average greater than the lifetime earnings of those of equal ability attending "low-quality" colleges. (College "quality" was measured by instructional cost per student and test ability

is measured by verbal scores on the Scholastic Aptitude Test.)
Their statistical results are shown in Table 43.

Table 43. Lifetime earnings of college alumni by quality of institution
and student ability

College Quality	Student Ability				
	Bottom 25%	Next 45%	Next 20%	Next 8.5%	Top 1.5%
High		$170,000	$178,000	$196,000	$200,000
Medium	$145,000	150,000	158,000	181,000	188,000
Low	129,000	138,000	150,000	169,000	
Earnings in high-quality colleges as percentage of earnings in low-quality colleges		123%	119%	116%	

Source: Daniere and Mechling (1970, p. 69).

Most studies confirm that students who go to colleges of
higher quality earn more money and are more successful in
graduate study (Hansen, 1971) than students of equal ability
and background who go to colleges of lesser quality. Similarly,
those who go to better graduate schools earn more than those
of equal ability and background who go to lesser graduate
schools (Solmon and Wachtel, 1975; Wachtel, 1976). The monetary return on investments in college quality appears to be of
the order of 7½ to 8½ percent.

Student and Alumni Evaluation of Their Colleges

Students' evaluations of their own colleges or universities and
their reactions to their experiences in higher education appear
to be fairly similar for different types of institutions. This was
shown in a survey conducted by the Carnegie Commission on
Higher Education (1972, appendix A). The survey revealed a
rough positive relationship between "quality" of institutions
and student evaluations, but the differences were not striking.
In another large survey of alumni, Bisconti and Solmon (1976,
pp. 15-19) found modest differences among institutions based

on institutional selectivity or affluence. Alumni of the more elite institutions were more likely to mention intellectual outcomes, such as general knowledge and ability to think clearly, and less likely to mention career outcomes than alumni of less elite institutions.

Conclusions

We have reviewed in some detail available studies describing differences in the impacts of institutions of various types. As usual, available data are scarce, fragmentary, and not wholly consistent. On the whole, the evidence supports the hypothesis that the differences in impact are relatively small—when impact is defined as "value added" in the form of change in students during the college years. But this conclusion hardly comes as a surprise, for the benefits from college education are so widely available, and the overlap among colleges in the environmental features they offer is so great, that striking differences in outcomes are unlikely. Clark Kerr observed (in Withey, 1971, p. xiii) that "it is the general impact of all colleges that matters more than the differential impacts of one type of college versus another type." In his pioneering study of *Changing Values in College* (1957, p. 14), Jacob concluded: "first, most American students share many values in common. There is a striking homogeneity of basic values throughout the country. Second, on issues where students do differ, they split in about the same proportions at most institutions. The patterns of value tend to be similar at American colleges, regardless of location, administration, size and background of student body, or character of the educational program."

Spaeth and Greeley (1970, p. 126), after reviewing the evidence and adding their own research results, reached this conclusion: "Attempts to show that specific institutions have specific effects on their students have usually failed. Assessments of the effects of going to college—any college—have come up with somewhat more positive results. Apparently the college experience produces people who are somewhat more independent, more tolerant, more open to new experiences, less rigid, and less prejudiced. . . . As far as we can tell, this kind of change is not much more likely to occur in one kind of an institution than in another, though a few well-known liberal arts colleges seem a little better at producing it. . . . On the whole, however, it seems to matter less what college one attends than that one attend college."

Chickering (1970, p. 2), on the basis of a longitudinal study in 1965 to 1969 of students in twelve small but varied colleges, concluded:

> But despite these dramatic differences among the institutions and among the students attending them, when the 1965 freshmen who were ready to graduate in 1969 were re-tested, several major areas of change were found at virtually all the colleges: increased autonomy, increased awareness of emotions and impulses and increased readiness to express them, increased personal integration, increased aesthetic sensitivity and interest in the arts and humanities, increased tolerance for ambiguity and complexity, increased religious liberalism, and decreased concern for material possessions and practical achievement. These changes occur at highly-organized institutions with numerous regulations and close adult supervision. They also occurred at a "student centered" college with little overt structure, few regulations, and minimal adult supervision. At two traditional colleges —one poor and relatively unknown operating with limited facilities, the other wealthy, prestigious with ample facilities and resources—similar changes occurred. Similar changes also occurred at two nontraditional colleges, one emphasizing independent studies and flexible programming developed by students themselves, the other with a highly structured curriculum using many required courses and a complex system of comprehensive examinations. These changes occurred among very liberal students and very conservative ones, among "authoritarians" and "antiauthoritarians," among the activists and the

alienated as well as among the silent majority and the apathetic.

In explaining these results, Gurin (in Withey, 1971, p. 46) wrote: "a common effect may reflect the fact that the American college in recent years has been an institution that encouraged and legitimized self-confrontation and the questioning and reevaluation of one's values, and the *current* values of society, and that this has been true to some extent regardless of the nature of the college."

The conclusion that differences among institutions in their power to change students are small may be disputed on several grounds. First, the findings of several economic studies reveal a significant correlation between institutional quality and lifetime income and suggest that the rate of return to investments in improved institutional quality may be of the order of 7½ percent or more. The economists may be finding interinstitutional differences that scholars in other fields are overlooking. Second, it is logically possible—and quite likely—that, whereas differences among institutions in *average* changes on various cognitive and affective variables may be negligible, significant differences may be occurring for students *viewed as whole persons*. In Chapter Seven we considered the tendency of averages to obscure the impacts of college. The same possibility exists in connection with the estimation of differences among institutions. Third, methods of measurement may be so crude that significant differences are overlooked—because either important variables are unwittingly ignored or because the recognized variables are not measured properly. Fourth, the judgments as to whether or not differences are important are relative to expectations that may be exaggerated. For all these reasons, we tend to be cautious in our conclusions about institutional differences.

On the one hand, we judge that the differences among institutions in their educational impact are much less than commonly supposed. This viewpoint leads to several inferences. It suggests that the claims of distinctiveness made by individual institutions may often be exaggerated; that choice of colleges by prospective students may for some students not be as signifi-

cant as they and their families believe; and that extra institutional costs intended to achieve exceptional outcomes may not
always be justified by the potential returns. The viewpoint that
differences among institutions are modest is also consistent with
our basic hypothesis that American higher education can, for
some purposes, be considered as a coherent system and that in
exploring outcomes it is not wildly unreasonable to consider the
system as a whole.

On the other hand, institutions clearly do differ in the degree and kind of change they effect among some, if not all, of
their students. The very fact that institutions differ implies that
some could do better in outcome achievement. Indeed, it is
largely through efforts at the institutional level that the system
can improve. Nothing in our analysis of institutional differences
justifies fatalistic acceptance of the status quo on the part of
institutions individually or of the system collectively.

Part Three

Consequences
for Society

In the preceding chapters of Part Two, we have considered the outcomes of higher education as changes in students during the college years and later. We have shown that college students as individuals are changed in knowledge, emotional and moral development, and practical competence. We have shown also that in later life college-educated persons exhibit values, attitudes, outlooks, and behavior patterns different from others. But the influence of higher education is not confined to its lifelong impact on its students as individuals. It also has direct and indirect consequences for society at large.

In the chapters of Part Three, we shall be concerned with these societal effects. Chapter Nine deals with the impacts upon society produced by the changes in individual students through education. Chapter Ten summarizes the societal impacts of research and public service. Chapter Eleven is devoted to the impact of higher education on social equality and inequality. Chapter Twelve examines the findings of economists concerning the monetary returns from investments in higher education. And Chapter Thirteen concludes this third part of the volume by weighing the views on these outcomes of social observers ranging from Ivan Illich to James Coleman.

9

Societal Outcomes
from Education

---

*Is it reasonable to suppose that a society with
a given set of values, beliefs and approved
methods of behavior is capable of creating an
educational system which convincingly
propounds and propagates another, opposing
set of values and beliefs?*

Louis Emmerij (1973, p. 42)

Dare the school build a new social order?

George S. Counts (1932)

Through its impact on students as individuals, higher education
undoubtedly generates change in society. Part of the societal
influence stems from the obvious fact that educated people are
members of society. To the extent that their attitudes, values,
and behavior patterns are modified by college education, society is changed spontaneously. As they take part in political discussion, as they vote, as they spend their money as consumers,
as they take their places in work, as they found families, as they
spend their leisure hours, and as they participate in religious
life—or do not do these things—they bring about social change.
As the number of college-educated people grows, their presence
in society and their impact expands. In 1974, about 13 percent

of the population over 25 years of age had graduated from college and another 12 percent had attended one to three years. Projections of the U.S. Bureau of the Census indicate that by 1990, the number of college graduates will rise to about 18 to 20 percent and those who have attended one to three years will rise to 14 to 15 percent of the adult population. (U.S. Bureau of the Census, *Statistical Abstract of the United States,* 1975, p. 119.) Thus, by 1990, about a third of the entire population will have been influenced by college education.

Moreover, college-educated people as members of society inevitably exert influences upon other persons in ways that modify their values, attitudes, and behavior patterns. Such influences may be strongest among relatives, friends, and associates, but may extend to the larger community as well. Such influences are mostly unintended. They occur simply through the presence in society of college-educated people with outlooks, ideas, and behavior patterns somewhat different from those of the general population. Without conscious intention, college-educated people may present to others new possibilities of thought and action, new standards, and new styles of life. In the longer run, the influence of college-educated people ultimately may result in changes in cultural patterns, social institutions and practices, and public policy; they may have consequences for the family, the school, the church, the economy, and the state. They may affect race relations, environmental policy, war and peace, and economic growth. Critics of higher education, recognizing that, on the average, the impacts of college on the abilities and characteristics of people tend to be small, are skeptical of the alleged social consequences of higher education. In response to this criticism, Freedman wrote (1967, pp. 5-6):

> The key to social change is that, in a dynamic system, slight changes in individuals can lead to profound changes in the system as a whole. Massive social change is compounded out of slight shifts in individual attitudes and beliefs. From this point of view, higher education can be seen to have exerted a pro-

found influence on American life and society, nota-
bly since the Depression years and especially since
World War II. Generations of students have emerged
... with a greater commitment to the liberal view
than they had at the time of college entrance. By
"liberal view," I mean appreciation of the complexity
of people and social events, openness to new experience, flexibility in thinking, comparison in judgment
of people, and the like.... few go through college
these days without acquiring at least a tinge of this
liberalization. And the social consequences of such
changes are enormous.

The societal influence of college-educated people is likely
to be enhanced because higher education attracts many persons
with exceptional leadership qualities and probably cultivates the
values, attitudes, and skills needed for leadership, and because
many of them occupy positions specifically concerned with influencing the thinking and behavior of clients. Such positions
include teacher, clergyman, business manager, public official,
lawyer, physician, accountant, social worker, librarian, jour-
nalist, advertising executive, writer, artist, and scientist. Thus,
the influence of the college-educated is not wholly accidental
but rather is a deliberate consequence of their professions. A
considerable literature has appeared in recent years on the role
of professional persons and "intellectuals" in modern society
and in the "postindustrial" society of the future. This literature
suggests that educated people are becoming increasingly influential in public affairs and in the shaping of public opinion. Some
authors have even ventured to refer to the intellectual class as a
new "estate" in society or a new aristocracy. (See, for example,
Schumpeter, 1950; Bell, 1973 and 1976; Brzezenski, 1970;
Daedalus, 1972a, 1972b; Ladd and Lipset, 1975.)
For higher education to have societal effects, every college-
educated person need not be a generator of social change. It is
only necessary that a significant number of persons be influenced by their education in ways that would have an impact on
society. The critical mass may be quite small. In some cases

even a single person may be enabled through education to exercise exceptional influence.

Not all college-educated people share the same outlooks or bring identical influences to bear upon society. For example, there are differences in ideologies among individuals and also among professional groups. For example, the influence of clergymen or professors may be quite different from that of physicians or businessmen. Yet there is a common element, based chiefly on the liberal component of higher education, that makes for some consistency of societal influence among many, if not most, college-educated people.

Unfortunately, quantitative evidence and detailed studies on the societal effects or benefits of teaching-learning are almost nonexistent. The causes of social change are so diverse and complex that it is almost impossible to trace out the effect of a single influence such as higher education. Friedman (1968) has argued that the social benefits are so tenuous and so hard to identify and measure that they ought not be considered in discussions of the economics of higher education. The same position has been taken by Hansen (in Solmon and Taubman, 1973, pp. 329-330):

> At the moment there exists an interesting intellectual impasse concerning external benefits. The predominant belief seems to be that significant external benefits do exist. . . . These views are not, however, based on any careful review of evidence; they reflect prevailing, constantly reaffirmed, beliefs. . . . The impasse arises because spokesmen for higher education argue that it is up to the critics to show that external benefits do not exist. Critics, on the other hand, argue that nobody has ever demonstrated that externalities do, in fact, exist; hence those who claim their existence should produce supporting evidence.

The subject is of special importance because the presumed existence of social benefits is part of the case for subsidies to higher education. As Hartman asks, with irony, "What is greater sweetness and light worth to the public at large?" (in Solmon and Taubman, 1973, p. 279). (See also Friedman, 1962; Schultz, 1972; Nerlove in Schultz, 1972; Johnson in Schultz, 1972).

Our approach to the subject necessarily will be analytical and judgmental rather than empirical. But the lack of rigorously verifiable evidence should neither inhibit rational exploration of the subject nor preclude tentative conclusions. Difficulty of measurement is no reason to gloss over important outcomes.

The Ethos of Higher Education

The basic educational task of colleges and universities is to help students achieve cognitive learning, emotional and moral development, and practical competence. Though most institutions have a strong tradition of freedom of thought for students as well as faculty and of aversion to overt indoctrination, in practice they are far from neutral in their influence on students. In most institutions, there is a prevailing conception of what the educated man or woman should be like. Most established curricula and degree requirements control the content of courses and the methods of instruction. And most institutions exert great influence on extracurricular life. Also, most academic communities engage in the consideration and analysis of values. They are involved in social and artistic criticism. They construct philosophical systems and ideologies and they appraise existing social policies and recommend new ones. Through all these processes, the academic community creates an ethos. This ethos is usually not promulgated officially; it is not necessarily shared by all members of the academic community; it often differs from views prevailing among the general public; and it changes over time. Yet one can say that, in a given period, the weight of academic influence is directed toward a particular cluster of values and toward a particular world outlook (see Bell, 1973; Cuninggim, 1969). In our time, the prevailing ethos of higher education includes several basic ideals or tendencies that influence the outlook and values of its students and through them influence social change.

The free mind is a foremost ideal of contemporary higher education. Great importance is attached to freedom of thought and communication, to the obligation to seek the truth through untrammeled inquiry, to tolerance of new and different ideas until proved false, to a disposition to explore and to experiment, and to a willingness to break away from conventions, traditions, superstitions, folklore, and myths. Tolerance is considered essential because knowledge is always contingent, ambiguous, complex, and therefore provisional. Emphasis is also placed on rationality, skeptical detachment, and scrupulous intellectual integrity in the search for knowledge and in the solution of problems both intellectual and practical. However, the vogue of logical positivism is on the wane, and intuition, revelation, criticism, and other avenues to the truth are gaining in acceptance.

Closely associated with the ideal of the free mind is the concept of individuality—the ideal that each person should have the chance to develop his personality according to his unique talents and interests. Also related to the free mind is the ideal of historical and geographic perspective. The academic community considers as one of its main duties to preserve the history of events, thought, and art and continually to reinterpret this history in relation to the concerns of the present. It seeks to cultivate in its students a sense of history and of historical perspective. Similarly, it encourages geographic cosmopolitanism, including a world outlook, a sense of cultural relativity, appreciation of different cultures, and international understanding. Cosmopolitanism is sometimes ringed with varying degrees of pacifism.

Another ideal of the academy is a humane outlook, expressed especially in broad social consciousness, social responsibility, and motivation toward betterment of the human condition. In recent years, the humane ideal has been extended to give greater weight to human equality, to promote amicable relationships among classes and races, and to discourage prejudice or discrimination based on sex, race, and religion. The academic community also usually favors the recognition of individual merit based on excellence of performance and the selection of people for various roles according to their qualifications. These meritocratic tendencies, however, exist in tension with the more recent egalitarian tendencies.

The academic community tends to be concerned with social issues and problems, engages in the study of them, and encourages free discussion of them. In recent years, the academic community has become more closely linked to the world of social affairs through internships and work-study programs, through consulting relationships, through increasing emphasis on the study of social issues and public policy, and through greater participation in social criticism. In some cases, these tendencies have compromised the objectivity of the academy. Because it places a high value on leadership, the academic community probably equips some of its students for leadership roles and also motivates them to assume such roles. In connection with social issues, the academic community has helped lead the way toward public concern for particular issues such as the Vietnam War, human inequality, and environmental deterioration. On the whole, the academic community stands for excellence in the arts and literature. It does not hesitate to commend Homer or Beethoven or Picasso over artists of lesser gifts. And it regularly practices critical discrimination with reference to recent works of art and literature.

The ideals of the academy are mostly radical ideals. Insofar as they are practiced, they are disturbing to superstition, prejudice, provincialism, ignorance, and discrimination, the enemies of change. They are not the ideals of an educational system that is intended to buttress the status quo by merely socializing its students. They are the very ideals which, if communicated to intelligent and energetic people, are likely to produce social change. On the other hand, the ethos of the academy is rooted in American political and social tradition and seldom functions as a source of violent social revolution.

The extent of social change resulting from college instruction will depend upon the number educated, the kind of education they received, and the depth of this education as reflected in the degree of personal change in knowledge, values, attitudes, motives, and competencies. Other things being equal, one would expect the amount of social change to be greater as the proportion of the population receiving higher education increases. Further, one would expect the amount of social change to be greater to the extent that the higher education system emphasizes the cultivation of free minds and of socially motivated people through liberal studies and less to the extent that it stresses socialization and training in skills for existing technologies. But it is difficult to imagine circumstances in which genuine higher education would produce little or no spillover in social change.

To assert that every college or university or every academic department shares all of these ideals or to claim that every student is strongly influenced by them would be utterly false. Higher education does perform little more than a socializing function for many students. It sometimes conditions them to be passive followers of instructions, to adjust themselves to the requirements of the labor market whatever they may be, and to fit comfortably into a conventional middle-class style of life. However, the more challenging ideals of the academy suffuse the environments of many institutions and, as documented in previous chapters, they do influence many—probably most—students. When young people become lifelong members of the general society, after having been part of a community that espouses these ideals, some of them are likely to become agents of social change and many of them are likely to be receptive to social change initiated by others.

To argue that the presence of educated people may exert an influence upon society does not imply that society is supinely receptive to a "higher truth" emanating from the academy and transmitted by its former students. Indeed, the general population sometimes reacts negatively toward the views and attitudes of educated people and resents their frequent arrogance. Nevertheless, when millions of persons have attended college and when many of them have been changed by it, the induction of these people into general society and their interaction with the general population will almost inevitably bring about social change. The societal impact of college-educated people does not necessarily operate through a simple and direct transference to society of what is learned in college. Rather, the societal impact of higher education is likely to be determined more by the kind of people college graduates become than by what they know when they leave college.

Some Probable Social Changes Derived from Higher Education

It is not difficult to cite examples of probable or plausible social changes that may be the result, at least in part, of the presence of college-educated people. Here are six examples:

The first and perhaps most important change may be greater openness to change itself. The influence of educated people may lead to wider realization that the prevailing conditions of society are not preordained, to greater appreciation of the possibility of change, to a breaking away from custom and tradition, to greater understanding of social problems, and greater willingness to apply knowledge to their solution.

Second, through the leadership of increasing numbers of college-educated persons, participation and involvement of citizens in public affairs may be extended, and as a result the responsiveness and accountability of government and of other social institutions may be strengthened. Politicians frequently mention changes in the political climate due to the increasing education and sophistication of the electorate. Also, as Trow has suggested (1975) the presence in the government of educated people tends to improve the quality of public administration.

Third, through the influence of college-educated people, various elements of the academic ethos may be transmitted to large sections of the general public. For example, humane values may become more pervasive, the concept of social responsibility may gain in influence, prejudice and discrimination among persons may be lessened, concern for conservation of natural resources and preservation of the environment may be increased (Ashby, 1976), and a cosmopolitan outlook may become more common. Trow (*Daedalus,* 1975, pp. 118-119) has written eloquently on the relation of education to race relations (see also Hyman and Sheatsley, 1964):

> One example of gains to a society that transcends the gains to individuals attending colleges or universities is the evidence that higher education increases the tolerance of citizens for unpopular political views, and decreases the racial prejudice and bigotry that have

been such powerful forces for ill in American political and social life. . . . It can be argued that the very great decline in prejudice against American Negroes in the past several decades, and the readiness to support legislation to affirm their equal rights before the courts, in the political process, and in various areas of social and educational life, have in part been the result of the widespread expansion of higher education during just these decades. . . . If the [predicted] backlash has not been more widespread and serious, it may well be because higher education has been systematically undermining the foundation of racial prejudice and misinformation on which such a backlash could be grounded and sustained. If that is the case, then the extension of higher education has made a contribution to the national life beyond any of its presumed economic benefits; it may indeed have enabled the country to hold together during our enormous racial revolution. . . . But this kind of gain is difficult or impossible to quantify, and thus is simply not taken into account in discussions of the benefits of higher education. Yet if we become a genuinely multiracial society, with the kind of full equality implied in that term, then surely higher education will be seen to have played a role in that achievement, and it may be its most important single contribution to American society in this century.

Fourth, through college education, the efficiency and growth of the economy may be increased in ways that benefit society at large. Educated people contribute new ideas for improvement of technology and organization applicable to business, government, and nonprofit institutions. Many of these ideas are not patentable and are quickly imitated, so that the benefit is widely diffused. Also, the presence of educated people in the economy facilitates the flow of information essential to the diffusion of new technologies (Nelson, Peck, and Kalachek, 1967). Indeed, all knowledge and technology ultimately find their way into the public domain and become part of the societal stock of information and wisdom which has accumulated over the ages. In his stimulating little book *Small Is Beautiful,* Schumacher describes a visit to an oil refinery (1973, pp. 155-156):

> As we walk around in its vastness, through all its fantastic complexity, we might well wonder how it was possible for the human mind to conceive such a thing. What an immensity of knowledge, ingenuity, and experience is incarnated in equipment! How is it possible? The answer is that it did not spring ready-made out of any person's mind—it came by a process of evolution. . . . What we cannot see on our visit is far greater than what we can see: the immensity and complexity of the [technological] arrangements . . . the intellectual achievements behind the planning, the organization, the financing and marketing. Least of all can we see the great educational background which is the precondition of all, extending from primary schools to universities and specialized research establishments, and without which nothing of what we actually see would be there.

Educated people perform large amounts of voluntary service in social, political, and civic organizations and activities, and many of them enter occupations having compensation below that in comparable occupations (see Ashby, 1976). Teaching, nursing, the ministry, social work, and public office provide obvious examples. In varying degrees, people who enter these occupations are motivated by sense of vocation or job satisfaction rather than by high monetary return. Another economic function—one of the most important of all—is the discovery and nurture of genius. As Alfred Marshall, the great Cambridge economist, observed (1930, p. 216):

> The wisdom of expending public and private funds on education is not to be measured by its direct fruits

alone. It will be profitable as a mere investment, to give the masses of the people much greater opportunities than they can generally avail themselves of. For by this means many, who would have died unknown, are enabled to get the start needed for bringing out their latent abilities. And the economic value of one great industrial genius is sufficient to cover the expenses of the education of a whole town; for one new idea, such as Bessemer's chief invention, adds as much to England's productive power as the labour of a hundred thousand men. Less direct, but not less in importance, is the aid given to production by medical discoveries such as those of Jenner or Pasteur, which increase our health and working power; and again by scientific work such as that of mathematics or biology, even though many generations may pass away before it bears visible fruit in greater material well-being. All that is spent during many years in opening the means of higher education to the masses would be well paid for if it called out one more Newton or Darwin, Shakespeare or Beethoven.

Fifth, the international exchange of students and faculty, which affects tens of thousands of Americans and foreigners each year, and frequent international communication among academic people, doubtless have some bearing on international understanding, the dissemination of knowledge and technologies, and the rate of economic and social development in the less-developed nations.

Sixth, the style of life, the tastes, and the behavior patterns of college-educated people may be diffused to some extent throughout society through imitation or emulation. For example, college-educated people tend to have smaller families than other groups, to pay greater attention to the nurturance of children, to be less prone to violent crime, to be more efficient, in coping with personal affairs and problems, to be healthier, to be more discriminating in consumer choice, etc. To the extent that others emulate their life patterns, the influence of college education may be transmitted to others. Further, the presence of college-educated people in the society may contribute toward graciousness of living and ease of social intercourse. It also may stimulate cultivation of the arts and learning and make feasible the publication of cultural magazines and books and the establishment of widely accessible cultural institutions, such as museums, libraries, symphony orchestras, and opera companies, all of which require a considerable scale of operation for economic feasibility. (See Clark and others, 1972; Benson and Hodgkinson, 1974.)

The kinds of social outcomes described in these six categories are secondary effects of higher education, spillovers from the initial changes in college students wrought directly by higher education. Their ultimate effect may be to modify widely prevailing ideologies and culture patterns as well as to encourage changes in such institutions as the family, school, church, government, and the economy (Emmerij, 1974; Counts, 1962). It is by no means certain that all of these changes will be universally regarded as desirable or even tolerable. For example, Yankelovich (1974b) has shown that, after a time lag, noncollege young people have tended to take on some of the "undesirable" attitudes and behavior patterns of college youth in such areas as religion, sex, and politics. A higher education based on freedom of the mind, historical perspective, cosmopolitanism, humane values, and egalitarianism is likely to discover disparities between social ideals and social realities, to produce criticism of existing social conditions, and to generate sympathy toward social change. The social outcomes of such higher education may be threatening to the established order. As Keniston and Gerzon (1972, pp. 66) have observed:

The college experience has demonstrably liberalizing effect on most students: college attendance tends to increase openmindedness, a perspectival view of truth, the individualization of moral judgments, psychological autonomy and independence; it decreases dogmatism, authoritarianism, intolerance, conformity, conventionalism, dependency, and so on. . . . If status and stability were the highest human or societal goods, then the effects of critical higher education would almost certainly be deemed costs, for critical education helps generate social change and often temporarily increases psychological tensions. It deliberately challenges students to reexamine assumptions, convictions, and world views that they previously took for granted. . . . Nor does critical higher education promote a conflict-free or unchanging society. In the last decade, American higher education has visibly helped produce millions of students who do not accept their society without question.

Society cannot be all change. It needs shared traditions, values, attitudes, symbols, myths, and loyalty to achieve social stability and cohesiveness. No society can work without them. In judging whether the social impact of higher education is favorable or unfavorable, one must keep in mind that higher education acts as a major custodian of the cultural heritage. More than any other institution in our society, it is in touch with the culture and thought of the past. Moreover, it finds room for many diverse points of view that are mutually self-correcting. It is constrained by its responsibility toward the truth and also by its dependence upon society. And it is conservative in its own procedures and methods. It is not therefore, a wildly radical institution. Yet, to the extent that it is true to its basic ethos—especially the ideal of the free mind—it is on balance an agent of social change.

For the university to serve at the same time as conservator of the ideas and values of the past and as a center of free thought is not a comfortable or secure position. As Kingman Brewster (1972, p. 8) has said:

When society itself is full of self-doubt, the tolerance of radical reappraisal is especially fragile. When the world is already upset, it is not always easy to gain support for centers of controversy; yet *the noncontroversial university is a contradiction in terms*. We badly need a significant number of each oncoming generation who have a talent for critical appreciation; an appreciation of the past that is stronger because it has survived the scrutiny of doubt; and a critical capacity that is capable of being an instrument of constructive change, because it has appreciated what has gone before. So our goal in higher education should be, first of all, to reaffirm the importance to society of protecting the university as a conservator of the past against the Philistines of the left and as an oasis for dispute, discovery, and creation, protected from assault from the Philistines of the right.

The 1960s: A Case History

The influence of higher education on society—ordinarily gradual and orderly—was dramatized during the student unrest of the 1960s. In that decade the colleges and universities became one of the major political forces of the nation. This remarkable episode was the work not of the institutions as official entities but of small minorities of students and faculty who succeeded in gaining ideological sympathy—if not active support—from large numbers of students and sizable numbers of faculty. As John D. Rockefeller, 3rd (1973, p. 30) pointed out, the youth of that period "affected a presidential election, changed universities in important ways, raised the visibility of the environment and population growth as major problem areas, provided the main impetus to the powerful antiwar sentiment, encouraged a more open and positive attitude toward sex, led the way in experimentation toward new social forms, sparked the eighteen-year-old vote, provided the backbone for consumerism and public-interest pressure groups, developed and carried forward a whole set of "new values" and acted generally as a goad and conscience to all of us in reflecting on our personal values and those we hold for our society." Similarly, Astin and others (1975, p. 190) remarked: "Indeed, it is difficult not to view the women's movement at least in part as an outgrowth of campus unrest. . . . This is not to suggest that the women's movement would not have occurred in the absence of campus unrest, but rather that its development was facilitated by the climate of protest and the array of tactical approaches and strategies that characterized the student movement. Furthermore, while the antiwar aspect of campus unrest was a transitory phenomenon . . . the women's movement is generating a series of societal changes that are presumably much more permanent and pervasive." Astin and his colleagues also documented the many changes in academic organization, governance, student rules, and so on that were initiated by the student movement (see also Ladd and Lipset, 1975).

During the 1960s the doctrines and the tactics of some of the actors in the drama of student protest were bizarre and in some ways utterly contrary to academic traditions. Yet, at the same time, the activist students and young faculty were expressing some of the basic ideals that had come to be accepted widely in the academic community and were pointing out the inconsistencies between these ideals and the realities of American life. In a few short years they managed to precipitate a radical reexamination of the values and policies of American society, a reexamination that has been going on (at a slower pace) ever since. No one who lived through the 1960s can reclaim older beliefs without at least *feeling* them differently.

The values underlying the student movement were related to some of those we have described as the ethos of higher education. In particular, the students were concerned with individuality. On the one hand, they sought to emancipate the individual from the tyranny of large impersonal organizations (including the large university and the "military-industrial" complex), from discrimination based on age, race, sex, and religion, from crassly materialistic values, and from conformity with restrictive patterns of middle-class life. On the other hand, they strove to free the individual to choose his own style of life and to "do his own thing." They were also troubled about the future of mankind and this—along with the draft—led them to concern about war, nuclear and other destructive weapons, population growth, resource depletion, environmental degradation, and consumer problems.

Though triggered by the Vietnam War and the draft, the

explosion of student activism brought issues latently present on the campus into the open. As Withey observed (1971, p. 30), the values of the fifties "undoubtedly provided the underpinning for the activism and commitment on the campuses of the sixties." Since 1970, when the student movement lost much of its momentum, it has become tinged with cynicism, but it is not dormant. For example, Astin (1975) identified twelve episodes of campus protests that were reported in the press in the Spring of 1975. Though the issues in these more recent cases were mostly different from those of the 1960s, the values that underlay the episode of the 1960s are still present in latent form on our campuses and among millions of people, not all of them young.

The interpreters of the student movement may be divided into at least three classes (Keniston, 1971): (1) those who construe it as a revolutionary thrust at the vanguard of new values, new attitudes, and new styles of life; (2) those who regard the movement as a futile counterrevolutionary effort in opposition to social developments sometimes referred to as the postindustrial or technetronic society; and (3) those who interpret it as an accidental aberration of no lasting significance. We reject the third of these interpretations, but for our present purposes it is not necessary to choose between the first two. The only conclusion we would offer is that the student movement of the 1960s was a concrete and vivid example of the influence of higher education upon the course of social history.[1]

Joseph Katz, who made detailed studies of college students during the 1960s, holds that society should take its adolescents more seriously. He writes (in Bloom, 1975, pp. 70-73): "The adolescent's rebelliousness often is a quite acute critique of the shortcomings of institutions and adult behavior. The adolescent's demand for action is not necessarily an incapacity to tolerate delay but a challenge to the procrastinating delays of

[1]The considerable literature on the student movement includes: Newfield (1966), Spender (1969), Toffler (1970), Reich (1970), Brzezinski (1970), Miles (1971), American Academy of Political and Social Science (1971), Harman (1972), Lystad (1973), Bell (1973), Clecak (1973), Ladd and Lipset (1975), Taylor (1975), Gouldner (1976).

adults, their settling into half-painful and half-deadening routines. . . . Adults often have concentrated on the style or incompleteness of adolescent expression and have missed the message; they have corrected the spelling and neglected the idea. . . . As one looks at the recent history of student activism, one may come to think that, far from being a disturbing social disruption, it was an expression of profound psychological needs of young people, an attempt at individual and social health rather than troublemaking."

The Discontents of Our Time, and Social Progress

The enormous expansion and enrichment of higher education in the United States was intended to bring about a new kind of society—a flourishing civilization, true democracy, and personal fulfillment in the lives of the masses of people. Yet today our nation seems to be floundering. It is unsure of its values and goals and lacks high confidence in its institutions and its leaders. Further, it is beset with grave and perplexing problems, most of them due to human error, human folly, or human neglect. Among these problems are overemphasis on material values, racial injustice, inequality between the sexes, wastage of natural resources, pollution of the environment, urban decay, overpopulation, preventable illness, drug abuse and crime, unemployment, inflation, poverty, and alienation. And one can add to these the worst problem of all, the constant threat of war and nuclear holocaust. We are uncertain and divided about how to deal with these problems. We are often stalemated by conflict among interest groups. The result is a kind of social paralysis.

In describing our present discontents, it is hard to believe that we are talking about the same nation that triumphed over Hitler, launched the Marshall Plan, restored democracy to Japan, overcame polio, invented the computer, harnessed nuclear energy, landed on the moon and on Mars, and doubled its real GNP at the rate of once every twenty years. Incidentally, most of these triumphs could not have been achieved without a well-developed higher educational system.

The discontents just described seemed to have reached a

new intensity almost precisely after the recent great upsurge in enrollments and expenditures for higher education (Heard, 1974). And comparative surveys of the "happiness" of the population covering the period 1957 to 1972 revealed a steady decline in the percentage of persons reporting that they were "very happy" (Campbell, Converse, and Rodgers, 1976, p. 26). This sequence of events raises some profound questions. Has our traditional faith in education been misplaced? Is it possible that the great expansion of higher education, so hopefully entered into, not only offered no solution but even intensified the problems? Would America have been better off to have restrained the genie of learning and to have clung to the intellectual innocence and the simple virtues of an earlier era?

It is sometimes believed that the many current social problems plaguing us today are new. This is not so. They have all been with the nation for a long time. Concern for overpopulation goes back to the time of Malthus. Among the environmental problems, the wanton wastage of natural resources has been a major characteristic of American society from the beginning; the pollution of air, water, and the visual environment have been known for centuries (all our older cities were black with coal soot and dust); urban decay has long been with us in the unbelievably squalid slums and unsightly industries of almost all our cities. Among the problems of human relations, racial injustice pricked the consciences of our ancestors over a century ago; the concern for inequality between the sexes goes back at least to the time of the suffragettes; and the alleged breakdown of the family has antecedents over centuries (Bane, 1976). The problems relating to health, crime, drug abuse, and general slackness of taste and refinement have a long history. The economic problems of unemployment and inflation have been with us intermittently since the founding of the republic. And problems of war and poverty are as old as the human race. Objectively, substantial progress is being made on many of these problems. The cult of economic growth is being questioned increasingly. The nation has awakened with new urgency to the need for resource conservation and pollution abatement. Population growth is stabilizing. Land planning and urban redevelopment are going on more intensively than ever before. Overt discrimination on the basis of religion, race, ethnic origins, and sex is declining.

The distribution of income (when transfer payments in cash and in kind are included) is becoming less unequal. Health continues to improve. And consumer protection is gaining ground. Moreover, great progress has been made in the last generation or two in such areas as social security, the conditions of work, and the standards of housing. The only areas for which progress is hard to substantiate are crime and the threat of war—that is to say, overt violence.

How does one reconcile the discontents of our time with the clear improvement in most objective conditions? The answer—at least in part—is that our subjective values and our aspirations have risen or expanded more rapidly than the improvements in objective conditions. Although sensitivity to the old problems has become more acute, we have acquired new aspirations relating less to economic progress and more to personal goals such as individual freedom and autonomy, cultivation of the inner human personality, and meaningful human relationships (Organization for Economic Cooperation and Development, 1974b). As Campbell, Converse, and Rodgers (1976, p. 2) have observed: "The quality of life has taken on new dimensions, and the national concern has turned increasingly from its focus on the needs of the 'ill-housed, ill-clad, and ill-nourished' to the needs of all the people for equity, participation, respect, challenge, and personal growth. The 'revolution of rising expectations' is not simply a desire for a larger house and a second car but a growing demand for the fulfillment of needs which are not basically material but are primarily needs of the 'spirit', needs for a larger and more satisfying life experience."

And as Merton has suggested (1970, pp. 6-9), these changes have almost certainly been associated with the rise of education, especially higher education.

> It is not, I venture to suggest, a newly acute deterioration in the structure and practice of our society which is producing our present discontents. Rather it

is the emergence of a new sensibility. Having raised our sights and moral expectations we become more sensitive to the long-existing inequities in our society and to its imperfectly realized potentials for a humane life. . . . In this process of collective self-scrutiny, the more we demand of our society, the more faults we naturally find. And we are becoming an exceedingly demanding people and a self-critical society. . . . As an expanding technology contributes to our discontent by enlarging our sense of what *could* be, vastly expanding higher education, with all its manifest deficiencies, contributes by enlarging our sense of what *should* be. Colleges and universities have long been both transmitters and critics of intellectual traditions and cultural values. They have made for both the continuity *and* change. But now, apparently for the first time, the scale of mass higher education has reached a critical mass which makes the decisive difference.

Inkeles (1967, pp. 32-33) has shown that the rate of disaffection toward society for persons between the ages of eighteen and twenty-four who have attended college is about double that for the rest of the population. He suggests paradoxically that one should not rush to the conclusion that college attendance produces lifelong dissatisfaction with American life, because in fact satisfaction is positively, though weakly, correlated with education. He does say that over the next decade or so, when the younger age groups will be an exceptionally large part of the population, there will probably be greater than average disaffection.

Campbell, Converse, and Rodgers (1976) apparently resolved the paradox of happiness in the midst of disaffection by distinguishing between "happiness" as an attitude toward one's overall life condition and "satisfaction" as an attitude toward such particular life "domains" as job, marriage, housing, and health. They suggested (p. 31) that happiness "seems to evoke chiefly an absolute emotional state," whereas satisfaction "implies a more cognitive judgment of a current situation laid against external standards of comparison." They reported (p. 167): "Persons who are young and well-educated are remarkably dissatisfied, in view of the happiness they express." And they indicated that happiness of college-educated people increases with age and of less-educated people decreases with age. They concluded (p. 168) with an interesting paradox: "The young may be happier exactly because they are hopeful, while their very hopefulness for the future leads them to more critical or dissatisfied evaluations of their current situations." At any rate, the authors found a clear negative correlation between education and satisfaction with the various life domains. This negative correlation persisted—indeed it became more pronounced—when various controls were introduced.

Campbell, Converse, and Rodgers explained the relative dissatisfaction of the educated by the effect of higher education in broadening their horizons and enriching the sense of alternatives (pp. 140-147). They found that people with constricted perspectives—for example, people who have always lived in the same kind of environment—are more satisfied and have lower ceilings on aspirations than those who have experienced varied environments (pp. 141, 147). They conclude (p. 209) that "aspiration levels can show net shifts within large populations without much change in overall circumstances of everyday life. Education and communication can serve to enlarge horizons, heighten the salience of alternatives, and, if the conditions of life remain constant, produce an erosion of satisfaction as a result."

Strumpel (1976, p. 272) surveyed some of the same territory with reference to economic satisfactions and reached a similar conclusion: "Although income and wealth are important factors in human welfare, there is only a loose association between an individual's or a nation's actual income and wealth and a subjective sense of well-being. The standards for evaluation differ interpersonally, interculturally, and they are intertemporally unstable."

In the words of Walt Whitman (quoted in Martin, 1968, p. 92): "It is provided in the essence of things that from any fruition of success, no matter what, shall come forth something to make a greater struggle necessary." And de Tocqueville (1947, p. 186) summed up the matter when he said: "The evil, which was suffered patiently as inevitable, seems unendurable as soon as the idea of escaping from it is conceived. All the abuses then removed seem to throw into greater relief those which remain, so that their feeling is more painful. The evil, it is true, has become less, but sensibility to it has become more acute. Feudalism at the height of its power had not inspired Frenchmen with so much hatred of it as it did on the eve of its disappearing."

A higher education that generates disaffection toward society among its students may be criticized; yet such disaffection may be a source of social change and, with luck, of social progress. It may be the "divine discontent" needed to advance civilization. Indeed, it has long been the hope of educators that their students would be moved to work toward societal improvement.

Professional Training

This chapter has been concerned mainly with the effect of higher education on the broad course of social evolution. Before leaving the subject of societal outcomes, however, it will be useful to consider the more mundane but nevertheless significant social consequences of practical professional training.

It has long been thought that the training of professional persons would confer important and broadly diffused benefits on society. For example, the training of clergymen may advance the cause of religion. A professional objective was in the minds of those who founded the first American college, Harvard, in 1636. The purpose, as stated in *New England's First Fruits* (1643), was as follows: "After God had carried us safe to *New-England,* and wee had builded our houses, provided necessaries for our liveli-hood, rear'd convenient places for Gods worship and settled the Civill Government; One of the next things we longed for, and looked after was to advance *Learning* and perpetuate it to Posterity; dreading to leave an illiterate Ministry to the Churches, when our present Ministers shall lie in the Dust." Similarly, the training of physicians and other health profes-

sionals may promote health and the relief of suffering, the training of lawyers may enhance order and justice, the training of
businessmen may encourage efficiency and enlightened standards of economic life, the training of journalists may promote
the flow of valid information, and the training of social workers
may ameliorate poverty and other social problems. Economists
have tended to ignore the possible spillovers to society from
professional education on the ground that professionally trained
persons are paid adequately for the social benefits they confer.
But if one lays aside the thorny question of how professional
services are (or should be) compensated, it becomes clear that
they do produce important social benefits. For example, the
lives of most of us are more pleasant and more secure because
of the presence of physicians and lawyers. Even in exuberant
good health, when we have no need of physicians' services, it is
good to live in a society where people are healthy, and it is com-
forting to know that doctors, nurses, and hospitals are ready to
serve us in case of need. They have very great standby value. So
do lawyers or journalists. As de Tocqueville (1966, p. 245) observed: "I hardly believe that nowadays a republic can hope to
survive unless the lawyers' influence over its affairs grows in
proportion to the power of the people." Similarly, concerning
journalists, it is good to live in a society where information is
communicated fully and accurately, even if as individuals we
never read the newspapers or watch television. A case can even
be made for the proposition that the leavening influence of educated persons on society, regardless of their professional qualifications, is a widely shared social benefit. It is more humane,
more pleasant, more interesting, more safe, and economically
more rewarding to live in a society where there are many people
with varied knowledge and skills than to live in one of widespread ignorance. It may be that educated people are adequately rewarded for their services—including the social benefits
they produce—and in some cases rewarded excessively, but that
does not vitiate the proposition that they do provide social
benefits derived in considerable part from higher education.
Actual or alleged inequities in the distribution of income do not

alter the fact that social benefits are produced through higher education.

Conclusions

In this chapter, we have explored the broad social effects of higher education. The causes of social change are exceedingly numerous and intricate, and it is not possible to isolate statistically the effect of a single influence, such as education. Yet when increasing numbers of individuals have been changed with respect to knowledge, emotional and moral development, and practical competence and are inducted into adult society, there can be little doubt that they will exert some influence over the course of social history. This influence is likely to be especially significant because many college-educated people occupy positions of leadership and engage in professional work involving advice to clients or discovery of new knowledge and technology. For education to have social repercussions, not every college-educated person need be a generator of social change—a small critical mass of innovators and leaders is enough.

Higher education influences many of its students through an ethos that permeates the life and thought of most academic communities. In our time, this ethos includes such ideals as the free mind, individuality, historical and geographic cosmopolitanism, social responsibility, human equality in tension with meritocracy, concern for social issues, and excellence in the arts. These are, on the whole, radical ideals, and the propagation of these ideals is probably conducive to social change. They probably lead to increasing concern for social issues and increasing participation in public and other community affairs, they are favorable to technological and organizational change and improved economic efficiency, they lead to greater international communication and understanding, and they encourage new styles of life. The ultimate effect of these ideals may be to bring about change in basic social institutions and culture patterns.

At the same time, the ethos of higher education has its conservative side. The academy has great respect for the cultural heritage and one of its main functions is to preserve and reinterpret this heritage. Higher education also finds room for many diverse points of view and encourages discussion and debate leading toward the resolution of differences. It is constrained by its responsibility to the truth and also by its dependence on society. Finally, it is deeply conservative with respect to its own procedures and methods. It is far from an ultra-radical institution. However, on balance, the ethos of the academy, especially in view of its central focus on the free mind, is an agent of social change.

The student unrest of the 1960s was an interesting case history of the influence of education upon society. This dramatic episode perhaps illustrates how—under the special conditions of the time—the ideals of the academy exerted influence upon student thought and behavior, and through them on the larger community. More generally, higher education probably heightens people's sensitivity to social problems and thus breeds both disaffection with the state of society and the will to bring about amelioration of social problems.

An important and very practical social benefit of education flows from professional training, in that the presence in society of a corps of competent professional persons may directly improve social conditions. For example, the presence of lawyers may advance the cause of freedom and justice, the presence of physicians may promote health and the relief of suffering, the presence of journalists may facilitate the flow of valid information, or the presence of clergymen may advance religious thought and practice. Moreover, the standby value of professional persons, for example, physicians and lawyers—even when they are not needed—may be substantial.

10

Societal Outcomes from Research and Public Service

The ideas of economists and political philosophers, both when they are right and when they are wrong, are more powerful than is commonly understood. Indeed, the world is ruled by little else. Practical men, who believe themselves to be quite exempt from any intellectual influences, are usually the slaves of some defunct economist. Madmen in authority, who hear voices in the air, are distilling their frenzy from some academic scribbler of a few years back. I am sure that the power of vested interests is vastly exaggerated compared with the gradual encroachment of ideas.

John Maynard Keynes (1936, p. 383)

American colleges and universities contribute to the quality and productivity of society not only indirectly through their influence on students but also directly through ramified activities that we call "research and public service." We use this term as shorthand for all of the functions or activities of higher education that

advance knowledge and the fine arts and serve the public directly. These include: scholarship; scientific research in the natural
sciences and social studies; philosophical and religious inquiry;
social criticism; public policy analysis; cultivation of literature
and the fine arts; and direct public service.

Research and Public Service in Higher Education

Higher education has no monopoly on the functions included
within research and public service. They are shared by government, business, private research organizations, labor unions,
churches, libraries, museums, performing arts organizations,
journalists, free-lance scholars and writers, various self-employed professional persons, and others. Nevertheless, colleges
and universities occupy a significant, perhaps dominant, position in the intellectual and artistic life of the nation, and they
perform many important public services. Indeed, their relative
importance in these functions has been growing. Moreover, the
role of higher education in research and public service is magnified because most of the persons who are engaged in these
activities received their own training in colleges and universities,
and many of them remain in constant communication with college and university faculties.

Various nations of the world differ in the degree to which
these functions are carried on within higher education. In the
United States the degree of responsibility borne by higher education for research and public service probably is greater than in
most other countries.[1] The result is the wide range of diversified activities that led Clark Kerr to coin the term *multiversity*.

The question of the most fruitful division of labor between
the academic world and other organizations is debated frequently. Some argue that American higher education has undertaken too much, to the detriment not only of instruction but of
research and public service as well. Perhaps a majority of Ameri-

[1] However, universities in many countries are expanding, relatively, their
activities in research and public service and are becoming more like their
American counterparts (*Organization for Economic Cooperation and Development*, 1975, pp. 62-74).

can academicians believe that research and public service bear a fruitful symbiotic relationship to instruction and, judging by results, that the American arrangement has not hindered the advancement of knowledge and the arts (see Ben-David, 1968; Wolfle, 1972). At any rate, American higher education is in fact heavily involved in research and public service. And since these activities produce important results for society, any appraisal of the outcomes of American higher education must take these results into account. The outcomes from research and public service cannot be measured with any precision, and so conclusions will inevitably be subjective and judgmental. It is possible, however, to describe these activities in some detail. Indeed, a mere recital of them strongly suggests that they yield important social benefits. While the same benefits doubtless could have been produced by organizations other than colleges and universities, the fact remains that in our society higher education does produce them.

It is sometimes assumed that academic research and public service are confined largely to major universities. Though they are much more heavily committed than other institutions, all sectors of higher education—even two-year colleges—are involved. Trow and Fulton (in Trow, 1975) investigated this matter through a massive 1969 survey of faculty. They found that substantial numbers of faculty members in all types of institutions are interested in and engaged in "research," and that teaching loads in all types of institutions are adjusted so that perceptible numbers of faculty could, if motivated, have time for research and public service. Their data are shown in Table 44. Fulton and Trow interpreted these figures (pp. 42-43) as showing "the diversity with which the different functions of teaching and research are spread across the American educational system. . . . there is no sharp differentiation of function between colleges and universities." However, they found (p. 45) that "only a very small minority of faculty are uninterested in teaching" and that "the *normative* climate in the United States, as reflected in academics' personal preferences, is far more favorable to teaching than most observers would have predicted" (see Parsons and Platt, 1968).

Table 44. Faculty involvement in research, by kind and quality
of institution

	Percentage of Faculty Members		
	With Heavy Involvement in Research	With One or More Publications in Past Two Years	With Teaching Loads of 10 Hours or Less Per Week
Universities			
High quality	50%	79%	91%
Medium quality	40	72	85
Low quality	28	57	72
Four-year Colleges			
High quality	26	54	72
Medium quality	12	37	52
Low quality	10	29	42
Two-year Colleges	5	14	22

Source: Fulton and Trow (in Trow, 1975, pp. 44, 46, 48).

There are, undoubtedly, differences in the kinds and elaborateness of research and public service conducted in the several types of institutions. University faculties may tend to emphasize large-scale and highly sophisticated studies and projects, four-year college faculties may concentrate on less ambitious efforts, two-year college faculties may limit their activities primarily to local projects. Yet all these activities occur to some extent in all types of institutions. The research function is shared also among faculty members of all disciplines (Trow, 1975, pp. 54-55). The biological sciences appear to surpass all other disciplines in "amount" of research activity as measured by publications. The amount in the humanities and fine arts and in professional fields is somewhat less than in the natural and social sciences. Nevertheless, substantial research activity occurs in all fields.

Research and public service as conducted in higher education are for the most part produced jointly with instruction. The two activities use the same faculties and facilities, complementing each other so closely that it is difficult, both conceptually and statistically, to separate the relative amounts of resources devoted to each. Some rough estimates, however, are possible.

One approach is to calculate the percentage of faculty time available for nonteaching activities. Using three different sets of data on classroom hours for all institutions, we have estimated that about three fourths of faculty time is devoted to teaching.[2] This leaves about one fourth of faculty time for nonteaching activities. Administrative work absorbs some of this time. Allowing for that, perhaps one fifth of total faculty time is available, on the average, for research and public service. In leading universities this fraction is, of course, much higher, perhaps 50 percent or more. From one study of 145 doctoral-granting universities, we calculated that as much as 40 percent of total faculty time in the natural sciences and engineering was available for research (Atelsek and Gomberg, 1976, p. 12), after allowing for administrative and other noninstructional activities. The institutions included were those granting the doctorate in at least one field of science and engineering in 1970-71 and receiving at least $1 million of federal aid for research and development in 1973-74. At the other extreme, in the four-year colleges of lesser "quality" and in two-year colleges, the teaching loads were higher and the fraction of time available for research and public service was smaller.

Analysis of the current fund expenditures of colleges and universities offers another approach to estimating the relative amounts of resources devoted to instruction and to research and public service. Though expenditures are not segregated neatly between the two activities, we have made some guesses based on official 1972-73 statistics, as shown in Table 45. These data

---

[2] This calculation is based on data relating to faculty teaching loads from the following sources: Trow and Fulton (1975), pp. 44, 46, 48; National Science Foundation, as reported in *The Chronicle of Higher Education*, May 24, 1976, p. 15; and American Council on Education, *Fact Book on Higher Education*, 3rd issue, 1975, p. 147. In calculating these percentages, it was assumed that a full-time teaching load is twelve classroom hours and that loads of less than this amount allow time for nonteaching activities. It should be observed that most studies of faculty working time find that the total time is far above the conventional forty hours a week.

Table 45. Institutional expenditures for instruction, research,
and public service, by functions

| | *(Millions of Dollars)* | | | |
	Instruction	*Research*	*Public Service*	*Total*
General administrative, general expense, and plant operation	$ 3,805	$1,405	$ 644	$ 5,854
Instruction, departmental research, and libraries	8,264	1,821	—	10,085
Extension, hospitals, and other public service	225	1,109	1,554	2,888
Research and other	1,552	2,395	523	4,470
Auxiliary enterprises and student aid	4,326	—	334	4,660
Total	18,172	6,730	3,055	27,957
Percentages	65%	24%	11%	100%

Source: U.S. Department of Health, Education, and Welfare, *Digest of Education Statistics*
(1965, p. 130).

suggest that about one third of the current expenditures of all
institutions of higher education are in support of activities that
can be classified as research and public service. These expenditures are financed in part from funds derived from the federal
government, individual and corporate donors, foundations, and
research fees. They are financed also in part from the general
funds of the institutions, largely in the form of low teaching
loads to allow faculty members to devote time to research and
public service.

Our tentative conclusion is that, taken as a whole, about
one fifth of all faculty time and one third of all institutional
expenditures in American higher education are devoted to research and public service. The fraction of faculty time and of
institutional expenditures devoted to research and public service
differ because some research projects make heavy use of expensive equipment (for example, high energy physics) and some
important public services use large numbers of nonacademic
personnel (for example, hospitals).

Scholarship

Scholarship, which refers to the preservation and interpretation of received knowledge, is obviously one of the most important functions of colleges and universities. Indeed, it is a bulwark of our culture.

Scholarship is primarily the work of faculty members who constantly study, review, synthesize, analyze, criticize, and expound received knowledge. Because of these activities, they are among the chief living repositories of what is known about a vast array of specialized subjects. And they are the chief interpreters of this knowledge to each generation. Faculty members are supported in these efforts by libraries and museums, which are storehouses of records, artifacts, and specimens representing the accumulated knowledge of the past and present. They are also frequently assisted by students.

The function of colleges and universities as conservators and interpreters of received knowledge is often overlooked or underrated. Without it, our accumulated knowledge—together with the truth, perspective, and wisdom it conveys—would dwindle away. Higher education is not the sole center of scholarship in our society but is surely preeminent in the field.

These functions are performed partly as an inevitable by-product of teaching and partly through special scholarly inquiries intended to illuminate and make accessible knowledge of the distant or recent past. Thus it is as impossible to abstract the cost of scholarship, because of its inextricable links with teaching, as it is impossible to estimate the value of scholarship to society, because of the intangibility of its results.

What *is* the value of keeping the works of Shakespeare, Dante, Kant, or Milton alive? Of recording the history of monetary and fiscal policy since the Keynesian revolution? Of reconsidering the critiques of American society by Emerson, de Tocqueville, Thoreau, and Veblen? Of reinterpreting the American revolution? Of discovering and interpreting the Dead Sea Scrolls? Of biblical criticism and interpretation? Of studies of the Newtonian revolution? Of the discovery of new works by Mozart or of knowledge casting his work in a new light? Of reconstructing the ancient culture of Greece or of the Seri Indians of Mexico?

The work of academic scholars is discovery and rediscovery of knowledge of the past, interpretation and reinterpretation of this knowledge, the preservation of texts and artifacts, and learning and transmitting this knowledge from generation to generation. When judged by their practical consequences, many of the specific results of scholarship are esoteric or even trivial. But the preservation of human experience and its constant reinterpretation in light of the circumstances of the present is of inestimable value. It interests people of every generation because it enables each generation to understand itself and its problems in the perspective of human experience. For human society to be cut off from its past would be to cast it adrift on a turbulent sea without compass, rudder, or navigational skills.

All institutions of higher education share the function of preserving and interpreting received knowledge. Faculty members cannot perform their work as teachers without becoming carriers and transmitters of the cultural heritage, without becoming repositories of received knowledge, discoverers of values and meanings and wisdom in it, and interpreters of it to the present generation. Moreover, this work cannot safely be entrusted to a small coterie of scholars who would become bastions of orthodoxy. It requires many approaches, fresh points of view, and ample room for originality and controversy.

If higher education performed no other function than to maintain fruitful continuity with the past, it might well be worth every dollar currently spent on it. However, granting the importance of scholarship, as nearly everyone does, cannot settle the question of how much of society's resources should be devoted to it.

Scientific Research: The Natural Sciences

Higher education is deeply involved in the natural sciences (including engineering and medical sciences). In carrying out its scientific mission, it traditionally has been at least partially exempted from concern for immediate practical results. Higher education has been allowed—and indeed expected—to pursue basic knowledge in quest of "truth" rather than applied knowledge in search of results. Faculty members, on the whole, have been free to choose their research programs in terms of intrinsic scientific interest rather than of practical outcomes. Experience shows that this freedom of choice often produces outcomes of great and unplanned practical value. For example, hybrid seed corn, the computer, polio vaccine, and the Pill were direct results of basic research conducted in universities. The academic contribution to these products alone probably added enough to national productivity or welfare to defray all the costs of higher education for years. University research also provided the knowledge base for unleashing and harnessing nuclear energy, a spectacular though controversial achievement.

The distinction between basic and applied research is fuzzy. Applied research often leads to basic knowledge and basic research often leads to practical application. Basic research, however, is characterized by interest in knowledge for its own sake and animated by a contemplative and philosophical spirit rather than by preoccupation with immediate results. These qualities are more at home in the university than in the corporation or governmental bureau. The increasing involvement of universities in applied research, which has been motivated by shortage of funds for basic research and by expediency under the pressure of war, cold war, and the space age, raises serious questions. Society should be served by at least one kind of institution that pursues scientific knowledge for its own sake rather than for practical results; the university is best equipped by tradition and temperament to fill this need.

Natural science for its own sake may be justified partly on the utilitarian ground that—despite the purity of its intentions —it turns out by serendipity to be vastly useful. It may be justified also because it is a rewarding cultural pursuit comparable to philosophical or historical learning or to artistic achievement (see Kaysen, 1969; Wolfle, 1972; Johnson in Lumsden, 1974). Kaysen (p. 37) refers to nuclear accelerators as "the cathedrals of the twentieth century." Oppenheimer (1959, quoted by Wolfle, p. 131) wrote: "Why, then, do we seek new knowledge, and ask for the help of others in enabling us to acquire it? To this question there is not one answer, there are two. They are disturbingly unrelated. . . . One answer is that new knowledge is useful; the other answer is that the getting of it is ennobling. Indeed it is ennobling, as anyone who has spent his life, or an honest part of it, in studying nature can attest. Science today, the study of nature and man as part of nature, is continuous, despite all that makes it unique in scope, brilliance, and virtuosity, with the long tradition of attempting to comprehend our situation in the world in which we live." If science for its own sake ennobles the scientist, is there anything in it for the citizen who pays the bill? One possible answer is that many people are intensely interested in science. Through science, man can explore inaccessible parts of the earth, plumb the ocean depths, venture into outer space, study exotic peoples, create new forms of life in the test tube, develop new wonder drugs, explode nuclear weapons, probe the depths of the psyche. These achievements arouse wonder, stimulate the imagination, satisfy curiosity, supply vicarious adventure, and confer a sense of national pride. They have about them the mystery and beauty of poetry and art and also the excitement of spectator sport. A recent editorial referred to the voyage to Mars of Viking I as "celestial Olympics." What is it worth to mankind to know for the sake of knowledge and to experience adventure vicariously? For example, were the manned space flights worth the $30 billion or more they cost?

Before extolling too uncritically the rewards and benefits of science, it may be well to consider, along with many social critics (for example, Barzun, 1964; Mumford, 1970), that our civilization may have overdone scientific modes of thought and experience that leave little room for the affective spheres of life and stress technological development so relentlessly as to endanger life on the planet. As Barzun (1964, pp. 282-283) observed:

> What we discover as the cause of our pain when we examine the burden of modernity is the imposition of one intellectual purpose upon all experience. To analyze, abstract, and objectify is the carrying out of a single, imperialistic mode of thought. That mode, the

scientific, is fully justified—as everyone grants—by many of its results. It is a triumph of mind, a masterpiece of symbolism, an unrivaled satisfaction of the ancestral curiosity of man about his surroundings. Its activity is a magnificent spectacle, a virtuoso juggling with ideas, things, numbers, instruments. . . . But science has a hold on our imagination and an ostensible alliance with technology which make it today not a profession among others but the head and power of a scientific culture. The consequence . . . is a cultural contradiction: from the undoubted flourishing of man's science and invention springs the lament of men over their success: Man is *not* flourishing.

Research and development. The science "industry" includes much more than basic research. The ultimate application of scientific knowledge involves the discovery of practical uses and the development of specific, useful products or methods of production. All this is preliminary to "developing" a marketable product or process. This complicated procedure—from basic knowledge to end product—is called research and development, or R and D. The data in Table 46 show expenditures for re-

Table 46. Expenditures for R and D in the United States in 1975, by type of institution conducting the R and D

	(Millions of Dollars)			
	Basic Research	*Applied Research*	*Development*	*Total*
Universities and colleges	$2,185	$ 780	$ 135	$ 3,100
Universities and colleges associated R & D centers	305	280	325	910
Other nonprofit institutions	280	605	390	1,275
Private industry	660	4,370	18,830	23,860
Federal government	655	1,955	2,590	5,200
Total	$4,085	$7,990	$22,270	$34,345

Source: U.S. Bureau of the Census, *Statistical Abstract of the United States* (1975, p. 548). These data include some research in social science.

search and development in the United States in 1975 (in millions of dollars). As shown in the table, over $22 billion are
devoted to development and nearly $8 billion to applied re-
search. These two categories account for over $30 billion, or 88
percent of the nation's R and D expenditures. Only $4 billion,
or 12 percent of the total are devoted to basic research. Universities and colleges have a negligible role in applied research and
in development. They perform about $2 billion worth of basic
research, a little more than half the total. In other words, higher
education has a quantitatively minor role in research and development. Its importance lies in its significant function as a center
for *basic* research, the foundation on which scientific and technological advancement is built. Moreover, it is probable that
higher education's share of the *most fundamental* scientific
work would be considerably more than half (Nelson, Peck, and
Kalachek, 1967, p. 60; Havelock, 1969, pp. 3-6).

Though undoubtedly significant, the contribution of academic science to technological advancement is not easy to identify. It is not always possible to link specific scientific discoveries made in university laboratories with particular new
products or processes. However, there are many stages and
many people involved in the complicated procedure that we
have come to call research and development. That is why the
combined expenditures for applied research and for development so greatly exceed the expenditures for basic research.
Each step in translating scientific knowledge into useful results
is indispensable. Though the academic community can claim
that its specialty of basic research has priority, each of the other
participants in the process of research and development can
rightly claim that its contribution is also indispensable. Moreover, higher education has no exclusive franchise on basic research. It conducts only a little more than half of it (as measured by expenditures). Thus, it behooves the academic
community to be conservative in its claims about the practical
results of its scientific research. Because some or all of the basic
research underlying, for example, hybrid seed corn, the computer, or polio vaccine, was conducted in universities does not
entitle the academic community to claim full credit for the

dramatic outcomes. On the other hand, it must not be over-looked that colleges and universities may claim some of the credit for most of R and D because colleges and universities train almost all of the scientists who conduct the work (Benson and Hodgkinson, 1974).

Some evidence on the outcomes from academic science. In judging the outcomes from academic science, one approach is to consider the progress of natural science in the United States in view of its relatively heavy reliance on higher education as a focal point of basic research. Wolfle (1972, pp. 65-83) gave special attention to this issue and drew on the comparative international studies of Ben-David (1968) and on commentaries by several European observers. Wolfle argued that the use of universities for basic research led to decentralization and competition within the scientific community and that these, in turn, promoted freedom and elicited strong motivation. He wrote (p. 65): "Decentralizing research in many universities instead of centralizing it in a few national research centers guaranteed a dispersed, competitive scientific community. The existence of many universities, all independent of each other and of the federal government, meant that no governmental or other centralized agency could control science, set limits, determine national priorities, or establish orthodoxies. Instead scientists were free to follow their own system of values, to choose the problems they wanted to investigate, and to reward those among them whose work they regarded most highly." Wolfle conceded that the extensive use of universities as "the home of science" may have had its disadvantages. He pointed out that science may have lost some of the public and legislative understanding that it might have had were it organized as specialized research institutes or governmental bureaus; that the schism between basic and applied science may be greater than it would have been under other circumstances; and that scientific problems requiring interdisciplinary cooperation might have been handled more expeditiously (see Clark and Youn, 1976). However, the removal of scientists from politics, by virtue of their position in the university, probably freed them from political distractions and allowed them to concentrate on science. Wolfle concluded (pp. 76, 83): "The university system, with scientists in control of scientific work, aided by large amounts of federal money in the past 25 years, has brought the United States acknowledged scientific leadership among the nations of the world. It is highly doubtful that the status would be as high had most of the scientific activity of the past 25 to 50 years been carried out in government laboratories. . . . It is the university that has been the home of the most creative scientists and the scene of most of the progress in basic science in the past hundred years."

Although Ben-David (1968) explained the technological superiority of the United States over other countries partly by differences in number of people and amount of money involved, he concluded that the main difference lay in underlying scientific superiority, which he attributed to the important role of higher education in basic research. Ben-David cited the statistics in Tables 47 and 48 to show that the technological superior-

Table 47. Percentage of major inventions and discoveries originating in the United States, 1880-1949

Time Period	Percentages
1880-1899	37%
1930-1939	54
1940-1949	88

Source: Ben-David (in Wolfle, 1972, p. 80).

ity of the United States was not merely a post-World War II phenomenon but a condition of long standing.

Data such as these tell us little about the precise contributions of universities and colleges but strongly suggest that the particular organization of science in the United States, where much of basic research is performed in higher education, has been conducive to the development of science.

Other statistics reveal that the United States occupies a predominant position in the world's scientific literature both in

Table 48. U.S. involvement in the fifty most significant
industrial inventions of the 20th century

	Basic Research	Development
Number for which development took place in one country		
United States	22	22
Other countries	11	10
Number for which development took place in two countries		
United States and one other country	13	16
Two countries not including United States	4	2
Total	50	50

Source: Ben-David (in Wolfle, 1972, p. 81).

the percentage of the world's research papers published in scientific and technical journals and in the frequency of citation of journal papers (National Science Board, 1975). The United States enjoys a highly favorable "balance of trade" with other countries in patents awarded, in payments for rights to use patents, and in trade in technology-intensive products (pp. 164-169). Also, ninety-seven of 230 Nobel prizes in the natural sciences between 1930 and 1975 were awarded to citizens of the United States (p. 162). Medical advances from 1940 to 1970, which together have increased life expectancy by 2.38 years, were partly the product of research in American universities (Terleckyj, 1976, p. 23). Finally, dramatic increases in United States crop yields, representing in most cases a doubling or tripling, were made possible in part by academic research (U.S. Bureau of the Census, *Statistical Abstract of the United States,* 1953).

Case studies of particular inventions have revealed important contributions of basic research conducted in universities. Examples are magnetic ferrites, the videotape recorder, the oral contraceptive pill, the electron microscope, the method of matrix isolation, penicillin, streptomycin, and electrical precipitation techniques (Nelson, Peck, and Kalachek, 1967; Illinois Institute of Technology, 1968). Other well-known cases are the ENIAC computer, neomycin, polio vaccine, hybrid seed corn, nuclear energy, and solid state electronics. According to Nelson, Peck, and Kalachek (p. 60), "The universities have played a prominent role in many inventive efforts. . . . University scientists and engineers have often played important roles as consultants to private companies and governments on R and D projects. The distinctive contribution of the universities, however, is as the *primary source of fundamental advances in understanding* that pave the way for major advances in technology in almost all fields." (Italics added.)

Mansfield (1968a, pp. 92-93) has pointed out that most commercial R and D is directed toward relatively short payout periods. One study reported that about 90 percent of firms expect to recover their R and D costs within five years or less, a period too short for the development and marketing of radically new products. Most, but not all, firms apparently confine their R and D activities to improvements and minor changes in products or processes and leave the pioneering to others, including universities, other nonprofit organizations, government laboratories, and independent inventors. Consistent with this finding, one study reported that laboratories of large corporations accounted for only twelve of sixty-one major inventions; another noted that they accounted for seven of twenty-seven major inventions since World War II.

Economic returns to research and development. The economic returns from research and development are another source of evidence about the role of higher education in the advancement of technology. Pertinent data are scarce but some scattered fragments are at least suggestive. Schultz (1971, p. 212) refers to "a branch of biological research that should be treated as *maintenance research*," the purpose of which is to keep agricultural yields from falling. Universities and colleges conduct much, but not all, of this research. Here are some examples cited by Schultz from an unpublished paper by A. H. Moseman:

The serious outbreak of Race 15-B of stem rust of wheat destroyed 65-75 percent of the durum wheat crop in the United States in 1953 and 1954; it was then brought under control.

The oat diseases from 1943 to 1953, caused by *Helminthosporeum septoria* and the new races of crown and stem rust, brought down the yield of oats.

The new virulent form of bunt in the Pacific Northwest resulted in a sharp increase in "smutty" wheat in the early fifties.

In tobacco in the Carolinas and Kentucky there were the losses from black shank disease.

In the western range lands, the spread of the poisonous weed "Halogeton" took its toll.

To this list of once-serious threats to output that have been brought under control by biological research, Moseman adds the outbreaks of green bugs or aphids on small grains, corn root worms, cereal leaf beetles, Mexican fruit fly, and the eradication of the screwworm, which had caused heavy losses in livestock production in parts of the United States.

Schultz (1971, pp. 242-243) estimated that the rate of return to investments in agricultural research by academic and other nonprofit organizations in the period 1940 to 1950 ranged from 35 to 170 percent. These rates are based on estimates of *investment*, defined as the cost of all nonprofit agricultural research, and estimates of *return*, defined as the "value of the agricultural inputs *saved* by the advances in the agricultural arts," that is, reductions in costs. Schultz thus suggests that, whereas the social rate of return to investments in physical capital was of the order of 10 to 15 percent, the rate of return to investments in nonprofit agricultural research was at least 35 percent and probably much higher.

In studies of rates of return from commercial research and development, Mansfield (1968b, pp. 70-77) found wide variations among different industries and also large differences between technological changes embodied in new plant and equipment and those not so embodied. The latter would be illustrated by new wage incentives based on time and motion study. After warning (p. 75) that, "in view of their roughness, it would be unwise to read too much into the results," he estimated marginal rates of return in individual chemical and petroleum firms of 30 to 60 percent (for the chemical industry 7 percent in the case of technological changes not embodied in physical capital). For ten major industry groups, he found marginal rates of return ranging from negative to more than 200 percent. The average was about 20 percent for technological changes embodied in new plant and equipment and 65 percent for other categories. These estimates are "lower bounds," that is, minimal estimates. They are based on the assumption that half the industry's technological change is due to its own R and D and that the other half is derived from outside. The monetary returns from most academic research are likely to be more uncertain and to be longer delayed than those from commercial research. However, if one assumed that investments in academic research produced rates of return of even half those cited by Schultz and Mansfield, the payout would amply justify the investment.

Advancement of knowledge and economic growth. One final bit of evidence on the outcomes from scientific research is supplied by Denison (1974) in his monumental studies of the sources of economic growth in the United States. He calculated the growth in annual national income between 1929 and 1969 (in constant 1958 dollars) at $438.2 billion (p. 11). Of this growth, he estimated that 31.1 percent was due to advances in knowledge (p. 128).[3] Applying this percentage to the dollar national income yielded $136.3 billion (1958 dollars) as the part of the growth in annual GNP due to advancement in knowledge. He provided no data on the portion of this increase that might be attributable to higher education. However, higher education was responsible for about 6 percent of the nation's total expenditures

---

[3] This figure also includes residual items not elsewhere classified. However, Denison indicates (p. 131) that these extraneous items "have individually been minor and have tended to be offsetting."

for research and development during the period 1929-1969. If one assumed that 6 percent of the $136.3 billion of growth due to advancement of knowledge had been attributable to academic science, then $8.2 billion of annual national income in 1969 would have been derived from research conducted in higher education. This result would have been achieved with expenditures for research in colleges and universities averaging considerably less than $1 billion a year during the period 1929-1969 (*Statistical Abstract of the United States,* 1975, p. 548). This calculation strongly suggests that the payout from academic science is substantial.

Conclusions. The arguments and data we have presented about the effects of, and the returns from, research and development do not yield accurate estimates of the dollar value of the scientific contributions of universities and colleges. They do lead to these conclusions.

1. The role of higher education in natural science is predominantly basic research, designed to discover knowledge and increase understanding and not necessarily to lead to immediate practical consequences. However, experience has shown that pure research conducted for its intrinsic scientific interest and without thought of practical results often proves to be practically significant.
2. Higher education accounts for a preponderance of the most fundamental research on which later technological achievements are based.
3. The general (but not universal) practice in the United States of using universities and colleges rather than specialized research institutes or government bureaus for basic research apparently has not been unfavorable to the advancement of science in this country.
4. Higher education has had a major part in the basic research, and some cases development, underlying major technological breakthroughs.
5. The rate of return to investments in research and devel-

opment has been very high relative to the returns to investments in physical capital.

6. The part of the growth of annual national income that may be attributed to academic scientific research probably is several times the annual cost of that research.

In interpreting these conclusions, it must be recognized that research and development, like any other application of resources to the productive process, are subject to diminishing returns (Mansfield, 1968b; Orlans, 1968). Because R and D may have produced high marginal returns in the past does not guarantee equal marginal returns in the present or in the future, when the amount of resources involved may be much greater.

Scientific Research: Social Studies

Higher education occupies a dominant position in both basic and applied research in the social studies and in related professional fields such as law, management, education, social work, journalism, communications, and library science. To some extent it shares this research function with government agencies, specialized research institutes, law courts, trade and professional associations, private business firms, and free-lance individuals. But in social studies research higher education is preeminent. Higher education is society's main source of new knowledge in this field.

The outcomes for society from expenditures on academic research in the social studies must be deduced from findings that tend to be less orderly, less general, and less reliably applicable to practical affairs than those of the natural sciences. Nevertheless, research in the social studies produces indisputable benefits for society (National Science Foundation, 1969).

The first of these benefits is simply the provision of knowledge of intrinsic value. Just as people are curious about the physical and biological world, so they are also curious about themselves, their own society, and other societies. They would be interested in such knowledge even if it had no practical utility whatever.

Second, knowledge of social studies helps people to understand themselves and their society. It gives them some conception of the nature, limitations, and potential of human beings and some perspective on the history, geography, culture, problems, and prospects of their own society. Without some systematic knowledge of society, the basis for rational decision making in personal and social affairs would be weak. Knowledge of society is, of course, not the exclusive province of the social studies. Such knowledge is derived from common observation, myth and folklore, literature, arts, and theology. But it is the social studies that extend, systematize, and objectify this knowledge.

Third, knowledge of society fosters perspective and openness to change. It is an antidote to narrow provincialism and rigid tradition. It teaches the concept of culture and cultural relativity as they relate to different periods in history and to different geographic areas. It raises consciousness of the possibility of cultural change and of individual or social action directed toward change. It predisposes people to be aware of possible choices and increases their capacity to identify and consider the various options before them. At the same time, it helps people to achieve an understanding and appreciation of tradition.

Fourth, social studies research is the source of much statistical data by which we monitor the condition of our society, judge its performance, and diagnose its problems. Examples are national income data; indexes of prices and production; labor force and employment data; demographic and actuarial statistics; data on public opinion and voting behavior; and data on crime and delinquency.

Fifth, research in the social studies can be applied variously to private and public policy. It has uses relating to organization of production, worker incentives, labor relations, and consumer behavior. It is applicable to education, mental health, race relations, poverty, crime and delinquency, social work administration, and legal decisions. It has been applied to the evolution of public policies relating to social security, taxation, inflation, unemployment, income distribution, monopoly, foreign policy, national defense, public budgeting, and mass communications. Virtually every kind of private and public policy calls to some extent upon research in the social studies.

Of the multitude of examples of specific social studies research that may have had a perceptible and direct bearing on policy or practical affairs or on thinking about policy (mostly after long time lags), these come to mind: Ruth Benedict's *Chrysanthemum and the Sword,* which was influential in American policy toward Japan during and after World War II; Gunnar Myrdal's *The American Dilemma,* which called attention to racial inequality and segregation; the development of intelligence and aptitude tests by Lewis M. Terman, E. F. Lindquist, and others; Thorstein Veblen's institutional critiques of American society; the many American economists who elaborated, applied, and propagated the doctrines of Lord Keynes; Edward H. Chamberlin's *Theory of Monopolistic Competition,* which shed new light on competitive relationships; Simon Kuznets' pioneering work on national income accounting; Wassily Leontief's input-output analysis, which provides a systematic framework for national economic planning; Charles Hitch's explorations of cost-benefit analysis; Chester Barnard's and Elton Mayo's research on the dynamics of interpersonal behavior in formal organizations; the development of surveys of public opinion and attitudes by George Gallup, Hadley Cantril, Paul Lazarsfeld, and Angus Campbell; John von Neumann's and Oskar Morgenstern's theory of games, and Noam Chomsky's structural linguistics. One could continue adding to this list.[4] All of the studies mentioned were carried on in American colleges and universities and, with the one exception of Myrdal, by American citizens.

Not all research in the social studies results in wise or successful policies. Social scientists do not always collect adequate data, take into account all the relevant variables, consider all political and psychological consequences, accurately assess side

[4] For an interesting list of major break throughs in the social sciences, see Deutsch, Platt, and Senghaas, 1971a and b. This list includes many methodological innovations such as "quantitative political science" or "statistical decision theory" as well as political innovations such as the "one party state" (Lenin) or "nonviolent political action" (Gandhi).

effects, or maintain complete objectivity. Moreover, the results of many social science studies or the recommendations flowing from them are controversial. They do not exempt decision makers from the obligation to use good judgment or to take political considerations into account. But in many cases, they do provide guidance or insight useful in the formulation of public policy.

As Orlans (1973, p. 262) points out, in the case of social research it is not necessary to limit "usefulness" to uses in which identifiable action follows from verified knowledge: "Social science has more uses than its scientific devotees will attest. For they would have to acknowledge its unscientific uses: its effect on our beliefs and values, and its subjective— personal, political, ideological, and in a very real sense, religious —uses. Thus man subjectivizes objectivity turning his feeble knowledge into reeds of belief." Bressler (1976) said more positively that the social sciences help to maintain "the delicate balance between that to which we aspire and that which is possible." One of its functions is "to limit the extravagance of dreams."

Philosophical and Religious Inquiry

In addition to seeking positive knowledge in the natural and social sciences, colleges and universities are deeply involved in the search for meanings and values through philosophical and religious inquiry. This work is the specialty of schools of theology and departments of philosophy but is by no means confined to them. Many faculty members in the humanities, social studies, and natural sciences are involved to varying degrees in the consideration and analysis of values, in the discovery of meanings, in the construction of philosophical systems, and in the formulation of ideologies, and also in the criticism of religious and philosophical ideas. Though philosophical and religious inquiry flourishes in the church, within journalism, among free-lance essayists, poets, and novelists, within political movements, and elsewhere, colleges and universities surely are also significant contributors. Through this work they add a thoughtful and influential voice to the formation of individual values and social goals.

In the past, men have been guided by priesthoods, churches, aristocracies, and custom in defining the good life, in setting standards and values for individual conduct, and in formulating social goals. Today the moral authority once exercised by churches, aristocracies, and tradition has lost much of its force. A partial vacuum has been created which gives rise to much of the lack of direction and the sense of meaninglessness that characterizes modern life. Higher education to a degree fills this vacuum—which it helped to create by establishing scientific modes of inquiry as dominant paradigms.

The university always has occupied an important place in the domain of values. It has engaged in the study of philosophy, religion, and the arts. Through the study of the history of man, his ideas, and his works, it has explored the meanings to be found in thought and action in most historic periods and most geographic areas. Through the biological and social sciences it has probed into the nature of man. And through the biological and physical sciences it has explored the universe and raised the great questions as to the origins and destiny of our world and of the universe. Yet most contemporary professors, even those in the humanities, see themselves as detached observers of phenomena within particular disciplines rather than as arbiters of value or as guides to social goals. They see themselves as concerned with what is, not what ought to be. This reluctance stems partly from commendable humility and partly from the enormous influence of "scientism" in current academic life. Its effects are not wholly beneficent, as described by Edna St. Vincent Millay (1941, p. 140):

> Upon this gifted age, in its dark hour
> Rains from the sky a meteoric shower
> Of facts . . . they lie unquestioned, uncombined.
> Wisdom enough to leech us of our ill
> Is daily spun, but there exists no loom
> To weave it into fabric . . .*

*From *Collected Poems,* Harper & Row. Copyright 1939, 1967 by Edna St. Vincent Millay and Norma Millay Ellis.

The university is not, however, as value-free or as uncompromisingly scientific in outlook at it may seem. In the area of esthetics and ideas the university is by no means reluctant to assert a major role as arbiter of values. It regularly distinguishes between the more worthy and the less worthy works of art. Similarly, it singles out thinkers and ideas that it considers to be touched with truth and greatness and relegates to the background or rejects those adjudged to be of lesser stature. In the study of history, judgments frequently are made about the efficacy of public policies and the motives of public leaders. In the social sciences and law, the study of what *is* always tends to shade into the study of what ought to be, and these fields are deeply implicated in public policy.

By suggesting that the university has a legitimate role in the realm of values and social goals, we do not imply that monolithic agreement can or should be reached, or that the university resembles a church, or that it should undertake moral crusades. We mean only that through patient and endless thought, discussion, and criticism, the academic community can reach useful but tentative conclusions about values and social goals—just as, through the same methods, it reaches tentative esthetic judgments or tentative scientific conclusions. The results of scholarly inquiry are never final, and they never win unanimous assent. Yet, when the academic community reaches tentative conclusions that gain substantial acceptance within that community, these conclusions tend to be widely disseminated, to gain substantial authority, and to be effective in private and public decisions. Walter Lippman (1966, p. 19) declared: "One of the great phenomena of the human condition in the modern age is the dissolution of the ancestral order, the erosion of established authority, and having lost the light and the leading, the guidance and the support, the discipline that the ancestral order provided, modern men are haunted by a feeling of being lost and adrift, without purpose and meaning in the conduct of their lives. The thesis which I am putting to you is that the modern void, which results from the vast and intricate process of emancipation and rationalization, must be filled, and that the universities must fill the void because they alone can fill it."

Social Criticism

Criticism has been defined as "judicious appraisal, analysis, and evaluation of works created or recorded by men" (*Columbia Encyclopaedia,* 3rd edition, pp. 512-513). The term is often applied to evaluations of works of art (literature, drama, music, art, architecture) but may be used with reference to society as well. Social criticism refers to reasoned explanation and evaluation of social conditions and social change. It is usually concerned with broad trends and developments in society as distinct from narrowly specialized analyses characteristic of the social studies. It draws upon and integrates moral, esthetic, and scientific judgments "contraposed or blended in varying quantities" (p. 513). The boundaries between criticism and scientific studies or between criticism and philosophical and religious inquiry are of course indistinct. Social critics, full-time or part-time, are to be found among natural scientists (Rene Dubos, Julian Huxley, Jacob Bronowski, Barry Commoner), social scientists (Daniel Bell, Kenneth Boulding, Kenneth Galbraith, Robert Heilbroner, Kenneth Keniston), philosophers (Charles Frankel, Ernest Nagel), theologians (Reinhold Niebuhr, John Cobb), humanists (Jacques Barzun, Northrop Frye), and historians (Christopher Lasch, Arthur Schlesinger, Henry Steele Commager). Social criticism is usually communicated through essays, books, and lectures intended for the educated public rather than for specialists.

Social criticism is not confined to academic people. It flourishes among journalists, free-lance intellectuals, and others. However, a large part of the reflective and critical examination of broad social conditions and trends that might be characterized as social criticism is conducted within colleges and universities, and social criticism must be counted as a valuable outcome of higher education.

By its nature, social criticism is controversial, especially because social critics tend to be concerned with significant issues at the forefront of social change. But social criticism is of inestimable value in a democracy because it is a major vehicle by which positive knowledge combined with philosophical or religious thought—representing varied points of view—enters

into the public discussion of social issues. Those who practice
the art of social criticism increasingly are referred to as "intellectuals"—persons of learning who are especially concerned with
the application of philosophical ideas and systems of thought to
social issues and to social evaluation.

Academic intellectuals are emerging as a highly influential
element in the leadership of our society. This degree of influence is being achieved partly through the increasing importance
of *ideas* (including those of natural science, social science, and
philosophy) in a complex technological society, and partly by
default, as family, church, school, and state have lost some of
their vitality and authority in the realm of values. The colleges
and universities have in a sense found themselves filling a
vacuum without having planned or intended to do so (Shils,
1975).

Keniston (1968, pp. 145-146, 154) summed up vividly the
role of higher education in social criticism:

> In the past fifty years, American higher education has
> become the prime source for critical analysis of our
> society. . . . By criticism, I mean above all the analy-
> sis, examination, study, and evaluation of our society
> at large, of its directions, practices, institutions,
> strengths, weaknesses, ideals, values, and character; of
> its consistencies and contradictions; of what it has
> been and what it is becoming, of what is becoming of
> it, and of what it might at best become. The critical
> function involves examining the purposes, practices,
> meanings, and goals of our society. . . . In this critical
> examination of modern society, American universities
> have quietly but nonetheless decisively assumed the
> leading role. Higher education has become the chief
> source of analyses, evaluations, and judgments of our
> society: our proposals for reform, our critiques and
> defenses of the *status quo,* our prophecies of doom
> and our utopias almost invariably originate from the
> academy. With but few exceptions, our modern
> vocabulary of social analysis, our rhetoric of social

criticism and reform, are the products of higher education. The university has given us our most powerful understandings of American social character, of the economy, of our psychology as a nation. Academics have analyzed emergent patterns of consumption and leisure, the human implications of technological revolutions of the past decades, and the meaning and portent of our new role in the world. The most cogent voices of criticism, rejection, and protest have emanated from the universities. So, too, the most powerful defenses of American life, of our ideals as a society, and of the viability of our traditions have come from the centers of higher education. And university students and teachers have intensified our reluctant awareness of the many discrepancies between the ideals we profess and the way we live.

In the same vein, Ladd and Lipset (1975, p. 313) concluded their remarkable study, *The Divided Academy*: "Almost certainly, the intellectual stratum will provide in a continuing fashion the principal nexus from which pressures for social change will emanate in postindustrial America." The connection between the academic world and the world of practical affairs appears to be growing closer and the time lag between the discovery or formulation of new ideas or the rediscovery of old ideas and the application of these ideas has diminished.

Public Policy Analysis

Closely related to social criticism is public policy analysis, a relatively new function of higher education, which encompasses studies, usually interdisciplinary, whose purpose is to reach specific recommendations on public policy. Such studies may be concerned with foreign policy, control of inflation, early childhood education, reform of public assistance, use of nuclear power, urban transportation, air pollution, health care, or any of a thousand other topics. Public policy often involves the melding of technical and scientific knowledge with exploration of values and priorities. It usually requires a consideration of alternative courses of action. There is scarcely a recognized problem in American society for which policy research is not going on somewhere in the academy. This considerable effort is almost surely an influential factor in social change.

Though colleges and universities have long conducted studies pertinent to public policy, such studies usually have been confined to single disciplines and have not examined all facets of particular policy issues. In recent years, however, colleges and universities have engaged increasingly in interdisciplinary policy studies—often through special institutes. Further, some individual faculty members have extended the scope of their interests across disciplinary lines.

It must be said, however, that universities and colleges have not always been able or willing to muster the interdisciplinary resources needed to apply knowledge to specific public policy issues. Indeed, much public policy analysis has been conducted within government or within specialized institutes such as The Brookings Institution, the Rand Corporation, the Hudson Institute, the Battelle Memorial Institute, and many others. The difficulty that universities experience in assembling interdisciplinary teams is surely not due to lack of talent, but is more probably due to the freedom accorded faculty members in their choice of research problems. However, this very freedom, as it turns out, is one of the major strengths of the university. In any event, there can be little doubt that colleges and universities play a significant part in the policy-making process in American democratic society.

Cultivation of Literature and the Fine Arts

A well-established and growing function of higher education is cultivation of literature and the fine arts. Through historical research and criticism in literature, music, art, drama, and other arts, college and university faculties help to keep alive and to reinterpret for each generation the great artistic works of the past. And they help to criticize and interpret new and emerging art forms. This work—in which higher education is predominant —is clearly of great value in a society that cherishes its cultural heritage.

Colleges and universities have long been active in the arts through a somewhat attenuated instruction in music, art, and drama. Recently, however, they have emerged clearly as hospitable and supportive centers and patrons of the arts. Today, in leading universities, both the creative and performing arts are taught and practiced at a high professional level. Colleges and universities now sponsor a majority of the performances of great musical artists and organizations. "Support by colleges and universities of the professional touring performing arts in the U.S. is probably around $370 millions annually" (*Higher Education and National Affairs,* December 13, 1974). They provide a rich fare of art exhibits, plays, operas, and dance performances. For example, more than 10,000 plays a year are produced on college campuses (*Chronicle of Higher Education,* April 4, 1977, p. 14). They include in their regular faculties important poets, novelists, essayists, critics, dramatists, composers, performing artists, painters, and sculptors. They provide a congenial environment for hundreds of artists-in-residence. They sponsor high-level performances and exhibits based on the work of students and faculty. And higher education is a significant resource for the training of future performing and creative artists, not only in the specialized conservatories and institutes but also in the many general universities and colleges. In the past several decades, as the role of higher education as patron of the arts has greatly expanded, quality has risen appreciably.

Direct Public Services

The public service activities of higher education are partly by-products of instruction and research. For example, medical and dental care are conducted within hospitals and clinics designed primarily for training professionals. Similarly, candidates for teaching certificates carry on elementary and secondary instruction. Today, clinical instruction is becoming increasingly common in law, social work, allied health professions, and college teaching. Universities and colleges also operate farms, dairies, hotels, restaurants, bookstores, and other enterprises— all available to the public—in conjunction with their instructional activities. Furthermore, now that many institutions accept experiential learning for credit, or sponsor work-study programs, many kinds of community service and work experience are being drawn into the orbit of higher education.

As a by-product of education, almost all colleges and universities provide recreational and cultural activities for persons in the surrounding community. These include dramatic and musical performances; libraries; museum exhibits; recreational facilities such as gymnasia, playing fields, golf courses, and tennis courts; summer camps; broadcasting; and spectator sports. Also, by their very existence, colleges and universities affect the character of nearby communities. As the turbulent history of town-gown relations testifies, academic institutions are not universally regarded as good neighbors. Yet many, perhaps most, communities are pleased to be hosts to colleges or universities and regard them as assets. As Solmon has said (1973a), Iowa City is a quite different community—surely more interesting and more cosmopolitan—from what it would be without The University of Iowa. And even great cities like New York or San Francisco are culturally enriched by the presence of many colleges and universities. Moreover, society at large probably derives some psychic satisfactions from the mere existence of higher education. There may be enjoyment and satisfaction from living in a society where knowledge, technology, ideas, the arts, and general culture are advancing. On the other hand, knowledge derived ultimately from academic pursuits may give rise to dissatisfactions. By raising people's aspirations more rapidly than their hopes can be fulfilled, it may lead to discontent. Yet this discontent may be the stimulus and the trigger for social reform.

Colleges and universities also engage in activities designed specifically to serve the public, usually in an educational or consulting capacity. The most important example is agricultural extension, which combines adult education with consulting services for farmers, agribusinessmen, and consumers. Some universities have similarly organized consulting services relating to local government, urban affairs, water supply, public health, business, management, organized labor, law, and engineering.

Most universities, both public and private, are on call from all levels of government to give advice or to conduct studies on numerous subjects, and most respond to inquiries from citizens. Many institutions or their faculties provide educational services through adult courses, conferences, public lectures, and writing and speaking through the mass media.

Perhaps the most important public service function of colleges and universities is the maintenance of a large pool of diversified and specialized faculty talent available on call for consultation on varied social problems (Peterson, 1975). Just as a hospital or an auto repair shop is of value on a standby basis, even if never used, so a college or university is valuable because of the talent it has in readiness to advise on technical questions or policy issues that may arise in government at any level, in the household, on the farm, in the business firm, in the labor union, or in the school. In fact, the advice is used widely. Some of it may be in the form of direct consultation, and some in the form of books and articles, public addresses, testimony before legislative committees and other public bodies, or statements in the press or on television. Havelock (1969, pp. 3-1, 3-6) has described the talent pool in this way: "The university is the *primary* source, storage point, and cultural carrier of expert knowledge in all fields, basic and applied. . . . The university as a whole provides a large institutional umbrella under which a great variety of 'experts' find shelter. For every field of endeavor without exception, the university is the place the experts call 'home'." For example, if the State Department needs to know some details of post-Sino-Russian relations, if a physician needs advice about a rare disease, if a museum or a citizen needs guidance in restoring a damaged painting, if a community wishes information on land-use planning, if a farmer needs assistance in overcoming an infestation of insects, people in colleges and universities somewhere will be able to help. Similarly, if there is need for information or advice on accounting methods for a cooperative society, national health insurance, preschool education of disadvantaged children, abatement of air pollution, or space exploration, college or university faculty members can be useful sources of information and advice.

Society looks to the academic community not only for information and advice but also, in many cases, for actual execution and administration of programs. Universities and colleges dispatch foreign technical missions, administer governmental laboratories, dispense technical services and training for private corporations and farmers, and provide a host of consulting services to government and industry. Some of this work is conducted officially under the auspices of the institutions and some by professors in their "spare time." Indeed, a new breed of professors has emerged who move easily between the academic world and business or government. Such professors are called upon to serve in the Cabinet and in the civil service, they are elected to public office, they become members of special commissions, they are sent on foreign missions, they are consulted on many kinds of political, technical, and diplomatic issues by government at all levels, by private business and by other organizations. Higher educational institutions are generous—some think too generous—in allowing their faculty members to do part-time consulting or to take leaves for the purpose of serving government, foundations, unions, corporations, trade associations, and other organizations over extended periods of time. American society and higher education probably are both enriched by the frequent interaction between the campus and public affairs—though the intellectual objectivity of the college or university can be compromised and its main business can be neglected through excessive involvement in practical affairs.

Many of the public service activities of higher education are akin to instruction. They are designed to foster learning in one form or another—the clientele in this instance being members of the general public rather than enrolled students. The relationship to the clients is usually less intensive than the relationship to regularly enrolled students, but the goals are nevertheless similar.

Havelock (1969, pp. 3-10, 3-11) sounded a note of restraint about the advisory functions of higher education:

> The university is very ambivalent about its role as universal expert and problem solver for the practical

world. Traditionally and particularly in England and Germany where the university came into being, applied work and "service" have been shunned altogether. In the more practically minded United States, however, the concept of a university as a center for teaching, research, *and* application came into being with the land-grant college legislation beginning in the 1860s. A century later, however, the image of the U.S. university is not clear even to itself. . . . A struggle goes on between teaching and research interests which virtually crowds out serious consideration of the university's role as the problem-solver and expert for the greater society. Meanwhile, the average citizen looking on from the sidelines insistently asks when the professors are going to stop "studying" problems and start "helping" the society by using what they know. (See Faiman and Olivier, 1972.)

Conclusions

In this chapter, an effort has been made to identify and describe the various contributions of higher education flowing from the varied activities we have called *research and public service.* About one fifth of faculty time and about one third of current institutional expenditures are devoted to research and public service. In dollars, this would be around $14 billion, of which about $10 billion would be devoted to research and around $5 billion to public service (in 1976-77).

It is assumed sometimes that the intellectual influence of higher education emanates exclusively from a few dozen major universities. Though the great "research universities" are major contributors to the intellectual capital of the nation, all branches of higher education are involved. There are active researchers, scholars, artists, philosophers, students of public policy, and social critics scattered throughout the newer state colleges and universities, the liberal arts colleges, and other primarily teaching institutions. The number of such people is increasing with the growth of the Ph.D. population and its wider diffusion to all parts of the country and all types of institutions.

The community colleges also perform the intellectual functions to a degree, especially for local community issues. The faculties in all branches of higher education are part of the system of communications by which the ideas of leading intellectuals—wherever they may be located—are diffused. Moreover, the colleges identify talent and stimulate interests, with the result that new blood flows into the major research centers.

The activities we have called *research* and *public service* produce many kinds of outcomes. First, they all serve as valuable—even essential—adjuncts to education. Instruction carried on in an environment devoid of inquiry and creativity, without a scholarly atmosphere, and without significant contact with the world, would be stultifying. Although faculty interest in research and public service may lead them to neglect teaching, many educators believe that on balance, some of the benefit of research and public service accrues to teaching itself (Nerlove in Schultz, 1972).

Second, through the function of scholarship, colleges and universities maintain constant contact with the cultural heritage; they conserve the knowledge, wisdom, and experience of the past; they reinterpret it and make it available to each successive generation.

Third, scholarship, research, and related activities produce knowledge of intrinsic value. Such knowledge needs no justification in terms of its application to practical affairs. Mankind is by nature curious and values knowledge for its own sake. An editorial in the *Los Angeles Times* (July 21, 1976), published on the day after Viking I landed on Mars, expresses this idea. "It is all, we think, unquestionably worthwhile, for what will be learned about Mars itself, for what insights may be gained about the evolution of our own planet. The search is only about to begin. The achievement already has been remarkable, the effort at discovery yet to come could be spectacular. No sentient person has ever looked to the heavens without wondering what was there. Viking I is a response to that sense of wonder, a tiny but momentous step toward a better understanding of the unimaginably vast universe, a great leap forward in scientific progress."

Fourth, scientific research contributes toward the advancement of technology. The particular niche of higher education, within the broad area of research and development, is basic research—especially the more fundamental kinds of basic research. There is evidence and authority for the conclusion that scientific research as organized in the United States, which gives a relatively important place to higher education, has not been unfavorable to the advancement of science. Also, it is well established that higher education has played a major part in the research underlying many technological breakthroughs. Furthermore, judging from studies of the rate of return to investments in research and development generally, and from studies of the role of knowledge in national economic growth, it is probable that the dollar returns to investments in academic science are worth several times the cost. Similarly, research in the social studies has many important practical uses. It provides much of the information by which we monitor social conditions and trends. It has many direct applications to public policy and practical affairs. It helps people to understand society and thus contributes to citizenship. It also helps people to understand themselves. Through enlarging perspectives, it encourages openness to change and counteracts the narrow provincialisms of time and space.

Fifth, philosophical and religious inquiry, social criticism, public policy studies, and cultivation of literature and the fine arts—all functions of higher education—help to define purposes, values, and meanings and thus to enhance civilized existence.

Sixth, public service—which includes such varied activities as medical care, art exhibits, advice to consumers, consultation on public and private problems, production of farm products, and football games—meets many needs of society.

The annual cost of these activities is of the order of $14 billion. Are they worth this outlay? No formula, no measuring stick, no sleight-of-hand will produce the answer. All we have to go on is judgment and common sense based on knowledge of the scope and significance of these activities for our material well-being and our culture. It must be evident to any informed observer that society receives an immense return from its investment in research and public service.

11

Progress Toward Human Equality

Education then, beyond all other devices of human origin, is the great equalizer of the condition of men—the balance-wheel of the social machinery.

Horace Mann

What's the use of a man working hard all his life and trying to get ahead if all he does is wind up equal?

Archie Bunker, *All in the Family*

One of the most compelling beliefs underlying American society is that glaring differences among people in freedom, power, status, and income are wrong and should be ameliorated. Though a reading of the Declaration of Independence or of de Tocqueville tells us that the quest for equality is an old feature of American life, perhaps at no time in the past has equality been pursued so pervasively or intensely as in the present generation. The demand for equality is expressed in the labor movement, the farm movement, the strivings of racial and ethnic groups, the women's movement, political action by the poor, the quest of teenagers for adult status, the gay liberation movement, the attempts to confer civil rights upon children, the

efforts of the handicapped to gain employment, the demand of
the elderly for first-class citizenship and dignity, the occasional
efforts to end discrimination based on physical appearance, and
even the restless assertiveness of prisoners and other institution-
alized persons. Virtually every group that experiences inferiority in social or economic status presses for equality. Responses
to this demand take the form of extending civil rights; outlaw-
ing discrimination based on race, sex, and religion; reforming
the tax system; broadening the coverage of social insurance and
public assistance; subsidizing health services, housing, and food;
and, not least, extending education to persons of all classes.

Education does not automatically mitigate human inequality. It may do so, it may work in the opposite direction, or it
may have little or no effect. The influence of education upon
inequality depends on the social origins of the students, the
numbers being educated, the capacity of the educational programs offered to meet the needs of persons of varying backgrounds and aspirations, and the degree to which egalitarian
ideas are conveyed through the attitudes and values it transmits.

In the United States, education has often been hailed as
the "great equalizer," a means of blurring, if not erasing, social
differences. In fact, though it has not always been at the vanguard of change, higher education has been involved deeply in
the egalitarian movement. For example, barriers to the admission of students and appointment of faculty based on income,
race, sex, and religion, have been lowered steadily. The total
number of students admitted has increased dramatically. The
range of programs offered has been widened to accommodate
people of different interests and aspirations—and also to meet
the changing needs of the economy. Higher education probably
has contributed to an awareness among underprivileged people
that customary social stratification is not inevitable. It has probably helped them to become effective in the political arena by
developing leaders and increasing the political awareness of the
rank and file. Higher education also may have helped to motivate privileged groups to work toward reducing inequality. It
has acquainted them with egalitarian ideas, it has helped them
to become aware of the objective conditions in society leading

to inequality, and it has informed them of proposals for ameliorating inequality. In these ways, many educators and public leaders have hoped and believed that opportunity would become diffused more widely; that inequality in competence, income, privilege, power, and status would be lessened; and that these goals would be achieved through "leveling up" the less privileged rather than "leveling down" the more privileged. Moreover, it was believed that these improvements would become permanent. They would extend to future generations by affecting the ability levels and motivations of the children of educated people; gradually, then, over generations, the cultural level and practical competence of the whole population would be raised and differences among classes lessened.

Recently, however, the idea that the diffusion of higher education would lessen inequality has been subjected to increasing doubt and intense criticism. For example, it has often been noted that the distribution of income has been remarkably stable over time, despite the advancement of higher education. Critics have often alleged that differences in social status, privilege, and power have not narrowed noticeably. Furthermore, it has been argued frequently that, by grading and labeling its students, higher education accentuates rather than reduces differences among persons. Finally, some have argued that persons of the highest ability and highest socioeconomic status receive the most education and profit most from it, and that higher education thus magnifies rather than lessens differences in income and status. Though not wholly consistent with one another, these allegations do raise formidable questions about the efficacy of higher education in reducing inequality. And they place the burden of proof on those who hold that education does promote human equality.[1]

---

[1] In many studies of the effects of higher education on human equality, comparisons are made between the distribution of benefits and the distribution of costs among various classes of the population. In this way, changes in the net position of different classes are calculated. Pechman (1970, 1972) has demonstrated that such studies present great difficulties, not simply because they require that the incidence of both benefits and costs be ascertained—a difficult enough task—but because they also involve

Before launching into our main discussion, it may be well to define equality and inequality as we shall use the terms. A human being may be regarded as a bundle of resources. Initially, these resources consist of a hereditary endowment in the form of physical, mental, and emotional characteristics. Throughout the individual's lifetime but especially in childhood and youth, these hereditary resources are developed and shaped by the person's unique life experiences in the family, the school, the church, the playground, and the workplace and by random events called "luck" or "destiny." The resources resulting from hereditary and environmental influences are *means* that are used by the individual to achieve *ends*, such as freedom, power, status, income, and psychic satisfactions. Though inequality may be considered in relation to either the means or the ends, we focus here on differences among individuals in the attainment of the ends. The several dimensions of inequality may be described as follows: *Freedom* is personal autonomy or choice enjoyed by the individual. *Power* is the influence of the individual over others. *Status* is the social standing of the individual relative to other persons. *Income* is the money or equivalent received by the individual. *Psychic satisfaction* is the inner psychic return people may receive from the whole of their experiences. Wealth and social class are often included among the criteria of social position. In our nomenclature, wealth is a source of power and income, and social class is a derivative of all five dimensions of inequality. In American society, freedom, power, status, income, and psychic satisfaction are all closely interrelated. Conceptually, the social position of an individual may be judged in relation to his or her combined position on

---

comparison of the costs, borne mainly by the people of one generation (taxpayers and parents), with the benefits reaped mainly by people of another generation. We have sidestepped these issues by focusing only on the question of how the distribution of social position within the population might be changed over time through higher education. We have ignored the question of how higher education is financed. Clearly, however, if the financing of higher education is on balance regressive with respect to income, it will tend to offset any egalitarian results from the education itself; conversely, if the financing is progressive, it will tend to enhance any egalitarian thrust of higher education.

the several dimensions of inequality. Thus, in this chapter, inequality among individuals will be defined as the degree of difference in *social position* among individuals or classes, reflecting the combined influence of freedom, power, status, income, and psychic satisfaction. Our main concern is to explore the relation between higher education and differences among people in social position. The degree of inequality of opportunity is seen as one factor determining differences in social position.

A Theory of Equality of Opportunity

In the American quest for human equality, the traditional ideal has been equality of *opportunity*. Education, including higher education, has been regarded as central to the attainment of this ideal. For this reason, we need to explore in some detail the place of education in the striving for equality of opportunity. In this section, we shall try to clarify the concept of equality of opportunity and to explore its relationship to education. We begin with three assumptions:

1. That within any human population, individuals differ with respect to their personal characteristics as derived from their heredity, socioeconomic backgrounds, and unique life experiences.
2. That substantial periods of time are required to bring about significant changes in the nature and extent of these differences; therefore, in the short run, these differences may be regarded as fixed.
3. That the opportunities for social position in the society —as determined by the basic technology, the underlying economic and social organization, and other cultural patterns—are given, and cannot be changed significantly in the short run.

Under these assumptions, people will tend to compete for social position and will be arrayed in hierarchies or classes— as though they occupy places on a huge totem pole on which they are ranked from bottom to top according to social position (Carnegie Commission, 1973c, p. 35). In fact, all modern industrial societies are characterized by such social stratification.

Given these assumptions, if some individuals near the bottom are promoted—for example, if male blacks are admitted in increasing numbers to preferred occupations—they will move up the totem pole. In doing so, they will move above others—perhaps uneducated poor whites—who thereby will be pushed farther down. Recent studies indicate that, in fact, the earnings of blacks have been rising more rapidly than those of whites during recent years when job discrimination has been on the wane (Smith and Welch, 1975; Freeman, 1976). Or, if some white women are admitted to preferred jobs, others—perhaps white men—will thereby be demoted. If all special privilege is stamped out and equal opportunity is extended to everyone, the result will be a general rearrangement of the population as to position on the totem pole. But in the end, the population will be arrayed again from highest to lowest social positions, and the social distance from top to bottom probably will be about as great as before. The process is akin to Pareto's theory of "the circulation of the elite." In the present context, it might better be called the circulation of the underprivileged.

Under the given assumptions, equality of opportunity would simply mean a condition in which all persons would have a fair chance—within the limits of their heredity, socioeconomic background, and unique life experiences—to compete on the basis of performance for a position anywhere along the continuum between highest and lowest social positions. Equality of opportunity would enhance fairness in the terms of competition. It would improve efficiency by placing talent where it is most productive. And it would allow mobility of individuals even if there were no net upward mobility (Bowman, in Solmon and Taubman, 1973, p. 390). These are goals well worth striving for, but, under our assumptions, equality of opportunity by itself would not lessen inequality of condition.

So far, we have assumed as given the hereditary and socioeconomic background of the population. This assumption may be valid in the short run but not in the long run. Let us now relax this assumption by postulating that, over time, the characteristics of the population might be changed. For example, the range of differences among people might be reduced through control of hereditary factors. Persons with known genetic defects of a crippling sort might be required or persuaded not to procreate, and defective genes might be repaired through "genetic engineering." Americans have little enthusiasm for pressing these methods very far, but some reduction in individual differences might be possible by diminishing the number of people with serious genetic defects. The range of differences among persons might be reduced also by overcoming the crippling effects of adverse socioeconomic backgrounds through changes in family and neighborhood influences, improvement in nutrition and health care, strengthening of childhood education, and expansion of higher education. It is true that efforts to ameliorate inequality through correcting socioeconomic disadvantage have not been, up to now, dramatically successful. The indifferent results have been due partly to deficient knowledge, partly to inadequate resources, and partly to the requirement that important gains can only be made by consistent effort over generations, not by sporadic programs over a few years. In view of the long-run possibilities of genetic and socioeconomic improvement, equality of opportunity requires fairness in access to the various *means of human improvement* as well as fairness in the rivalry for social position on the totem pole.

Let us then assume that access to the means of human improvement becomes widely available, so that people differ less than formerly in the resources they bring to the competitive fray. If the range of opportunities the society affords remains unchanged—that is, if technologies, economic and social organization, and cultural patterns are the same as before—then the people competing for the given social positions on the totem pole will end up arrayed as before, except that the relative positions of particular individuals may be changed. Some of those previously privileged in hereditary endowment and socioeconomic background will have dropped down on the totem pole and some of those previously underprivileged will have risen. In the end, the degree of inequality will be the same as before, despite the fact that the individual differences in personal characteristics will have narrowed. Given the assumptions, the society will offer the same degrees of individual freedom, the same positions of power, the same positions of status, the same jobs, the same sources of income, and the same opportunities for psychic satisfaction. In this situation, a population in which the distribution of personal characteristics has been changed must be fitted into an old social structure designed for people with the original pattern of personal characteristics. This state of affairs is illustrated today, after several decades of rapid growth of higher education enrollments, in the disparity between the job expectations of college graduates and the actual jobs some of them are forced to accept (Freeman, 1976).

To assume that the social structure would remain static in the face of significant changes in the characteristics of the population is implausible. Let us then drop the assumption that the basic technology, economic and social organization, and other cultural patterns will remain fixed, and let us assume, instead, that over time they would adjust to changes in the characteristics of the people who make up the society. These adjustments might take any of several forms. The degree of personal freedom might be enlarged and power might become correspondingly less centralized. The increased freedom might affect personal life styles, degree of autonomy in work, and extent of political participation. Authoritarian power in the workplace, the body politic, the university, and the church might be checked. The criteria for status might be broadened to give less importance to money and more to excellence in the arts, learning, professional skill, human relations, and other aspects of human life. The character of work might be changed.

In fact, social changes of this nature have been going on in American society for a long time and have accelerated in recent decades with increased access to education and other means of human improvement. Many menial tasks have been mechanized or eliminated, and professional services have become more widely available and increasingly utilized. Some distribution of income has occurred as the number of persons qualified for the more skilled and demanding jobs has increased and the number of persons willing to engage in menial or routine tasks has declined. Indeed, the expansion of effects of higher education has been so rapid that the social structure has not been able to adjust fully to the new levels of education. A disjunction has arisen between the social structure and the characteristics of the people who make up the society. It is not unreasonable to hope that, over time, this disjunction may be corrected by mutual accommodation between the social structure and the characteristics of the people. As this accommodation occurred, the distribution of the population on the totem pole might become less dispersed. Progress toward human equality might be achieved.

From this analysis of equality of opportunity, we draw three major conclusions:

1. That equality of opportunity in the sense of nondiscrimination in the competition for places on the totem pole will not reduce inequality of social position. It will only rearrange the relative positions of individuals and classes.
2. Equality of opportunity in the sense of equal access to the means of human improvement also will not reduce inequality of social position unless the social structure adapts to the changes in the characteristics of the population. If the social structure does adapt, then changes in the degree of inequality of social position corresponding to changes in individual differences are likely.
3. Because long periods of time are needed to change the distribution of personal characteristics of a population and because even longer periods of time are needed to change the social structure, the effects of education or other means of human improvement must be reckoned in decades or generations, not in years. Much of the disappointment about the effects of programs for human improvement is that people expect quick results (Husén, 1974b).

These conclusions raise two additional questions. First, given equality of access to the means of human improvement, how many people will in fact take advantage of the opportunities that access affords? The answer depends in part on the multiple meanings of "access." At one extreme, it could mean merely formal access on a take-it-or-leave-it basis without assistance or encouragement. At the other extreme, it could mean mandatory participation (as in the case of required school attendance). Between these extremes, access can include such incentives as moral suasion, free or below-cost service, financial aid to defray personal costs, or even financial rewards for participation. For example, to achieve equal access to nursery school or to college may require an elaborate system of subsidies, penalties, rewards, or—possibly—requirements. Moreover, genuinely equal access may require a variety of services suited to different clients and yet of equal efficacy. The number of people who will avail themselves of their opportunities will depend upon the kinds of barriers imposed and incentives offered. Obviously, contemporary American society falls far short of providing true equality of access. Many people cannot or do not take advantage of available opportunities to the same extent as others. Thus, egalitarian trends are held in check. Edward Denison (1971, pp. 7-10) made a trenchant criticism of the present practice in American higher education of concentrating social investment on the more capable students as measured by grades and test scores and slighting the less capable. He advocated (p. 9) "providing equality of public support to all youth, regardless of ability as well as of race and sex." Harrington (1975, p. 94), in commenting on open admissions, observed, "It is the political question of whether or not the society is willing to make the investment required to liberate the intelligence of a large number of young people from the stunting environment in which it is confined."

The second question is this: If there were true equality of access to the means of human development, would this equality result in a narrowing of differences among individuals in their ability to compete for positions on the totem pole? The answer is almost certainly affirmative. If individual differences due to environmental influences were lessened, the population would be clustered closer together on the totem pole. (See Okun,

1975.) Genetic differences almost surely are less than the differences resulting from a combination of genetic and environmental factors.

It must be conceded that American society has made only rudimentary advances in the direction of true equality of opportunity. These efforts have somewhat reduced discrimination on the basis of race, sex, and religion (Freeman, 1976), and they probably have brought about a slight reduction in inequality of opportunity for the whole population. However, the net effect of the nation's policies has been mainly to change the ease of mobility and the rank order of different persons on the totem pole, not to change the dispersion or social distance from top to bottom. This is an accomplishment of no small significance, but it has not reduced inequality of condition very much.

Although efforts to improve the socioeconomic backgrounds of the disadvantaged have been made for generations and have been intensified in the past two decades, the results are far from reassuring; change among the disadvantaged is slow, and gains made among persons at the lower end of the social scale are often matched by gains among persons at the upper end, so that the overall degree of inequality remains unchanged.

Also, immigration—legal and illegal—tends to replace those persons who were formerly at the bottom of the totem pole and who have moved up, thus offsetting the effect of egalitarian policies. To conclude that efforts to improve socioeconomic background of the disadvantaged will not pay off in the long run, however, is premature. The resources devoted to changing socioeconomic conditions and the length of time over which they have been applied have been inadequate in relation to the magnitude of the task. The belief that millions of people can be changed quickly through crash programs with limited resources is patently false. Even with well-conceived programs and adequate resources, significant progress is bound to be slow. Success requires appropriate and diversified methods and adequate resources, applied consistently over several generations. Progress should be measured not in years but in decades or even centuries. Nevertheless, some gains have been achieved (Ribich, 1969). As Levitan and Taggart (1976, pp. 274-275) concluded after a thorough review of the Great Society programs: "The Great Society did not eliminate poverty, but the number of poor was reduced and their deprivation significantly alleviated. The Great Society did not equalize the status of blacks and other minorities, but substantial gains were made which have not been completely eroded. Significant redistribution of income was not achieved or sought, but the disadvantaged and the disenfranchised were helped. The Great Society did not have any magic formula for prosperity, but its policies contributed to the longest period of sustained growth in the nation's history. It did not revamp education, or assure health care for everyone, or feed all the hungry, but as a result of its efforts, the disadvantaged were considerably better educated, fed, and cared for."[2]

Despite the modest gains of recent decades, history teaches us that some skepticism is in order about even the possibility of substantial progress toward equality of condition. Most industrial societies—capitalist and socialist alike—have been characterized by wide dispersion in social position among their people. Inequality of condition has a way of surviving even the most well-intentioned and thoroughgoing welfare programs, educational efforts, religious and moral crusades, and even violent social revolutions. The inertial forces are potent and temporary gains have a way of vanishing in the long run. The idealism behind programs for equality is usually no match for the forces of human avarice, pride, and lust for power. Indeed, some economists and critics hold that progress toward equality of condition should not be pressed too far lest they be achieved at exorbitant cost, or at the expense of cultural and intellectual

---

[2] In two illuminating articles, Paglin (1975) and Browning (1976) have shown that when taxes, transfer payments in money, and transfer payments in kind are taken into account, substantial progress toward equality of income has occurred over the period since World War II. In a companion article, Schiller (1976) has shown that there is much mobility from year to year among persons in the various income classes and that the apparent stability of the distribution of money income conceals great changes in the identity of the particular people who occupy the various income classes. He implies that the distribution of *lifetime* income, rather than the customary annual income, would be a better indicator of the meaningful distribution.

excellence, or at the cost of incentives needed for productivity, or at the risk of government controls that jeopardize freedom (de Jouvenel, 1951; Okun, 1975). Moreover, objective changes in the degree of inequality may not be *perceived* by the population, because people are highly sensitive to differences among them and statistically small differences can be the basis for enormous invidious distinctions. Status probably is judged psychologically by ordinal rather than cardinal numbers. For example, if the ratio of average income in the richest tenth to that in the poorest tenth changed over time from 20:1 to 10:1, the sense of inequality and injustice might not change at all. The "rich" would still be comparatively so far ahead of the "poor" that the perceived social distance from top to bottom would seem very wide.

Though social equality may be elusive, human beings have a saintly side that values brotherhood, charity, and justice. The egalitarian thrust in contemporary society expresses this altruistic side of human nature. It calls on the rich, the proud, and the powerful to share with the poor, the lowly, and the weak, and it entitles the latter to press for brotherhood and justice. And it calls upon all to seek equality in the faith that greater justice—both in fact and in perception—is possible and that justice can be reconciled with cultural excellence, incentives for productivity, and freedom. The call is especially compelling for educators.

Education and Human Equality

The main conclusion from our sortie into the theory of equality of opportunity is that greater equality of access to the means of human improvement would lessen individual differences in ability to compete for social position on the totem pole and therefore would ultimately lessen inequality of condition. One of the most important means to human improvement is education at all levels. Education carries within it the possibility of reducing the differences among people; it is one instrument, among many others, for combatting inequality among persons or classes.

In the recent past, the efforts to raise up people at the lower end of the scale through education seem to have lessened inequality very little, because people at the upper end of the scale also were advancing and differences remained about the same. But the recent past has been a transitional period. What occurred then was not true of the distant past and will probably will not be true of the future.

The development of education in the United States may be viewed in three stages. The first stage was typified by the American frontier, where differences in education were small because no one had very much. With few exceptions, the range was from illiteracy to fourth grade. There were differences, of course, in other aspects of socioeconomic background and in learning from experience. But differences in formal education were on the whole quite small.

The second stage, covering the period from perhaps 1920 to 2000 and through which we are now passing, is a period in which at least some elementary education has been extended to virtually all the population, secondary education has been extended to a majority of the people, and advanced graduate and professional education have been growing rapidly. During this stage, differences among people in educational level have become very great and have been accentuated by a steady flow of immigrants, many of whom have little education. The population is now arrayed from illiterates to persons with Ph.D.s and M.D.s, with many persons at every intermediate level, including elementary school, high school, and college. During the second stage, the whole population has not been advancing together in educational level, one grade at a time. Rather, the educational level of young people has increased rapidly, while that of old people has not changed; the educational progress of some groups of young people has been much more rapid than that of others, the difference being related in large part to differences in socioeconomic background, including race. And large numbers of immigrants of low educational attainment have steadily filled in at the bottom of the educational ladder. The result is a very unequal distribution of educational attainment.[3]

---

[3]Heilbroner (1976, p. 70) properly warns that "it would be hasty to jump from the fact of a larger 'quantity' of education bestowed upon the labor force to the conclusion that the stock of 'knowledge' of society has increased in like degree."

We now may be slowly approaching a third stage, in which virtually the entire population will have completed several years of high school, and a half to two thirds will have attended college. Thus differences in educational attainment can be expected to diminish over the next several decades.

The two-century trend is illustrated in Table 49. Education was probably rather equally distributed at Stage I in that

Table 49. Percentage distributions of the adult population by years of formal education, 1825-2025

	Grade School			High School		College		
	0-4	*5-7*	*8*	*9-11*	*12*	*13-15*	*16 or more*	*Total*
Stage I (1825—hypothetical)	80	10	5	3	1	0.5	0.5	100
Stage II (1975)	4	7	10	16	36	12	14	100
Stage III (2025 or later—hypothetical)	0	1	2	7	30	25	35	100

most of the population had very little of it; it will probably again be distributed quite equally at Stage III in the future, when most of the population will have a great deal of it; but at present, in the transitional Stage II, differences in educational level have been and will continue to be very great.[4] The process of raising the educational level of a whole population cannot be accomplished quickly. It must be carried out over several gen-

[4]There are several ways of comparing the degree of inequality of various distributions. The most common uses the Lorenz curve. This arrays the population in classes from those having the least amount of the object under discussion (for example, income or education) to those having the greatest amount. It then compares the cumulative numbers of the population with the cumulative amount of the object. Using Lorenz curves, the distribution of education has become more equal over the years. This, however, compares *amounts* of education, not *levels* of education. In our opinion, the more relevant comparison relates to levels of education. On this basis, dispersion among the several educational levels is the appropriate measure of inequality. Clearly, using our hypothetical data, the dispersion is greater in 1975 than in either 1825 or 2025. On the problems of comparing the degrees of inequality for various distributions, see Boulding (in Smith, 1975, pp. 15-19).

erations. One of the costs of going through Stage II is a widening of educational differences and of concomitant differences in social position. Little wonder that human inequality is a major social issue today. As the figures in Table 50 clearly show, the

Table 50. Distribution of adult population (25 years of age and over) by educational attainment, 1940-1990

	Grade School			High School		College		
	0-4	*5-7*	*8*	*9-11*	*12*	*13-15*	*16 or more*	*Total*
1940	14%	18%	28%	15%	14%	5%	5%	100
1950	11	16	21	18	21	7	6	100
1960	8	14	18	19	25	9	8	100
1970	5	9	13	17	34	10	11	100
1975	4	7	10	16	36	12	14	100
1980 (projected)	3	6	9	17	38	12	14	100
1990 (projected)	2	4	6	15	40	15	18	100

Source: U.S. Bureau of the Census, *Statistical Abstract of the United States* (1964, p. 113; 1973, pp. 114, 117); *Educational Attainment in the United States:* March 1975, Current Population Reports, Series P-20, No. 296, 1976; p. 60. The projections are those of the U.S. Bureau of the Census.

process of transition by which the population is changing from Stage II, one of very unequal educational level, to Stage III, one of high and fairly equal educational level. The transitional Stage II is something the society must go through in the process of moving from a generally low to a generally high educational level.

It may be supposed that the transitional Stage II will go on indefinitely—that as the average level of education rises, more people will seek advanced degrees and recurrent adult education. This supposition may be correct to a degree (Thurow, 1975, pp. 75-97). However, formal education, like any other use of resources, is subject to diminishing returns. As a person's educational level is raised, the incremental gains in desired abilities, traits, and skills tend to diminish. A person cannot "improve" himself or herself very much by going on and on to school or college indefinitely. Diminishing returns are also manifest when advanced education is extended to more people. On the one hand as enrollments expand, the additional students drawn into the higher educational system may have less academic ability and motivation than those previously in college, and the returns to their education may be less. On the other hand, as enrollments expand, the supply of college-educated people available for the preferred ranks in society increases and the returns to people in these ranks—in the form of earnings, freedom, power, status, and psychic satisfaction—tend to fall; correspondingly, the number of less-educated people available for the less desirable ranks declines and their returns rise. These effects are seen clearly in the case of personal earnings. With few exceptions, the rate of return on investments in education is lower at the secondary level than at the primary level, lower at the college level than at the secondary level, and lower at the graduate than at the college level. The reason for this diminishing effect is that the rudiments of literacy and numeracy acquired in elementary school are absolutely essential for functioning in our society and that, at each subsequent stage, the costs of education rise and the relative importance of what is added declines (Schultz, 1972; Marin and Psacharopoulos, 1976).

The monetary return to investments in higher education probably has declined in recent years. Freeman (1976, pp. 26, 204), using various methods of computation, shows that the rate of return in 1968, which was in the range of 10 to 13 percent, had fallen by 1973 to 7 to 10 percent. The recent decline is not necessarily due exclusively to diminishing returns, ordinarily a gradual influence. Indeed, the effect of diminishing returns has probably been obscured during the period since World War II by large increases in demand for college-educated people due to technological changes (for example, the introduction of computers), governmental activities (for example, the space program), demographic changes (for example, the increased birth rate leading to a huge demand for teachers). In recent years, these influences have subsided, and the number of college-educated people entering the labor market has increased substantially at the same time. The result has been a fairly sudden decline in returns on college education.

In Stage III, as differences in educational attainment within the population become narrower, one would expect that the role of higher education in grading and labeling people for job placement might become less important. For example, if almost everyone were a high school graduate and large numbers had college degrees, then these particular credentials would lose much of their significance for discriminating among persons. Specific qualifications relating less closely to formal education would become more important. It is possible, however, that the relevant credentials would become not degrees but "quality" of institutions attended, particular subjects studied, and grades earned.

To conclude, as America progresses toward Stage III in the educational attainment of its population, inequality of social position could be ameliorated. This is a *potential* long-range outcome of higher education, not an already realized or near-term outcome (see Vaizey, 1962; Thurow, 1975). However, if the spread of higher education is curtailed, as is often advocated on grounds that there are not enough jobs of the kind traditionally reserved for the college-educated, then present differences in educational level will be maintained and the present degree of inequality will tend to persist. Unless the growth of higher education proceeds, the American dream of equality through education will have been effectively frustrated. If America is sincerely egalitarian, it will carry on the long tradition of extending higher education to ever-increasing numbers. To maintain the situation at Stage II would tend to perpetuate the present degree of inequality (Carnegie Commission, 1970; Wren, 1975).

Higher Education and the Distribution of Income

The view that the spread of higher education may be expected to bring about a leveling of differences in social position has gained considerable, if not universal, acceptance. Most of the discussion of the subject has been focused on money income or earnings (rather than the more vague notion of "social position"). What may be the prevailing opinion was expressed by the Carnegie Commission (1973c, pp. 34-35) in terms reminiscent of our totem pole:

> Higher education is a major means by which individuals seek to locate themselves and do locate themselves among the income classes, some moving up and others moving down; by which they vary their locations from those held by their parents; by which ability and interest rather than inheritance determine location. Thus higher education is more important to equality of individual opportunity in finding a place among the established occupational and income classes, than it is in closing remuneration gaps among these classes—even though it also does this in the long run. . . . Higher education . . . reduces the scarcity of highly trained manpower and thus, slowly over time and through the imperfect operations of the labor market, diminishes the premiums paid for such skill. It educates people out of reliance on common labor for an income, and thus, by creating a scarcity of people willing to do disagreeable manual work, slowly raises the comparative compensation paid to them. The inevitable consequence is a narrowing of differentials in income originating from employment.

Schultz (1972, pp. 6-10) shared this view. He noted a slow secular trend toward equality in the distribution of income and attributed it to increasing investment in "human capital" relative to investment in physical capital. He noted that the trend toward equality had slowed down in the postwar years. This he attributed to the growth of demand for educated people owing to the rapidly increasing use of knowledge in production. He implied that he expected diminishing returns from education to reappear in the future and for the trend toward equality to be resumed.

Chiswick and Mincer (in Schultz, 1972) concurred with Schultz's assessment. In explaining long-term changes in income distribution, they concluded that the most significant variables were the composition of the population with respect to education, age, and employment. They found that income distribution during the period from 1939 to the early postwar years had been becoming more equal but that thereafter it had remained unchanged. They explained the negligible influence of education during the postwar years by the *distribution* of education among the population, which remained fairly constant. Chiswick and Mincer concluded, however, that inequality of income might be ameliorated in the future by a decline in the rate of return to education as the relative number of educated people in the population increased. Their argument was that the distribution of education among the population was nearly constant at Stage II but that, with the approach of Stage III, the distribution of education would become more equal and consequently the distribution of earnings also would tend to equalize.[5]

The view expressed by the Carnegie Commission, Schultz, and Chiswick and Mincer is based on the marginal productivity theory of wages—namely, that the earnings of each worker will be determined in the long run by the money value of his incremental addition to product. According to this theory, if the supply of a given type of labor is increased, the marginal product of that labor will fall (partly because of diminishing returns and partly because of the increased supply of its product); employers will then pay lower wages to that class of labor. Thus, an increase in the relative number of college-educated people would bring about a reduction in their per capita earnings in the long run.

[5] Colin Clark (1957, pp. 521, 542-555) assembled data from various countries showing secular trends toward reduced relative earnings for white-collar workers associated with the expansion of education. Brittain (1977, p. 5) concluded on the basis of empirical studies that "despite the substantial influence of his background on a man's chance of economic success, public policies aimed at reducing the inequality of educational attainment would have an independent effect alleviating the inequality of economic status." Similarly, Marin and Psacharopoulos (1976) concluded on the basis of data for the United States and Mexico that income inequality may be lessened as a population's education increases. They attribute this effect to the well-known decline in returns to education as the level of education rises.

This line of reasoning has been subject to criticism in recent years, and several alternative labor market theories have been advanced (Rivlin, 1975a, pp. 8-11). One such alternative theory is simply that education has no relation to income except for the coincidence that the personal qualities that enable people to succeed in education are the very same qualities that enable them to succeed in work (Arrow, 1973). Education, in this view, merely provides credentials on the basis of which employers can select workers for various jobs. Thurow (1975) proposed to replace the marginal productivity theory of wages with a "job-competition" model based on several novel assumptions about the labor market: (1) that most skills are learned on the job and employment is essentially an offer of an opportunity to be trained; (2) that employers have a strong incentive to maintain a stable work force with continuity and low turnover and that adjusting wages and employment to changing market conditions is contrary to the interests of employers; (3) that the work force may be regarded as a vast queue in which the workers are arrayed from least trainable to most trainable; (4) that the preferred workers in terms of trainability get the best jobs, and these tend to be the workers with the most education; (5) that the wage structure (the pattern of relative wages for different occupations) tends to remain constant over time because deviations from the established wage structure are unsettling to the labor force.

With these assumptions, Thurow (p. 119) concluded: "A larger supply of college workers would extend the college work force farther down the distribution of job opportunities. In the process the average college wage would fall. With more college workers, high school workers and grade school workers would be forced farther down the distribution of job opportunities and their average wages would also fall. Changes in relative earnings would depend upon the shape of the earnings distribution and the changes in net earnings due to lower training costs . . . the entire distribution of earnings might become more or less equal."

The Thurow hypothesis is intriguing; it may well help to explain the behavior of earnings as related to education in the short run. However, it is based on data for the years 1950 to 1970—a relatively short period on which to base a theory of income distribution. Moreover, during this period, the *distribution* of educational attainment changed very little (as suggested by Chiswick and Mincer), and the demand for educated workers increased because of the rapid growth in applications of knowledge to production (as suggested by Schultz). The data, then, are not necessarily inconsistent with the marginal productivity theory. Moreover, Thurow's concept of trainability is not unlike the concept of productivity. Indeed, his theory might be called the marginal trainability theory of wages. The Thurow hypothesis implicitly assumes that available jobs do not change with changes in the characteristics of the working population. This may be a valid picture of reality in the short run, but it is scarcely plausible in the long run. There is the further assumption that the wage structure is stable over time. This also may be true only in the short run.

These considerations suggest some caution in accepting Thurow's conclusions for the long run. Thurow might respond by invoking Lord Keynes' dictum, "In the long run we are all dead." However, when the subject under study is the effect of education on the distribution of income the only "run" that is relevant is the long run. Fundamental changes in the characteristics of populations can occur only over generations, not decades. Admittedly, there are powerful institutional and attitudinal obstacles to change in income distribution. We see them today in the tendency to shut off the expansion of higher education as the earnings of college graduates begin to decline. But over historic eras, profound social changes do occur, and there is no reason to suppose that the extension of higher education to a larger portion of the population would not have significant influence, not only on the distribution of income but also on many other features of social life. Perhaps the most telling criticism of Thurow's hypothesis is that, within the past several years, the relative earnings of college graduates have in fact begun to decline (Freeman, 1976). In commenting on the decline, Freeman (pp. 189-190) observed: "Income distribution is likely to become more egalitarian as a result of the relative surplus of the educated. . . . While detailed calculations are needed to measure the impact, inequality in incomes among workers is likely to diminish."

Educability

A common argument against the theory that the spread of higher education would work toward equalization of incomes is that only a fraction of the population, perhaps a small minority, is qualified for higher learning. On this assumption, higher education inevitably would accentuate differences among various classes of the population by adding to the competence of the most capable people and leaving the masses of people untouched. Higher education has functioned this way in the past, but it need not do so in the future. If the general educational attainment of the population could be raised to the level of Stage III—a large majority college-educated and most of the rest having completed high school—then the effect of education would be strongly egalitarian. But are abilities so distributed that the achievement of Stage III is feasible?

On the basis of data from the Army General Classification Test, the President's Commission on Higher Education (1947, pp. 40-41) judged that, in 1947, "1. At least 49 percent of our population has the mental ability to complete at least 14 years of schooling with a curriculum of general and vocational studies that should lead either to gainful employment or to further study at a more advanced level. 2. At least 32 percent of our population has the mental ability to complete an advanced liberal or specialized professional education." The Commission added that a wide variety of institutions and programs would be needed to accommodate youth in these numbers.

Differences in "scholastic aptitude" are due in part to socioeconomic background (Guilford, 1967, p. 468), not merely to inherent hereditary differences—though the latter undoubtedly have a substantial effect. Moreover, abilities develop with use. Thus, as standards of living have risen and secondary education has expanded, the percentage of the population with ability up to college admissions standards has probably grown steadily. Taubman and Wales (1972) collected data on average ability (IQ) levels of high school graduates who entered college over the period 1925 to 1961. They found that despite the enormous growth in college enrollment over this period, the average ability level of those entering college rose from the 53rd to the 62nd percentile of all high school graduates. The authors concluded (p. 19): "On the basis of these data it is apparent that the quality of college students has not declined. In fact, throughout this period of forty years, during which a substantially greater percentage of high school graduates entered college, it has even noticeably increased." Since the turn of the century, "intelligence" tests have been administered periodically to large samples of the American population. The average scores have risen consistently over time—suggesting that environmental influences are steadily pushing up ability levels. For example, the Educational Testing Service assembled 186 cases of tests given during the decades of the 1950s and 1960s to comparable groups at different times. In all but ten of these cases, those taking the tests later scored higher than the comparable earlier groups (U.S. Department of Health, Education, and Welfare, *Toward a Social Report,* 1969b, p. 67). Husén (1974b, p. 141) expressed the view, on the basis of past experience, that "we can expect the average 18 to 20 year old person in Europe of the year 2000 to score at least 110 on the IQ scale of the 1960s." A similar view was expressed by Schwebel (1968, pp. 207-214). He judged (following Bloom, 1964) that with an "abundant environment" two thirds of the population would have an IQ of 105 or higher, with the average IQ considerably above 105. He concluded (p. 212): "The fact is that educability is not a finite quality; its limits are unknown." Schwebel pointed out that, with an IQ of 105, a student has a 50-50 chance of graduating from high school; with an IQ of 110, he has a 50-50 chance of graduating from college. The average IQ of college graduates is 120 and of persons receiving the Ph.D., 130.

A fact that may cast doubt on the likelihood of future increases in academic ability is the recent and highly publicized decline in scores on college entrance examinations. The reasons for the decline are not well understood. It is to be hoped that investigations now under way will dispel the mystery. The decline may be due to changes in elementary and secondary education; to changes in modes of communication giving greater emphasis to television, radio, and stereo and less to the written word; to the nature of the tests; to the increasing divorce rate; to changes in the size of families and spacing of children; to changes in the population of students attending college; to general social malaise. The decline in SAT scores probably is not due to the fact that we have reached a ceiling on academic aptitude. Had this been the case, the scores would slowly have leveled off, not declined.[6]

More persuasive is the clear-cut evidence that millions of young people who are not attending college are more capable, actually or potentially, than many who are. For example, 930,000 fewer women than men were in college as degree-credit students in 1975 (American Council on Education, *A Fact Book on Higher Education*, 2nd issue, 1975, p. 64).[7] The relative number of low-income persons attending is far below that for high-income persons. Only 15 percent of persons eighteen to twenty-four years of age from very low-income families were attending in 1972, as compared with 56 percent of those from families with incomes over $15,000 (National Commission on the Financing of Postsecondary Education, 1973, p. 27). The relatively low enrollments among Chicanos is well known. Similarly, there are surprisingly wide variations among the states in college attendance. To mention the extremes, in Arkansas, Alaska, and Georgia 25 percent of persons eighteen to twenty-four years of age are in college; in Oregon, California, Utah, and Arizona, the student population is more than 50 percent of the eighteen-to-twenty-four-year-old group (Carnegie Commission on Higher Education, 1973b, pp. 101-102). The experience of higher education with students beyond the usual college age also suggests that there are many academically able people

[6]I have benefited from correspondence with Leo Munday of American College Testing Program regarding the decline in test scores.

[7]Including degree-credit and non-degree credit students, there were 1,133,000 fewer women than men attending.

in the population who have not attended college. For example, educators learned from the GIs following World War II (and from older adult students generally) that many people who had not been motivated or "ready" for higher education in their teens become capable students after achieving some maturity.

On the basis of his review of the evidence, Schultz (1972, pp. 16-17) summed up the matter as follows: "the *proportion* of youth of college age who have this capacity to learn *increases* as relatively more of the members of this age group benefit from precollege investments that add to their acquired ability. At some point, however, as this process continues, the innate abilities that are required to benefit from college work will become exhausted. But it is hard to believe that we are close to this point . . . the supply of the relatively high level of innate ability distributed among the college-age population is as yet less scarce than the supply of acquired abilities that is necessary to a sufficient capacity to learn enough to warrant the investment in college work."

Marxists often suggest that individual differences are largely due to environmental factors, most of which ultimately would be removed in a classless society. Levitas (1974), for example, rejects the notion that the number of educable persons is significantly limited and argues that all but a tiny minority with obvious genetic defects can learn to use their minds. Gartner, Greer, and Riessman (1974) offer trenchant criticisms of intelligence tests as measures of critical abilities. Without going to the Marxist extreme, which seems clearly contrary to evidence about hereditary influences—evidence derived, for example, from studies of twins (Taubman, 1976a, 1976b; Nichols and Loehlin, 1976)—data on the distribution of abilities within the population and the facts concerning present college attendance strongly suggest that the achievement of Stage III by 2025 is not unattainable. At this stage, 60 percent of the population would have had some college education and another 37 percent would have had some high school education (and, of the latter, most would have graduated).

In considering the educability of the population, one must recognize that the percentage qualified will depend on the prevailing conception of higher learning. That conception has been expanding steadily as the nation has moved from a classical education characteristic of the nineteenth century to an education that encompasses natural sciences, social studies, many interdisciplinary fields, and many professional and vocational areas. The conception has been expanding also as methods of instruction have been diversified to include various forms of independent study, self-paced learning, internships, experiential learning, mechanized instruction, and so on. And the prevailing idea of higher learning has been broadening as higher education has become increasingly available to part-time students of all ages according to their readiness to learn, the circumstances of their lives, and convenience of time and place. There are possibilities of enlarging the conception even further. Higher education is still mainly centered on the learning of abstract ideas of a kind that can be expressed in written or spoken words. If greater recognition were to be given to the development of interpersonal skills and of ability to work with things—as well as the ability to deal with abstract knowledge—higher education would be broadened still further and would serve an increasing percentage of the population. Patricia Cross, in her books *Beyond the Open Door* (1971) and *Accent on Learning* (1976), eloquently elaborated this theme. In an address given in 1974, she said: "If we persist in thinking that the ability to perform academic tasks is a measure of human worth, then we face the prospect of creating a new group of 'disadvantaged' that consists not necessarily of minority groups or poor people, but of all those from any stratum of society with below-average academic aptitude.... We must begin now to look beyond academic ability as the sole determiner of human contribution. There are other talents of equal importance in creating a humane society." She then suggested that education for all students should be concerned with the three domains—knowledge, people, and things—but that each student might choose one domain in which to concentrate and excel.

The same concept has been enunciated by many other writers. For example, John Gardner (1961, pp. 131-132) wrote: "A conception which embraces many kinds of excellence at many levels is the only one which fully accords with the richly varied potentialities of mankind; it is the only one which will permit high morale throughout the society." Schrag (1970, p. 93) sounded the same theme: "By definition, no society with but one avenue of approved entry into the mainstream of dignity can be fully open. When that single instrument of entry is charged with selecting people out, and when there are no honorable alternatives for those who are selected out, we are promising to all men things that we cannot deliver." Okun (1975, p. 87), in the same vein, remarked: "Many participants now measure their success in dimensions other than money incomes. Harvard professors hardly feel inferior to the president of U.S. Steel. Nor do sculptors feel inferior to college professors. The same self-respect can extend to good landscape gardeners and good plumbers, to mothers who prefer full-time home management, and to those who delegate home management in order to earn paychecks. Society can run contests without adding to frustration, so long as people engage in many contests and use many criteria to judge their own contributions. The more criteria they employ, the more they will tend to give themselves high grades. And that is good for self-respect." Brim and others (1969, p. 6) warned that the standardized tests by which entry to college is regulated and student achievement evaluated may foster conformity, penalize unusual or creative talents, and set arbitrary standards based on the range of abilities within the population at a given point in history. They asked: "Do these standardized tests available for measurement of abilities have a narrow range of application, selecting, so to speak, only a small portion of talent (say, verbal fluency) from the broader spectrum of human abilities which might include imagination, creativity, or artistic gifts; with the consequence that the recruitment, selection, and training of persons in the United States favors a group with only a single type of ability?" Brim and his colleagues added that the wide use of tests may set arbitrary standards based on the range of abilities within the population at a given point in history and may obscure "the true limits of human abilities . . . and severely restrict our aspirations about the heights to which human intelligence might be brought." (See Husén, 1974b, pp. 25, 95-101, 127; Ginzberg, 1974, p. 40.) Some Marxists hold the view that distinctions between mental and physical labor will cease to have meaning in a classless communist society and that education will eventually also drop this distinction (Levitas, 1974).

Academic conservatives (like the authors of this book) may recoil from a kind of higher education that would encompass every conceivable human activity and interest and that would not assign first place to academic excellence as historically and conventionally defined. Conservatives argue that liberal learning should be the firm foundation on which the entire higher education edifice should rest. As we understand Dr. Cross's position, she would agree. In addition, she would probably point out that there is growing support for the view that liberal learning could be acquired by a vast majority of people. Benjamin Bloom is perhaps the leading exponent of this view (Bloom, 1968; Bloom, Hastings, and Madaus, 1971). Bloom (1968), following Carroll, argued that "aptitude is the amount of time required by the learner to attain mastery of a given task," and "given sufficient time (and appropriate types of help), 95 percent of students . . . can learn a subject up to a high level of mastery." He concluded: "Most students can master what we have to teach them, and it is the task of instruction to find the means which will enable our students to master the subject under consideration. Our basic task is to determine what we mean by mastery of the subject and to search for the methods and materials which will enable the largest proportion of our students to attain such mastery. . . . One basic problem for a mastery learning strategy is to find ways of reducing the amount of time required for the slower students to a point where it is no longer a prohibitively long and difficult task for these less able students . . . individual students may need very different types and qualities of instruction to achieve mastery."

From quite a different perspective, Robert M. Hutchins (1974, p. 32) argued that a near-universal liberal education would be practicable. He wrote: "I have always thought that the basic requirement for the formation of a political community is a common liberal education. The liberal arts are the arts of communication and the arts of using the mind. They are the arts indispensable to further learning. . . . They have a timeless quality, for they are indispensable no matter what happens in any state of the world. . . . I believe in liberal education for everybody. Nor have I ever seen any evidence that it is beyond the reach of everybody, nor any evidence that educational institutions are incapable of imparting it if only they will, but they don't." (Compare Bruner, 1960; Cremin, 1965.)

Our judgment on these matters is that the ideal of liberal learning in some depth for everyone, or nearly everyone, is an admirable objective but the hope of attaining it—in the foreseeable future—is utopian. With a broadening of the content of higher education and with diverse methods of instruction suited to students of varied characteristics, however, it is by no means visionary to look forward to the time when as many as 60 percent of the population will have had some college education as projected in Stage III (see Russell, 1965, pp. 67, 80-83 and McGrath, 1975, pp. 45-47).

In considering future possibilities, one must remember that higher education is now at Stage II, where differences in educational attainment within the population are at a maximum. One of the main tasks of higher education in this stage is to induct many first-generation students into the secondary and higher educational systems and thus into the mainstream of American society. As this process goes on, differences in the educational attainment of the population will be narrowed. Future generations of students will become gradually less diverse, and educational programs can become correspondingly less varied. It is of the utmost importance for educational policy that the present system of higher education be recognized as a transitional one, designed for a nation that is moving from elitist to mass to universal higher education, and not a final form designed for a society in which educational levels will be higher on the average and more equal (see Trow, 1974b).

A concept of Ruth Benedict is useful in considering the scope or range of interests encompassed by higher education. She pointed out, with reference to the total culture of a society, that social life presents innumerable possibilities in the form of interests, behavior patterns, values, and attitudes. Each culture must confine itself to those that it can manage. As she said (1959, p. 24):

> In culture too we must imagine a great arc on which are ranged the possible interests provided either by the human age-cycle or by the environment or by man's various activities. A culture that capitalized even a considerable proportion of these would be as unintelligible as a language that used all the clicks, all the glottal stops, all the labials, dentals, sibilants, and gutturals from voiceless to voiced and from oral to nasal. Its identity as a culture depends upon the selection of some segments of this arc. Every human society everywhere has made such selection in its cultural institutions. Each from the point of view of another ignores fundamentals and exploits irrelevancies. One culture hardly recognizes monetary values; another has made them fundamental in every field of behavior. In one society technology is unbelievably slighted even in those aspects of life which seem necessary to ensure survival; in another, equally simple, technological achievements are complex and fitted with admirable nicety to the situation. One builds an enormous cultural superstructure upon adolescence, one upon death, one upon after-life.

As Benedict (pp. 251-277) observed, the great cultural arc cannot encompass every interest and every temperament; otherwise the society would lose its coherence and integrity. But the range of permitted interests need not be so narrow as to condemn large numbers of people to the role of deviants or misfits. If differences are measured in terms of a single criterion, such as income, differences are bound to be pronounced. But if other qualities are valued along with income—values such as learning, moral virtue, religious commitment, sociability, talent for art and handicrafts, green thumb, patriotism, civic participation, athletic ability, mechanical skill, and adventurous spirit—then overall inequality can be lessened and the potential incompatibility between equality and excellence can be reconciled.

If education serves people of varying talents, if it helps them to discover their interests, and if it assists them in developing along lines compatible with their individual interests, then education can be an instrument for widening the range of human expression and reducing inequality among persons. It is through extending the cultural arc, through broadening the dimensions of human worth, that higher education can help to reconcile equality and excellence.

A final comment concerning actual versus perceived inequality is in order. Actual inequality is measured by the objective differences among people in freedom, power, status, income, and psychic satisfactions. Perceived inequality is measured by these same differences as *sensed* by these people. Actual and perceived inequality may not be the same. Progress in objective conditions may not enhance the sense of social justice or ameliorate envy and division among people unless these changes are perceived and understood by the persons affected.

Also, progress toward equality of condition is likely to involve sacrifice of values such as freedom, economic efficiency, and cultural excellence (Okun, 1975; de Jouvenel, 1951). To the extent that the trade-offs among various fundamental values are understood, people might accept some degree of inequality without a concomitant sense of injustice. Education, especially higher education based on liberal learning, should contribute toward greater knowledge of the objective facts about inequality and greater appreciation of multiple social goals, of which greater justice in the distribution of freedom, power, status, income, and psychic satisfaction is only one.

Conclusions

The discussion in this chapter leads to skepticism about the conclusion that past higher education has brought about a narrowing of the differences among people with respect to their social positions. Indeed, higher education may have widened these differences, since it mainly has served people who were already relatively privileged and has enhanced their advantages. We have argued, however, that if higher education were extended to more people and if it were changed to serve students of increasingly diverse backgrounds, it could become an instrument for eventual progress toward egalitarian objectives. That is, higher education has the capacity to influence the degree of human equality or inequality (as to freedom, power, status, income, and psychic satisfactions), and this capacity could be used to reduce inequality. It could also be used, however, to maintain the status quo or to increase inequality.

Marxist critics argue that in a capitalist society, higher education is unlikely to be used for egalitarian ends, rather that it will probably be used to maintain present inequalities in the distribution of social position from the bottom to the top of the totem pole (Bowles and Gintis, 1976). They hold that only through a fundamental restructuring of society can egalitarian hopes be realized. Only then would education become one of the instruments for bringing about a narrowing of human differences. Others hold that widespread higher education would not reduce inequality but would only shift the criteria by which inequality is measured.

Our conclusion is more hopeful. It is that a democratic-capitalist society could use education at all levels (including especially higher education) as one means of gradually reducing inequality of the human condition. There is at least a good chance that it can be effective within the prevailing democratic-capitalist system without a radical overhauling of the social structure. As the number of persons with higher education steadily increases relative to the number with less education, the earnings and status of the more educated can be expected to fall and of the less educated to rise. It should be no surprise that truck drivers and coal miners are paid more than teachers or junior bank officers or that people with college education find their way into blue-collar work. There is an old saying that "education raises the earnings of the uneducated." The obverse is that it lowers the relative earnings and status of the educated. This result is exactly what a society that proclaims egalitarian values should hope for and work for.

In the long run, education could be an effective and acceptable means for changing the distribution of social position. Because of its possible carry-over to future generations, its impact may be multiplied over time. It may produce valuable side effects both for individuals and for society. It may stimulate economic growth and thus generate the revenue to pay for further increments of education. It may avoid the dependence and the stigma attached to welfare and other more direct forms of income distribution. And most important of all, education may enhance the general culture and quality of life.

Education need not be the sole or even the main social instrument for achieving egalitarian ends. It is only one of several possibilities, among them progressive taxation, transfer payments, distribution of goods in kind, and others. But it is superior to these other possibilities in that it not only changes what people get but also what they can contribute and what they are.

12 Gordon K. Douglass

Economic Returns on Investments in Higher Education

Nothing in modern economics is more speculative than quantitative empirical research.

Fritz Machlup (1970, p. 10)

The preceding chapter reviewed evidence on the outcomes of American higher education in terms of social equality and inequality. This chapter examines outcomes in terms of economic returns to investments as revealed through the methods and the data of economics. Generally, economists have focused on those effects of higher education which are measurable in money—those which produce money income to individuals or yield higher levels of gross national product for society. Admittedly, these results leave out some very important outcomes that are not reflected in market transactions and cannot be measured in money. Nevertheless, the perspective of economics adds a useful dimension to the study of higher educational effects. Moreover, economists are beginning to venture beyond the realm of market phenomena and to produce results that do not depend on monetary measurement. In this chapter, we shall review and assess the findings of economists about both monetary and nonmonetary returns on higher education.

Interest of economists in the effects of higher education can be traced historically at least to the writings of Adam Smith, who commented in some detail on the social and economic benefits of education. But intense professional interest in the economics of education did not truly begin until about 1960, when empirical investigations of the American economy confirmed that the output of goods and services had been growing much more rapidly than the quantity of labor, capital, and materials used to produce it. This difference in the values of input and output came to be known as the "residual," and was variously ascribed to advances in knowledge, enlargement of markets, education of the labor force, and other "growth-producing" factors. This finding led to attempts to estimate empirically the effect on output of changes in each potential source of the residual, including college education, and it was only a small step from there to begin trying to estimate the monetary payoff from investments in higher education and in other means of building "human capital."

Physical and Human Capital

The concept of human capital is in all respects analogous to the economist's traditional concept of physical capital. Physical capital, in the lexicon of economists, includes all useful physical assets—other than unimproved land and natural raw materials—that are used in the production of goods and services. Thus turret lathes and fork-lift trucks, factory smoke stacks and office towers, warehouse supplies and dwelling units all are classed as capital. These man-made assets are valuable because they enhance "productivity," that is, the volume of real output per unit of productive input.

When new capital is formed, economists say that "investment" takes place. Investment is the act of committing resources to the production of producer goods rather than consumer goods. It may take the form of business decisions to replace worn-out or obsolete old capital, or it may involve net additions to the capital stock, as when inventories expand or new real estate subdivisions are created. Society's capital stock may be compared with a lake and its stream system. The lake is like the capital stock, a body of productive assets that can rise or fall, depending upon the rate new assets are being accumulated and old assets are becoming valueless. The flow of water from the inlet is analogous to investment; the flow of water from the outlet is comparable to depreciation and obsolescence. If the pool of capital assets receives more inflow than outflow, it grows in size and productive power. If the stream of new investments falls short of the wearing-out rate of existing capital stock, the capital stock is diminished.

Capital assets have finite working lives. They come into the working force through the process of production, they serve for a period of time, and then leave it through depreciation and retirement. During the period of productive life, capital assets are employed in quite specific ways to help produce goods and services. Some have longer productive lives than others because they are more efficient or wear out more slowly, but all eventually lose their vitality and usefulness.

Capital assets yield over their productive lifetimes a stream of earnings equivalent to their contribution to the value of output produced. Their "wages" tend to be equal to their "marginal productivity." Suppose, for example, that a piece of capital equipment could be purchased today for $1,000 and that, over its expected lifetime of twenty years, it is likely to yield earnings of $100 annually over and beyond its costs of operation and an allowance for depreciation. Should this asset be purchased? A rational decision maker would need to know the present value of the future income. Because income today is more valuable than income tomorrow (it may be lent at interest and earn additional income), incomes in future periods must be discounted with an appropriate rate of interest before one can calculate the true present value of the capital asset. If our decision maker thinks that 6 percent is the appropriate interest rate, then reference to a compound interest table will tell him that the present value of the sample asset is $1,147.00. In this case he should buy the asset and use it, because its discounted present value exceeds its costs of acquisition. It will pay off as an investment.

Another way to look at this decision would be to calculate

the rate of return of a $1,000 investment that would yield $100 net income annually over a period of twenty years. This would be the equivalent of the interest rate that would bring the capital value of an asset to equality with its cost of acquisition. To break even, an investor could not afford to pay more than this rate of interest for funds borrowed to make the investment. In the case of the sample asset, the rate of return would be 7.75 percent. Accordingly, the investment should be made because the expected rate of return would exceed the prevailing interest rate of 6 percent. This rate-of-return concept is used extensively in what follows.

In recent decades, the idea that capital is composed only of physical assets has been breaking down. In its place has gradually emerged a more inclusive view that capital is *any* asset—physical or human—that has the capacity to generate a flow of earnings in the future. In this view, the skills of workers and the abilities of executives are regarded as particular kinds of capital "equipment" employed in the production process. Their skills and abilities were developed by investment, that is, by diverting some of society's scarce resources in earlier times toward their education, on-the-job training, and health care in much the same way that resources commonly are diverted to create physical capital assets. Human capital yields, over its productive lifetime, a stream of earnings that could not have been generated so fully without these prior investments. Thus the acquired skills and abilities of people are recognized along with the traditional forms of physical capital to make up society's capital stock, swelling it greatly, at least for more advanced societies, and raising a variety of new issues for investment planning. It is to these issues that we now turn.

Human capital, as most economists define it, consists of the acquired energy, motivations, skills, and knowledge possessed by human beings, which can be harnessed over a period of time to the task of producing goods and services. It may include abilities acquired through some more or less formal system of instruction, such as colleges and graduate professional schools. But, just as likely, it includes competencies learned less formally in the home, on the job, and around the community. Good health enhances productivity also, as does full knowledge about employment opportunities and easy access to the most attractive opportunities. Outlays on health care, nutrition, communications, and transportation therefore may also contain elements of human capital investment.

Perhaps the most remarkable feature of the concept of human capital is its narrowness in relation to the totality of human life. In human capital, economists have fashioned a concept that leaves no room for the traits of individuals that produce such ineffable outcomes as happiness, love, friendliness, humanitarian impulses, spirituality, knowledge for its own sake, and so on. These are simply left out of any assessment of the value of human capital except to the extent that they significantly influence the earning capacity of individuals or the productive capacity of the economy. Economists do not deny the existence of nonmonetary values. Rather, they merely choose to concentrate attention on those attributes of human beings which yield outputs measurable in dollars.

Having taken this first definitional step—perhaps grudgingly and with serious reservations—the reader, like economists generally, can be forgiven the next step, which reveals the considerable similarities between investments in human capital and investments in physical capital. At first glance, anyway, both investment processes create income-producing assets that can be employed to raise the volume or quality of goods and services. Both sets of investment decisions presumably are made after careful consideration of alternative investment opportunities and both are expected to yield maximum returns after adjusting for the degree of risk involved. By the same token, calculations of rates of return can be used interchangeably in determining the wisest human or physical capital investments. Both kinds of investments produce capital assets that are durable, in the sense of possessing relatively long (though finite) productive lifespans, and both require maintenance expenditures in order to keep the assets in working order. The similarities are numerous and intriguing—so much so, indeed, that the theoretical apparatus traditionally employed to analyze capital investment decisions has been adapted by economists for use on human capital problems with only minor modifications.

Private Monetary Returns

According to the theory of human capital, individuals will spend time and money on more education when they judge that the present value of expected future benefits from the investment exceeds the cost (or when the expected rate of return exceeds the prevailing interest rate). The benefits they seek need not always be in the form of higher salaries or earnings—though this is the form of benefits that has proven to be the most easily measured and most often analyzed—but may be in some non-monetary form of present or future personal satisfaction or in a combination of the two.

Consider first the case of private monetary returns to higher education, schematically represented in Figure 3 (Davis and Morrall, 1974, p. 11; see Eckaus, 1973, p. 73). Suppose that the lower curve running from C to D traces out the average working-lifetime earnings profile for a high school graduate of certain qualifications, and that the upper curve anchored at A and B represents the same individual's age-earnings profile if he

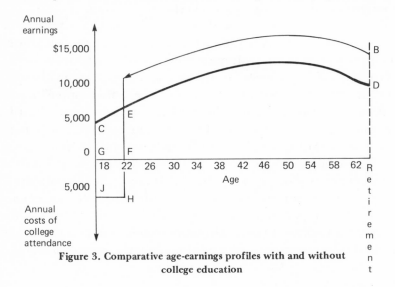

Figure 3. Comparative age-earnings profiles with and without college education

or she finishes four years of college. According to the diagram, this individual could invest in a college education at a cost equal to the area CEHJ, made up both of direct college costs of GFHJ and of indirect costs in the form of forgone income of CEFG, and expect lifetime benefits in the form of extra income equal to the area ABDE between the upper and lower curves. Assuming no other benefits or costs, the individual would seek to find out whether the present discounted value of ABDE exceeds that of CEHJ and, if so, would consider delaying entry into the workforce and going instead to college for four years.

Much of the economics literature about higher education in recent years has reported on empirical research designed to find out whether individuals do in fact realize significant monetary returns from their private investments in schooling and do, therefore, behave as if they were guided by some cool-headed calculation of benefits and costs as posited in the theory of human capital. This literature is perhaps best divided into three periods of scholarly activity, each distinguishable from the other by dramatic changes both in the questions being asked by researchers and in the sophistication of research designs. The periods, grouped by publication date of scholarly works, correspond roughly to 1956-1965, 1966-1972, and since 1973.

The early period, 1956-1965. Attempts during this period to measure private monetary returns to investments in American higher education were somewhat rudimentary. In addition to certain technical deficiencies, they did not provide adequate controls for such noneducational sources of earnings as native ability, wealth, parental education, social background, hours of work, and ambition or perseverance. The calculated rates of return on investments in education almost surely overstated the effect of education on earnings, since part of the income superiority attributed to education was the result of other factors.

Even so, these early rates of return are of great historical significance, because they seemed at the time to confirm scientifically the common assumption that investments in more education were worth what they cost. They suggested that the private monetary rate of return to higher education—net of

costs and without inclusion of nonmonetary benefits—were in
the neighborhood of 12 to 15 percent for higher education, and
some estimates were even higher (Becker, 1960; Miller, 1960;
Schultz, 1961, 1963; Hansen, 1963). The important study by
Becker (1964), for example, suggested that private rates of return were quite stable for investments in four years of college,
yielding, from four different sets of American census data, rates
between 12.4 and 14.8 percent per annum extrapolated over
the working lifetimes of college-educated people. Since these
figures probably were higher than the returns then available to
investments in physical capital of comparable risk, they suggested to educators and public policy makers that investments
in higher education were "paying" and certainly that there was
no overinvestment in higher education. Accordingly, these earlier findings confirmed the then current inclination to expand
access to higher education in America and encouraged important public policy revisions to bring this about.

The middle period, 1966-1972. In the middle period of research
on educational returns, interest in the field widened greatly, and
a multitude of studies were made, some based on better data
than the earlier studies[1] and some better equipped to correct
rate-of-return estimates for the effects of age, social class, and
unemployment. This was also the period when studies of educational returns in other countries began to appear and when rates
of return for particular subgroups of the total population, defined by race, sex, and region, were developed for the first time.

For urban men completing four years of college, private
monetary rates of return estimated during this period ranged between 9.6 percent (from Hanoch, 1965) and 13.6 percent (from
Hines, Tweeten, and Redfern, 1970). The somewhat lower results as compared with earlier estimates came about principally
because of the rising private costs of higher education. Most
studies suggested that returns in the South were marginally
higher than in the North (Hanoch, 1967; Lassiter, 1966); that

[1]See especially Giora Hanoch (1965) for the best data and estimation
techniques then available.

the returns to whites were substantially higher at given levels of educational attainment than for nonwhites (Hanoch, 1967; Lassiter, 1966; Welch, 1967; Landes, 1968); and that the returns to men were greater than to women (Hanoch, 1967; Malkiel and Malkiel, 1973).

In most studies, the estimated rates of return varied inversely with educational level—highest for primary school education, next highest for secondary education, lower still for college, and lowest for postgraduate education. The explanation of these differences seems simple enough: grade school and high school education are more necessary to successful functioning in society than college education. Moreover, education is doubtless subject to diminishing returns, each additional year adding less than the preceding one in skills and abilities useful in the labor market. A special factor tending to increase the value of education at the elementary and secondary level is that each step up the educational ladder is a prerequisite to the next step. For example, one of the values of a high school diploma is that it is an entry ticket to college. Not only do benefits decline with additional years of schooling, but costs increase, further weakening rates of return. Individuals personally incur rising educational costs as they ascend the academic ladder, partly because public subsidy of educational costs is less for higher grades than for lower and partly because forgone income rises as individuals grow older and as they receive more education. Accordingly, estimates of the private payoff from primary schooling were found to range upwards from 20 to 150 percent or more; for secondary schooling, from 14 to 20 percent; for college, from 9 to 14 percent; and for advanced degree work, from 2 to 8 percent (except for a few privileged occupations like medicine).

Estimated rates of return in the ranges indicated, though somewhat lower than those obtained in earlier studies, were presented frequently as evidence that resources were allocated between higher educational capital and physical capital in a reasonably efficient manner, since measured returns to physical capital investments with comparable degrees of risk were thought to be in the range of 9 to 14 percent. But some implied that there might have been underinvestment in grade school and high school education, overinvestment in programs of graduate education, but about the right investment in undergraduate higher education (if one considered only monetary returns). The question of what rate of return to physical capital to use for comparisons with returns to human capital is an awkward one. From the point of view of the students and their families, the alternatives (savings accounts, stocks and bonds, houses, and so on) yield from 5 to 8 percent. Business investments in capital equipment may yield from 10 to 15 percent or even 20 percent. Indeed, the question of the rate of return to be used in deciding on social investments is controversial. When a positive rate of return beyond an allowance for risk and uncertainty is required, the implication is that a dollar of income for posterity is worth less than a dollar of income for the present generation—an idea that we are reluctant to promulgate in the present work. For an interesting discussion of this issue, see Samuelson (1976, pp. 475, 487-488).

Recent studies, 1973-1977. In the third and most recent period, estimates of private monetary returns from educational investment have become more sophisticated. Great effort and ingenuity have been devoted to sorting out the influence of education from other variables that affect earnings, such as individual ability and family background, both of which are linked closely with educational attainment. A substantial portion of recent research has made use of a unique set of time-series data—the so-called NBER-Thorndike sample—initiated in 1943 when 75,000 men were given a standardized battery of United States Air Crew Aptitude Tests. Periodically since 1943, a sample of 10,000 of these men has been resurveyed to obtain data on earnings, occupational history, education, family background, nonmarket behavior patterns, and sociopolitical attitudes. Since the respondents were all males, were willing to volunteer for military service, and were better-educated and probably brighter than the general population, considerable caution is needed to generalize from findings based on the data. The fact that it is being used extensively, despite obvious sources of biases, testifies to the frustrations felt by scholars in trying to construct income-age profiles with cross-sectional data.[2] Both kinds of data, however, suffer from the limitation that they reflect only past experience and do not forecast income-age profiles for the distant future as affected by education and other influences of the present, particularly the increasing proportion of the population with college education.

Becker (1964, p. 82) had tried in 1964 to separate the effects of "innate ability" from the effects of education in explaining earnings. He had estimated that perhaps 20 percent of the income difference between high school and college graduates (and a small percentage of the corresponding rate of return) might be accounted for by differences in the average ability of the two groups. Recent research findings suggest that the proportion may be higher (Taubman and Wales, 1974; Hause, in Juster, 1975; Wachtel, in Juster, 1975). But other recent studies cast some doubt on the possibility of measuring ability independent of education. Griliches (1970), for example, whose views a number of investigators recently have embraced, has concluded that available tests that purport to measure ability really amount to tests of achievement (Eckaus, 1974; Psacharopoulos, 1975, ch. 3). Accordingly, because of differing conceptions of "ability," estimates of the amount by which rates of return on higher education should be adjusted downward to eliminate the influence of "ability" range widely—from none at all to as much as 35 percent of the total return (Taubman and Wales, 1974, p. 77).

In recent research, efforts have been made to isolate the effects of "family background" on earnings. Parents' and in-laws' education and income have been found to have a modest influence on lifetime earnings; religious preferences also have some effect. But studies to date have not successfully controlled for other background characteristics, such as the possible influence on earnings of different amounts of parental time spent with preschool or school-age children.[3] Thus, the inability to

[2]See a new study by Fägerlind (1975) based on especially rich Swedish longitudinal data.

[3]Initial attempts to deal with this relationship empirically made use of such biased data that the results cannot be used to draw generalizations.

control fully for family background may still produce bias in calculated returns to educational attainment. Indeed, some radical political economists contend that family background is the major factor determining earnings (Bowles, in Schultz, 1972; Bowles and Gintis, 1976).

By disaggregating data on the relation of education to earnings, Eckaus (1973, ch. 1) pointed the way to two additional kinds of adjustment needed to estimate truer rates of return. In one investigation, he found that some differences in calculated rates of return are a result of differences in hours of work that are associated with education (see also Mincer in Juster, 1975, pp. 71-94; Lindsay, 1973). With controls for hours of work, rates of return to investments in primary education tended to rise, in secondary education to fall dramatically, and in college and graduate school education to decline modestly. At the college level the adjustment for hours of work reduced calculated rates of return by about 10 percent.

Eckaus also showed that differences in rates of return among occupations are extraordinarily large. For example, he found that rates of return from a four-year college education for different occupations ranged from 20 percent or more to negative (Eckaus, 1973, ch. 2; Eckaus, 1974, pp. 345-350; see also Blank and Stigler, 1957). This finding is important because the relative size of each occupational group and its treatment in the labor market changes over time. Disaggregating by occupations would enable economists to take these changes into account by adjusting the relative weight of each occupation in computing average rates of return.

The rate of return has been found also to vary according to the "quality" of education experienced by people of similar educational attainments. On the premise that higher-cost schools also are higher-quality ones, one study found that the returns to the extra investment associated with quality are in the 10 to 15 percent range, even though the returns to under-

See Leibowitz (1974); see also her suggestive article about the relationships between women's education and child care in "Education and the Allocation of Women's Time," in Juster, 1975, pp. 187-194.

graduate education found in this study were lower than in most other studies (Wachtel, in Juster, 1975, pp. 151-170. See also Solmon and Wachtel, 1975; Psacharopoulos, 1975; Wachtel, 1976). Differences in outcomes among different institutions is discussed at length in Chapter Eight.

Recently, a considerable body of evidence has been assembled to show that the link between earnings and differences in the amounts of human capital embodied in people is forged partly by the experience people have in school and college and partly by two other factors: (a) learning experiences after completing school and (b) grading and labeling (or screening) of students. Both factors deserve attention.

Mincer's work is central to the question of postcollege influences on earnings differences (Mincer, 1962a, 1974, 1975). He suggested that human capital is built up throughout most of life—from the earliest years when parents are primarily responsible, through years of education, and finally through on-the-job training. His research on earnings differentials shows that, at least for white urban men, only about 25 percent of differences in earnings can be attributed to formal education; differences in institutional costs (which may be related to quality) explain perhaps another 10 percent of observed differences; and at least another 25 percent is probably traceable to on-the-job investments in training after leaving school or college. Mincer found also that more highly educated persons tend to invest more than less-educated people in opportunities after formal education to build human capital, suggesting, though not proving, that education and postschool investments may be complementary (Mincer, 1974, pp. 131-132). Accordingly, rate-of-return analyses that previously related income differentials directly to years of education may have overstated the direct impact of formal education on earnings. In Mincer's findings, formal education exerts its effect on earnings partly through its direct impact, partly through encouraging individuals to engage in adult study and other forms of self-improvement, and partly through increasing the effectiveness of on-the-job training. Education is thus seen as intensifying learning throughout adult life. (See also Knapp, 1977.)

Another factor to be considered in estimating rates of return is the "screening hypothesis," to the effect that a major (or even sole) influence of education on earnings arises from its role in grading and labeling its students and thus determining their placement in the labor force. (This hypothesis was considered in Chapter Five and will be reviewed only briefly here. For a complete bibliography on this subject, see Blaug, 1976.) The basic concept underlying this hypothesis is that differences in earnings at different educational levels might arise, other things equal, not only because education imparts various useful cognitive and affective characteristics, but also because employers regard educational attainment as an inexpensive way, as compared with alternatives, to identify potentially productive workers for specific jobs. If so, some extra earning accruing throughout working life to college-educated people might be a fee for being credentialed rather than a return for being productive; by the same token, the shortfall of income earned by noncollege workers might not reflect true inferiority of productive capacities, as assumed by the theory of human capital, but exclusion by employers from access to some higher-paying occupations.

To test for the existence of screening, Taubman and Wales compared the actual occupational distribution of individuals at various educational levels with the distribution that might have been expected under conditions of free entry into occupational labor markets. Their findings, though tentative and controversial, seem to confirm a major role for grading and labeling, or screening, in the setting of interpersonal income differences. They suggest that the rates of return to investments in a college bachelor's degree might be reduced by as much as 50 percent when corrected for screening, at least for their sample, which contained men who are brighter and better-educated than average.

The screening hypothesis has recently come under attack (Layard and Psacharopoulos, 1974; Blaug, 1976). Perhaps the most telling criticism is that employers are too adroit to settle for a credential alone when selecting among potential workers. They want new employees who possess scarce cognitive skills, desirable personality traits such as self-reliance and drive, and perhaps a willingness to play by the organizational rules. In a sense, therefore, they want trainable people with gifts of intelligence and personality who will learn quickly and grow in their jobs. They want people with credentials not just because they went to college but because college changed them in desirable ways. Moreover, granting that employers might rely heavily on educational credentials in initial employment decisions, there is no reason to suppose they would not look to actual work experience in decisions about promotion or about the employment of experienced workers. A second criticism of the screening hypothesis is that those who advocate it have not examined in any detail what actually happens in college to the students who are being educated. They have simply ignored the evidence that college changes people in ways that would clearly enhance their productivity and justify employers in paying attention to educational credentials. If college did not have such effects, employers would long ago have found other devices for testing the suitability of workers to take up particular occupations (Blaug, 1976).

Lest the reader think that all proposed adjustments in the calculated rates of return to higher education are in the downward direction, he should consider also the likely impact of adjusting returns for differences in fringe benefits earned by people with differing levels of education. Fringe benefits, as a percentage of basic salary, increase typically as the level of basic salary increases. Therefore, money wage differentials, on which (until recently) all previous rates of return had been calculated, clearly understate the true differentials in compensation. Psacharopoulos (1975, pp. 134-161) reported that the resulting understatement of earnings differentials is very significant indeed, pushing the calculated rates of return upward by one fifth when adjusted for the value of paid holidays and vacations alone. Stern (1975) found that the midcareer return on a college education was increased by 25 percent when earnings were adjusted for six nonpecuniary job characteristics: making less physical effort, making more of own decisions, being more creative, having less repetition, having more say, making more friends. Similarly, Duncan (1976, p. 481) concluded: "When pecuniary and nonpecuniary variables are combined into a single composite earnings measure, the estimated coefficient on education is considerably greater (25 percent in one data set, 10 percent in the other) than when earnings are measured by the wage rate alone. This added importance of education persists even when cognitive ability, achievement motivation, and socioeconomic background are taken into account." As data for literally dozens of other kinds of fringe benefits become available by educational level, surely calculated rates of return on education will balloon. However, Quinn and Baldi de Mandilovitch (1975, p. vi) found that education per se has little direct effect on job satisfaction. That is, people of different levels of education in the same jobs do not exhibit significant differences in satisfaction, and, indeed, those persons with jobs incommensurate with education tend to be highly dissatisfied. The effect of education on job satisfaction is indirect. It "provides workers with generally 'better,' and hence more satisfying jobs."

Most studies have been concerned with white males and have been silent about minority groups and women. The few recent studies of nonwhite males suggest that the rate of return for them may be comparable to that for white males, but studies of women usually show that the rate of return for them is lower than that for men (Becker, 1964; Mincer, 1962b, 1974b). Madden (1975) found that the rate of return to women was *greater* than that for men and that the rate for black men was slightly higher than that for white men. Madden pointed out that the lower return to women in most studies is due to the fact that women devote fewer hours each year to remunerative work and fewer years in a lifetime. Her more favorable results were obtained by using data on hourly earnings and confining her study to a young age cohort. She added that the returns on women's education tend to be understated because they do not take account of the substantial effect of the education of wives on their husband's earnings (Benham, 1974).

Recent trends in rates of return. After remaining remarkably constant over a period of at least two decades, estimated rates of return on investments in college education have recently been falling. This decline is due partly to new sophisticated methods and concepts that permit controlling for such variables as ability, family background, and screening. The 1974 estimates of Taubman and Wales (1974, pp. 2-3), based on the NBER-TH sample, was 7½ to 9 percent. This rate applied to college dropouts as well as college graduates and applied also to persons of varying mental abilities. But when allowance was made for the use of education as a screening device, it was found that such screening accounted for "up to one-half of (net) earnings differentials," leaving the return from education itself at perhaps 4 to 5 percent.

The decline in calculated rates of return was also due to a downward trend in the estimated lifetime earnings of college graduates after 1969. Freeman (1975, p. 296) estimated that the decline was from 11.1 to 11.5 percent in 1968 to 7.5 to 8.5 percent in 1973 (see Freeman, 1976, pp. 26, 204). In explaining the decline, Freeman cited a slackening of the growth rate of occupations using relatively large numbers of college graduates and a very large increase in the number of graduates. One could mention also the rapid increase of college costs. Witmer (1976) however, challenged the findings of Freeman and argued that the return on college-going has not declined, though it may do so over the next twenty-five years. He argued also that it is likely to recover by the end of the century.

On balance, these most recent estimates of the rates of return may be even lower than roughly comparable estimates of return on investments in physical capital (Jorgenson and Griliches, 1967). This possibility suggests to some that overinvestment is occurring in higher education—if the criterion of returns is money earnings. Before drawing that conclusion, however, it would be well to keep in mind that scholars even yet have not been able to take account of several important variables affecting the true rate of return. The unexplored territory includes some elements of cultural and family background; the impact of certain personality traits, such as motivation, drive, and risk aversion; aspects of the linkage between early-childhood and on-the-job training on the one hand and formal schooling on the other; the relationship between educational level and fringe benefits; and the intricate influence of past experience on the future. The appropriateness of the screening adjustment also remains in doubt. Accordingly, rate-of-return estimates still are subject to potentially large uncertainties, and it is not at all clear which way further adjustments will push them.

Then, too, the calculations summarized above do not include private *non*monetary returns on investment in education, including the significant consumption benefits realized by students during the college years and throughout adult life. These, too, deserve evaluation when estimates of the potential benefits of education are being made. Finally, economists who attempt to calculate rates of return almost invariably try to control for the effect of socioeconomic background, which is itself largely a product of education in an earlier generation, or (and it may amount to the same thing) they fail to take into account the effects of education in the present generation or the socioeconomic background that will be reflected in the earnings of future generations. Similarly, the benefits may be private, composed primarily of the after-tax earnings individuals receive as a result of having gone to college, or they may be social, including, in addition to private benefits, any benefits that accrue to third parties and to society at large. Most third-party and societal benefits cannot be estimated in quantitative terms, however, and so the only adjustment to private benefits usually made is to add back the income taxes excluded from private benefits as a measure of society's extra gain from enhanced productivity. As thus estimated, social rates of return are usually lower than the corresponding private ones. The reverse would be true only when educational subsidies are very low and income taxes are exceedingly progressive.

Estimates of social rates of return, rather than private rates, ought to be used by public authorities when planning educational outlays. Since they more accurately reflect social costs and benefits, they ought to provide planners with better tests of the "profitability" of alternative proposals. But they are not used widely because their reliability is even less than that of private rates of return. The problem is mainly the impossibility, at this time, of accurately estimating the added monetary returns that neighbors, fellow workers, and others in the community and nation receive when more highly educated people join their ranks (Weisbrod, 1964). In addition, the data on educational costs are inadequate. Until further progress is made on these fronts, social rates of return probably should be regarded skeptically as practical guides to public policy. Their usefulness for theorizing about public choices, of course, remains high.

Nonmonetary Returns

In recent years, economists have begun to turn their attention to the benefits produced by education that are not direct monetary returns. Most of the work done so far has been concerned with private nonmonetary benefits, though the distinction between the private and the social in the case of nonmonetary benefits has not yet been specified clearly. Various studies have shown that education affects consumer choice, saving, family planning, crime, and job satisfaction, and the ability generally to adjust to disequilibria in the economy. Since these matters have been discussed in earlier chapters of this book, we shall not dwell on them here. Suffice it to say that still other potential relationships between education and human behavior are being explored, among them, household decisions about the amount and content of leisure activities, the efficiency and frequency of investments in good health, the degree of family stability, the readiness of family members to participate actively in voluntary activity, the incidence of gambling behavior, various social and political attitudes, and others. As these studies accumulate, we suspect that additional evidence on nonmonetary returns from educational attainment will be amassed.[4]

One area of nonmonetary return that warrants examination here, however, is that of "consumer" benefits. According to traditional economic theory, consumer goods and services differ from investment goods and services in that they do not contribute to the accumulation of greater productive powers

---

[4] Much of the leadership in opening up this new territory to economic analysis has come from Gary Becker. See his "A Theory of Social Interactions" (1974).

but rather yield direct satisfactions. They are valued for their own sake—not for their capacity to boost flows of future income or other future benefits. The key question is whether outlays on higher education yield direct *consumer* benefits, in addition to future monetary benefits deriving from human capital.

As the literature of human capital has grown and matured, previously clear distinctions between production and consumption have been blurred more and more. When originally conceived, human capital theory viewed individuals as part of the machinery of production; they contributed basic physical vitality in the form of labor services and also special skills, talents, and knowledge from their storehouses of acquired human capital. They were paid a money income, presumably equivalent to their productivity, which included a return for pure "labor" plus a return for human capital. Then new sources of return on investments in human capital were recognized, some of them related to household decisions about uses rather than sources of income and none easily measurable in monetary terms. To incorporate these household returns into the existing theory, the so-called new home economics emerged, in which households were regarded as firms purchasing consumer goods and services in the market to be combined with homemakers' time in the "production" of goods and services for final consumption. Thus, a family might buy a lawn mower to produce the satisfaction from a well-groomed lawn, or might devote its savings and acumen to building an investment portfolio to achieve financial security, or might buy music lessons for a child to give the child and the family the benefit of present and future musical enjoyment. A better education would help households to make these and other "production" decisions more efficiently, and so to raise the level of well-being within the household. Thus, in this revision of the theory of consumer behavior, consumption was transformed into production. But this raises the question: What proportion of household production leads to the accumulation of still more human capital rather than to direct satisfaction from improved access to varied consumer goods and services? Consumption, then, is limited to the flow of "final" satisfactions and does not necessarily occur with the purchase of goods in the market or the production of "capital" in the household (Bowen, 1977, pp. 84-118).

The distinction between production and consumption is made even more confusing by the facts that the level and content of consumption affect our labor power and that our experiences in remunerative work affect our personal well-being and the quality of our lives. The question must ultimately be asked: Do we eat to work or work to eat? The answer is that our well-being is determined by the totality of our lives in the work place, in the home, and in the community. Our lives cannot be divided meaningfully between production and consumption— between means and ends. The activities we call means are as much a part of our lives and as much an influence on our well-being as the activities we call consumption.

Whatever solution is reached in distinguishing between production and consumption, all economists—and educators as well—recognize that higher education may yield direct satisfactions at the time the education is taking place. These satisfactions may be in the form of the experience of learning, the pleasures of campus life, and the satisfaction of personal development. It is also widely recognized that higher education may yield future direct benefits to individuals in the form of elevated taste. Students acquire new interests and broadened horizons that may bring about future national or community betterment. Economists recognize that the results may sometimes be negative as well as positive, but they are still some distance from being able to assess either benefits or drawbacks with total confidence.

The allocation of any substantial fraction of total costs of higher education to direct benefits would have the effect of raising the observed rates of return. Until now, economists have ignored these benefits by assuming that all costs of higher education are devoted to enhancing private and public productivity. If, later on, the direct benefits can be included in the calculation of rates of return, then these rates probably will balloon. Meanwhile, one can only assert (on the assumption that the direct benefits are positive) that the calculated rates of return are lower than the true rates of return.

Higher Education and Economic Growth

Rates-of-return analyses focus primarily upon education as a form of investment, yet most of them fail to spell out a direct causal connection between rates of return and growth of the national income. But some economists have created rather sophisticated "growth accounting systems" to show explicitly how outlays on education might affect national economic growth.

Studies of the sources of economic growth usually recognize five potential factors increasing the national income: the use of more labor; the use of more physical capital; improvement in the productivity of labor; improvement in physical capital; and more effective organization of these resources in production. Thus, growth in the capacity to produce requires either additions to the supply of productive resources or more effective methods of utilizing given resources. Educational outlays clearly are most directly related to the third of these possible sources—improvement in labor productivity—but there are indirect links between education and most of the five sources. Education may raise labor quality by imparting greater discipline and reliability, better health, increased efficiency, prompter reactions to new information, and heightened mobility. Education also may influence the amount of available labor by altering the age of entry and exit from the labor force, the labor force participation rate, the pattern of workdays and vacations, and so on. It may alter the amount of available physical capital as well, by boosting the rates of saving and investment. Then, too, it may improve the quality of physical capital by creating a population better attuned to the needs and uses of machinery and equipment and more capable, through research and development efforts, of designing, adapting, installing, and using new equipment. Finally, educated people are essential to the tasks of improving the organization and management of production (Machlup, 1970).

Most empirical studies of the sources of economic growth have begun by trying to isolate the influence of greater supplies of labor and capital on growth of national income over a period of time. This technique results in a "residual" amount of national income at the end of the period which cannot be explained by incremental growth of labor and capital. Since the residual presumably includes various influences of education operating through improvements in the quality of labor and capital and in the organization of production, scholars who have wished to trace the influence of education on the behavior of national income have tried to dissect this residual. In a series of influential studies, Schultz (1962, 1971) and Denison (1962, 1967, 1974) pioneered the development of growth accounting systems designed to do exactly that (see also Abramovitz, 1962). Drawing upon early work on rates of return, Schultz posited that the influence of education on growth might be captured by multiplying the social rate of return by the annual increment in investments in education and dividing the product by the national income. Thus, if either the social rate of return or the amount of educational investment rose relative to the total national income, education's contribution to growth would rise. Reduced rates of return or rates of investment, similarly, would lower education's contribution.[5] By limiting the values of educational investment and rate of return to those only attributable to higher education, one also could estimate relative contributions of higher education to national income growth. Using Schultz' formula, Psacharopoulos (1973) calculated that educational outlays accounted for about 18 percent of America's national income growth during the early 1960s and that *higher* education investments were associated with

---

[5]Mathematically, let I_H represent educational investment outlays, including an estimate of forgone income; r_H, the social rate of return on educational investment; Y, the value of national income or output. Then the contribution of education to growth is equal to:

$$\frac{I_H \times r_H}{Y}$$

Sometimes this formula is multiplied by the labor force participation rate, π, to adjust for the fact that not 100 percent of students become members of the labor force. Higher education's contribution to growth can be represented by disaggregating the formula into components representing each level of education, for example, by using I_h terms rather than I_H and r_H.

about one fourth of the 18 percent—or with about 4 to 5 percent of the observed growth. He also estimated that education's
contribution to growth in most other countries, rich and poor
alike, was significantly lower than in America over the same
period of time. The average contribution for developed countries was 11.2 percent and for developing countries 14.5 percent
(1973, tables 7.1, 7.2, Appendix D; see Denison, 1967; Patrick
and Rosovsky, 1976).

Making use of a much more sophisticated model Denison
(1974) found that "potential" national income of the United
States (the value of national income assuming aggregate demand
at a sustained high level) rose at an average annual rate of 3.41
percent during the forty-year period ending in 1969. (See also
Denison, 1967.) Of this growth, he found that slightly more
than half had been due to increasing quantities of primary inputs, such as labor and physical capital, and slightly less than
half from increases in output per unit of labor and capital input.
Table 51 highlights his findings.

**Table 51. Sources of U.S. economic growth, 1929-1969,
in percentages of average annual growth rate**

	1929-1969	*1948-1969*
Potential national income	100.0	100.0
Advances in knowledge and changes not else-where classified	31.1	34.1
More work done, with account taken of the characteristics of workers except education	28.7	23.9
More physical capital	15.8	21.6
INCREASED EDUCATION PER WORKER	14.1	11.9
Improved resource allocation	10.0	9.0
Dwelling occupancy ratio and irregular factors	0.3	−0.5

Source: Denison (1974, p. 130).

The table suggests that education has a modest but significant role in the generation of economic growth. For the
period 1929-1969, the accumulation of education per worker

(after adjusting for known ability and socioeconomic differences among workers) accounted for 14.1 percent of total growth (p. 128). Since Denison's educational indices were constructed from data on workers employed in the business sector only, they probably understate the true impact of advances in educational attainment for the whole population. Moreover, his methods of estimation raise the question also of whether the very large shares of growth attributed to "advances in knowledge," "more work done," and "improved resource allocation" were not also heavily influenced by availability in the American work force of skilled and well-educated technical personnel and managers. In other words, this estimate of 14.1 percent may be minimal.

In interpreting this percentage, it is important to note that, if education added 14.1 percent to the national income over the period 1929-1969, it added much more than that to the potential output *per worker*. As Denison shows, educational attainment added 24.6 percent to potential output per worker.

Assuming that the 14.1 percent figure is valid and that Psacharopoulos was justified in assigning to *higher* education one fourth of the economic growth due to education at all levels, then perhaps 3.5 percent might be traced to higher education. Annual national income (in 1958 dollars) grew from $161.4 billion in 1929 to $599.6 billion in 1969, an increase of $438.2 billion. If 3.5 percent of this growth could be attributed to education, then in 1969, education in the past would have been yielding annually $15.3 billion of national income, considerably more than the annual cost of higher education in the decades prior to 1969. These estimates refer only to the effects of education and do not include the effects of research (which are considered in Chapter Ten).

Conclusions

The literature on investment in human capital clearly does not produce a simple conclusion as to whether education is worth what it costs. It begins with a leap of faith, asserting that man's economic qualities, especially as a producer of goods and services, can be isolated from other aspects of his personality and that private and public policies may be guided by the findings of human capital research without prejudicing the attainment of nonmarket educational objectives. It proceeds by likening humanity's productive powers to those of a machine, so that a familiar theory of capital may be employed to assess human worth and to explain the place of education in augmenting it. Grudgingly at first, but then perhaps too easily, it declares the usefulness of human capital theory to analyses of nonmonetary returns from education. And it culminates in a set of estimates about the net returns from investments in education that is hostage to weak data and numerous methodological doubts. The question now at hand is whether real understanding about the economic worth of higher education can be gained from this literature's heroic and sometimes contradictory testimony.

The easier part of the question to answer, perhaps, is whether calculated rates of return are plausible. By now literally hundreds of econometric studies have been carried out around the world, calculating both private and social rates of return on investments in formal schooling. Many of these have focused on American higher education and some have incorporated one or more of the adjustments to earnings functions reviewed in this chapter. Surprisingly, with few exceptions, the various approaches yield about the same results, which is to say that most studies report positive private and social rates of return from higher education in the 8 to 15 percent range—with one recent study showing a return of below 5 percent (Taubman and Wales, 1974). These rates *are* plausible, and many have interpreted them as reflecting a certain underlying "rationality" in both private and public decisions about education (Hanoch, 1967, p. 308; Griliches, 1970, p. 110; Psacharopoulos, 1973, p. 17).

Testing calculated rates of return by criteria of plausibility or "reasonableness" does not meet very high standards of scientific inquiry, however, and a goodly number of skeptics continue to claim that economists are far indeed from finding "true" rates of return on higher education. Their skepticism is especially anchored in two sets of reservations. The first is their view that the kinds of data available to measure costs and returns do not permit careful identification of the extra amounts of income associated with extra amounts of education. The discussions above of how educational returns must be controlled for differences in ability, family background, hours of work, occupation, school quality, postschool experiences, and perhaps screening illustrate this reservation. The skeptics especially do not believe that it is possible to separate the effects of differences in "innate ability" from those due to differences in education—nor, for that matter, do a majority of economists, who generally take more optimistic views of the usefulness of rate-of-return analysis.

A second source of skepticism is the view that calculated rates of return fail to account for certain costs and benefits of education. The skeptics note, for example, that it is virtually impossible to evaluate properly the costs of public or private education because neither operates under a price system that would give reasonably accurate signals about the scarcity values of the resources employed. They point out also that educational outlays produce many returns that go uncounted in dollar estimates of educational returns. Some uncounted effects redound directly to the benefit of people investing in their education, while others yield benefits that spill over to the general population. The latter group of effects are called "externalities" or "spillover effects." Most of the effects described above in the section on nonmonetary returns on education are a mixture of direct and spillover effects that have escaped the attention of the econometricians prospecting for higher-grade rates of return. The ability to spend money more efficiently, to save more and invest it wisely, to plan family growth more effectively, to enjoy work more completely, and to adapt more quickly and efficiently to changes in the personal environment undoubtedly enhances the lives of educated people as well as of society as a whole. One easily can imagine the existence of many other externalities. Society surely must benefit enormously, for example, when greater supplies of educational capital create a scientific environment conducive to more successful research and development activities. And the general population surely must gain when rising levels of education create better neighborhoods and more alert citizens. On the other hand, additional education may produce certain kinds of externalities that may not be regarded as desirable—for example, the propensity of American college campuses in the late 1960s and early 1970s to incubate violence and neoradical movements.

Since market transactions do not take account of externalities, no one has yet succeeded in estimating their significance. And if a definite value cannot be placed on them, the skeptics argue, it is impossible to know by how much those externalities that are positive may outweigh those that are negative. A trustworthy set of rates of return, therefore, is a will-o'-the-wisp, they say, an objective that already has lured far too many resources into a futile task of "scientifically" demonstrating whether or not investments in education are worth what they cost.[6]

The skeptics have a point, yet in their very insistence on the relevance of externalities to a judgment about the usefulness of rates-of-return analyses, they offer an opportunity to take one more step toward answering this important question. Is it not possible, from the evidence presented in this and other chapters of this book, at least to make an informed judgment about the existence of externalities generated by investments in higher education and about the net balance of possible positive and possible negative externalities? We think so. In our judgment, the evidence strongly favors the existence of numerous externalities, predominantly positive in value and generally very significant when compared to the market values of the direct private returns with which they are associated. The evidence is of two kinds: First, there is the reasonably well-documented economic evidence that the availability of substantial numbers of highly educated people capable of developing and managing advanced productive and social systems yields significant productivity advantages shared broadly with the general population. Second, there is the behavioral evidence summarized in Chapter Nine suggesting that the induction of more college-

---

[6] For an appraisal of the human capital approach to the study of educational outcomes, see Blaug (1976) and Welch (1975).

educated people into society may, through "neighborhood" and other kinds of effects, increase openness to social change, enhance the responsiveness and accountability of government and other social institutions, change the values and attitudes of the general population in desirable ways, increase concern for education and rearing of children, enhance the graciousness of social intercourse, and variously alter the style of life.

This evidence is sufficient in our view to establish calculated rates of return as a kind of lower boundary to the range of possible "true" rates of return that would fully reflect all costs and benefits of higher education. To be sure, precise estimates of true rates of return probably cannot be made, since they would require measuring essentially unmeasurable variables. The skeptics once again have a point. But to ignore the existence in fact of heretofore uncounted costs and benefits is equal folly. Surely the inclusion, if only at the conceptual level, of nonmonetary as well as monetary returns, indirect as well as direct costs and benefits, and consumption as well as production effects in the assessment of true rates of return is the next logical step in deciding whether investments in higher education are worth what they cost. Having taken that step into essentially uncharted terrain, we conclude that the answer is "yes": economically, higher education is a good investment.

Peter Clecak

Views of
Social Critics

*Each man judges correctly those matters with
which he is acquainted; it is of these that he
is a competent critic. To criticize a particular
subject, therefore, a man must have been
trained in that subject: to be a good critic
generally, he must have had an all-round
education.*

Aristotle

Thus far, this book has reviewed evidence about the outcomes
of American higher education for individuals and for American
society. In this final chapter of Part Three, we move beyond the
evidence of outcomes to the views of social observers and thinkers about whether these outcomes are good or bad, adequate or
inadequate, socially beneficial or destructive. We move, in other
words, from social science to social criticism.

Social Criticism and Social Science

The idea of paying sustained attention to critics of higher education may seem at first a desperate ploy in a book concerned
with what we now know about the consequences of college. In
a way, it is. Administrators, faculty members, and large segments of the public display a deep ambivalence about the value

of social criticism; and many social scientists raise strident objections to it as a useful mode of inquiry, regarding it as an exercise in mere opinion rather than a disciplined search for objective truths. None of these reservations is without some foundation. Much criticism of postwar American society and its system of higher education has been intemperate, uninformed, and unreflective. Some of it has been politically and socially irresponsible. Moreover, as social scientists rightly contend, criticism is interpretive at best.

Despite these caveats, social criticism remains an indispensable tool in the examination of the outcomes of higher education. Two reasons dominate: First, as earlier chapters of this book show, the growing supply of hard knowledge concerning outcomes is incomplete and less than definitive. Nevertheless, important decisions that will shape future outcomes of higher education cannot be deferred, endlessly awaiting solid evidence. At least until more hard data are posted, then, the critical act will constitute a tenuous link between imperfect knowledge and intelligent educational policy. Second, even if all the results were in (and future outcomes could be predicted confidently on the basis of past and present ones), the issue could not be settled fully within the parameters of science. We should still have to decide how much knowledge, of what sort, is valuable for individuals, for various groups, and for society as a whole. For this, only a philosophical and critical mode of inquiry that includes a consideration of conflicting values will do.

Social science and social criticism are symbiotic elements of the untidy search for approximate answers to questions concerning outcomes. Whereas the study of higher education within and among the disciplines of social science is concerned mainly with causal theory, the relation among facts (Kateb, 1968), social criticism of education deals with its subject from a broadly moral point of view. Hard knowledge helps to discover the actual outcomes; criticism helps to determine what these outcomes might mean and how they ought to be valued.

Let us quickly recall the nature of social criticism. Social/cultural criticism is fundamentally a transdisciplinary enterprise whose broad scope includes the description, analysis, interpretation, and evaluation of changing social structures. Although the analytic component of social criticism presupposes a knowledge of social theory, the whole activity does not lie exclusively in the province of the social sciences. Interpretation and evaluation finally require humanistic perspectives—theological, historical, philosophical, psychological, and literary. The social critic lives within the changing structures he examines. In part shaped by these structures, he may hope also to influence them through his interpretations of the past and present. Social criticism is thus highly subjective but not merely subjective. At its best, it uses and illuminates the subjective, personal dimension of experience in an attempt to understand the quality of individual and social life of a particular society.

There are usually four basic elements of critical argument. First, the critic must characterize a social problem and estimate its causes. It may be a relatively isolated, specific problem (for example, whether to abolish or restore a system of grading on a campus). It may be a larger dilemma (for example, how or whether to expand higher education in America). It even may be a collection of problems calling into question the basis of an entire social order or civilization.

Second, using the powers of reason, observation and imagination, the critic offers (or assumes) a version of social reality, a characterization of what is and what is emerging out of the present historical moment (which is, itself, some combination of chance, choice, and necessity shaped in the past). Previous criticism, formal theory, empirical evidence, hunches, literary metaphors, analogies, and even myths comprise the materials out of which versions of social reality and visions of future possibilities are fashioned.

A third element of the critical act involves a characterization (often an implicit one) of a set of values and assumptions concerning the just organization of social life, the moral aptness of means in relation to ends, and the ethics of individual freedom and social responsibility. Various proposals to alleviate the problem or problems under consideration are assessed in terms of these normative assumptions.

Finally, through an exercise of imagination and judgment,

the critic must connect versions of social reality with visions of an ideal order. He advances a proposal—or at least an agenda—and suggests which values may be realized through its adoption, in what hierarchical order, and with what probable trade-offs. Unless the exercise is to be a utopian reverie, this judgment must include a plausible estimate of historical trends and of factors, such as the limits of plasticity in human nature, that may advance, alter, or wholly redirect these trends. On the basis of these considerations, the critic may assess the chances of this or that proposed politics of transition.

Social criticism, then, is ultimately a special form of art composed of argument and rhetoric. It is an exercise of the moral imagination disciplined by an estimation of human, historical, and political possibilities.

Caught in an Ezekiel's wheel of their own design, critics must live with their inability to separate objective social facts, conditions, and processes from subjective perceptions and characterizations of them. In a culture as heterogeneous as ours, then, criticism may generate more confusion than consensus, especially on a topic so broad as the outcomes of higher education. Critics regularly disagree over the definition, measurement, and evaluation of outcomes. They offer quite inconsistent assessments of the disparity between aims and perceived outcomes. And they differ wildly in their estimates of the system's chances of substantially reducing the gap between goals and outcomes. Whatever progress critics make is more often in a circle than a straight line. Moreover, since they tend to dwell on negative outcomes or on desired outcomes that have not been achieved, critics may add to the stock of public pessimism. In fact, criticism thrives on various sorts of exaggeration; though some strive for balance and moderation, many important critics are highly partisan. Despite its many limitations, however, we are driven back to criticism, perhaps with some embarrassment, even in a scientific age.

In the subsequent pages of this chapter, we shall summarize, specify, and assess the state of criticism about college outcomes by examining social critics in two major groups: first, those who regard American higher education as a social disease requiring radical surgery (or even decapitation) and then those who consider it a flawed mixture of positive and negative outcomes in need of constant criticism and renewal. Though this division between radical and mainstream critics lacks precision, it will help to illuminate the complex terrain of critical discussion of outcomes. In surveying this landscape of contemporary criticism, it is hard to avoid the impression that, for radicals and centrists alike, an earlier faith in American higher education has lapsed into a labored belief—if not outright skepticism.

Radical Critics

Radical critics of American higher education display marked differences. They assume various ideological positions—neo-Anarchist, neo-Marxist, revisionist, socialist. They differ in their theoretical approaches to the assessment of higher education, in their estimates of present outcomes, and in their recommendations for change. In fact, such figures as Paul Goodman, Ivan Illich, Edgar Z. Friedenberg, John Holt, Theodore Roszak, Charles Reich, Samuel Bowles, and Herbert Gintis frequently disagree as passionately with one another as they do with critics on the other side of the ideological spectrum. Despite significant individual variations, however, radical critics do inhabit one side of this spectrum. Though numerically small, the radicals are important. Using a framework of social premises that differs markedly from those employed by most American students of outcomes, the radicals call attention to assumptions and values normally taken for granted in discussions of higher education. To bring the radical section of the critical landscape into perspective, we need to focus initially on their broad similarities.

Radical critics generally regard basic American articles of faith in education, including higher education, as one of the central myths of twentieth-century American capitalism. Cast in their most general terms, the fundamental elements of this social myth are clear. (See Greer, 1972, pp. 13-22.) Education is intrinsically good, because it helps individuals to realize their capacities for knowledge and self-expression. Moreover, advocates of the liberal mystique suggest that the historical trend toward widening and deepening educational opportunity in America contributes to economic progress, thereby advancing the values of order, security, democracy, liberty, equality, fraternity, and cultural excellence—the most important cluster of social values.

The myth has still other dimensions. Since universal primary and secondary education—and more recently, mass higher education—enlarges the scope of individual freedom by reducing ignorance and expanding choice, it presumably strengthens the fragile political system of democracy, itself the main social guarantor of liberty. At the same time, steady expansion of educational opportunities contributes to the social realization of the ideal of egalitarianism in several ways. First, when fully implemented, the widening and deepening of education will insure each individual an equal chance to develop unequal talents. Second—and here tensions between liberty and equality surface —education equalizes opportunities for achieving rewards in society because it places the competition on a fairer basis, superseding ascriptive criteria of noble birth or privileged class. By reducing capricious social inequities inherent in the larger world, then, American education moves society toward the goal of a fair meritocracy. Third, over the past century education has contributed to economic growth and hence to the gradual betterment of all classes. It helps to redistribute wealth, power, and privilege in each generation. And, at a certain point perhaps not too far off, the universalization of higher education may be expected to act as a major redistributive force, permanently flattening out the class structure. As more and more people take degrees, it is assumed, the economic advantages of higher education to individuals will level off, reducing differentials of salary and status throughout society. Education, then, may yet redeem its old promise by becoming the vehicle of a classless society.

Finally, another feature of the myth is that the widening and deepening of education also may contribute to the classic goal of fraternity, by consolidating elements of a common national culture while preserving parts of the various subcultures.

In this dominant view—or better, in this composite sketch

of many views—education is regarded either as a primary component of a basically healthy society or as a (perhaps *the*) principal corrective force for a potentially far healthier and more humane society. Radical critics spend much of their energy attacking this belief system, terming it an ideology in the classic Marxian sense of false or inverted consciousness. Formal education as currently organized, they claim, is the handmaiden of a corrupt society. At worst, it produces negative outcomes that mirror corruption in the larger society. At best—usually in the more renowned institutions of higher learning—it professes desired outcomes (or goals) that benefit a few, while concealing both the negative outcomes it produces and the massive social ills of a society in need of a fundamental transformation. This transformation, some radical critics contend, must include the abolition of capitalism, bureaucracy, representative democracy, a repressive "elitist" culture—and most of the present system of higher education.

Let us examine two sorts of radical critics of education— neo-Anarchist and neo-Marxist—using as representative examples the work of Ivan Illich, Samuel Bowles, and Herbert Gintis. (The prefix *neo* is used rather loosely, to distinguish contemporary anarchists and Marxists from their nineteenth- and early twentieth-century predecessors.)

Neo-Anarchists. Ivan Illich claims that schools impoverish individuals rather than enriching them and that contemporary education reinforces the inequities of class structure rather than reducing or eliminating them. Though by now utterly familiar, these charges until recently were the property of a few radical predecessors of Illich, such as Goodman, Friedenberg, Holt, Marcuse—and of Rousseau and Marx, their spiritual ancestors. At the level of description, then, Illich commands our attention as a representative of one increasingly influential if relatively small stream of contemporary criticism of education. Moreover, he is a trenchant and lucid exponent of the most radical *explanation* of the social and psychological factors that sustain elements of the liberal mystique. His diagnosis—and proposed cure —are radical in the traditional sense of going to the roots.

Indeed, with Illich, we reach the circumference of educational criticism; beyond him there is nowhere to go, except back toward the ideological center.

Along with other radical critics, Illich finds the liberal myth perverse, an inverted image of social reality that conceals its actual dimensions. Schooling, by which he means an "age-specific, teacher-related process requiring full-time attendance at an obligatory curriculum," is harmful to individuals and to society (Illich, 1972, p. 38). To account for the persistence of the myth that formal education produces positive outcomes, Illich remolds the classical Marxian theory of alienation to fit the contours of the welfare state. Penetrating the stale crust of the familiar comparison between schools and factories, Illich argues that the development of a welfare state within the structure of twentieth-century capitalism inflicts a "psychic impotence" on its victims, enlarging the scope of alienation and refining its shapes to include the sphere of culture (Illich and others, 1973, p. 11).

A kind of romantic irony operates here, reminiscent of Herbert Marcuse's notion of one-dimensionality (Marcuse, 1964). Culture, which formerly afforded a relatively free mental space, a source of potential opposition to the grimy social world, is closed off steadily through the institutionalization of individual, family, education, and community life in late capitalist society. This extension of alienation into education simultaneously promotes evil and prevents good. Through their "hidden curricula," schools enforce a series of negative outcomes: They emphasize competition, submission to the personal authority of teachers, and acceptance of an impersonal hierarchy enforced through the processes of sorting, grading, and certifying. Schools standardize norms and deny individual differences. They discourage creativity and love while promoting imitativeness and fear. They favor abstract categories over concrete, sensuous experience. Moreover, the structure of schooling convinces people that education must come in discrete particles, graded units to be sequentially consumed. In societies where consumption takes on a sacramental quality, the school system assumes "the threefold function common to powerful churches throughout history. It is simultaneously the repository of society's myth, the institutionalization of that myth's contradictions, and the locus of the ritual which reproduces and veils the disparities between myth and reality" (Illich, 1972, p. 54).

When schooling becomes an ideological narcotic, demand for the commodity continuously outstrips supply. Rather than advancing equality, organized education insures permanent inequality because, as each level of schooling approaches universality, demands for more advanced packages of knowledge inevitably arise. Since these new levels can be opened initially only to a few, inequality must be the normal condition of the educational system as a whole, despite its egalitarian pretensions. This pattern of education operates as long as citizens remain addicted to an ethic of consumption.

This sweeping indictment and the accompanying analysis call for a bold remedy—for nothing less than the deschooling of society. "Deschooling," according to Illich, is at the root of any movement for human liberation (1972, p. 69). Like most radicals, he displays some ambivalence about the value of discarding all of the current structure. But not much: "Equal educational opportunity is, indeed, both a desirable and a feasible goal, but to equate this with obligatory schooling is to confuse salvation with the Church" (1972, p. 15). He concedes that reforms may help in small ways; more importantly, the quest for piecemeal change may transform consciousness, thereby preparing the way for fundamental social change. As a prophetic critic, however, Illich concentrates on the need for revolutionary change—in the schools and in the social order as a whole. A social revolution without deschooling would more or less rapidly betray its promise of liberation. Deschooling without a social revolution probably would increase inequality. And it certainly would leave intact the harmful values, attitudes, and institutions that preclude the free expression of man's essential powers. Illich thus assumes that the removal of oppressive institutions and the abandonment of their accompanying ideologies will usher in a new age, a human community or association of autonomous individuals, genuinely free and fundamentally good.

In Illich's view, genuine individual freedom is the primary human value. Without it, no society can be just. With it, individuals will exhibit inherent goodness. Since education, as opposed to schooling, can occur only in an atmosphere of freedom, Illich proposes constitutional guarantees: "The State shall make no law with respect to the establishment of education" (1972, p. 16). In a free society, a good educational system would "provide all who want to learn with access to available resources at any time in their lives; empower all who want to share what they know to find those who want to learn it from them; and finally, furnish all who want to present an issue to the public with the opportunity to make their challenge known" (1972, p. 108). A philosophical anarchist who articulates many political themes, Illich emerges as a libertarian in his politics.

He holds unorthodox views on the value of higher education to individuals and society. Universities produce needlessly complex technological knowledge that becomes a repressive power over the majority who pay for it. And they produce privileged people: "Students see their studies as the investment with the highest monetary return, and nations see them as a key factor in development" (1972, p. 52). Rather than questioning the rate of economic return to individuals—or even trying to measure it—he condemns the *idea* of an economic payoff from education. The intangible benefits that defenders of liberal learning usually celebrate are, for Illich, largely illusory, because the hidden curriculum subverts the humanistic tradition of knowledge (1972, p. 51).

Illich makes only one concession to higher education: the university, he observes, still provides a space for discovery and dissent. But the "hotbeds of heresy" are small and, more often than not, the university co-opts and contains dissent, enveloping it within the folds of its larger myths and rituals. Nevertheless, the surviving pockets of intellectual resistance strengthen the argument that "the existence of the university is necessary to guarantee continued social criticism" (1972, p. 53). In Illich's view, then, the only unambiguously positive outcome of the present system of higher education is the chance it offers selected individuals to understand why the whole system ought to be abandoned.

Neo-Marxists. From critical vantage points of nonradicals, those whom I have loosely labeled neo-Anarchists and neo-Marxists do not differ appreciably in their conclusions concerning the generally negative outcomes of American higher education. At the level of description, similarities are striking. At the level of analysis and prescription, however, differences become significant enough to warrant discussion. Neo-Anarchists believe that American education should not be bound to any state; neo-Marxists believe that it is tied to the wrong state. In an extensive critique of *Deschooling Society,* Herbert Gintis examines the major variances between neo-Anarchists and Marxists (Gintis, in Illich and others, 1973, pp. 29-76).

According to Gintis, Illich mistakenly locates the sources of present social and educational crises primarily in the reproduction of alienated patterns of consumption in the cultural superstructure, rather than identifying these as "merely manifestations of the deeper workings of the economic system" (1973, p. 31). Beginning with this failure to understand the centrality of the mode of production, Gintis claims, Illich goes off the tracks of Marxian analysis at every crucial juncture. Assuming that the ideology of consumerism derives from manipulative indoctrination by corporate bureaucracies through the sales effort, Illich simplifies and distorts the problem of transforming individual consciousness, schools, and society. According to Gintis, Illich presupposes a romantic and ahistorical view of human nature, which leads him to a libertarian rather than a revolutionary socialist conception of politics. Positing a felicitous human essence that is prior to contemporary existence and badly distorted by it, Illich (in Gintis's view) mistakenly argues that individuals may liberate themselves one by one, through a sort of ideological exorcism and, further, that the entire society may be freed by removing the offending institutions.

The Marxian thesis developed by Bowles and Gintis centers on "contradictions," or pressure points, of advanced capitalism whose sources reside deep in the mode of production (Gintis, in Illich and others, 1973; Bowles, 1973; Bowles and Gintis, 1975). The synthesis, or solution, turns upon a vague politics of socialist revolution. Neo-Marxist critics of education analyze the development of American society in terms of interrelationships between the classic subcategories of the mode of production: the forces of production, "the productive capacities of the economy," and the social relations of production—"the rules of authority among those engaged in production, the system of control over the work process, and the relations of property that govern the ownership of the product" (Bowles, 1973, p. 141). In this framework, the development of American capitalism through its various stages can be viewed as a long process of capital accumulation requiring a vast expansion of the forces of production and a more or less continuous transformation of the social relations of production—of the values, beliefs, attitudes, and behavior of the people who form the most crucial components of the economic machine. By the end of World War II, the drive to accumulate capital included nearly everyone in the wage-labor system. The expansive drive of the system entailed the "proletarianization" of such previously exempt groups as white-collar workers and self-employed persons.

At a remote level of abstraction, this argument provides the theoretical underpinnings of Marxist interpretations of American higher education. According to Bowles, "higher education has aided in the expansion of the productive capacities of the nation, the reproduction of the social class system, and the legitimation of the resulting inequalities" (p. 143). Using these assumptions concerning the central functions of higher education in America, neo-Marxists are bound to take a pretty grim view of the outcomes. Consider the Archimedian value of egalitarianism which, when applied to present circumstances, implies —for Marxists, at any rate—the need to redistribute income, wealth, opportunity, responsibility, and status. Bowles does concede that "higher education in the United States has made a major contribution to economic growth"—that is, to the expansion of the forces of production (p. 143). But in the process of imparting a wide variety of technical skills, thereby expanding human capital, higher education also promotes an array of attitudes appropriate to an ever more differentiated social hierarchy.

Thus, in Bowles's view, the trend toward mass higher education since 1945 does not represent an advance toward equality or toward greater realization of such other social values as democracy, liberty, and fraternity. Quite the reverse. First, the entire structure of education supports an inequitable economic and social order. Indeed, the evolving structure of higher education faithfully reproduces the class structure (Bowles, 1973, pp. 144-145). With few exceptions, women, minorities, and lower echelons of the working class systematically are accorded less prestigious places in the educational and social hierarchies. Second, the existence of some mobility permits the recruitment of talent for the middle and upper reaches of the capitalist hierarchy and robs the working class of potential revolutionary leadership. Finally, the proliferation of higher education lends some plausibility to the myth of equal opportunity. In so doing, however, it legitimizes the class system by providing an ostensibly fair means through which the inequitable privileges and benefits of society are parceled out in seemingly objective ways. In good times, the entire system grows, demonstrating a capacity to produce that commands the allegiance of all sectors. In leaner times, working people bear the brunt of restricted expansion. And through every economic phase, the entire social system sustains an inequitable pattern of distribution.

Neo-Marxists find clear sources of social inequality in the postwar shapes of higher education as well as in its increased size. What many mainstream critics celebrate as a diversity of institutions and curricula established to meet the variegated needs of an ever larger constituency strikes neo-Marxists as a partly successful adaptive response to developing contradictions between the forces and social relations of production. The growth of first-rate universities and second-line state universities and the spectacular emergence of community colleges only corresponds to the complex needs of the evolving mode of production, not to the complex needs of people.

According to Marxist critics, colleges and universities no longer merely train elites. They also—perhaps primarily—train masses. Attempts to accomplish both sorts of tasks in the campus culture of, say, small liberal arts colleges or major research universities only reveals and intensifies the contradictions of advanced capitalist society. The desired outcomes in the form of changes in personality traits, say, for future corporation executives and computer programmers must be different if the complex social organization is to run harmoniously. The creation of a multitiered system of higher education has relieved some of the pressure, permitting various types of institutions to perform very different acts of socialization. According to Bowles, "Structural change in educational processes has ... been necessitated by two parallel movements: the growth in enrollments and the continuing change in the social relations of production, manifested in the fragmentation and routinization, in short, in the proletarianization of white-collar labor" (1973, p. 150).

Neo-Marxists contend that only a revolutionary transition to socialism can reverse this dynamic pattern in which inequality persists through vast internal change. But inequality, along with such other negative outcomes as the diminution of personality required by the capitalist division of labor, receives different emphasis according to the status of the economy. Thus, in the sixties, when the economic system delivered relatively more goods, the working class, especially its upper reaches, received more, and the classic issue of exploitation receded before the theme of alienation. Disparities between the unlimited needs of the system for ever more specialized personnel and the growing needs of individuals for interesting and socially useful jobs intensified alienation. Though college graduates could take money and status for granted then, the system did not provide enough rewarding work. This incongruity, along with the deliquescence of campus life resulting from disparate economic and social imperatives—and a disastrous foreign war—provided the middle-class impetus to the campus unrest and revolts of the 1960s.

Although Marxists hoped that middle-class youths and other oppressed groups might coalesce into the beginnings of a revolutionary movement, the contradiction did not come to a boil. It merely fizzled out under the impact of stagflation and declining expectations of future abundance in the seventies. Such dramatic reverses, however, do not trouble Marxists much.

Like phases of the moon, new economic configurations require only a shifting stress among the ensemble of contradictions. In a period of slower economic expansion, the main emphasis shifts from alienation back to exploitation. More higher education has promoted alienation. The threat of less intensifies exploitation. Both contribute to inequality. Despite variations governed by the seasons of the economy, then, Marxists assess desired and actual outcomes with a set of shifting assumptions that insures a single negative conclusion.

The Marxists maintain that cognitive and affective learning contributes to forces and social relations of production that must be revamped totally if education is ever to produce genuinely positive outcomes for individuals and society. Insofar as tensions in the mode of production promote inequality, submission, exploitation, and alienation, they are evil. Insofar as the system of higher education fails to educate, it does not meet people's needs. Performance subverts capitalist pretensions. Capitalist pretensions subvert the potential performance of socialism and inhibit the formation of revolutionary consciousness, the only acceptable outcomes for neo-Marxists. In this political project, higher education plays an accidental role: it yields positive outcomes only through the efforts of radical faculty and students to make others aware of the inhumane character of the entire social system, including, of course, higher education. Despite its narrow final focus, Marxist criticism is suggestive of certain themes that in recent years have claimed the attention of mainstream critics. As we shall see, chunks of radical critique now are carried along the surface of mainstream criticism of higher education by populist undercurrents.

Of course, not all radicals inhabit closed mythologies. As editor of *Dissent*, the major American journal of democratic socialist opinion, Irving Howe represents a significant radical tendency outside the rigidities of many contemporary Marxists and Anarchists, yet not at the center of the mainstream. Howe thus provides a convenient transition, a way toward the center. Primarily a critic of literature, politics, and culture, Howe nonetheless is an interesting voice in the debate over outcomes, having long experienced the dilemma of being a political radical committed to individual liberty, to social egalitarianism, and to the preservation and extension of liberal learning. In attempting to clarify this dilemma, Howe preserves some elements of classical Marxism that have been neglected by its recent exponents and ignored by most mainstream critics. This enables him to sort out, at least theoretically, distinct elements of tradition and class without denying their relationships: "In the 19th century ... there appeared two revolutionary ideas of education, one emerging out of the democratic upheavals in France and America, the other out of the socialist movement. Both of these were necessarily marked by ambivalence toward traditional kinds of education: they saw it as a rationalization for the power of a ruling class but also as a valued heritage that the masses had been unjustly deprived of. Some liberal democrats succumbed to contempt for the 'dead past,' some socialists to contempt for 'bourgeois culture.' But there were also the wiser persuasions of Melville and Whitman that the mission of America was to absorb and transcend European culture, and of Marx that the workers must 'conquer' and elevate traditional culture" (Howe, 1975, pp. 9-10).

Evoking this historical background, Howe suggests that the egalitarian ideal of mass higher education must be pursued, even though the quest now seems more costly and more complicated than it did in the late nineteenth and early twentieth centuries. Its abandonment would have grave consequences for education and for democracy (whether capitalist or socialist). It would deprive those "who bear the stigmata of decades, centuries of American outrage" of material opportunity as well as of their right to share the legacy of political and cultural achievement and to add to it. Because he is committed also to the "widespread diffusion of learning," Howe (1975, p. 10) advocates "preservation of the highest standards of learning." But he does not countenance a return to the arid elitism of "those harrumphing Old Humanists who shield themselves behind the armor of 'standards' . . ." using the imperatives of the new fiscal conservatism to justify the contradiction of liberal learning. Nor does he pretend that genuine liberal learning and the pursuit of universal higher education can proceed without conflict. Recognizing its theoretical and practical difficulties, Howe insists on the value of maintaining an ambivalent vision: "In the short and perhaps the long run there occurs a wrenching conflict between high culture and universal education, to both of which we are devoted and between which we would hardly know how to choose" (1975, p. 10). The problem of making imperfect choices among desired outcomes of higher education, which Howe approaches from a radical view of history, also plagues mainstream critics.

The Mainstream

In an era of limits, critics in the mainstream—those in and out of the academy, and those physically or psychically on the outside—have come to accept the idea that higher education, like other public enterprises, promised more than it conceivably could deliver during the postwar phase of affluence, relatively rapid growth, and anticipated abundance. If higher education cannot be all things to all people, however, critics wonder what it reasonably can offer various clienteles during a time of relative economic scarcity (which may be only temporary) and increased competition for public and philanthropic funds (which may be expected to persist).

The current critical debate has several fundamental dimensions. The first involves a critique of the disparity between the desired outcomes of higher education and its performance, as perceived by critics. How wide *is* the gap between desired and actual outcomes? Second, debate centers on the problem of which values ought to be pursued through formal education—and which sacrificed—during the rest of this century. What ought to be the shape of our educational desires in the coming period of limits?

To illustrate the central directions of the debate, I should like to focus initially on Caroline Bird's *The Case Against College,* a popular exposé of the pretensions of American higher education. Bird's book has weaknesses stemming especially from her ignoring many of the significant and well-documented positive outcomes of higher education. Nevertheless, the book is important. For one thing, she has the courage to address head-on the vital question of whether American higher education really is worth what it costs—a problem that few mainstream critics approach so directly. For another, her negative answer gives public shape as well as a measure of legitimacy to what seems to be the increasingly popular sentiment that college may be, after all, only a luxury, appropriate for a sizable minority but not for the masses.

Bird argues the proposition that only the minority of perhaps 25 percent who "love learning for its own sake. . . . those who would rather read a good book than eat" ought to enroll in college immediately upon completing high school (1975, pp. 3-4). The chief reason for seeking a college education—and the only sensible one, according to Bird—is pleasure. But, she reasons, college cannot be enjoyable for the 75 percent of the population who lack the intellectual equipment that might enable them to love learning (p. 186). On the basis of these assumptions, Bird assumes what those concerned with the identification and measurement of actual outcomes take as their primary problem—namely, that college has very little positive impact on most people. It "doesn't make people intelligent, ambitious, happy, liberal, or quick to learn new things. It's the other way round" (p. 122). Specifying her claim that college has only slight impact on individuals, Bird produces along the way an indictment of both the public elements of the liberal myth and the complementary notion of higher education as the key to personal success.

First, she considers the purely economic considerations. Surveying the inconclusive literature on economic outcomes, Bird concludes definitely that college is "the dumbest investment you can make." To elucidate this flat assertion, she relies on a variant of the old laissez-faire argument against Social Security: If a 1972 Princeton freshman (male) had banked the $34,181 that his diploma would ultimately cost him at "7.5 percent interest compounded daily, he would have at the retirement age of sixty-four a total of $1,129,200 or $528,200 more than the earnings of a male college graduate" (p. 64).

Bird then argues that college has been oversold greatly as a means to a rewarding career: "Whatever college graduates *want* to do, most of them are going to wind up doing what there *is* to do" (pp. 87-88). Colleges do not prepare students to do anything, she declares; most graduates perform jobs not directly related to their majors. Even professional schools, often spared the wrath of philistines, fail to prepare students adequately to perform particular tasks: "The plain fact is that what doctors, nurses, lawyers, journalists, social workers, broadcasters, librarians, and executives do all day long isn't taught in classrooms" (p. 103).

Having seriously questioned the presumed connections between higher education and employment, augmented earnings, higher status, and satisfying work, Bird proceeds to examine intangible outcomes. In her view, the advertised benefits of liberal education—familiarity with a tradition of masterworks, heightened esthetic sensibility and deepened intellectual powers, the formation of humane attitudes and values—are all so much pious doubletalk (p. 109). In her view, both liberal learning and the extracurricular facets of the college experience ought to be classed as elements of a larger category—the transition from youth to adulthood. She concedes that college may be useful, to some, in this metamorphosis. The "real benefits," according to the students she interviewed, are "getting away from home, living on their own, making friends different from themselves, exploring knowledge, trying a field of work, training for a job, growing up" (p. 136). But if a chance to mature constitutes the principal payoff for most, as she maintains, then higher education in its present forms becomes just one of many possible alternatives open to graduating seniors. In fact, it emerges as a very expensive option that provides only limited independence to young people still partially indentured to parents.

All this clears the way for a consideration of alternatives for the 75 percent who presumably cannot benefit greatly from higher education. Bird begins with a quaint passage on success, defined by the solid criterion of amassing a million dollars through individual initiative. For those who do not fit the mold of Horatio Alger, however, there are lesser options: vocational training, college work-study programs, business, the armed forces, "helping people," subsistence jobs, and the like. In fact, about half of the nation's high school graduates routinely elect these alternatives to college. And, it should be added, a percentage of the other half elect college as a barely preferable alternative to this thin array of outside choices. Bird suggests that the alternatives to college need to be widened and deepened. And she would finance this operation with some of the billions saved by cutting the present higher educational establishment down to an appropriate size.

However, her case against mass higher education articulates a serious popular assault on the still dominant set of beliefs concerning the interconnected monetary and nonmonetary values of higher education to individuals. By defining college as a special case of the transition to adulthood, factoring out the categories of benefits to individuals, and presenting them as separable both in theory and plausible practice, Bird suggests a glacial shift in the entire *conception* of the problem of outcomes.

A more careful conception and elaboration of this emerging framework for assessing the outcomes of higher education may be found in *Youth: Transition to Adulthood* (1974), in which Coleman and others on the Panel on Youth of the President's Science Advisory Committee address the problem of outcomes in higher education. They approach it obliquely, considering it as one facet of the complex process of the socialization of youth, a stage of life between fourteen and twenty-four which separates childhood from adulthood. In this category of youth, secondary schools, higher education, and other socializing environments are assessed with reference to the gap between desired and actual outcomes.

Coleman sees two main classes of objectives that the environments of youth ought to advance: self-enhancement and social maturation. The principal class of objectives having to do with self-enhancement includes, first, "cognitive and non-cognitive skills necessary for economic independence and for occupational opportunities," that is, marketable skills; second, the "capability of effective management of one's own affairs"; third, "capabilities as a consumer, not only of goods, but more significantly, of the cultural riches of civilization." Finally, environments for youth should facilitate "capabilities for engaging in intense concentrated involvement in an activity" such as scholarship, performance, or the "creation of physical objects" (pp. 3, 4).

The second, equally important class of objectives centers on activities "directed toward other persons." Here an enlargement of perspective may be gained first by "experience with persons differing in social class, subculture, and age." Another dimension of social maturation concerns "the experience of having others dependent on one's actions." Finally, the social maturation of individuals requires a context of "interdependent activities directed toward collective goals, where the outcomes for all depend on the coordinated efforts of each." To complete the transition from youth to adulthood, individuals need experience as leaders and followers. From these two classes of objectives—self-enhancement and social maturation—young people ought to develop "a sense of identity and self-esteem" (pp. 4, 5).

Coleman finds schools, the chief formal institution to facilitate the transition to adulthood, inadequate. "At their best," he observes, "schools equip students with cognitive and noncognitive skills relevant to their occupational futures, with knowledge of some portion of civilization's cultural heritage, and with the taste for acquiring more such skills and knowledge" (p. 146). But schools do not "provide extensive opportunity for managing one's affairs; they seldom encourage intense concentration on a single activity, and they are inappropriate settings for nearly all objectives involving responsibilities that affect others" (p. 146). Indeed, in Coleman's view, formal institutions of education "retard" youth in these important areas by "monopolizing their time for the narrow objectives that schools have" (p. 146).

The Coleman report centers on identifying important "unmet objectives" and suggesting possible alternatives. This widens the context of the debate over outcomes. Indeed, the selection of youth as the primary object of inquiry entails a joint consideration of secondary and higher education. Coleman, however, does distinguish between high school and college, noting similarities but stressing differences. Segregation by culture and race persists in college, though in a far less rigorous manner. Segregation by age also continues, though in much diluted form. In contrast to the rigidities of the secondary system, four-year colleges and universities exhibit a healthy pluralism. And community colleges fall somewhere between the ends of this continuum (p. 89). These important caveats notwithstanding, the problems of transition affect all formal educational institutions to some degree.

Coleman fundamentally objects to the dominant pattern of a long, uninterrupted period of schooling designed to foster self-development, followed by useful social activity in "the form of a full-time job." Because it thwarts social maturation, this pattern needs revision. Coleman recommends that schools emphasize what they presumably do best—the cognitive aspects of development—while claiming less of the time and attention of youth. Periods of schooling should be punctuated by periods of activity in the larger society aimed at providing opportunities for social maturation. Coleman proposes an enlargement of current options: continuing education, which permits individuals to interweave learning and social activity throughout life; recurrent education, or the alternation of "full-time work and full-time education"; career education, which entails a shift in locale —and emphases—of vocational education from schools to the workplace; and "learning at work," a constant interplay of learning and work carried out wholly at the workplace (pp. 137-139). Coleman finds some merit in each of these patterns: "To satisfy the dual needs for activity directed inward and outward, some such environment, involving both learning and some public service work directed toward a shared goal, would be optimum. But environments of this sort are now seldom available to youth" (p. 139).

To insure the widest possible choice for youth, Coleman and his associates endorse a voucher system for everyone over sixteen as an alternative to the current arrangement, which in their view provides inequitable subsidies—and "bribes"—to those who continue in school. The voucher plan sketched out by Coleman would make young people directly responsible for educational decisions after they pass the compulsory school age of sixteen. Vouchers "equivalent in value to the average cost of education through four years of college" would be presented to all young people "to be used at their discretion for schooling and other skill acquisition at any subsequent time of their life" (pp. 169-170).

Though far more sophisticated in conception and detail than Bird's popular tract, Coleman's report proposes similar outcomes. Together, they express one strong current of mainstream criticism and popular opinion that involves a major redefinition of the problem of outcomes. In this view, higher education no longer should be regarded as the primary (and most desirable) formal institution for socializing the young (fourteen to twenty-four), for sorting and certifying people, and for advancing the egalitarian ideal.

The implications of this analysis for higher education are significant. Adoption of Coleman's proposals would result in lowered expectations concerning the functions of higher education, thereby bringing desired outcomes more in line with actual outcomes. It would preclude the further expansion of higher education as a major means of equalizing opportunity, knowledge, and rewards. It would entail a reorientation of priorities within higher education (at least in the nonelite sectors) away from liberal education toward versions of the new vocationalism. The more ambitious dimensions of such schemes, however, provide compensations: Liberal education may be preserved in the more prestigious institutions and through lifelong learning programs. And the ideal of equality may be advanced somewhat through a voucher system.

Other critics in the mainstream—single voices within the academy—take on colorations of the pervasive mood of pessimism and weariness without reaching such negative assessments of present outcomes as Bird's and Coleman's. A two-part issue of *Daedalus,* "American Higher Education: Toward an Uncertain Future" (1974, 1975), prompted Norman Birnbaum to remark: "Our uncertainties are more collective than individual. Taken singly, each of the contributors professes to know what

ought to be done. Taken together, they speak past each other"
(1975, p. 15). Despite their differences, these critics—eighty-five
in all—do represent a major force in American higher education.
The list includes presidents of important American universities
(Martin Meyerson, Derek Bok, Robben Fleming, Richard Lyman, and Theodore Hesburgh); nationally recognized spokesmen for higher education (Clark Kerr, Daniel Moynihan); prestigious students of higher education (Martin Trow, Carl
Kaysen); and distinguished scholars from other disciplines (C.
Vann Woodward, Charles Frankel, John Hope Franklin, Frank
Manuel, Talcott Parsons, Robert Coles).

Linked directly to the upper reaches of American higher
education, these figures represent the politically moderate, aca-
demically elite, largely white, predominantly male, middle-aged,
primarily Eastern solid center of respectable opinion. Although
this center does not hold together very well, it does display
critical patterns distinctly different from those of the radicals
and rather different from those of various publics outside the
academy. Whereas Bird and Coleman suggest a reorientation of
outcomes and a consequent reorganization of social institutions,
most of the mainstream critics in the *Daedalus* symposium still
regard higher education as the principal agency for socializing
and cultivating the young.

They thus operate in the shadowy zone between the dominant liberal myth and its radical negation. In this area some
agreement exists concerning fundamental problems. Contributors generally believe that the system is in deep crisis and that
old ways must be modified. They find the undergraduate curriculum in a shambles. They maintain that graduate education
must be recast and professional education revised. Faced with
fiscal crises and leveling enrollments in the youth sector, the
system somehow must be adapted to new clienteles in a more
competitive market. Goals and purposes, no less than organization and governance, require serious reexamination within and
among institutions. Though there is no consensus about solu-
tions, most of the contributors believe—or assume—that these
problems ought to be resolved primarily within the system of
higher education, not through a wholesale reorganization of the

social system. All of the issues raised in the symposium affect the question of outcomes, but the issue of curriculum lies at the center of things.[1]

Viewed from perspectives within the academy, the vast social and cultural changes of the past quarter-century call former structures and goals of higher education into question. Martin Trow's scheme of "autonomous" and "popular" functions conveniently identifies the main external causes of internal shifts. Such activities as the transmission of high culture, pure research, and the development of elites can be considered autonomous in that they "are intrinsic to the conception of the university and the academic role as these have been evolved in Europe and America over the past 150 years" (Trow, 1970, p. 2). Popular functions such as service to larger social institutions and the education of everyone to the limits of his or her desire and ability have been assumed in response to "external needs and demands." In the evolution of higher education, tensions between autonomous and popular functions quite predictably arose. These conflicts have been attenuated primarily through a complex division of academic labor within and among institutions, enabling American higher education to fulfill both sorts of purposes surprisingly well, compared with, say, European universities, which until recently stressed autonomous functions exclusively.

Higher education has evolved from a minority privilege to a mass right and, in Trow's view soon may become a nearly universal obligation. This rapid expansion of popular functions raises the question of the compatibility between the two sorts of purposes. Indeed, it leads many to wonder whether the autonomous functions can survive the rest of the century in any recognizable form. Indicating the depth of uncertainty, Trow observes that "many academic men no longer really believe they have a right to define a curriculum for their students or to set

[1] In discussing curriculum I follow Peter Caws' admonition that "All arguments of detail about the curriculum are absolutely pointless. . . . Arguments of principle, centering on what to do instead of lining up courses end to end until graduation, might be helpful" (Peter Caws, 1974).

standards of performance, much less to prescribe the modes of thought and feeling appropriate to 'an educated man' " (p. 35).

Few critics of higher education find curricula rational. The curricular disarray constitutes a major artifact that permits several inferences. It testifies to the loss of confidence among faculty. It confirms the enlargement of popular functions summarized by Trow. And it provides archeological evidence of the vast transformation of the amount and shape of knowledge—what there is to teach—over the past century. "The comfortable center of knowledge," Steven Muller (1974, p. 149) observes in the *Daedalus* symposium, "disintegrated under the centrifugal forces of professionalization and specialization that were induced by the technological explosion." A century ago, Muller recalls, "advanced knowledge could still be thought of as an orderly mansion. One could move from a foundation of literacy and elementary mathematics through the chambers of the arts and sciences and the learned professions, the whole roofed over by philosophy. The entirety was visible and comprehensible." Instead of a mansion, advanced knowledge now resembles "a labyrinth still under construction. It lacks both wholeness and a center. Tunnels extend in all directions, crossing one another occasionally, and the best and the brightest are at work extending them" (pp. 149-150). Specialized scholars in various tunnels do not communicate with one another. Beginners dig their way a short distance into one or two tunnels, and then either give up or press ahead in one. "There is," Muller concludes, "no longer a body of higher learning." As a consequence, "the graduates of colleges and universities may be highly skilled technologically, but they are no longer civilized or well-grounded in the traditional sense" (p. 150).

These dramatic changes in the functions of higher education and in the extent and structure of knowledge have seriously eroded the traditional university ideal articulated by Newman, Mill, and Arnold. And they have given rise to alternative ideals of technical and professional knowledge. Though the traditional liberal ideal has been undercut by changing realities, as even its most ardent defenders concede, both models have their advocates in the academy. Most of the participants in the debate agree that liberal learning and specialized training—what Muller calls "skilling"—in the advanced disciplines, as well as in professional and vocational curricula, have a place in contemporary higher education. Disagreements center on the relative importance and the degree of compatibility among the major thrusts, as well as on their social implications. Though there are purists among both traditionalist defenders of liberal learning and professionalists, most favor or at least acquiesce in some sort of political compromise. A third group, the fusionists, favor compromise at the level of principle. Taken together, these three emphases—traditionalist, professionalist, and fusionist—define the broad parameters of mainstream critical opinion concerning outcomes as it unfolds in the debate over curricular rationales.

Traditionalists. In contrast to neo-Marxist critics of higher education, traditionalists do not share a distinct theory of society, persons, politics, and education. There is no single traditionalist position, nor is there even a common set of assumptions from which the usual arguments proceed. To speak of *the* traditionalist position, then, is a verbal convenience. We nevertheless can identify a traditionalist tendency in the current debate over outcomes that may be distinguished usefully from other views of the purposes of higher education.

Traditionalists usually defend images of higher education, culture, and personality fashioned largely in the nineteenth century (or earlier). Inasmuch as these images seem increasingly at odds with current realities, traditionalists cast their criticism in somber tones, ranging from moods of regret to embattled rage. In part defenders of humanistic modes of liberal education, traditionalists also criticize those dominant tendencies that have shaped posttraditional contours of higher education. They find the rapid and indiscriminate adoption of popular functions by higher education inimical to its proper functions. And they regret the proliferation of science and technology, especially its seemingly endless division of new knowledge into increasingly specialized fields and subfields. Though not unified politically, they often display conservative biases.

Ironically, traditionalists are more deeply aware of history than other mainstream critics and more wounded by its odd turns. In their view, the multiplication of the functions of higher education over the past century has distorted the central core and rationale of humanistic study. Few seriously believe that older visions can be restored, and even the most optimistic expect no more than the preservation of ideals of liberal learning within the larger, essentially hostile system of higher education. Inasmuch as social and educational history appears as a steady deliquescence, a falling away from original aims, traditionalists tend to judge current outcomes of undergraduate (not to mention graduate and professional) education harshly. The present confusion, they argue, arises largely from a failure of will, a refusal to assert classically simple images of the academy against the gathering forces of contemporary life.

Beginning with a confused present and moving toward a less complex past, traditionalists account for contemporary troubles by rerunning their versions of history. In this reversed cinematic image, the academic enterprise appears healthier as it sheds extraneous functions, each of which exacts a high, often unacknowledged price. Most critics showing this outlook endorse a lean image of the university whose fundamental mission, as Robert Nisbet put it, ought to be "a unique fusion of the quest for knowledge through scholarship and the dissemination of this knowledge through teaching (quoted in Woodward, 1974, p. 36). Though vague, the notion of liberal learning can be defined with some precision. It consists principally in the transmission of knowledge and values through careful study of a tradition of masterworks, from antiquity through the present or at least into the recent past. Note that the ends—the cultivation of reason, the formation of values, and the enrichment of sensibility—are tied closely to disciplined study of significant books. As Allan Bloom puts it, "Philosophy and liberal studies, in general, require the most careful attention to what are frequently called the great books. This is because they are expressions of teachers such as we are not likely to encounter in person, because in them we find the arguments for what we take for granted without reflection, and because they are the sources for forgotten alternatives. They make it possible for us to carry on our discussion on a high level. Thus, liberal education consists largely in the painstaking study of these books. This study requires long and arduous training, for these books are not immediately accessible to us. Without such a training, an impoverishment of our intellectual discourse necessarily results" (Bloom, 1974, p. 60). Properly pursued, the intrinsic goals and conditions of liberal learning benefit individuals directly and society obliquely: The best citizen, then, "is the person who has learned from the great minds and souls of the past how beautiful reason and virtue are and how difficult to attain" (Trilling, 1974-75, p. 56).

Operating against the dominant currents of culture, politics, and society in the postwar period, traditionalists claim that the main road to genuine self-enhancement—the centerpiece of contemporary culture—must pass through the difficult terrain of humanistic learning. This view is elitist in intellectual terms and probably so in social terms as well. It accepts the authority of tradition and the professoriate's right to define tradition. And it implies that the liberally educated segment of society must be a minority who possess "promise," "ambition," and "interest" in the great tradition (Chalmers, 1948-49, p. 44). Most significantly, traditionalists reject popular neo-romantic conceptions of self-enhancement based on the notion that "each student should express his unique self and find his own interests" (Bloom, 1974, p. 61). They believe that formal learning ought to cultivate sense and sensibility rather than celebrating the affective self.

Bloom finds the consequences of a system of higher education based on the root assumption of what he terms "radical egalitarianism" predictably disastrous. The curriculum becomes a shambles, since it does not proceed from any coherent body of knowledge. Every popular fad, whether initiated from below or from above, becomes grist for the curricular mill. The fragmented parts lack depth; courses become mere pap, which bore the bright and the dull alike. Standards of excellence and performance lose their meaning. Gordon Craig (1974, p. 144) terms this the "age of the Green Stamp University, in which the student receives the same number of stamps for a course on Bay Area Pollution or Human Sexuality as he does for American History or The Greek Philosophers, sticks them happily into his book, and gets a diploma when it is filled. Whether he has received an education in the course of all this is doubtful." Higher education expanded largely in this random fashion during the postwar years; it now enters a period of retrenchment, in Bloom's view, "without an 'order of priorities' or any view of what should be cut out—just drift and random choice as circumstance dictates" (1974, p. 62).

If traditionalists lament the invasion—indeed the near triumph—of neo-romantic notions of self-enhancement that define every activity as educational without sanctifying any, they also trace the fragmentation of liberal education to the burgeoning of specialized knowledge, the erosion of the house of intellect by a labyrinth of tunnels. In earlier decades, humanists feared the encroachment of science, even though a grounding in its methods has been a fundamental element of liberal education since the eighteenth century. Echoing Mill's view, traditionalists warned that specialization, if entered upon too early, "has a narrowing effect not only upon vision, but also upon values." Generations of scientists and professionals, with no more than a smattering of liberal learning, seemed nearly as threatening to democracy as their counterparts—the neo-romantic refusers of any specialized knowledge. Together they would unravel the fabric of an orderly society and bury the memory of human excellence in an unmarked grave of vulgar egalitarianism, a democracy of ignorance.

In its purer forms, the traditionalist position exhibits deeply conservative biases. Many traditionalists hold to a rather low estimate of human nature and its potentialities. Only a small minority—indeed, an elite composed of a presumed aristocracy of intellect—are capable of pursuing genuine liberal learning. In this view, attempts to widen the student base beyond a certain point inevitably result in the decline of universities and colleges, a confusion of purpose that dilutes performance. Higher education, therefore, should not attempt to be the popular agent of an egalitarian society because such hazy aims either fail or, worse, succeed in bringing about equality at the price of mediocrity. Though some traditionalists lament the absence of an aristocratic class, most are worldly enough to recognize that, in America, elites must be recruited in a somewhat haphazard fashion from various echelons of society. When universities abdicate this social responsibility, democracy tends to become misrule by an uninformed populace.

Since discrimination on the basis of race, ethnicity, or sex works against the development of talent, traditionalists favor equality of opportunity, including encouragement and support (preferably in the form of loans) of talented young people without financial means. Equality of opportunity constitutes the traditionalist's main concession to the spirit of egalitarianism. Though it falls short of most contemporary versions of equity, with their stress on equality of access and result, this position fits well enough with the imperatives of the new fiscal conservatism. A policy of liberal education to meet the needs of a deserving minority would preclude expansion of the present sprawling system. The less gifted, according to traditionalists, require postsecondary training, some of it in formal settings and the rest in informal social environments, but education and training should not be mixed indiscriminately or expanded in hybrid forms.

Traditionalists often consider the failure of the university the consequence of liberal politics operating in a popular democracy. According to Bloom, "disinterested love of the truth is particularly threatened in democracy" (1974, pp. 58-59). Traditionalists who profess this view often display conservative politics of moral outrage. They hold the democratic system, which aims at utility, responsible for tendencies toward corruption of truth. But they also accuse liberal politicians—and liberal colleagues—of betraying their good sense. Liberal academics, they charge, yield too easily to pressures to adopt popular functions and accept too cheerfully a dubious correlation between the new labyrinthine shape of knowledge and an incoherent curriculum. By identifying the genuine goals of liberal education, then, traditionalists isolate desired outcomes that ought to be pursued in the academy. And by implication, they expose dubious popular ideals that have guided liberal practices over the past decades.

In their somber assessments of the largely negative outcomes of the hybrid institutions of higher education, then, traditionalists often locate sources of failure primarily in the political system or in a debasement of earlier forms of competitive capitalism. Some also find sources of decline in more subtle cultural shifts. As Lionel Trilling observes, currently fashionable notions of self-enhancement exhibit "the tendency of our culture to regard the mere energy of impulse as being in every mental and moral way equivalent and even superior to defined intention" (1974-75, p. 66). Having rejected what Robert Frost terms the pleasure of taking pains, large numbers of people no longer accept the challenge of fashioning a well-proportioned life, of making "a good self." The liberation of the self from disciplines that once bound and defined it renders liberal education and its discipline stifling, irrelevant. Education becomes a pleasurable mode of affective therapy, a celebration of emotion, intuition, and expressiveness rather than an ordeal, an initiation into a moral and intellectual minority. Trilling concludes that "the assimilation that contemporary culture has made between social idealism, even political liberalism, and personal fluidity—a self without the old confinements—is as momentous as it is recalcitrant to correction. Among the factors in the contemporary world which militate against the formulation of an educational ideal related to the humanistic traditions of the past, this seems to me to be the most decisive" (p. 67).

I do not, of course, mean to imply that the most consistent version of the traditionalist position is also the most widely held. In fact, few people cling to all fundamental elements of this outlook. Moreover, the traditionalist position has lost ground in the postwar period, though it shows some signs of partial recovery. It no longer provides a remotely accurate image of higher education (and probably never did; Martin Meyerson (1974, p. 173) observes in *Daedalus*, "Universities have mostly been centers of professional education"). It has ceased to supply a unifying image of what higher education ought to be. Moreover, a majority of academics reject its conservative philosophical presuppositions and political implications. And yet elements of the traditionalist position continue to exert a powerful, often semiconscious influence on intellectuals and critics within the academy and beyond. The traditionalist ideal remains the touchstone against which changes of purpose are measured, the icon toward which proponents and rationalizers of educational change must bow, if only perfunctorily.

Professional-vocational models. Less philosophically unified than traditionalists and far less embattled, professionalists represent a strong voice in the debate over outcomes. Many of the essential tenets of this cluster of positions may be found in Carl Kaysen's contribution to the *Daedalus* symposium. Rather than engaging traditionalists at the philosophical level of desired outcomes, Kaysen (1974) begins by describing contemporary versions of the actual (or perceived) consequences of liberal education. The surviving practice of liberal education represents an "adaptation of the older classical and humanistic learning to the rise of experimental sciences, as opposed to the older natural philosophy, and to the slightly later development of the social sciences as distinct from history and moral philosophy" (p. 181). In Kaysen's view, it constitutes a maladaptation, the preservation of hollow, anachronistic forms that conceal a confused substance. Undergraduates shop around in an increasingly meager supermarket of courses with few guidelines for their intellectual diets other than the requirement—in many instances now, the mere suggestion—that they choose courses from the four main intellectual food groups: natural sciences, social sciences, humanities, and the nonverbal arts. They are further encouraged to concentrate on one discipline, usually related only tenuously to the subsequent requirements of an occupation or to choices among leisure pursuits.

This ruling concept of liberal education represents an accommodation to the basic social facts summarized by Trow and Muller. It is an attempt to preserve the most abstract rhetoric of older desired outcomes of liberal education in the context of new realities: large numbers of diverse students and the labyrinthine contours of knowledge that emerged within and across disciplines in the late nineteenth and twentieth centuries. Kaysen accepts these social facts of change but rejects the current organization (or disorganization) of curricula as the most suitable means of reaching the vague goals of an ideal undergraduate education. He suggests that major changes in clientele and in the organization of knowledge destroy the possibility of any shared notion of what ought to comprise a liberal education. According to Kaysen, the entry of more than one half of the postsecondary cohort into higher education subverts the earlier traditionalist ideal of developing an intellectual elite. And with the explosion and specialization of knowledge, the representative faculty member is no longer a teacher but a scientist or scholar. Few academics, therefore, possess both the talent and the inclination to participate in the formation or execution of a solid liberal arts curriculum.

Inasmuch as these trends seem irreversible, Kaysen proposes that "we should offer some kind of professional training as the central means toward securing the results that we seek: the creation of the critical, inquiring, and informed mind" (p. 183). Several lines of supporting argument emanate from a pragmatic and instrumental core of values. Whereas the elite model of the traditionalists lacks much sustenance outside the academy, Kaysen (p. 184) notes, the idea of professional training would be consonant with the prevailing elite culture "of rational problem-solving by the application of organized knowledge" shared by leaders of government, business, the professions, and a large sector of the academy.

Kaysen predicts that students and teachers would engage the challenges of professional training more seriously than they do the current liberal arts curricula. (Many traditionalists would agree, though for different reasons.) Indeed, in Kaysen's view, liberal learning might be prized more highly, and therefore more seriously pursued, *after* training and experience in professional life. Professional training thus fits the needs of students. And it suits their desires for economic security, higher occupational status, and interesting work.

The contrasts between Kaysen's professional model and

traditionalist positions hardly could be more stark. Traditionalists support autonomous functions—dissemination of high culture, pure disciplinary research, and the development of intellectual elites. Kaysen advocates shuffling these to the bottom of
the deck in order to get at the high cards, the very popular functions that traditionalists abjure. Whereas traditionalists regard
the academy as a place apart—connected to society through a
healthy tension—Kaysen wants people within the academy to
lead (or ratify) its transformation into the form and image of a
"rational problem-solving culture" and to train individuals to fit
into the current scheme of things. In effect, he wants higher
education to pursue more efficiently those desired outcomes
that Marxists believe it now accomplishes all too well. In Kaysen's view, dissonance between ideal and actual outcomes may
be reduced by trimming desired ends to fit the mold of commonly held utilitarian purposes and by reorganizing curricula to
conform to these common purposes.

By redefining higher education as essentially the transmission of skills under the organizing curricular principle of professional training, Kaysen fashions an implicitly multivalent
rationale with wide appeal to various publics. The idea of re-
labeling higher education and rationalizing its structure along
the lines of a professional-vocational model is consistent with
the pragmatic cast of American culture: Comparatively few
people oppose work on philosophical grounds. Moreover, the
concept of professional training is familiar to all people—to parents and students, to college graduates and others. Unlike the
traditionalist rationale, it does not evoke an irritated response
from many sectors of the public. The proposal blends well with
the new mood of fiscal conservatism. Training may be conducted in formal centers of learning—indeed, in the existing
ones—and elsewhere throughout society. And it need not lead
to a costly expansion of the current system.

Fusionist models. Out of conviction or necessity, everyone in
the mainstream is something of a fusionist. With the possible
exception of a few traditionalist holdouts, all mainstream critics
acknowledge that the functions of liberal and professional learn-

ing at least must continue to coexist in the academy. Disagreements surface quickly, however, over the elements to be fused and their proper proportions. It makes a considerable difference whether a proposed fusion occurs at the level of purposes or organization—whether it involves a redefinition of desired outcomes or a reordering of disciplines and departments. In its broadest construction, the fusionist category cuts across traditionalist and professional models, encompassing elements of both. In this sense, the category is theoretically trivial. But it is also of considerable practical importance, inasmuch as a good deal of the critical debate over outcomes occurs within its sprawling, untidy space.

Among explorations of the possibilities of fusion in the *Daedalus* symposium, Martin Meyerson's piece, "Civilizing Education: Uniting Liberal and Professional Learning," strikes me as the most skillful (1974, pp. 173-179). According to Meyerson, a fusion of liberal learning and professional education might be achieved by restoring the ideas of vocation and service to their central place in the hierarchy of educational values. Liberal learning, he observes, ought not exist in isolation, divorced from "the instrumental, the utilitarian, the professional" (p. 174). Nor should professional training be concerned primarily with preparation for a career in the narrow sense. They rather need to be synthesized, cross-fertilized, and animated by the notion of service. This requires, first of all, "interaction," the cultivation of "creative tension between the concrete and the theoretical, the rationalistic and the empirical" (p. 175). Beyond its traditional purposes, liberal learning needs to be driven by a greater concern for the immediate, the practical, the historical present. And professional education "needs to be made more intellectual, reflective, and liberal, by increasing theoretical understanding, by sharpening research and methodology, by questioning accepted practices, and by educating men and women to be flexible, civilized, and responsible" (p. 175).

But interaction is not enough; liberal arts and the professions "must also recreate in themselves a devotion to their imaginative responsibilities to man. Faculty in both the professions and the liberal arts ought now more than ever to devote themselves to exploring how their calling serves civilization" (p. 176). By refurbishing the notion of vocation or calling, imagining it as a vehicle for satisfying both personal and social needs, faculties might bring new energy to their tasks. They might devise fresh curricula that go beyond sterile mechanical proposals to rearrange courses and requirements in accordance with abstract schemes of outcomes. As Myerson observes, "Imaginative teaching that links the arts, sciences, and professions can satisfy the inner hunger for moral commitment and self-expression, while answering the outer call for service by providing a vehicle for social regeneration" (p. 175). Myerson offers several illustrative examples of fusion drawn from law, medicine, and engineering.

In addition to the usual training in cases, law students ought to study legal history and social thought. They should read Voltaire, Hume, Locke, Berkeley, Burke, and Bentham. They should study Plato's *Republic* and Aristotle's *Poetics,* Augustine's *City of God* and Machiavelli's *Prince,* Hooker's *Of the Laws of Ecclesiastical Polity* and Hobbes' *Leviathan,* not simply because these are classics but because they have shaped contemporary values, social forms, and legal concepts. Without an immersion in the philosophy of law and its historical development, students cannot acquire a deep understanding of their vocation. Similarly, if a student in the health sciences "does not comprehend that a soul and a body inhabit the same space and that a patient is also a member of a community," then he or she "cannot truly treat the whole person" (p. 178).

Meyerson's general rationale for a fusion of liberal and professional learning is intellectually authentic, clearly the idea of a cultivated mind rather than the gesture of accommodation that many fusionist proposals seem to be. The balance of careerist and humanitarian elements in this proposal should attract students. And it might stir faculty significantly if the current structure of academic rewards favoring specialists can be amended. Meyerson goes so far as to ask "that every teacher aspire to be a Roscoe Pound, a William Osler, or a Lionel Trilling—to contribute significantly to the culture as he passes it on. We ought to reward . . . those who, like Aristotle, think metaphysics is a natural sequel to physics" (p. 179). After so many critical probes in pessimistic keys, Meyerson's sober optimism comes as a pleasant change of mood.

Conclusions

We have come a long way: from the peripheries of the social criticism of higher education to the center; across a great ideological spectrum from radicalism to amelioratism; and, to vary the metaphor once again, through important tributaries and a considerable distance down the mainstream. What, if anything, does this odyssey lead us to conclude about contemporary critics' views of the consequences of college?

First, there is general pessimism and uncertainty regarding these outcomes and the possibility of their improvement. To one degree or another, most social critics doubt claims that higher education acts as a principal catalyst of economic abundance, a democratic polity, a more egalitarian society, and a rich culture accessible to all. That is to say, most critics seem discouraged by what they perceive variously as large disparities between promise and current performance and by even larger disparities between the long-term goals of higher education and restricted sources of funding.

Nonetheless, every grouping—and to some extent, every critic—advances different analyses and different answers to the fundamental question of what should be done. Radical critics find the system both inefficient and ineffective, not worth the cost of upkeep. Among mainstream critics, Bird, and to a lesser extent Coleman, represent an increasingly popular view that the higher education establishment ought to be reduced in scope and size. Other critics in the mainstream, principally the "insiders," believe that the system might be made more effective (and more efficient) through redefinition of goals and a corresponding reordering of institutional parts rather than through reduction in size.

Second, from this welter of conflicting views, it should be obvious that criticism cannot replace or bypass the orderly, disciplined pursuit of hard knowledge that higher education as a field of study may supply. In his introduction to the *Daedalus* symposium, Stephen Graubard (1974, p. ix) observes that criticism and autobiographical reflection do "nothing to alter the fact that higher education needs desperately to be developed as a subject of sustained and deliberate scholarship." Nevertheless, those engaged in fashioning the field of higher education ignore the rich tapestry of criticism at the risk of impoverishing whatever sure knowledge they produce. In fact, the body of social criticism ought to be made one important facet of the formal study of higher education.

Third, taken together, the varied critiques constitute a prism that exaggerates, refracts, but also illuminates aspects of the central question of the value of higher education. Students of this field cannot afford to neglect any critical tendency, for no single group has sufficient intellectual or political power to displace the others. And no group articulates completely the public interest. Moreover, something may be learned from each group, even—perhaps especially—from those who represent positions outside the mainstream. Anarchists remind us that in an ideal world we probably could get along very nicely without large institutions such as schools, which probably *oppress* individuals in the process of *pressing* them into disciplined shapes. Marxists (among others) help us, indeed compel us, to reconsider the rhetoric of the liberal mystique, to wonder whether higher education systematically discriminates against classes and whether it intensifies social inequalities endemic to the American social order. Presenting images of academic worlds that probably never existed, traditionalists offer up dreams of a civilized academy—and a civilized nation—devoted to higher standards of intellectual excellence, moral probity, and good taste.

Fourth, it should be remembered that the critical debate itself complexly affects outcomes. By characterizing ideals, critics constitute constellations of desired outcomes, throw them into social existence, if you will. Or they articulate and connect values that others hold in amorphous ways. Insofar as critics help to shape the range of desired goals, they affect judgments of actual outcomes. Outcomes, desired and actual, finally depend largely upon how we think and feel about what we do in education. In this sense, there are no unobtrusive measures; once a statement about outcomes becomes public, it enters the debate as an active element. Social criticism, then, is a significant outcome of American higher education.

Fifth, despite the mood of pessimism and uncertainty among critics, the liberal myth has survived various critiques surprisingly well. One might go so far as to say that, under the pressure of withering criticism, the liberal myth has been largely demythicized, ground down to a more reasonable form, and in the process, greatly enriched. It is now a more realistic, less pretentious, though in some ways more ambitious, ideal than it was in the Progressive Era, or even during the late 1950s and early 1960s. Thus, for example, few would still argue that universal higher education will assure perfect democracy, the spread of high culture, or a classless society. But many critics still find it reasonable to hope that a more educated citizenry will increase the chances for the survival and development of fragile democratic institutions. Moreover, universalization of higher education within a diverse, multitiered system may bring about greater equality in the long run. And a more educated citizenry also may be expected to display greater understanding of the diverse people and cultures of America and greater tolerance for those who prefer the rigors of high culture. In its demythicized form, then, the liberal ideal still constitutes the basic structure of belief (or hope) among critics of American higher education. No longer commanding universal or easy assent, it must be debated constantly, taken as a problematic rather than as an unquestioned ideal. But it is a generous, flexible, open-ended vision, subject to enriching radical and conservative revisions of its parts, and consistent with a broader range of moods than it once encompassed.

Part Four

Conclusions

In these final two chapters we seek to tie together the evidence from all the previous chapters. We have reviewed the evidence from research about the effects of college in the first twelve chapters and in Chapter Thirteen we have weighed the criticisms of a variety of social observers about these effects. But are the consequences of American higher education worth their cost? And what suggestions can be offered concerning the future of American higher education? The following pages present our answers.

14

Is Higher Education Worth the Cost?

*Support of universities is like adherence to a
religion or a church—the payoff from doing so
is incalculable and problematical, but it is wise
to buy insurance against unknown risks.*

Harry G. Johnson (in Lumsden, 1974)

Thus far in this book, we have assembled and interpreted a great
deal of evidence about the actual and potential consequences of
American higher education. Despite the skepticism of social
critics, the evidence almost all points in the same direction—that
is, to significant positive effects of higher education on both
individuals and society. This evidence is found in hundreds of
empirical studies and in numerous critical analyses as well as in
firsthand observation. It stems not from dramatic findings of a
few studies but from the cumulative piling up of many small
pieces of data on many facets of higher education. Even though
the significance of any particular fact or study is likely to seem
small by itself, the final impact of this mass of evidence is overwhelming: The story we have told can lead only to the conclusion that higher education, taken as a whole, is enormously
effective.

In this chapter, we review the many outcomes of higher

education that lead to this conclusion and that have been revealed through our explorations, and then we offer a final accounting in answer to our original question of whether American higher education is worth what it costs.

Outcomes as Specific Changes in Individuals

The primary purpose of higher education is to change people in desirable ways. These changes may, in turn, have profound effects on the economy and the society and even on the course of history. But in the first instance the objective is to modify the traits and behavior patterns of individual human beings. This is not to imply that higher education tries to fit every student into the same mold. Far from it. It is rather thought of as a source of opportunities to which individual students will respond in different ways according to their talents, interests, and aspirations. College is intended to give its students a chance to work out their destiny in an environment that encourages certain ranges of outcomes, rather than specific preprogrammed outcomes. Nevertheless, college does produce, on the average, certain clearly identifiable effects on its students, and these can be discovered at least to a degree. Psychologists, sociologists, scholars in the field of education, public opinion analysts, and economists have written a vast—but scattered and fragmented—literature on the impacts of college on its students. This literature is the raw material from which we have made estimates of the outcomes of higher education. The interpretation of this literature is always uncertain, especially because of the difficulty of isolating the effects of college education from hereditary and socioeconomic factors, and from the normal process of maturation. Our main findings are summarized in the following paragraphs.

On the average, college education significantly raises the level of knowledge, the intellectual disposition, and the cognitive powers of its students. It produces a large increase in substantive knowledge; moderate increases in verbal skills, intellectual tolerance, esthetic sensibility, and lifelong cognitive development; and small increases in mathematical skills, rationality, and creativity.[1] These generalizations are based primarily upon studies describing changes in students from the freshman to the senior years or comparing college-educated people with others. Mostly, however, these studies do not reflect the cognitive residue of a college education after the detailed knowledge is forgotten and only the larger principles, ideas, cognitive abilities, and intellectual and artistic interests have survived. Shockingly little is known about the cognitive residues of college education. There is urgent need for further research in this area. Yet, direct evidence on the knowledge and traits of alumni and the considerable indirect evidence on the opinions, attitudes, and behavior patterns of alumni all point to significant cognitive changes that endure throughout life.

More information is available about the impact of college on the affective aspects of human personality than on the cognitive aspects. The evidence supports the following broad conclusions: on the average, college education helps students a great deal in finding their personal identity and in making lifetime choices congruent with this identity. It increases moderately their psychological well-being as well as their understanding, human sympathy, and tolerance toward other ethnic and national groups and toward people who hold differing opinions. It may have a small impact on refinement of taste, conduct, and manner. And it produces a moderate decrease in religious interest and observance, though the current resurgence of Evangelical Christian and Far Eastern religious thought may raise questions about this finding. College increases relativism, tolerance, and flexibility in the area of personal morality. It also appears to narrow the traditional differences between the two sexes: masculine traits decrease for men and increase for women; and feminine traits increase for men and decrease for women.

---

[1] The intended meanings of the adjectives denoting degree of change are as follows:

    small — .10 to .39 of a standard deviation
    moderate — .40 to .69 of a standard deviation
    large — .70 to .99 of a standard deviation
See the appendix at the end of Chapter Three.

Higher education greatly enhances the practical competence of its students as citizens, workers, family members, and consumers. It also influences their leisure activities, their health, and their general ability to cope with life's problems. Perhaps the main influence of college on practical competence is that it helps students to develop skills and traits of general applicability such as verbal facility, substantive knowledge, rational approach to problems, intellectual tolerance, future orientation, adaptability, and self-confidence. All these are widely useful in practical affairs. In the domain of citizenship, college-educated people are politically more liberal than others, better informed, and more likely to vote and to participate in community affairs. In the area of economic productivity, college assists its students in the process of self-discovery and helps them find careers congruent with their talents, interests, and aspirations. It also provides specific vocational training for a large minority of its students. In addition, college-educated people (especially women) are more likely than others to be in the labor force. College-educated people on the average work longer hours and experience less unemployment. They have greater "allocative ability," that is, ability to adjust promptly and appropriately to changing economic demands, technologies, and resource supplies.

In the domain of family life, higher education affects the selection of marriage partners. It probably tends to delay the age of marriage and to reduce the birth rate. And, most important, it clearly increases the thought, time, energy, and money devoted to the rearing of children. As consumers, college-educated people get more return than others from given incomes. Their orientation is more toward home and the nurturance of children. They save more. They cope better with the myriad practical problems of life. And they have better health than others.

The gains in practical competence associated with higher education may be summarized as follows: citizenship—moderate; economic productivity—moderate; family life—large; consumer behavior—small; leisure—small; and health—moderate.

Outcomes as Changes in Personality Structure of Individuals

Cutting across these specific effects of college on its students are important changes in personality structure. Most research scholars in human development find that personality is not fully formed in childhood, as was supposed previously; rather, it continues to change during the college years and after. They point to several major personality changes that occur for many students during college and that presumably persist wholly or in part in later life.

First, they consider liberation of the personality as the most distinctive and important outcome of college. As compared with others, college-educated people on the average are more open-minded toward new ideas, more curious, more adventurous in confronting new questions and problems, and more open to experience. They are likely to be more rational in their approach to issues. They are more aware of diversity of opinions and outlooks, of the legitimacy of disagreement, and of the uncertain and contingent nature of truth. They are more tolerant of ambiguity and relativity, and more willing to think in terms of probabilities rather than certainties. They are less swayed by tradition and convention. They are less authoritarian, less prejudiced, and less dogmatic. At the same time, they are more independent and autonomous in their views, more self-confident and more ready to disagree. They are more cosmopolitan.

This liberation, so evident in ways of thinking and in general outlook, carries over into liberalism in religion, personal morals, and social views. During the college years students become religiously less orthodox, on the average, and less consistent in religious commitment and practice, though they continue to be interested in religion and religious ideas. They become more flexible and relativistic in their own moral judgments and less moralistic in their judgments of others. And they become more liberal in their political and social views. All these liberal tendencies presumably carry over into later life, though with maturity the personality becomes more entrenched and integrated and views and attitudes become less strident and less volatile. Summing up the liberating influence of college, Trow (1974, p. 40) observed: "Whatever its nominal goals or content, higher education tends to erode narrow ethnic, regional, national, or group identifications, that is to say, all kinds of non-rational loyalties that are incompatible with rapid social and geographic mobility and change. Modern higher education is a universal solvent; it generates, in the people exposed to it, a skepticism toward all received values and allegiances."

Second, researchers in the field of personality development find that students become more independent and self-sufficient during the college years. Seniors are more self-confident, assertive, and autonomous than freshmen. They are more ready to express impulses, more spontaneous, more venturesome, more self-confident, and more poised. They are less sociable, less gregarious, and less extroverted. They have less need for active and intense emotional expression and self-indulgence. They are more resourceful, organized, motivated, fully involved, and persistent. Their emotional and psychological stability increases.

Third and finally, college influences the values and interests of its students. They become more interested in ideas—in general education, as distinguished from specific vocational education. They become more concerned with self-expression and other intrinsic returns from careers, as distinguished from returns in the form of income and security. They develop interests in esthetic experience and awareness; in sensitivity to inner feelings and experiences; in tolerance toward persons and groups of different ethnic, religious, national, and socio-economic backgrounds; in involvement in political and community affairs; and in the careful rearing and education of children. On the other hand, college education appears to reduce interest in formal religious observance. Its effect is uncertain on such values as intellectual integrity, observance of law, and refinement of taste, conduct, and manners. Its effect on altruism leading to kindness, sympathy, unselfishness, friendliness, and sociability appears to be more positive toward groups of persons in the abstract than toward fellow human beings as individuals.

These questions must be asked: (1) To what extent are

these many changes in individuals actually due to the influence of college and to what extent are they due to native ability and socioeconomic background? (2) To what extent are these results due to maturation that would have occurred without the influence of college? (3) How large are the college-induced changes? These questions cannot be answered with finality. However, most of the generalizations stand up in studies that control for noneducational variables and compare the college-educated with other people. The amount of average change, however, is quite modest in most cases. Our rough estimate is that the average change on various aspects of personality is never more than one standard deviation unit, that it is in a few cases zero (in one case negative), and that it is less than half a standard deviation unit overall.

The Whole Person

For two reasons, these average changes tend to understate the total impact of higher education. First, the changes observed for the various dimensions of cognitive, affective, and practical development obscure significant changes for individual students regarded as whole human beings. Each individual draws different consequences from college. Some gain a great deal along particular dimensions, others lose ground or are unchanged along these same dimensions. For example, while some may make large gains with respect to verbal skills, others may make no gains on this dimension, either because their skills were highly developed on entry to college or because their course of study did not make high demands in this field. The average gain, then, will tend to be fairly modest. At the same time, those who gained on the verbal dimension may slip in mathematical skill, while those who made little verbal progress may achieve large gains in mathematical skills. Again the average gains may turn out to be modest. Meanwhile, students will be achieving widely different rates of progress (ranging from zero or less to several standard deviations) on esthetic sensibility, personal self-discovery, religious interest, citizenship, and other dimensions. As a result, the average change on each dimension considered separately will tend to be small, but the change in students as whole persons may be very great as they shore up particular weaknesses, avoid those areas in which they have achieved adequate development, and pursue their particular interests. Time and energy prevents any student from achieving large gains on every single dimension. Selection is inevitable, and different students make different choices as to the dimensions on which to concentrate.

A second qualification applies to averages: the changes in individuals during college, as measured by the averages, do not include intergenerational effects as the outcomes from college are transmitted to the children and even more distant descendants of college students. Thus, the total impact of college on its students is almost surely much greater than the average changes on the several dimensions would signify.

The Worth of Changes in Individuals

What is the worth of the changes in individuals wrought by higher education? It is of interest to present some illustrative numerical calculations.

One may argue that whatever is being spent on higher education is a measure of its worth. Just as we might say that the nation's output of automobiles is worth what people individually and collectively are willing to pay for them, so one could argue that higher education is worth whatever people are willing to pay for it. That is to say, the total expenditure on higher education would not have been made unless the students and their families, the citizenry, and philanthropic donors collectively thought the returns justified the outlays. This approach, however, begs the question because the purpose of the present study is to judge whether the American people are spending too much, too little, or the right amount for higher education. Nevertheless, that the American people do devote $85 billion of resources each year to higher education is some evidence that they value it highly.

A second approach is to find out the reactions of the clients to their own college education. Numerous studies conducted over many years consistently have shown that two thirds or more of students and alumni hold favorable attitudes toward their college educations—toward the academic programs to which they were exposed or toward their overall college experience, including the direct satisfactions associated with attendance. This evidence is far from conclusive—especially because the clients do not pay the whole cost. Yet the overwhelmingly favorable reactions of clients can only mean that something of great value was received by a large majority of students.

A third approach is to consider the possible increases in the capital value of human beings resulting from higher education. These estimates can only be rough guesses, but they may give some idea of orders of magnitude. It may seem repugnant to speak of human beings in terms of capital value, yet in the course of practical affairs human lives are often implicitly assigned a dollar value. For example, they are valued in connection with claims for damages in cases of death and disability; they are valued by implication when decisions are made about expenditures intended to save lives, as in air or highway travel or work places; and people value their own lives when they make decisions to accept premium pay for risky work assignments. In fact, a modest literature has grown up around the concept of valuing human lives. Without going into further detail, we may reasonably estimate the value of a college-age person at $400,000 to $700,000 in 1977 dollars.[2] Given this value, assume that through higher education students achieve a 10 percent overall "improvement" in the realization of their human potentialities and in their capacities as workers, citizens, family members, and consumers. This improvement would be over and above any improvement achieved by comparable persons who

---

[2] Fromm (1965, p. 196) assigned a value of $373,000 to $422,000 for an air fatality, age 40, in 1960 dollars. Converted to 1977 dollars, these figures would be about $686,000 to $775,000 and, when adjusted to the age of a college graduate, would be well over $800,000. Carlson reported values for lives saved (based on U.S. defense expenditures for pilot safety and on pilot compensation for risky missions) ranging from $200,000 to $1,000,000. Thaler and Rosen (1975, p. 294) concluded on the basis of a study of premiums paid for risky work that the value of a life is around $200,000 in 1967 dollars, which would be around $400,000 in 1977 dollars. Schelling (1968) suggested that the value might be several times lifetime earnings.

did not attend college. The addition to their value would then be 10 percent of $400,000 to $700,000, or $40,000 to $70,000. This amount would equal or exceed the cost per student of four years of higher education, which is about $40,000 (including institutional costs plus forgone income and incidental costs borne by students). It should be emphasized, however, that these calculations are no more than guesses. Both the capital value of human beings and the percentage of "improvement" wrought by higher education are unknowns. These calculations do no more than illustrate the possibilities and indicate general orders of magnitude.

A fourth approach to estimating the value of college education is to draw upon the findings of Denison (1974) regarding the sources of the growth in U.S. national income over the period 1929-1969. Denison estimated that potential annual national income (at full employment levels) grew over this period from $161.4 to $599.6 billion (in constant 1958 dollars), an increase of $438.2 billion. He also estimated (p. 130) that about 14.1 percent of this growth, or $62 billion, was due to education. Assuming that *higher* education was responsible for one fourth of this growth (after Psacharopoulos, 1973), the annual national income in 1969 ascribable to higher education would be $15.5 billion. This figure would be an underestimate, because it does not include that part of the national income in 1929—at the beginning of the period—that was due to higher education. Nor does it allow for growth that may have taken place in government, nonprofit institutions, private homes, and other parts of the economy where changes in productivity are not measured. Thus, it would be reasonable to increase the figure of $15.5 billion to at least $20 billion. Over the years 1929-1969, we have estimated that the average annual cost of higher education, including institutional instructional costs, forgone income, and incidental expenses (in 1958 dollars), was about $11 or $12 billion. (Instructional costs were estimated at two thirds of current fund expenditures; forgone income was estimated at two thirds of average annual earnings in nonagricultural employment.) On this basis, the instructional activities of higher education have handsomely paid their way in the past.

A fifth approach to estimating the value of college education is to estimate the "rate of return" on investments in higher education. The investments are the sum of the costs of operating colleges and universities, the forgone income of students, and the incidental costs of college attendance. The return consists of the discounted stream of increased earnings enjoyed by students as a result of attending college. The rate of return is the annual increment in earnings as a percentage of the investment after allowance for depreciation of the investment. Economists have made innumerable calculations of the rate of return both in the United States and abroad. These calculations have referred to different classifications of students and have based their studies on varied sources of data and diverse assumptions. As might be expected, these calculations have produced many different estimates of rates of return, ranging from 4 percent or less to 20 percent. The great majority, however, have been of the order of 8 percent to 15 percent. This percentage is in the same range as the rate of return on investments in physical capital with comparable degrees of risk. And it compares very favorably with rates of return available to private savers who invest in stocks, bonds, savings accounts, and the like. If investments in higher education produce rates of return comparable to those derived from physical assets, when the return includes only money earnings, then the total returns on higher education, including all the nonmonetary benefits, must be substantially higher than those earned by physical capital. McMahon (1974) estimated the total rate of return, including both monetary and nonmonetary returns, by investigating the rate of return *expected* by students in the form of enhanced income, job satisfaction, personal satisfaction, service to society, and service to the next generation through more competent rearing of children. He found the combined expected rate of return to be 22 percent, whereas the expected monetary rate of return alone was 14.5 percent for men and 7.5 percent for women. Since he did not include some significant nonmonetary returns, his findings suggest that the true combined returns might be much more than 22 percent.

The clear inference from these exceedingly rough estimates

is that higher education probably pays off in monetary returns alone and that the many nonmonetary returns are a handsome bonus that makes higher education a high-return industry. However, the calculations of monetary returns must be taken with reservations. They are only rough guesses based on inadequate data and heroic assumptions. They are based on past experience that may not be duplicated in the future. In particular, they refer to a period when the number of college-educated persons in the population was limited to a small minority. Today, that number is still relatively small. In 1974, those who had attended college made up 25.2 percent of the population, and those who were college graduates made up only 13.3 percent. But if higher education continues to expand, the incremental earnings due to college may tend to decrease. As a result, the rate of return in dollars, and in status as well, may be expected to decline. Indeed, this decline may have already set in, and so one cannot assume that future rates of return will match those of the past. However, if in the future the expansion of higher education raises the relative earnings of the less-educated and lowers those of the more-educated, then the benefits accruing to the less-educated will have to be considered among the outcomes of higher education.

Outcomes as Consumer Satisfactions

Higher education is, in part, a consumer good that may be valued for its own sake. The experience of attending college is rewarding for many students. It offers the satisfaction of learning, the stimulus of interesting people and ideas, sociability, recreation, pleasant surroundings, and memorable experiences. Most students enjoy their college years and the alumni look back on them as an agreeable episode in their lives. Moreover, college education opens up to many people new interests, new awareness, and new understandings which are an important source of enjoyment and satisfactions throughout their lives. Most alumni report that they gained lasting personal benefits from college. The direct satisfactions are not restricted exclusively to young full-time students but are shared by part-time students, young and old. For many of them, higher education is an attractive leisure-time pursuit—a meaningful alternative to playing bridge or watching television. Attending college—full-time or part-time—is also a desirable activity for people who otherwise would be unemployed. Finally, its benefits are shared by relatives and friends of students who receive vicarious satisfactions from it. Higher education cannot be justified solely as a leisure-time activity. It is too costly for that. Considering that four years of college are about 5 percent of an average lifetime, however, its contributions to the quality of life are far from trivial.

Outcomes as Changes in Society

There is little precise information on the specific impact of higher education on societal change. The course of history is influenced by a multitude of causes, of which higher education is only one, and it seems doubtful that this influence can ever be sorted out satisfactorily from all the others. Yet, it is beyond belief that higher education has no significant part in the drama of social change. In this book, we have tried to isolate the probable social effects of higher education in the past and to speculate about its potential effects in the future.

One effect of higher education upon society is exerted through the change it produces in its students who eventually become members of society. When well-educated, cultivated persons are received into society, their presence will almost inevitably modify the general social environment. They may influence the prevailing patterns of interests, values, attitudes, and behavior. This may happen even if the educated persons are passive toward others and intend no influence over them. But if the educated persons take on professional and leadership roles, as they are likely to do, the influence may be magnified. Through these informal processes, a general leavening of society may occur. For example, the general level of esthetic imagination, respect for personal uniqueness, civilized behavior, and interpersonal communication may be raised. Family planning may be encouraged and the rate of population growth reduced. Child care and the home training of children may be improved, the quality of the schools may be raised and children may be stimulated to gain more from their education and to seek more education. Appreciation of the arts and learning may be deepened and the cultivation of both encouraged. The quality of health services may be raised and the health practices of the community improved. Participation in and concern for political, civic, religious, and cultural organizations and activities may be increased, the understanding of political and community affairs may be deepened, and humane influences in politics may be encouraged. The understanding of specific social issues and problems in fields such as international relations, environment, and tax reform may be increased. Willingness to seek and to accept social change may be enhanced, and the values underlying personal, community, and political decisions may become more humane and more influenced by considerations of basic morality and social responsibility. Finally, a sense of common culture and social solidarity may be enhanced.

These social changes may occur as a result of higher education. They are not inevitable. Their occurrence will depend partly on the numbers of college-educated people introduced into the community—the more, the greater the influence. They will depend also on the character of the higher education. If it is narrow and technical, then social effects of the kinds mentioned may not be realized. Furthermore, if colleges and universities produce selfish, arrogant, and status-conscious people who set themselves apart from the larger community, who have little sense of social responsibility, and who create social division, envy, and hostility rather than communication, then the social effects of higher education may be negative or destructive. The civilizing and liberating influence of higher education as it now exists easily can be exaggerated. Even in institutions that stress liberal learning, perhaps only a minority of students are influenced deeply and achieve a strongly humane outlook and a keen sense of social responsibility. Yet the introduction of millions of educated people into society is bound to exert a civilizing influence. Moreover, it is almost certain they would enhance the productivity of the economy. Not only are college-educated people themselves likely to be more productive than they would have been with less education but their influence radiates out to the whole economy. They are receptive to change and responsive to changing demands, technologies, and resource supplies; they can discover and apply new methods of production and new modes of economic organization; they can create and conduct the elaborate communication systems essential to large-scale organizations and division of labor.

A second effect of higher education on society is achieved through the manifold activities that we have called *research and public service*. Basic research in the natural sciences as conducted in higher education produces an exceptionally high return on the investment. Its return alone probably compensates for the expenditures on all research and public service activities. Research in the social studies and related disciplines has many uses, though it is hard to put a dollar value on it. It is essential to the people's understanding of themselves and of their society. It fosters perspective and openness to change. It provides the data to monitor the performance of our society. It has many applications to practical decision making in both public and private affairs. And it provides knowledge of value for its own sake.

The varied activities of colleges and universities in the areas of scholarship, philosophical and religious inquiry, social criticism, public policy analysis, and cultivation of the fine arts are all enormously valuable in preserving the cultural heritage and advancing the civilization—but there is no way of placing dollar values on the outcomes of these functions. Who can tell the value of preserving and interpreting literature and artifacts of the past, of discovering and defining the meanings and purposes of human life, of explaining and appraising broad social trends, of formulating considered recommendations for public policy, and of fostering the fine arts? These are tasks for which higher education bears primary responsibility in our society. These tasks are carried on quietly and steadily, year in and year out. They often are not noticed or understood by the public and often are underrated even by academic people themselves. However, if they were stopped, their absence would soon be noticed. Winston Churchill was once asked, "Why are we fighting this war?" He answered, "If we were to stop, you would know why." So it is with education. To avoid cultural deterioration, society would be obliged at great cost to find substitute institutions for carrying on these varied functions.

The direct public services rendered by higher education also contribute substantially to societal welfare. These include health care, libraries and museums, dramatic and musical performances, recreational facilities and programs, consulting in a wide range of fields, and maintaining a standby pool of knowledge and expertise to be drawn upon when needed. In addition, all of the activities of higher education—instruction as well as research and public service—are one of the bases of national prestige and national military power. They also are a source of enjoyment and satisfaction to the general public, who find interest and pride in living in a world of advancing knowledge and dramatic scientific breakthroughs.

Third, higher education may contribute to the quest for human equality. This, however, is a potential, not an actual, effect. Since higher education in the past has served mainly the privileged classes—those privileged by virtue of income, social status, and (to some extent) native ability—it probably has not had a leveling effect. Indeed, the range of differences in educational level among the American people today may be at an all-time high. In the early history of the nation, educational levels were relatively equal because few had much education; in the next fifty years, educational levels may again become more equal because nearly everyone will have a great deal of education. But today, we stand almost precisely at the point where inequality of educational attainment is at a maximum. If, in the future, higher education in its many forms could be extended steadily to more people, the incomes and social status of the less-educated might rise, and progress toward human equality might be achieved. This would happen, however, only if attitudinal, political, and institutional obstacles to mobility—upward and downward—were kept at a minimum. It cannot be asserted with confidence that a leveling of human income and status will come about through the expansion of higher education. Rather, this is a potential outcome and a goal toward which to strive. At present, the nation is unsure about pushing ahead with the historic expansion of higher education. If it does not, the quest of greater equality will be confined to redistributive techniques, such as taxes at graduated rates, public welfare, social security, and housing subsidies. These may reduce the inequality of what people get, but they will do little to reduce the inequality of what they are and of what they can contribute.

We cannot emphasize too strongly that in our consideration of possible expansion of higher education, we are thinking not merely of expanding colleges and universities precisely as they now exist but also of increasing the whole range of opportunities for higher education, possibly through new institutional forms, new programs, and new methods.

Conclusions: The Consequences of Higher Education

From the above summary, a tidy dollar comparison of costs and benefits is conspicuously absent. There is no "bottom line." It is hard to imagine, however, that a thoughtful person could review this summary and the underlying documentation as presented in this book without reaching the conclusion that the sum of the benefits exceeds the total cost by a factor of three or more. The monetary returns alone, in the form of enhanced earnings of workers and improved technology, are probably sufficient to offset all the costs. But over and above the monetary returns are the personal development and life enrichment of millions of people, the preservation of the cultural heritage, the advancement of knowledge and the arts, a major contribution to national prestige and power, and the direct satisfactions derived from college attendance and from living in a society where knowledge and the arts flourish. These nonmonetary benefits surely are far greater than the monetary benefits—so much greater, in fact, that individual and social decisions about the future of higher education should be made primarily on the basis of nonmonetary considerations and only secondarily on the basis of monetary factors. Unfortunately for the future of the nation, the pattern of decision making is too often reversed. As Harold Howe II commented (1975, pp. 7-8):

> There is a danger for both individuals and for the society as a whole in overplaying the economic arguments about higher education's future and in allowing

those arguments alone to control that future. . . . there are two major considerations that much of the economic analysis tends to neglect because they cannot be quantified—the contribution of advanced education to the personal lives of American citizens and its contribution to their lives as citizens of our republic. . . . The practical consequence emerging from the economic analysis of advanced education in recent years is the impression that we cannot afford it and should not have to pay for it unless the results can be added up in hard economic gains. It is a narrow, questionable, and potentially dangerous notion. In effect, we find ourselves selling out to one system of judging value largely because it can be quantified in dollars while other indices of judgment about higher education are forced out of the conversation.

These, then, are the major conclusions of this book: First, the monetary returns from higher education alone are probably sufficient to offset all the costs. Second, the nonmonetary returns are several times as valuable as the monetary returns. And third, the total returns from higher education in all its aspects exceed the cost by several times. In short, the cumulative evidence leaves no doubt that American higher education is well worth what it costs.

15

The Future of American Higher Education

That there should one man die ignorant who had the capacity to learn, this I call a tragedy.

To impart the gift of thinking to those who cannot think, and yet who could in that case think: this one would imagine, was the first function a government had to set about discharging.

Thomas Carlyle

America has thus far in its history had a love affair with education. The widening and deepening of educational opportunity has been pursued steadfastly, and it has been held by many Americans that the end of the road to opportunity will be reached only when every person can be educated up to his full capacity as a unique human being. Today, however, the nation is engaged in a great debate about the future of higher education, especially about the wisdom of expanding it still further to serve new classes of students. Critics claim that Americans are overeducated and that higher education is overbuilt. What light can be shed on this debate from the evidence of this book that the total return from higher education is greater than the total cost?

The Current Debate

America's enthusiasm for education has derived from a deep faith in education as the foundation of a workable democratic society and from the belief that every individual should have the chance, and even the obligation, for personal fulfillment through learning. It has been reinforced solidly by the desire of submerged groups to get ahead and by the economic need for trained manpower.

At first, the effort to diffuse learning meant the overcoming of illiteracy through the spread of free public elementary schools. Later, it meant the provision of public secondary education to virtually all our people and the steady growth of higher education. The growth of higher education occurred initially through the founding of hundreds of private colleges and state universities as the frontier moved westward. Later came the land-grant movement, the establishment of scores of normal schools which eventually became state colleges and universities, and the extension movement which recently has taken on new life as nontraditional study. More recently came the community college movement, the G.I. Bill, the federal grants to institutions for research and many other purposes, and finally, massive federal aid to students. This history has been based on the principle that colleges and universities should be readily accessible to successive waves of new students on easy and inviting terms. Supply has been made available, not just in response to demand, but in anticipation of demand. And demand has responded time and time again.

The outcome of all this effort is a network of about 3,000 colleges and universities of widely diverse types, serving about 11 million students (of whom about 7 million are full-time). The average level of formal education in the United States surpasses that in virtually all other countries. The current annual cost for all this we estimate as shown in Table 52.

At each stage in the past development of higher education,

Table 52. Costs for higher education in the U.S., 1976-77

	Billions	*Percentage*
Institutional expenditures, including capital		
Instruction	$31	36%
Research and public service	15	18
Subtotal	46	54
Expenses borne by students		
Forgone income	34	40
Incidental expenses	5	6
Subtotal	39	46
Grand total	$85	100%

there have been those who believed that the three Rs are enough, that only an elite minority of people were educable beyond a few years of school, or that the nation could not "afford" additional education. Today, many believe that education has been overdone. We hear allegations that a large proportion of our people are uneducable, that there are not enough jobs for educated people, or that the nation cannot afford the heavy costs. Yet, it is quite clear that the enormous growth of colleges and universities has taken us only partway toward the long-held ideal of education for every person up to the limit of his potentialities. The number of women attending is substantially below the number of men; the proportion of low-income and minority youth attending is far below the number of middle- and high-income youth; the attendance rates in some states is half that in other states; and the number of adults attending, though growing, is far from ideal. It takes little imagination to realize that total enrollments could thus conceivably double over the next generation if the nation chose to offer incentives and learning opportunities relevant to the needs of new clienteles. Moreover, the mere extension of higher education to more people is not the only possibility. Education also could be deepened for those already involved. Indeed, the ignorance in our land suggests that education is far from the saturation point.

The question we face, then, is whether the historic development of higher education should be resumed, whether the amount of higher education should be stabilized at about its present level, or whether it should be cut back. There are proponents with persuasive arguments for all three views. Indeed, in considering the future of American higher education, these proponents probably would agree only that higher education of the twenty-first century should *not* be exactly like that of the present. Even its most ardent defenders would admit that the higher educational system as now constituted is not wholly suited to its prospective responsibilities and that some modifications are in order—whether or not higher education is destined for expansion.

Our conclusion that the total return from higher education is today several times greater than the total cost does not necessarily imply that it would pay the nation to expand the higher educational system. Expansion can be justified only if successive increments of cost will produce equal or greater increments of benefit. The limit of economical expansion is reached at the point where incremental cost and incremental benefit are equal.[1]

A Moral Imperative

In terms of incremental analysis, would growth in the number of educated people significantly increase economic productivity or enhance the quality of life? Would expansion of research and public service speed up technological progress or enrich the culture?

Some believe the answers may be "no" or "not much." And their viewpoint is supported by the fact that some countries having relatively small higher educational establishments—such as Britain or Switzerland—manage nevertheless to achieve visibly advanced economies and high cultures. It is indeed possible that provision of college education to an increasing propor-

---

[1] Since higher education is not a single homogeneous commodity, however, expansion might be carried out to different degrees for the different "products" of higher education.

tion of the American people or the expansion of research and public service might contribute little to the growth of the economy or the enhancement of the culture. In our judgment, these negative assessments of the potential economic and cultural impacts of expanded higher education greatly underrate the possibilities of incremental advantage. But the future of higher education should not and need not rest on guesses about such possibilities. It should be decided on *moral* grounds based on the following propositions:

1. That higher education contributes to the cognitive and affective qualities and the practical competence of people as individuals and is therefore conducive to their full development as whole human beings.
2. That higher education enhances the quality of social life in many ways.
3. That the number of persons who could benefit from higher education greatly exceeds the number who now partake of it, especially if innovative programs suited to diverse clienteles were available.
4. Given these three propositions, a moral imperative follows. It is that, on moral (not economic) grounds, each person should have the opportunity, and the obligation as well, to develop fully his or her unique personal powers.

As Cremin has suggested (1965, p. 48), the foreseeable future may be the first time since the dawn of civilization when appreciable cultural advantages could be conferred upon a substantial proportion of the whole population. The incremental benefit from expanded education would be the extension of learning and personal development to all those people who could be helped by it. Educational "output" would be simply the augmentation of human life on this planet. The many secondary outcomes would be regarded as welcome by-products but not as the primary goals. But even if there were no by-products, a moral imperative would still demand that human beings should have a right and a duty to achieve full development of their powers. No one knows how many people ultimately would be able and willing to benefit from higher education if the impediments derived from underprivileged socioeconomic backgrounds could be gradually overcome. It is clear, however, that the number would far exceed present enrollments (Rever, 1971).

Some Practical Considerations

The proposal to push ahead with the expansion of higher education raises important practical considerations. The expansion of higher education might increase the supply of people aspiring to technical, professional, and managerial jobs beyond the capacity of the economy to employ them. It is often argued that the expansion would lead to unemployment and discontent, and at worst to social upheaval. This argument raises a serious moral issue, implying as it does that a large part of the population with the potential for personal development through higher education should be held down deliberately to lives of relative ignorance. Such an outcome would be indefensible. The argument also is questionable from the economic standpoint. It assumes that the economy offers a more or less fixed inventory of jobs to which the labor force must adjust. On the contrary, there is a mutual adjustment process between the jobs the economy provides and the jobs the workers want. The economy can and does adjust to the workers that are available. For example, in the past, as the numbers of people presenting themselves for manual work has decreased and the numbers seeking white-collar work has increased, the economy has adjusted its technology and its product mix to accommodate the labor supply. Millions of unpleasant and monotonous jobs have been automated, and many goods and services that are dependent on menial labor have virtually disappeared from the market—for example, household service, ditch-digging, and shoe-shining. Indeed, the continued existence of many menial jobs has been due to immigration of uneducated and unskilled workers. Meanwhile the relative number of white-collar jobs has increased steadily until now these jobs represent more than half of total employment, yet unemployment among college-educated people has been consistently less than among noncollege workers. The argument that education will lead to a suplus of white-collar workers is dubious also because it is based on the widespread but obsolete assumption that blue-collar work is in some sense inappropriate for educated men and women. This assumption is a carryover from an aristocratic conception of both work and higher education. This attitude will probably disappear as the skill requirements and earnings of many blue-collar jobs exceed those of many white-collar jobs. The electrician or the truck driver who earns $10 an hour need not defer to the junior bank officer or the school teacher who earns $7.50 an hour. In both social status and right to education, the blue-collar worker need not be a second-class citizen.[2]

Granting that expansion of higher education is desirable, will students actually attend in ever-increasing numbers? Judging from past experience, the numbers will depend on the terms on which higher education is offered. These terms include tuitions and fees, student aid, the quality and variety of programs, the convenience of time and place, arrangements for released time from work, the state of the labor market, the general level of economic prosperity, and, not least, the accepted ideology of college attendance. One thing is certain: If the earnings from jobs traditionally reserved for college graduates decline, the incentive to attend will be weakened and the need for public subsidy will increase. Nevertheless, as young women have demonstrated for generations (when most of them had expected to become housewives), many people will elect to attend college even though the return in the form of lifetime monetary earnings promises to be small. But the attendance of women always has been less than that of men, suggesting that prospective monetary rewards are one among many factors determining college attendance.

Though higher education may be clothed with a pervasive moral imperative, it does not have unlimited claims on resources. There are important competing values. In extending higher education, therefore, the higher educational community

---

[2] For a more extended discussion of these issues see Bowen (1973, 1974c).

is heavily obliged to be efficient in the use of resources. Some of the resources needed for expansion will have to be bought with improved efficiency in existing operations. The need for efficiency calls not only for prudence in the operation of each institution but also for imaginative innovation in the overall organization and operation of higher education. As we have said repeatedly, in considering the expansion of higher education, we do not imply that it should grow in precisely its present form. The higher educational establishment is not well equipped for the tasks that lie ahead, and new conceptions, new forms, and new methods are needed. And at best, the cost of extending higher education will be high.

For several reasons, the next two decades will be an ideal period in which to press ahead toward opening higher education to an increasing proportion of the population. First, well-known demographic trends will tend to reduce traditional enrollments and make room for population groups not previously represented. Second, the relatively heavy unemployment of the recent past, which may persist into the future, could be ameliorated if more people—especially uneducated youth among whom unemployment rates are severe—could fill idle time by learning. Third, in meeting the twin problems of natural resource depletion and pollution, the nation will be forced to reduce the relative share of the national product derived from goods-producing industries and to increase the share from service-producing industries. Higher education happens to be a service industry of great value that makes minimal claims on scarce natural resources and generates little environmental pollution.[3]

[3]The cost of expanding higher education along the lines we have suggested has been estimated in an important study of Terleckyj, *Improvements in the Quality of Life* (1975b, pp. 116-128). In this study, he identified twenty-eight possible ways by which the quality of life in America might be enhanced, and he estimated the cost of each over the period 1973-1983, subject to the constraint set by the total resources likely to be available to the American economy. Among his proposed "improvements" he placed considerable emphasis on the expansion of higher education in accordance with the concept of "universal access." He proposed that, by 1983, higher education should be geared up to award about 2,000,000 de-

Conclusions: A Possible Future for Higher Education

Our exploration of outcomes suggests that the historic growth of higher education in the United States has been beneficial and, further, that future returns may be reaped through the widening of higher education to include more people and the deepening of higher education to intensify personal development of those already included. In the future, however, the potential incremental returns will be mainly in the fulfillment of individual lives and the building of a humane civilization rather than in raising the earnings and status of individuals and in augmenting the gross national product. Given this change in emphases, let us consider a possible future for higher education in the United States.

Since the regular work of the world will still need to be done, people will require training for a wide range of conventional jobs. To meet the special needs of the future, however, great cadres of scientists, engineers, physicians, other health workers, social scientists, teachers, social workers, humanists, and other vocationally trained persons will be needed to help find ways to conserve resources, clean up the environment, restore the cities, overcome racial injustice, improve health, eradicate poverty, and achieve economic stability. There will be no shortage of work to be done if the nation is dedicated to

---

grees—as compared with 946,000 actually awarded in 1973 or about 1,100,000 projected for 1983 in the absence of any new expansionary program. He also offered other proposals that would affect the production of college degrees, among them remedial programs for disadvantaged children, job training, and improvements in educational technology and organization.

Terleckyj estimated the additional cost of universal access over the entire decade 1973-1983 at $273 billion. This figure included institutional costs, forgone income of students, and other student expenditures, and it was expressed in 1973 dollars. One might guess that the *annual* additional cost at the end of the decade would be around $50 billion. This amount would be an addition to the approximately $85 billion of cost in 1976-1977.

In our judgment, such a buildup of higher education by the year 1983 would be quite unrealistic. From every point of view—political, financial, and educational—several decades will be needed to achieve universal access. But Terleckyj's concept and his cost estimates are useful in judging what the cost will be whenever the transition to universal access occurs.

solving these problems and building a better—not necessarily more opulent—life. Indeed, the nation would lack the amount of trained manpower needed to achieve goals stated in terms of the requirements of a good life rather than in terms of market demand for ordinary goods.[4] Moreover, if the people were prepared for and dedicated to the jobs that would make America better, not just richer, the likelihood of appropriate political decisions would be increased.

The activities we have called research and public service would be intensified and not curtailed as is so often proposed. Higher education would give increasing attention to the advancement of basic knowledge, to the preservation of the cultural heritage, to the exploration of means and values in a contemporary setting, to the analysis and evaluation of public policies and societal trends, and to the cultivation of the arts.

Open access and strong encouragement would be given to all the people to achieve education commensurate with their capacities. This would be done on the premise that learning is essential both to personal fulfillment and to cultural advancement. The extension of education in this way would not mean that everyone would graduate from a conventional college at age twenty-one but rather that each person would be given the genuine opportunity and encouragement to develop himself during his whole lifetime. To this end, the educational system would adjust and diversify its programs so that it could accommodate persons of varying backgrounds, interests, talents, and ages. Such education would provide an array of programs suited to a large majority of people. These programs would be available in convenient times and places. They would be supplied at low cost to the students, and thus they would allow for appropriate financial aid and released time from work. Higher education would be recurrent and would serve adults of all ages from 18 years to 100. (Already about 1,000,000 persons over the age of 35 are attending college (Young, 1975b).) It would serve blue-collar workers, housewives, and the elderly as well as

[4]For a careful statistical study of the resource requirements for improving the quality of life in America, see Terleckyj (1975b).

middle- and upper-class youth. It would be flexible in admissions requirements and in prerequisites. It would recognize learning from all sources, and it would include both degree and nondegree programs. It would meet vocational as well as personal needs, but its underlying emphasis would be on liberal learning—redefined to fit twenty-first century conditions and needs. Over several generations it would expect to draw millions of disadvantaged persons into the mainstream of American society. The overriding purpose of higher education would change from that of preparing people to fill particular slots in the economy and of adding to the GNP to that of helping them to achieve personal fulfillment and of building a civilization compatible with the nature of human beings and the limitations of the environment. Vocational education would continue to be an essential function, but it would be combined in symbiotic relationship with liberal education.

At present, the higher educational system is not geared fully to this challenge. However, great progress has been achieved in recent decades—especially through the establishment of scores of community colleges, the progress of the continuing education movement, the enormous growth of student aid, the invention of new instructional techniques, and the provision of special programs and facilities for the "new students." The basic task is to modify the system of higher education so that it can continue to accommodate traditional students and to cultivate exceptional talent and, at the same time, to reach out to the new students of all ages whose educational needs, at least during a transitional phase, may be different from those of traditional students. This does not mean that every single institution should shift gears, though many should. It means rather that the system as a whole should adjust to the needs of students of many backgrounds, interests and ages. New kinds of institutions, new modes of delivering educational services independent of college and universities as we know them, new methods of instruction, and new subjects of study will be needed in this transition.

We are suggesting that the nation embark on an educational adventure that has never before been attempted in human history—an adventure designed to banish ignorance so far as it can be banished, and to maximize human *life*. As Ruskin said in *Unto This Last* (1960, pp. 155-156): "Production does not consist in things laboriously made, but in things serviceably consumable; and the question for the nation is not how much labour it employs but how much life it produces. For as consumption is the end and aim of production, so life is the end and aim of consumption. There is no wealth but life."

References

Note: Sources of particular value in compiling the goals of higher education (as presented in Chapter Two) are marked with an asterisk.

Abramovitz, M. "Economic Growth in the United States." *American Economic Review,* September 1962, pp. 762-782.

Adelson, J. "Psychological Research on a Profound Issue." *Science,* December 26, 1975, p. 1288.

*Adler, M. J., and Mayer, M. *The Revolution in Education.* Chicago: University of Chicago Press, 1958.

Advisory Commission on Intergovernmental Relations. *Changing Public Attitudes on Governments and Taxes.* Washington, D.C.: 1976.

Akin, J. S., and Garfinkel, I. *Economic Returns to Education Quality.* Madison: Institute for Research on Poverty, University of Wisconsin, 1974.

*Allen, M. G. "The Development of Universal Criteria for the Measurement of the Health of a Society." *The Journal of Social Psychology,* 1962, pp. 363-382.

American Academy of Political and Social Science. "Student Protest." *The Annals,* Vol. 395. Philadelphia: 1971.

American Council on Education. *A Fact Book on Higher Education.* Washington, D.C., periodical.

American Council on Education. *Higher Education and National Affairs.* Washington, D.C., periodical.

Anderson, A., Bowman, M. J., and Tinto, V. *Where Colleges Are and Who Attends.* New York: McGraw-Hill, 1972.

*Arnold, M. *Prose and Poetry.* New York: Scribner's, 1927. See particular essays: "Literature and Science"; "Sweetness and Light"; "Barbarians, Philistines, Populace"; "Hebraism and Hellenism"; "Equality."

Arrow, K. J. "Higher Education as a Filter." *Journal of Public Economics,* 1973, pp. 193-216.

*Ashby, E. *Technology and the Academics.* London: Macmillan, 1963.

*Ashby, E. *Adapting Universities to a Technological Society.* San Francisco: Jossey-Bass, 1974.

Ashby, E. "A Case for More Mass Education." *London Times Higher Education Supplement,* January 23, 1976, p. 5.

*Assembly on University Goals and Governance. *A First Report*. Cambridge: American Academy of Arts and Sciences, 1971.

Astin, A. W. "Undergraduate Achievement and Institutional 'Excellence.'" *Science*, August 1968, pp. 661-668.

Astin, A. W. "Institutional Selectivity and Institutional Outcomes." Paper presented at the 137th meeting of the American Association for the Advancement of Science, Chicago, December 27, 1970.

Astin, A. W. "The Measured Effects of Higher Education." *The Annals of the American Academy of Political and Social Science*, November 1972, pp. 1-20.

Astin, A. W. "The Impact of Dormitory Living on Students." Unpublished paper, 1973a.

Astin, A. W. "Measurement and Determinants of the Outputs of Higher Education." In L. C. Solmon and P. J. Taubman (Eds.), *Does College Matter?* New York: Academic Press, 1973b.

Astin, A. W., Astin, H. S., Bayer, A. E., and Bisconti, A. S. *The Power of Protest: A National Study of Student and Faculty Disruptions with Implications for the Future*. San Francisco: Jossey-Bass, 1975.

Astin, A. W., and Lee, C. B. T. *The Invisible Colleges*. New York: McGraw-Hill, 1972.

Astin, A. W., and Panos, R. *The Educational and Vocational Development of College Students*. Washington, D.C.: American Council on Education, 1969.

Atelsek, F. J., and Gomberg, I. L. *Faculty Research: Level of Activity and Choice of Area*. Washington, D.C.: American Council on Education, 1976.

Auster, R., Leveson, I., and Sarachek, D. "The Production of Health, an Exploratory Study." *The Journal of Human Resources*, Fall 1969, pp. 411-436.

Bachman, J. G. *Young Men in High School and Beyond*. Washington, D.C.: U.S. Office of Education, Department of Health, Education, and Welfare, 1972.

*Bailey, S. K. *The Purposes of Education*. Bloomington, Ind.: Foundation Monograph Series, Phi Delta Kappa, 1976.

Bane, M. J. *American Families in the Twentieth Century*. New York: Basic Books, 1976.

Barfield, R., and Morgan, J. *Early Retirement*. Ann Arbor: University of Michigan Press, 1969.

Barlow, R., Brazer, H. E., and Morgan, J. N. *Economic Behavior of the Affluent*. Washington, D.C.: Brookings Institution, 1966.

*Barzun, J. *The House of Intellect*. New York: Harper & Row, 1959.

Barzun, J. *Science: The Glorious Entertainment*. New York: Harper & Row, 1964.

*Barzun, J. *The American University*. New York: Harper & Row, 1968.

Bauer, R. A. (Ed.). *Social Indicators*. Cambridge: M.I.T. Press, 1966.

Baumol, W. J., and Bowen, W. G. *Performing Arts: The Economic Dilemma*. New York: Twentieth Century Fund, 1966.

Bayer, A. E. "College Impact on Marriage." *Journal of Marriage and the Family*, November 1972, pp. 600-609.

Bayer, A. E. "Faculty Composition, Institutional Structure, and Students' College Environment." *Journal of Higher Education*, September-October 1975, pp. 549-565.

Bayer, A. E., Royer, J. T., and Webb, R. M. *Four Years After College Entry*. Washington, D.C.: American Council on Education, 1973.

*Becker, E. *Beyond Alienation: A Philosophy of Education for the Crisis of Democracy*. New York: George Braziller, 1967.

Becker, G. S. "Underinvestment in College Education." *American Economic Review* (Supplement), May 1960, pp. 346-354.

Becker, G. S. *Human Capital: A Theoretical and Empirical Analysis, with Special Reference to Education*. New York: National Bureau of Economic Research and Columbia University Press, 1964.

Becker, G. S. "Comment on S. Bowles, Schooling and Inequality from Generation to Generation." *Journal of Political Economy* (Supplement), 1972, 252-255.

Becker, G. S. "A Theory of Social Interactions." *Journal of Political Economy*, November-December 1974.

Beecher, G., Chickering, A. W., Hamlin, W. G., and Pitkin, R. S. *An Experiment in College Curriculum Organization*. Plainfield, Vt.: Goddard College, 1966.

*Bell, D. *The Reforming of General Education*. New York: Columbia University Press, 1966.

Bell, D. *The Coming of Post-Industrial Society*. New York: Basic Books, 1973.

Bell, D. *The Cultural Contradictions of Capitalism*. New York: Basic Books, 1976.

Ben-David, J. *Fundamental Research and the Universities*. Paris: Organization for Economic Cooperation and Development, 1968.

*Ben-David, J. *American Higher Education*. New York: McGraw-Hill, 1972.

Benedict, R. *Patterns of Culture*. Boston: Houghton Mifflin, 1959.

Benezet, L. T. *College Organization and Student Impact*. Washington, D.C.: Association of American Colleges, 1976.

Benham, L. "Benefits of Women's Education with Marriage." *Journal of Political Economy*, March-April 1974, pp. 57-71.

Benson, C. S., and Hodgkinson, H. L. *Implementing the Learning Society: New Strategies for Financing Social Objectives*. San Francisco: Jossey-Bass, 1974.

Benson, G. C. S., and Engeman, T. S. *Amoral America*. Stanford: Hoover Institution Press, 1975.

Berelson, B., and Steiner, G. A. *Human Behavior: An Inventory of Scientific Findings*. New York: Harcourt Brace Jovanovich, 1964.

Berg, I. *Education and Jobs: The Great Training Robbery*. New York: Praeger, 1970.

*Berman, R. S. "Culture and Society." *ACLS Newsletter*, Winter 1975, pp. 3-11.

Best, F. *The Effect of Work and Free-Time Scheduling upon Worker Time-Income Trade-Off Preferences*. Washington, D.C.: Quality of Life Research Associates, 1976.

Betz, E. L., Starr, A. M., and Menne, J. W. "College Student Satisfaction in

Ten Public and Private Colleges and Universities." *Journal of College Student Personnel,* September 1973, pp. 456-461.

Bidwell, C. E. "Proposal for a Study to Investigate Relationships Between the Social and Normative Structures of American Colleges and Universities." Unpublished report, 1975.

Bird, C. *The Case Against College.* New York: McKay, 1975.

Bird, C., and Boyer, E. L. "Is College Necessary?" *Change,* February 1975, pp. 32-37.

Birnbaum, N. "Higher Education's Self-Portrait: Not Entirely Flattering." *Chronicle of Higher Education,* May 5, 1975.

Bisconti, A. S., and Solmon, L. C. *College Education on the Job—The Graduate's Viewpoint.* Bethlehem, Pa.: CPC Foundation, 1976.

Blank, D. M., and Stigler, G. *The Demand and Supply of Scientific Personnel.* New York: National Bureau of Economic Research, 1957.

Blau, P. M., and Duncan, O. D. *The American Occupational Structure.* New York: Wiley, 1967.

Blaug, M. "The Empirical Status of Human Capital Theory: A Slightly Jaundiced Survey." *Journal of Economic Literature,* September 1976, pp. 827-855.

Blaug, M., Peston, M., and Ziderman, A. *The Utilization of Educated Manpower in Industry.* Toronto: University of Toronto Press, 1967.

Bloom, A. "The Failure of the University." *Daedalus,* Fall 1974, pp. 58-66.

Bloom, B. S. *Stability and Change in Human Characteristics.* New York: Wiley, 1964.

Bloom, B. S. "Learning for Mastery." *Evaluation Comment.* Los Angeles: Center for the Study of Evaluation of Instructional Programs, University of California, 1968.

*Bloom, B. S., Englehart, M., Furst, E., Hill, W., and Krathwohl, D. *Taxonomy of Educational Objectives: Handbook I, Cognitive Domain.* New York: McKay, 1956.

*Bloom, B. S., Hastings, J. T., and Madaus, G. F. *Handbook on Formative and Summative Evaluation of Student Learning.* New York: McGraw-Hill, 1971.

Bloom, B. S., and Webster, H. "The Outcomes of College." *Review of Educational Research,* October 1960, pp. 321-333.

Bloom, B. T. (Ed.). *Psychological Stress in the Campus Community.* New York: Behavioral Publications, Inc., 1975.

*Bok, D. "On the Purposes of Undergraduate Education." *Daedalus,* Fall 1974, pp. 159-172.

*Bondi, H. "The Dangers of Rejecting Mathematics." *London Times Higher Education Supplement,* March 26, 1976.

Boudon, R. *Education, Opportunity, and Social Inequality.* New York: Wiley, 1974.

Boulding, K. E. "The Pursuit of Equality." In J. D. Smith (Ed.), *The Personal Distribution of Income and Wealth.* New York: National Bureau of Research and Columbia University Press, 1975.

Bowen, H. R. "The University in America: 2000 A.D." In R. W. Roskens and R. I. White (Eds.), *Paradox, Process and Progress.* Kent, Ohio: Kent State University Press, 1968.

Bowen, H. R. "Manpower Management and Higher Education." *Educational Record*, Winter 1973, pp. 5-14.

Bowen, H. R. (Ed.). *New Directions for Institutional Research: Evaluating Institutions for Accountability*, no. 1. San Francisco: Jossey-Bass, 1974a.

Bowen, H. R. *Financing Higher Education: The Current State of the Debate*. Washington, D.C.: Association of American Colleges, 1974b.

Bowen, H. R. "Higher Education: A Growth Industry." *Educational Record*, Summer 1974c, 147-158.

*Bowen, H. R. (Ed.). *Freedom and Control in a Democratic Society*. New York: American Council of Life Insurance, 1976.

Bowen, H. R. *Toward Social Economy*. Carbondale: Southern Illinois University Press, 1977.

Bowen, H. R., and Minter, W. J. *Private Higher Education: Second Annual Report on Financial and Educational Trends in the Private Sector of American Higher Education*. Washington, D.C.: Association of American Colleges, 1976.

Bowen, H. R., and Seryelle, P. *Who Benefits from Higher Education and Who Should Pay?* Washington, D.C.: American Association for Higher Education, 1972.

Bowen, W. G., and Finegan, T. A. *The Economics of Labor Force Participation*. Princeton: Princeton University Press, 1969.

Bowles, S. "The Integration of Higher Education into the Wage-Labor System." In M. B. Katz (Ed.), *Education in American History*. New York: Praeger, 1973.

Bowles, S., and Gintis, H. *Schooling in Capitalist America*. New York: Basic Books, 1976.

Boyer, E. L., and Michael, W. B. "Outcomes of College." *Review of Educational Research*, 1965, pp. 277-291.

Bradshaw, T. K. "The Impact of Education on Leisure: Socialization in College." Unpublished doctoral dissertation, University of California, Berkeley, 1974.

Bradshaw, T. K. "The Impact of Peers on Student Orientations to College: A Contextual Analysis." In M. Trow (Ed.), *Teachers and Students*. New York: McGraw-Hill, 1975.

*Brawer, F. B. *New Perspectives on Personality Development in College Students*. San Francisco: Jossey-Bass, 1973.

Breneman, D. W. "Conceptual Issues in Modeling the Supply Side of Higher Education." Paper presented to the annual meeting of the Southern Economic Association, November 15, 1974.

Breslow, L., and Klein, B. "Health and Race in California." *American Journal of Public Health*, April 1971, pp. 763-775.

Bressler, M. Address to American Council of Life Insurance, Arden House, Harriman, N.Y., June 1976.

*Brewster, K. "Four Paradoxes in Higher Education and How to Deal with Them." *Chronicle of Higher Education*, May 1, 1972, p. 8.

*Brewster, K., Price, D. K., Wood, R. C., and Frankel, C. *Educating for the Twenty-First Century*. Urbana: University of Illinois Press, 1969.

Brigante, M. E. "A Trans-Generational Study of Sex Roles in Marriage in

Middle-Class America." Unpublished doctoral dissertation, Claremont Graduate School, Claremont, Calif., 1972.

Brim, O. G., Jr., Glass, D., Neulinger, J., and Firestone, I. *American Beliefs and Attitudes About Intelligence*. New York: Russell Sage Foundation, 1969.

Brittain, J. A. *The Inheritance of Economic Status*. Washington, D.C.: Brookings Institution, 1977.

Browning, E. K. "How Much More Equality Can We Afford?" *The Public Interest*, Spring 1976, pp. 90-110.

*Bruner, J. S. *The Process of Education*. Cambridge: Harvard University Press, 1960.

Brzezenski, Z. *Between Two Ages*. New York: Viking Press, 1970.

Burn, B. B. *Higher Education in Nine Countries*. New York: McGraw-Hill, 1971.

*California, University of (Berkeley). Report of Select Committee on Education. *Education at Berkeley*. Berkeley: University of California, 1966.

Campbell, A., Converse, P. E., Miller, W., and Stokes, D. E. *The American Voter*. New York: Wiley, 1960.

Campbell, A., Converse, P. E., and Rodgers, W. L. *The Quality of American Life: Perceptions, Evaluations, and Satisfactions*. New York: Russell Sage Foundation, 1976.

Carnegie Commission on Higher Education. *A Chance to Learn: An Action Agenda for Equal Opportunity in Higher Education*. New York: McGraw-Hill, 1970.

Carnegie Commission on Higher Education. *Reform on Campus*. New York: McGraw-Hill, 1972.

Carnegie Commission on Higher Education. *Higher Education: Who Pays? Who Benefits? Who Should Pay?* New York: McGraw-Hill, 1973a.

*Carnegie Commission on Higher Education. *Priorities for Action: Final Report*. New York: McGraw-Hill, 1973b.

*Carnegie Commission on Higher Education. *The Purposes and Performances of Higher Education in the United States*. New York: McGraw-Hill, 1973c.

Carroll, J. "A Model of School Learning." *Teachers College Record*, 1963, pp. 723-733.

Caws, P. "Instruction and Curriculum." *Daedalus*, Fall 1974, pp. 18-24.

Centra, J. A., and Rock, D. A. "College Environments and Student Academic Achievement." *American Educational Research Journal*, 1971, pp. 623-634.

Chalmers, G. K. "The Social Role of Education." *American Scholar*, Winter 1948-49, pp. 41-49.

*Chandler, J. W. "The Liberal Arts College in Postindustrial Society." *Educational Record*, Spring 1974, pp. 126-130.

*Cheit, E. F. *The Useful Arts and the Liberal Tradition*. New York: McGraw-Hill, 1975.

Chickering, A. W. "Institutional Size and Student Development." Paper presented at the Council for the Advancement of Small Colleges Conference on Factors Affecting Student Development in College, 1965.

Chickering, A. W. *Education and Identity.* San Francisco: Jossey-Bass, 1969.

Chickering, A. W. "College Experience and Student Development." Address given at the meeting of the American Association for the Advancement of Science, 1970.

Chickering, A. W. "The Best Colleges Have the Least Effect." *Saturday Review,* January 16, 1971, pp. 48-50.

Chickering, A. W. *Commuting Versus Resident Students: Overcoming Educational Inequities of Living Off Campus.* San Francisco: Jossey-Bass, 1974.

Chiswick, B. R. "Schooling, Screening, and Income." In L. C. Solmon and P. J. Taubman (Eds.), *Does College Matter?* New York: Academic Press, 1973.

Citicorp, press release, Public Affairs Department, June 23, 1975.

*Clark, B. R., and others. *Students and Colleges: Interaction and Change.* Berkeley: Center for Research and Development in Higher Education, University of California, 1972.

Clark, B. R. and Trow, M. *Determinants of College Student Subculture.* Berkeley: Center for Research and Development in Higher Education, University of California, 1962.

Clark, B. R., and Youn, T. I. K. *Academic Power in the United States.* Washington, D.C.: American Association for Higher Education, 1976.

Clark, C. *The Conditions of Economic Progress.* London: Macmillan, 1957.

Clecak, P. *Radical Paradoxes.* New York: Harper & Row, 1973.

Clecak, P. "Caroline Bird's Hypothetical Class Action Suit Against Higher Education." *Chronicle of Higher Education,* March 31, 1975, pp. 15-16.

*Clecak, P. *Crooked Paths.* New York: Harper & Row, 1976.

*Cleveland, H. *Seven Everyday Collisions in American Higher Education.* New York: International Council for Educational Development, Occasional Paper No. 9, 1974.

*Cleveland, H. "The Little League and the Imperatives of Interdependence." *Educational Record,* Winter 1975, pp. 5-9.

Clinard, M. *The Black Market.* New York: Holt, Rinehart and Winston, 1952.

Clinard, M. *Sociology of Deviant Behavior.* New York: Holt, Rinehart and Winston, 1963.

Cobern, M., Salem, C., and Mushkin, S. *Indicators of Educational Outcome, Fall 1973.* (Publication No. (OE) 73-11110, Department of Health, Education, and Welfare) Washington, D.C.: U.S. Government Printing Office, 1973.

*Cohen, A. A. (Ed.). *Humanistic Education and Western Civilization: Essays for Robert A. Hutchins.* New York: Holt, Rinehart and Winston, 1964.

Cohen, M., and March, J. *Leadership and Ambiguity.* New York: McGraw-Hill, 1974.

*Coleman, J. S., and others. *Youth: Transition to Adulthood.* Chicago: University of Chicago Press, 1974.

Collins, R. "Schooling and Social Inequality." *The Center Magazine,* November-December 1976, pp. 66-74.

The Columbia Encyclopaedia. (3rd ed.) New York: Columbia University Press, 1963.

*Committee on the Student in Higher Education. *The Student in Higher Education.* New Haven: Hazen Foundation, 1968.

Conley, B. C. "The Value of Human Life in the Demand for Safety." *American Economic Review,* March 1976, pp. 45-55.

*Conrad, C. "University Goals, An Operative Approach." *Journal of Higher Education,* October 1974, pp. 502-516.

Correaa, H. *The Economics of Human Resources.* Amsterdam: North Holland Publishing Company, 1963.

*Cosand, J. P. "Setting National Goals and Objectives." In J. F. Hughes (Ed.), *Education and the State.* Washington, D.C.: American Council on Education, 1975.

Cottle, T. J. "The Effects of College on Individuals: Three Life Studies." In L. C. Solmon and P. J. Taubman (Eds.), *Does College Matter?* New York: Academic Press, 1973.

Counts, G. S. *Dare the School Build a New Social Order?* New York: John Day, 1932.

*Counts, G. S. *Education and the Foundations of Human Freedom.* Pittsburgh: University of Pittsburgh Press, 1962.

*Craig, G. A. "Green Stamp or Structured Undergraduate Education." *Daedalus,* Fall 1974, pp. 143-147.

*Cremin, L. A. *The Genius of American Education.* Pittsburgh: University of Pittsburgh Press, 1965.

*Cross, K. P. *Beyond the Open Door: New Students to Higher Education.* San Francisco: Jossey-Bass, 1971.

Cross, K. P. "Looking Beyond Academic Ability." *The Chronicle of Higher Education,* April 22, 1974, p. 24.

*Cross, K. P. "The Elusive Goal of Educational Equality." In J. F. Hughes and O. Mills (Eds.), *Formulating Policy in Postsecondary Education: The Search for Alternatives.* Washington, D.C.: American Council on Education, 1975.

*Cross, K. P. *Accent on Learning: Improving Instruction and Reshaping the Curriculum.* San Francisco: Jossey-Bass, 1976.

Cuninggim, M. "The Integrity of the University." *Educational Record,* Winter 1969, pp. 37-46.

Daedalus. "Intellectuals and Tradition." (S. R. Graubard, Ed.) Spring 1972a.

Daedalus. "Intellectuals and Change." (S. R. Graubard, Ed.) Summer 1972b.

Daedalus. "American Higher Education Toward an Uncertain Future." (S. R. Graubard, Ed.) Vol. I, Fall 1974; Vol. II, Winter 1975.

Daniere, A., and Mechling, J. "Direct Marginal Productivity of College Education in Relation to College Aptitude of Students and Production Costs of Institutions." *Journal of Human Resources,* Winter 1970, pp. 51-70.

Davis, J. A. *Great Aspirations: The Graduate School Plans of American College Seniors.* Chicago: Aldine, 1964.

Davis, J. A. *Undergraduate Career Decisions: Correlates of Occupational Choice.* Chicago: Aldine, 1965.

Davis, J. R., and Morrell, J. F., III. *Evaluating Educational Investment.* Lexington, Mass.: Heath, 1974.

Deacon, R., and Shapiro, P. "Private Preference for Collective Goods Revealed through Voting on Referenda." *American Economic Review,* December 1975, pp. 943-955.

de Jouvenel, B. *The Ethics of Redistribution.* Cambridge: Cambridge University Press, 1951.

Denison, E. F. *The Sources of Economic Growth in the United States.* New York: Committee for Economic Development, 1962.

Denison, E. F. *Why Growth Rates Differ: Postwar Experience in Nine Western Countries.* Washington, D.C.: Brookings Institution, 1967.

Denison, E. F. "An Aspect of Unequal Opportunity." *The Brookings Bulletin,* Winter 1971, pp. 7-10.

Denison, E. F. *Accounting for United States Economic Growth, 1929-1969.* Washington, D.C.: Brookings Institution, 1974.

DePalma, D. J., and Foley, J. M. (Eds.). *Moral Development: Current Theory and Research.* New York: Halsted Press, 1975.

de Tocqueville, A. *Democracy in America.* (G. Lawrence, Trans.) New York: Harper & Row, 1966.

de Tocqueville, A. *L'Ancien Regime.* (M. W. Patterson, Trans.) Oxford: Blackwell, 1947.

Deutsch, K. W., Platt, J., and Senghaas, D. "Conditions Favoring Major Advances in Social Science." *Science,* February 5, 1971a, pp. 450-459.

Deutsch, M. "On Making Social Psychology More Useful." Social Science Research Council *Items,* March 1976, pp. 1-6.

*Dewey, J. *On Education.* (R. D. Archambault, Ed.) Chicago: University of Chicago Press, 1974.

*Dobbins, C. G., and Lee, C. B. T. *Whose Goals for American Higher Education?* Washington, D.C.: American Council on Higher Education, 1968.

Dressel, P. L., and Lehmann, I. J. "The Impact of Higher Education on Student Attitudes, Values, and Critical Thinking Abilities." *Educational Record,* Summer 1965, pp. 248-258.

Drew, D. E., and Patterson, M. "Noah's Ark in the Frog Pond: The Educational Aspirations of Male and Female Undergraduates." Paper presented at annual meeting of American Sociological Society, New York, August 1973.

Dubin, R., and Taveggia, T. C. *The Teaching-Learning Paradox.* Eugene: Center for the Advanced Study of Educational Administration, University of Oregon, 1968.

*Dugger, R. "If I Were a Trustee." *Change,* Winter 1975-76, pp. 8-9.

Duncan, B. "Trends in Output and Distribution of Schooling." In E. B. Sheldon, and W. E. Moore (Eds.), *Indicators of Social Change.* New York: Russell Sage Foundation, 1968.

Duncan, G. G. "Earnings, Functions and Nonpecuniary Benefits." *Journal of Human Resources,* Fall 1976, pp. 462-483.

Duncan, O. D., Featherman, D. L., and Duncan, B. *Socioeconomic Background and Achievement.* New York: Seminar Press, 1972.

Easterlin, R. A. "Relative Economic Status and the American Fertility

Swing." In E. B. Sheldon (Ed.), *Family Economic Behavior*. Philadelphia: Lippincott, 1975.

Eckaus, R. S. *Estimating Returns to Education: A Disaggregated Approach*. Berkeley: Carnegie Commission on Higher Education, 1973.

Eckaus, R. S., El Safti, A., and Norman, V. D. "An Appraisal of the Calculations of Rates of Return to Higher Education." In M. S. Gordon (Ed.), *Higher Education and the Labor Market*. New York: McGraw-Hill, 1974.

*Eddy, E. D., Jr. *The College Influence on Student Character*. Washington, D.C.: American Council on Education, 1959.

Elgin, D., and Mitchell, A. "The Trend to Simpler Life Styles." *Los Angeles Times*, February 28, 1977, Part IV, p. 1.

*Elliott, H. S. R. (Ed.). *The Letters of John Stuart Mill*. London, 1910.

Emmerij, L. "Education and Employment: Some Preliminary Findings and Thoughts." *International Labour Review*, January 1973, pp. 31-42.

*Emmerij, L. *Can the School Build A New Social Order?* Amsterdam: Elsevier, 1974.

Entwistle, N., and Hounsell, D. "How Do Students Learn?" *London Times Higher Education Supplement*, April 6, 1976, p. 15.

Erikson, E. H. *Childhood and Society*. New York: Norton, 1963.

*Eurich, A. C. (Ed.). *Campus 1980*. New York: Dell, 1968.

Executive Office of the President: Office of Management and Budget. *Social Indicators, 1973*. Washington, D.C.: U.S. Government Printing Office, 1973.

Fägerlind, I. *Formal Education and Adult Earnings*. Stockholm: Almquist and Wiksell, 1975.

Faiman, R. N., and Olivier, M. E. (Eds.). *A Question of Partnership: Institutions of Higher Education As a Resource in the Solution of National Problems*. Washington, D.C.: National Association of State Universities and Land-Grant Colleges, 1972.

Farnsworth, D. L. "Social Values in College and University." *Daedalus*, Fall 1974, pp. 297-301.

Fay, M. A., and Weintraub, J. A. *Political Ideologies of Graduate Students*. Berkeley: Carnegie Commission on Higher Education, 1973.

Feldman, K. A. *Research Strategies in Studying College Impact*. Iowa City: American College Testing Program, 1970.

*Feldman, K. A., and Newcomb, T. M. *The Impact of College on Students*. 2 Vols. San Francisco: Jossey-Bass, 1969.

Ferman, L. A. "Religious Change on a College Campus." *Journal of College Student Personnel*, 1960, pp. 2-12.

Fetters, W. B. *National Longitudinal Study of the High School Class of 1972: Student Questionnaire and Test Results by Sex, High School Program, Ethnic Category, and Father's Education*. U.S. Department of Health, Education, and Welfare, National Center for Education Statistics, publication number NCES75-208. Washington, D.C.: U.S. Government Printing Office, 1975.

Finegan, T. A. "Hours of Work in the United States: A Cross-Sectional Analysis." *Journal of Political Economy*, October 1962, pp. 452-470.

*Frankel, C. *The Democratic Prospect*. New York: Harper & Row, 1962.

Frankel, C. *Education and the Barricades.* New York: Norton, 1968.

Freedman, M. B. *The College Experience.* San Francisco: Jossey-Bass, 1967.

Freeman, R. B. *The Market for College-Trained Manpower.* Cambridge: Harvard University Press, 1971.

Freeman, R. B. "Overinvestment in College Training?" *Journal of Human Resources,* Summer 1975, pp. 287-311.

Freeman, R. B. *The Over-Educated American.* New York: Academic Press, 1976.

Freeman, R. B., and Hollomon, J. H. "The Declining Value of College Going." *Change,* September 1975, pp. 24-31.

Friedman, M. *Capitalism and Freedom.* Chicago: University of Chicago Press, 1962.

Friedman, M. "The Higher Schooling in America." *The Public Interest,* Spring 1968, pp. 108-112.

Fromm, G. "Civil Aviation Expenditures." In R. Dorfman (Ed.), *Measuring Benefits of Government Investments.* Washington, D.C.: Brookings Institution, 1965.

Fuchs, V. R. *Who Shall Live?* New York: Basic Books, 1974.

*Fuller, E. (Ed.). *The Christian Idea of Education.* New Haven: Yale University Press, 1957.

Gaff, J. G. "Making a Difference: The Impacts of Faculty." *Journal of Higher Education,* November 1973, pp. 605-622.

*Gagnon, P. "The Right to Culture." *Change,* Winter 1975-1976, pp. 36-40.

Gallup, G. *Attitudes of College Students on Political, Social, and Economic Issues.* Princeton: The Gallup Poll, 1975.

*Gardner, J. W. *Excellence: Can We Be Equal and Excellent Too?* New York: Harper & Row, 1961.

*Gardner, J. W. *Self-Renewal.* New York: Harper & Row, 1963.

Gardner, J. W. Remarks at the Inauguration of James A. Perkins as President of Cornell University, October 4, 1965.

*Gardner, J. W. *The American Commitment.* New York: National Conference of Christians and Jews, 1966.

Garrett, H. E., and Woodworth, R. S. *Statistics in Psychology and Education.* (6th ed.) New York: McKay, 1966.

Gartner, A., Greer, C., and Riessman, F. *The New Assault on Equality: IQ and Social Stratification.* New York: Harper & Row, 1974.

Gilroy, C. L. "Investment in Human Capital and Black-White Unemployment." *Monthly Labor Review,* July 1975, pp. 13-21.

Gintis, H. "Toward a Political Economy of Education: A Radical Critique of Ivan Illich's Deschooling Society." In I. Illich and others, *After Deschooling, What?* New York: Harper & Row, 1973.

Ginzberg, E. "Strategies for Educational Reform." *Teachers College Record,* September 1974, pp. 39-45.

*Givens, P. R. "Toward a New Emphasis on Human Values in Higher Education." *Liberal Education,* December 1974, pp. 409-427.

Goethals, G. W., and Klos, D. S. *Experiencing Youth.* Boston: Little, Brown, 1970.

*Goldwin, R. A. (Ed.). *Higher Education and Modern Democracy.* Chicago: Rand McNally, 1967.

*Goodman, P. *Compulsory Miseducation.* New York: Horizon Press, 1964.

Gouldner, A. "Ideology and University Revolt."*London Times Education Supplement,* August 18, 1976, p. 15.

The Graduate Magazine. The Senior in 1974: A Growing Seriousness. Knoxville, Tenn.: Approach 13-30 Corporation, 1974.

Graubard, S. R. (Ed.). "Intellectuals and Tradition." *Daedalus,* Spring 1972a.

Graubard, S. R. (Ed.). "Intellectuals and Change." *Daedalus,* Summer 1972b.

*Graubard, S. R. (Ed.). "American Higher Education: Toward an Uncertain Future." *Daedalus,* Vol. I, Fall 1974; Vol. II, Winter 1975.

*Graubard, S. R. "Thoughts on Higher Educational Purposes and Goals." *Daedalus,* 1974, Vol. I, pp. 1-11.

Greenberg, J., and Greenberg, H. "Predicting Sales Success—Myths and Reality."*Personnel Journal,* December 1976, pp. 621-627.

Greer, C. *The Great School Legend: A Revisionist Interpretation of American Public Education.* New York: Basic Books, 1972.

Griliches, Z. "Notes on the Role of Education in Production Functions and Growth Accounting." In W. L. Hansen (Ed.), *Education, Income, and Human Capital.* New York: National Bureau of Economic Research and Columbia University Press, 1970.

*Gross, E., and Grambsch, P. V. *University Goals and Academic Power.* Washington, D.C.: American Council on Education, 1968.

*Gross, E., and Grambsch, P. V. *Changes in University Organization, 1964-1971.* New York: McGraw-Hill, 1974.

Grossman, M. "The Correlation Between Health and Schooling." In N. E. Terleckyj (Ed.), *Household Production and Consumption.* New York: National Bureau of Economic Research and Columbia University Press, 1975.

Guilford, J. P. *The Nature of Human Intelligence.* New York: McGraw-Hill, 1967.

Gurin, G., Veroff, J., and Feld, S. *Americans View Their Mental Health.* New York: Basic Books, 1960.

Halberstam, D. *The Best and the Brightest.* New York: Fawcett World Library, 1973.

*Handlin, O., and Handlin, M. F. *The American College and American Culture.* New York: McGraw-Hill, 1970.

Hanoch, G. *Personal Earnings and Investment in Schooling.* Chicago: University of Chicago Press, 1965.

Hanoch, G. "An Economic Analysis of Earnings and Schooling." *The Journal of Human Resources,* Summer, 1967, pp. 310-329.

Hansen, W. L. "Total and Private Returns to Investment in Schooling." *Journal of Political Economy,* April 1963, pp. 128-140.

Hansen, W. L. "Prediction of Graduate Performance in Economics." *Journal of Economic Education,* 1971, pp. 49-53.

Hansen, W. L., and Weisbrod, B. A. *Benefits, Costs and Finance of Public Higher Education.* Chicago: Markham, 1969.

Hansen, W. L., and Witmer, D. R. "Economic Benefits of Universal Higher Education." In L. Wilson, and O. Mills (Eds.), *Universal Higher Education.* Washington, D.C.: American Council on Education, 1972.

Harman, W. "Changing United States Society: Implications for Schools." In Organization for Economic Cooperation and Development (OECD), *Alternative Educational Futures in the United States and in Europe: Methods, Issues, and Policy Relevance.* Paris: OECD, 1972.

Harrinton, M. "Keep Admissions Open." *New York Times Magazine,* November 2, 1975.

Harrington, T. F., Jr. "The Literature on the Commuter Student." *Journal of College Student Personnel,* November 1972, pp. 546-550.

Harris, J., and Hurst, P. "Does College Assure Academic Growth?" *Change,* February 1972, pp. 8-9, 60.

Harris, L. "American Public's Confidence in Higher Education Declines." *Chronicle of Higher Education,* October 14, 1974.

*Harris, W. V. "Jencks and the Carnegie Commission." *Journal of Higher Education,* March-April 1975, pp. 213-225.

Hartman, G. W., and Barrick, F. "Fluctuations in General Cultural Information Among Undergraduates." *Journal of Educational Research,* December 1934, pp. 255-264.

Hartnett, R. T. *Accountability in Higher Education.* Princeton: Educational Testing Service, 1971.

*Harvard Committee. *General Education in a Free Society.* Cambridge: Harvard University Press, 1945.

Hause, J. C. "Ability and Schooling as Determinants of Lifetime Earnings." In F. T. Juster (Ed.), *Education, Income, and Human Behavior.* New York: McGraw-Hill, 1975.

Havelock, R. G. *Planning for Innovation through Dissemination and Utilization of Knowledge.* Ann Arbor: Institute for Social Research, University of Michigan, 1969.

Havemann, E., and West, P. *They Went to College.* New York: Harcourt Brace Jovanovich, 1952.

*Heard, A. "The Modern Culture of Higher Education: Many Missions and Nothing Sacred." The Wilson Lecture. Nashville: Board of Higher Education, United Methodist Church, 1973.

*Heard, A. "The Consequences of Knowing." *Educational Record,* Spring 1974, pp. 75-78.

Heath, D. H. *Growing Up in College: Liberal Education and Maturity.* San Francisco: Jossey-Bass, 1968.

*Heath, D. H. "What the Enduring Effects of Higher Education Tell Us About a Liberal Education." *Journal of Higher Education,* March-April 1976, pp. 173-190.

Heath, R. *The Reasonable Adventurer.* Pittsburgh: University of Pittsburgh Press, 1964.

*Heilbroner, R. L. *An Inquiry into the Human Prospect.* New York: Norton, 1974.

*Heilbroner, R. L. *Business Civilization in Decline.* New York: Norton, 1976.

Heist, P. (Ed.). *Education for Creativity: A Modern Myth.* Berkeley: Center for Research and Development in Higher Education, University of California, 1967.

*Heist, P. (Ed.). *The Creative College Student: An Unmet Challenge.* San Francisco: Jossey-Bass, 1968.

Heist, P., McConnell, T. R., Matsler, F., and Williams, P. "Personality and Scholarship." *Science,* February 10, 1961, pp. 362-367.

Heist, P., and Yonge, G. *The Omnibus Personality Inventory Manual.* New York: Psychological Corporation, Inc., 1968.

*Hesburgh, T. M. *The Humane Imperative.* New Haven: Yale University Press, 1974.

Heston, J. C. "Educational Growth as Shcwn by Retests on the Graduate Record Examination." *Educational and Psychological Measurement,* 1950, pp. 367-370.

Higher Education Research Institute. "Education and Work." Unpublished report, University of California, Los Angeles, 1976.

Hill, C. R., and Stafford, F. P. "Allocation of Time to Preschool Children and Educational Opportunity." *Journal of Human Resources,* Summer 1974, pp. 323-341.

Hines, F., Tweeten, L., and Redfern, M. "Social and Private Rates of Return to Investment in Schooling by Race-Sex Groups and Regions." *Journal of Human Resources,* Summer 1970, pp. 318-340.

Hinkle, L. E., Jr., and others. "Occupation, Education, and Coronary Heart Disease." *Science,* July 19, 1968, pp. 238-246.

Hodgkinson, H. L. *Institutions in Transition.* New York: McGraw-Hill, 1971.

Hodgkinson, H. L. "Encouraging Change and Significance in Higher Education." In R. H. Kroepsch (Ed.), *Legislative Decision Making in Higher Education, A Report on the Legislative Work Conference on Higher Education.* Boulder: Western Interstate Commission in Higher Education, 1972.

Hodgkinson, H. L. "Adult Development: Implications for Faculty and Administrators." *Educational Record,* Fall 1974, pp. 263-274.

Hoffmann, B. *The Tyranny of Testing.* New York: Crowell, 1962.

Hoge, D. R. *Commitment on Campus: Changes in Religion and Values Over Five Decades.* Philadelphia: Westminster Press, 1974.

*Holsten, R. W. (Ed.). *The Requirements for Leadership.* A Symposium with Fred Hoyle, John Cogley, Harold D. Lasswell, and Howard W. Johnson. Chapel Hill: University of North Carolina, 1968.

*Hook, S. *Education and the Taming of Power.* LaSalle, Ill.: Open Court, 1973.

*Howe, H., II. *The Value of College: A Non-Economist's View.* New York: Ford Foundation, 1975.

Howe, I. "Living with Kampf and Schlaff: Literary Tradition and Mass Education." *The American Scholar,* Winter 1973-74, pp. 107-112.

Howe, I. "Beyond Turmoil, Beyond Torpor." *Chronicle of Higher Education,* January 27, 1975, pp. 9-10.

Howes, R. F. (Ed.). *Vision and Purpose in Higher Education.* Washington, D.C.: American Council on Education, 1962.

*Huff, R. A. *Inventory of Educational Outcomes and Activities.* Boulder: Western Interstate Commission for Higher Education, 1971.

Hunt, S. "Income Determinants for College Graduates and Return to Educational Investment." Unpublished doctoral dissertation, Yale University, 1963.

Husén, T. "Comparative Research on Higher Education." In *Higher Education: Crisis and Support*. New York: International Council for Educational Development, 1974a, pp. 109-115.

*Husén, T. *Talent, Equality and Meritocracy*. The Hague: Martinus Nijhoff, 1974b.

*Hutchins, R. M. *The Higher Learning in America*. New Haven: Yale University Press, 1962.

Hutchins, R. M. *The Learning Society*. New York: Praeger, 1968.

*Hutchins, R. M. "On Political Maturity." *Change*, November 1974, pp. 32-33.

Hyman, H. H., and Sheatsley, P. B. "Attitudes Toward Desegregation." *Scientific American*, July 1964, pp. 16-23.

Hyman, H. H., Wright, C. R., and Reed, J. S. *The Enduring Effects of Education*. Chicago: University of Chicago Press, 1975.

*Illich, I. *Deschooling Society*. New York: Harper & Row, 1972.

Illich, I., and others. *After Deschooling What?* New York: Harper & Row, 1973.

Illinois Institute of Technology. *Traces: Technology in Retrospect and Critical Events in Science*. A report prepared for the National Science Foundation, Chicago, 1968.

Inkeles, A. "Rising Expectations: Revolution, Evaluation, or Devolution." In H. R. Bowen (Ed.), *Freedom and Control in a Democratic Society*. New York: Institute of Life Insurance, 1976.

*Jacob, P. E. *Changing Values in College*. New York: Harper & Row, 1957.

Jefferson, T. *Notes on the State of Virginia*. (W. Peden, Ed.) Chapel Hill: University of North Carolina Press, 1955.

*Jencks, C. *Inequality*. New York: Basic Books, 1972.

*Jencks, C., and Riesman, D. *The Academic Revolution*. Garden City, N.Y.: Doubleday, 1968.

*Jones, H. M. *One Great Society*. New York: Harcourt Brace Jovanovich, 1959.

Jorgenson, D. W., and Griliches, Z. "The Explanation of Productivity Change." *Review of Economic Studies*, July 1967, pp. 249-283.

Juster, F. T. (Ed.). *Education, Income, and Human Behavior*. New York: McGraw-Hill, 1975.

Kagan, J. (Ed.). *Creativity and Learning*. Boston: Houghton Mifflin, 1967.

Karweit, N. *Life History Data on the Occupational Effects of Obtaining Educational Credentials Through Alternate Routes*. Washington, D.C.: National Institute of Education, 1976.

Kateb, G. *Political Theory: Its Nature and Uses*. New York: St. Martin's, 1968.

Katona, G., Mandell, L., and Schmiedeskamp, J. *1970 Survey of Consumer Finances*. Ann Arbor: Institute for Social Research, University of Michigan, 1971.

Katona, G., Strumpel, B., and Zahn, E. *Aspirations and Affluence*. New York: McGraw-Hill, 1971.

Katz, A. "Schooling, Age, and Length of Unemployment." *Industrial and Labor Relations Review*, July 1974, pp. 597-605.

Katz, D., and others. *Bureaucratic Encounters*. Ann Arbor: Survey Research Center, Institute of Social Research, University of Michigan, 1975.

Katz, J. (Ed.). *Growth and Constraint in College Students: A Study of The Varieties of Psychological Development.* Stanford: Institute for the Study of Human Problems, 1967.

*Katz, J. "Psychodynamics of Development During the College Years." In B. L. Bloom (Ed.), *Psychological Stress in the Campus Community.* New York: Behavioral Publications, Inc., 1975.

*Katz, J. "Benefits for Personal Development from Going to College." Paper presented at the annual meeting of the Association of Professors of Higher Education, Chicago, March 6-7, 1976.

Katz, J., and Associates. *No Time for Youth: Growth and Constraint in College Students.* San Francisco: Jossey-Bass, 1968.

Katz, M. B. (Ed.). *Education in American History.* New York: Praeger, 1973.

*Kaysen, C. *The Higher Learning, the Universities and the Public.* Princeton: Princeton University Press, 1969.

*Kaysen, C. (Ed.). *Content and Context.* New York: McGraw-Hill, 1973.

Kaysen, C. "What Should Education Do?" *Daedalus,* Fall 1974, pp. 180-185.

*Kaysen, C. "Setting National Goals for Higher Education." In J. F. Hughes (Ed.), *Education and the State.* Washington, D.C.: American Council on Education, 1975.

Keeton, M. T. *Models and Mavericks.* New York: McGraw-Hill, 1971.

Keeton, M. (Ed.). *Reflections on Experiential Learning and Its Uses.* Working Paper, Cooperative Assessment of Experiential Learning, Princeton: Educational Testing Service, December 1974.

Kelsall, R. K., Poole, A., and Kuhn, A. *Graduates: The Sociology of an Elite.* London: Methuen, 1972.

Keniston, K. "Responsibility for Criticism and Social Change." In C. G. Dobbins and C. B. T. Lee (Eds.), *Whose Goals for Higher Education?* Washington, D.C.: American Council on Education, 1968a.

Keniston, K. *Young Radicals: Notes on Committed Youth.* New York: Harcourt Brace Jovanovich, 1968b.

Keniston, K. *Youth and Dissent: The Rise of a New Opposition.* New York: Harcourt Brace Jovanovich, 1971.

*Keniston, K., and Gerzon, M. "Human and Social Benefits." In L. Wilson and O. Mills (Eds.), *Universal Higher Education.* Washington, D.C.: American Council on Education, 1972.

Keniston, K., and Lerner, M. "Campus Characteristics and Campus Unrest." *Annals of the American Academy of Political and Social Science,* May 1971, pp. 39-53.

*Kerr, C. *The Uses of the University.* Cambridge: Harvard University Press, 1963.

Keynes, J. M. *The General Theory of Employment Interest and Money.* London: MacMillan, 1936.

King, S. H. *Five Lives at Harvard: Personality Change During College.* Cambridge: Harvard University Press, 1973.

Kinsey, A. C., Pomeroy, W. B., and Martin, C. E. *Sexual Behavior in the Human Male.* Philadelphia: W. B. Saunders Company, 1948.

Kitagawa, E. M., and Hauser, P. M. *Differential Mortality in the United States: A Study in Socioeconomic Epidemiology.* Cambridge: Harvard University Press, 1973.

Klemp, G. O., Jr. "Three Factors of Success in the World of Work: Implications for Curriculum in Higher Education." Paper presented to the American Association for Higher Education, March 21, 1977.

Klitgaard, R. E. "Going Beyond the Mean in Educational Evaluation." *Public Policy,* Winter 1975, pp. 59-79.

Knapp, C. B. "Education and Differences in Postschool Human Investment." *Economic Inquiry,* April 1977, pp. 283-289.

*Kohlberg, L., and Mayer, R. "Development as the Aim of Education." *Harvard Educational Review,* November 1972, pp. 449-496.

Kohlberg, L., and Turiel, E. "Moral Development and Moral Education." In G. S. Lesser (Ed.), *Psychology and Educational Practice.* Glenview, Ill.: Scott, Foresman, 1971.

Koon, J. *Types, Traits, and Transitions: The Lives of Four-Year College Students.* Berkeley: Center for Research and Development in Higher Education, University of California, 1974.

Kosobud, R. F., and Morgan, J. N. (Eds.). *Consumer Behavior of Individual Families over Two and Three Years.* Ann Arbor: Survey Research Center, University of Michigan, 1964.

*Krathwohl, D. R., Bloom, B. S., and Masia, B. B. *Taxonomy of Educational Objectives* (Handbook 2, Affective Domain). New York: McKay, 1964.

*Ladd, E. C., Jr., and Lipset, S. M. *The Divided Academy: Professors and Politics.* New York: McGraw-Hill, 1975.

Landes, W. M. "Economics of Fair Employment Laws." *Journal of Political Economy,* July-August, 1968, pp. 507-552.

Lando, M. E. "The Interaction between Health and Education." *Social Security Bulletin,* December 1975, pp. 16-22.

Lannholm, G. V. "Educational Growth During the Second Two Years of College." *Educational and Psychological Measurement,* Winter 1952, pp. 645-653.

Lannholm, G. V. "Trends in Liberal Arts Outcomes in Seventy-Nine Colleges During a Five-Year Period." Mimeograph. Princeton: Educational Testing Service, 1962.

Lannholm, G. V., and Pitcher, B. "Achievement in Three Broad Areas of Study During the Second Two Years of College." Mimeograph. Princeton: Educational Testing Service, 1956.

Lannholm, G. V., and Pitcher, B. "Achievement in Three Broad Areas of Study During the First Two Years of College." Mimeograph. Princeton: Educational Testing Service, 1957.

Lannholm, G. V., and Pitcher, B. "Mean Score Changes on the Graduate Record Examinations Area Tests for College Students Tested Three Times in a Four-Year Period." Mimeograph. Princeton: Educational Testing Service, 1959.

Lansing, J. B., and Mueller, E. *The Geographic Mobility of Labor.* Ann Arbor: Institute for Social Research, University of Michigan, 1967.

Lassiter, R. L. *The Association of Income and Educational Achievement.* Gainesville: University of Florida Press, 1966.

*Lawrence, B. "Issues Related to the Purposes of Postsecondary Education." In L. Glenny and G. Weathersby (Eds.), *Statewide Planning for Postsecondary Education: Issues and Design.* Boulder: Western Interstate Commission for Higher Education, 1971.

Lawrence, B., Weathersby, G., and Patterson, V. W. (Eds.). *Outputs of Higher Education: Their Identification, Measurement and Evaluation.* Boulder: Western Interstate Commission for Higher Education, 1970.

Layard, R., and Psacharopoulos, G. "The Screening Hypothesis and the Returns to Education." *Journal of Political Economy*, September-October 1974, pp. 985-998.

Learned, W. S., and Wood, B. D. *The Student and His Knowledge.* New York: The Carnegie Foundation for the Advancement of Teaching, Bulletin Number 29, 1938.

Lebergott, S. "Labor Force and Employment Trends." In E. B. Sheldon and W. E. Moore (Eds.), *Indicators of Social Change.* New York: Russell Sage Foundation, 1968.

Lehmann, I. J., and Dressel, P. L. *Critical Thinking, Attitudes, and Values in Higher Education.* East Lansing: Michigan State University, 1962.

Lehmann, I. J., and Dressel, P. L. *Changes in Critical Thinking Ability, Attitudes, and Values Associated with College Attendance.* East Lansing: Michigan State University, 1963.

Lehmann, I. J., and Payne, I. K. "An Exploration of Attitude and Value Changes of College Freshmen." *Personnel and Guidance Journal*, January 1963, pp. 403-408.

Leibowitz, A. "Home Investments in Children." *Journal of Political Economy* (Supplement), March-April, 1974.

Leland, C. A., and Lozoff, M. M. *College Influences on the Role Development of Female Undergraduates.* Stanford: Institute for the Study of Human Problems, Stanford University, 1969.

*Lenning, O. T. *The Benefits Crisis in Higher Education.* Washington, D.C.: American Association for Higher Education, 1974.

*Lenning, O. T. *An Overview of the Outcomes Structure: Its Application in Postsecondary Education Institutions.* Boulder: National Center for Higher Education Management Systems, Western Interstate Commission for Higher Education, 1976.

*Lenning, O. T., and others. *The Many Faces of College Success and Their Nonintellective Correlates: The Published Literature Through the Decade of the Sixties.* Iowa City: American College Testing Program, 1974.

*Lenning, O. T., and others. *A Structure for the Outcomes of Postsecondary Education.* Boulder: National Center for Higher Education Management Systems, Western Interstate Commission for Higher Education, 1976.

Lenning, O. T., Munday, L. A., and Maxey, E. J. "Student Educational Growth During the First Two Years of College." *College and University*, 1969, pp. 145-153.

Levin, H. M. *The Costs to the Nation of Inadequate Education.* A report prepared for the Select Committee on Equal Educational Opportunity, U.S. Senate, 92nd Congress, 2nd Session. Washington, D.C.: U.S. Government Printing Office, 1972a.

Levin, H. M. *The Effects of Dropping Out.* A report prepared for the Select Committee on Equal Educational Opportunity, U.S. Senate, 92nd Congress, 2nd Session. Washington, D.C.: U.S. Government Printing Office, 1972b.

Levin, M. R., and Shank, A. (Eds.). *Educational Investment in an Urban Society: Costs, Benefits, and Public Policy.* New York: Teachers College Press, Columbia University, 1970.

Levitan, S. A., and Taggart, R. *The Promise of Greatness.* Cambridge: Harvard University Press, 1976.

*Levitas, M. *Marxist Perspectives in the Sociology of Education.* London: Routledge and Kegan Paul, 1974.

Linden, F. (Ed.). *Market Profiles of Consumer Products.* New York: National Industrial Conference Board, 1967.

Linder, S. B. *The Harried Leisure Class.* New York: Columbia University Press, 1970.

Lindsay, C. M. "Real Returns to Medical Education." *Journal of Human Resources,* Summer 1973, pp. 331-348.

*Lippmann, W. *Preface to Morals.* New York: Macmillan, 1929.

*Lippmann, W. "The University." *The New Republic,* May 28, 1966, pp. 17-20.

Lipset, S. M., and Dobson, R. B. "The Intellectual as Critic and Rebel: With Special Reference to the United States and the Soviet Union." *Daedalus,* Summer 1972, pp. 137-198.

Lipset, S. M., and Ladd, E. C., Jr. "College Generations—from the 1930s to the 1960s." *The Public Interest,* 1971, pp. 99-113.

Lumsden, K. G. (Ed.). *Efficiency in Universities: The LaPaz Papers.* Amsterdam: Elsevier, 1974.

*Lyman, R. W. "The Search for Alternatives." *Educational Record,* Fall 1974, pp. 217-222.

Lystad, M. *As They See It: Changing Values of College Youth.* Cambridge, Mass.: Schenkman, 1973.

Lytton, H. *Creativity and Education.* London: Routledge and Kegan Paul, 1971.

*MacArthur, B. *Beyond 1980: The Evolution of British Higher Education.* New York: International Council for Educational Development, 1975.

McCarthy, J. L., and Deener, D. R. *The Costs and Benefits of Graduate Education: A Commentary with Recommendations.* Washington, D.C.: Council of Graduate Schools, 1972.

McClelland, D. C. *The Achieving Society.* New York: Van Nostrand, 1961.

McClelland, D. C. "Does Education Accelerate Economic Growth?" *Economic Development and Cultural Change.* April 1966, pp. 257-278.

McClelland, D. C. *Motivational Trends in Society.* New York: General Learning Corporation, 1971.

McConnell, T. R. "Differences in Student Attitudes Toward Civil Liberties." In R. L. Sutherland and others (Eds.), *Personality Factors on the College Campus.* Austin: Hogg Foundation for Mental Health, University of Texas.

McDaniel, T. R. "The Cognitive and Affective in Liberal Education: Can We Have Both?" *Liberal Education,* October 1976, pp. 465-471.

*McDanield, M. A. "Tomorrow's Curriculum Today." In A. Toffler (Ed.), *Learning For Tomorrow*. New York: Vintage Books, 1974.

McEaddy, B. J. "Educational Attainment of Workers, March 1974." *Monthly Labor Review*, February 1975, pp. 64-69.

McGrath, E. J. (Ed.). *Universal Higher Education*. New York: McGraw-Hill, 1966.

*McGrath, E. J. "The Time Bomb of Technocratic Education." *Change*, September 1974, pp. 24-29.

*McGrath, E. J. *Values, Liberal Education, and National Destiny*. Indianapolis: Lilly Endowment, Inc., 1975.

*McGrath, E. J. *General Education and the Plight of Modern Man*. Indianapolis: Lilly Endowment, Inc., 1976.

McKeachie, W. J., and Stephens, J. J., III. "Final Report: Research Opportunities in Postsecondary Education for the National Institute of Education." Mimeograph. Washington, D.C.: National Institute for Education, April 7, 1976.

McMahon, W. W. "Policy Issues in the Economics of Higher Education and Related Research Opportunities in Britain and the United States." *Higher Education*, 1974, pp. 165-186.

Machlup, F. *The Production and Distribution of Knowledge in the United States*. Princeton: Princeton University Press, 1962.

Machlup, F. *Education and Economic Growth*. Lincoln: University of Nebraska Press, 1970.

MacRae, D., Jr. *The Social Function of Social Science*. New Haven: Yale University Press, 1976.

*Madden, J. F. "The Role of Wages and Occupation in Determining the Education of Young Women and Men Workers." Unpublished manuscript, 1975.

Madison, P. *Personality Development in College*. Reading, Mass.: Addison-Wesley, 1969.

Malkiel, G. B., and Malkiel, J. A. "Male-Female Pay Differentials in Professional Employment." *American Economic Review*, September 1973, pp. 693-705.

Mandell, L. *Credit Card Use in the United States*. Ann Arbor: Institute for Social Research, University of Michigan, 1972.

Mandell, L., and others. *Surveys of Consumers 1971-72*. Ann Arbor: Institute for Social Research, University of Michigan, 1973.

Mansfield, E. *The Economics of Technological Change*. New York: Norton, 1968a.

Mansfield, E. *Industrial Research and Technological Innovation*. New York: Norton, 1968b.

Marcuse, H. *One-Dimensional Man: Studies in the Ideology of Advanced Industrial Society*. Boston: Beacon Press, 1964.

Marin, A., and Psacharopoulos, G. "Schooling and Income Distribution." *Review of Economics and Statistics*, August 1976, pp. 332-338.

Marshall, A. *Principles of Economics*. (8th ed.) London: MacMillan, 1930.

*Martin, W. B. *Alternative to Irrelevance*. Nashville: Abingdon Press, 1968.

*Martin, W. B. "Education as Intervention." *Educational Record*, Winter 1969, pp. 47-54.

*Maslow, A. H. *Toward a Psychology of Being.* Princeton: Van Nostrand, 1962.

Masters, S. H. *Black-White Income Differentials.* New York: Academic Press, 1975.

Merton, R. K. "Thoughts on Our Discontents." Paper presented at Kalamazoo College, June 1970.

Metropolitan Life Insurance Company. *Statistical Bulletin.* January 1976.

Meyerson, M. "Civilizing Education: Uniting Liberal and Professional Learning." *Daedalus,* Fall 1974, pp. 173-179.

*Micek, S. S. *Preliminary Summary of the Higher Education Outcome Measures Identification Study Pilot Test.* Boulder: National Center for Higher Education Management Systems, 1973.

*Micek, S. S., and Arney, W. R. *Outcome-Oriented Planning in Higher Education: An Approach or an Impossibility?* Boulder: National Center for Higher Education Management Systems, 1973.

*Micek, S. S., and Arney, W. R. *The Higher Education Outcome Measures Identification Study.* Boulder: National Center for Higher Education Management Systems, 1974.

*Micek, S. S., and Wallhaus, R. A. *An Introduction to the Identification and Uses of Higher Education Outcomes Information.* Boulder: National Center for Higher Education Management Systems Technical Report 40, 1973.

*Michael, D. N. *The Unprepared Society: Planning for a Precarious Future.* New York: Basic Books, 1968.

Michael, R. T. *The Effect of Education on Efficiency in Consumption.* New York: National Bureau of Economic Research, 1972.

Milbraith, L. *Political Participation.* Chicago: Rand McNally, 1965.

Miles, M. W. *The Radical Probe.* New York: Atheneum, 1971.

*Mill, J. S. *Dissertations and Discussions: Political, Philosophical, and Historical,* Vol. IV. London: Longmans, Green, Reader, and Dyer, 1875.

Millay, E. St. V. *Collected Sonnets.* New York: Harper & Row, 1941.

Miller, H. P. "Annual and Lifetime Income in Relation to Education: 1939 to 1959." *American Economic Review,* December 1960, pp. 962-986.

Mincer, J. "On-the-Job Training: Costs, Returns, and Some Implications." *Journal of Political Economy* (Supplement), October 1962a, pp. 50-79.

Mincer, J. "Labor Force Participation of Married Women: A Study of Labor Supply." In National Bureau of Economic Research, *Aspects of Labor Economics.* Princeton: Princeton University Press, 1962b.

Mincer, J. "The Distribution of Labor Incomes: A Survey with Special Reference to the Human Capital Approach." *Journal of Economic Literature,* March 1970, pp. 1-27.

Mincer, J. *Schooling, Experience, and Earnings.* New York: National Bureau of Economic Research and Columbia University Press, 1974.

Mincer, J. "Education, Experience, and the Distribution of Earnings and Employment: An Overview." In F. Thomas Juster (Ed.), *Education, Income, and Human Behavior.* New York: McGraw-Hill, 1975.

Mincer, J., and Polachek, S. "Family Investments in Human Capital: Earnings of Women." *Journal of Political Economy,* March-April 1974, pp. 76-108.

Mitchell, D. F. *Preferences for the Two-Child Family Among Student Fathers.* Paper presented at the Southern Sociological Association, Atlanta, 1973.

Mitchell, W. C. *The Backward Art of Spending Money.* New York: McGraw-Hill, 1937.

*Moberly, W. *The Crisis in the University.* London: SCM Press, 1949.

*Monsour, K. J. *The Annual Report of the Counseling Center.* Claremont, Calif.: Claremont University Center, 1974, 1975, 1976.

*Morehouse, W. *A New Civic Literacy: American Education and Global Interdependence.* Princeton: Aspen Institute for Humanistic Studies, 1975.

Morgan, J. N. *Income and Welfare in the United States.* New York: McGraw-Hill, 1962.

Morgan, J. N. "The Achievement Motive and Economic Behavior." *Economic Development and Cultural Change.* April 1964, pp. 243-267.

Morgan, J. N. (Ed.). *Five Thousand American Families—Patterns of Economic Progress.* 3 vols. Ann Arbor: Survey Research Center, Institute for Social Research, University of Michigan, 1974.

Morgan, J. N., and Sirageldin, I. A. "A Note on the Quality Dimension in Education." *Journal of Political Economy*, September-October 1968, pp. 1069-1077.

Morgan, J. N., Sirageldin, I. A., and Baerwaldt, N. *Productive Americans: A Study of How Individuals Contribute to Economic Progress.* Ann Arbor: Institute for Social Research, University of Michigan, 1966.

Moss, M. (Ed.). *The Measurement of Economic and Social Performance.* New York: National Bureau of Economic Research and Columbia University Press, 1973.

Mosteller, F., and Moynihan, D. P. (Eds.). *On Equality of Educational Opportunity.* New York: Vintage Books, 1972.

Mueller, E., and others. *Technological Advance in an Expanding Economy: Its Impact on a Cross-Section of the Labor Force.* Ann Arbor: Institute for Social Research, University of Michigan, 1969.

Muller, S. "Higher Education or Higher Skilling?" *Daedalus*, Fall 1974, pp. 148-158.

Mumford, L. *The Myth of the Machine: The Pentagon of Power.* New York: Harcourt Brace Jovanovich, 1970.

Munday, L. A., and Rever, P. R. "Perspectives on Open Admissions." In P. R. Rever (Ed.), *Open Admissions and Equal Access.* Iowa City: American College Testing Program, 1971.

Murphy, G., and Likert, R. *Public Opinion and the Individual: A Psychological Study of Student Attitudes on Public Questions, with a Retest Five Years Later.* New York: Harper & Row, 1938.

Murphy, L. B., and Raushenbush, E. *Achievement in the College Years.* New York: Harper & Row, 1960.

*National Board on Graduate Education. *Graduate Education: Purposes, Problems, and Potential.* Washington, D.C.: National Board on Graduate Education, 1972.

National Commission on the Financing of Postsecondary Education. *Financing Postsecondary Education in the United States.* Washington, D.C.: U.S. Government Printing Office, 1973.

National Science Board, National Science Foundation. *Science Indicators, 1974.* Washington, D.C.: U.S. Government Printing Office, 1975.

National Science Foundation. *Knowledge into Action: Improving the Nation's Use of the Social Sciences.* Report of the Special Commission on the Social Sciences of the National Science Board. Washington, D.C.: U.S. Government Printing Office, 1969.

Nelson, R. R., Peck, M. J., and Kalachek, E. D. *Technology, Economic Growth and Public Policy.* Washington: Brookings Institution, 1967.

New England's First Fruits: in Respect of the Colledge, and the Proceedings of Learning Therein, 1636. Reprinted as Old South Leaflet Volume III, No. 51. Boston: Directors of the Old South Work, undated.

Newfield, J. *A Prophetic Minority.* New York: New American Library, 1966.

*Newman, J. H. *The Scope and Nature of University Education.* New York: Dutton, 1958.

Nichols, R. C. "Effects of Various College Characteristics on Student Aptitude Test Scores." *Journal of Educational Psychology,* 1964, *55* (1), 45-54.

Nichols, R. C. *Heredity and Environment: Major Findings from Twin Studies of Ability, Personality, and Interests.* Mimeograph. Buffalo: State University of New York, 1976.

Nichols, R. C., and Loehlin, J. C. *Heredity, Environment, and Personality.* Austin: University of Texas Press, 1976.

Nollen, S. D. "The Economics of Education: Research Results and Needs." *Teachers College Record,* September 1975, pp. 51-77.

Ohmann, R. "The Decline in Literacy is a Fiction, if Not a Hoax." *Chronicle of Higher Education,* October 25, 1976.

Okun, A. M. *Equality and Efficiency.* Washington, D.C.: Brookings Institution, 1975.

Orcutt, G. H., and others. "Does Your Probability of Death Depend on Your Environment? A Microanalytic Study." *American Economic Review,* February 1977, pp. 260-264.

Opinion Research Corporation. "Is College Worth the Cost?" *ORC Public Opinion Index,* September 1972.

*Organization for Economic Cooperation and Development (OECD). *Alternative Educational Futures in the United States and in Europe.* Paris: OECD, 1972.

*Organization for Economic Cooperation and Development (OECD). *Indicators of Performance in Educational Systems.* Paris: OECD, 1973a.

*Organization for Economic Cooperation and Development (OECD). *Recurrent Education: A Strategy for Lifelong Learning.* Paris: OECD, 1973b.

*Organization for Economic Cooperation and Development (OECD). *Policies for Higher Education* General Report of Conference on Future Structures of Post-Secondary Education. Paris: OECD, 1974a.

Organization for Economic Cooperation and Development (OECD). *Subjective Elements of Well-Being.* Paris: OECD, 1974b.

Organization for Economic Cooperation and Development (OECD). *Toward Mass Higher Education: Issues and Dilemmas.* Conference on Future Structures of Post-Secondary Education, June 26-29, 1973. Paris: OECD, August 1974c.

Organization for Economic Cooperation and Development (OECD). *Patterns of Resources Devoted to Research and Experimental Development in the OECD Area, 1963-1971.* Paris: OECD, 1975.

Orlans, H. (Ed.). *Science Policy and the University.* Washington, D.C.: Brookings Institution, 1968.

Orlans, H. *The Nonprofit Research Institute.* New York: McGraw-Hill, 1972.

Orlans, H. *Contracting for Knowledge: Values and Limitations of Social Science Research.* San Francisco: Jossey-Bass, 1973.

*Ortega y Gasset, J. *Mission of the University.* (Howard Lee Nostrand, Trans.) Princeton: Princeton University Press, 1944.

*O'Toole, J. "The Reserve Army of the Underemployed." *Change,* May 1975, pp. 26-33.

*O'Toole, J., and others. *Work in America.* Cambridge: M.I.T. Press, 1973.

*Ottoway, A. K. C. *Education and Society.* London: Routledge and Kegan Paul, 1962.

Oulton, N. "The Distribution of Education and the Distribution of Income." *Economica,* November 1974, pp. 387-402.

Pace, C. R. *They Went to College.* Minneapolis: University of Minnesota Press, 1949.

Pace, C. R. "The Environment as a Factor in the Criterion of College Success." Paper presented at the 65th annual meeting of the American Psychological Association, 1957.

Pace, C. R. *Analyses of a National Sample of College Environments.* Los Angeles: University of California, 1967.

Pace, C. R. *Education and Evangelism.* New York: McGraw-Hill, 1972.

*Pace, C. R. *The Demise of Diversity.* Berkeley, Calif.: Carnegie Commission on Higher Education, 1974a.

*Pace, C. R. *Evaluating Liberal Education: A Report Prepared for the Lilly Endowment.* Los Angeles: Graduate School of Education, University of California, 1974b.

Pace, C. R. "A Contextual Model for Evaluating Educational Benefits." Paper presented at the annual meeting of the Association of Professors of Higher Education, Chicago, March 6-7, 1976.

*Pace, C. R., and Associates. *Higher Education Measurement and Evaluation Kit.* Los Angeles: Laboratory for Research on Higher Education, Graduate School of Education, University of California, 1975.

Pace, C. R., and Stern, G. G. "An Approach to the Measurement of Psychological Characteristics of College Environments." *Journal of Educational Psychology,* October 1958, pp. 269-277.

*Page, E. B. "Effects of Higher Education." In L. C. Solmon and P. J. Taubman, *Does College Matter?* New York: Academic Press, 1973.

Paglin, M. "The Measurement and Trend of Inequality: A Basic Revision." *American Economic Review,* September 1975, pp. 598-609.

Parnes, H. S., and Kohen, A. I. "Occupational Information and Labor Market Status: The Case of Young Men." *Journal of Human Resources.* Winter 1975, pp. 44-55.

Parnes, S. J. "Creativity: Developing a Human Potential." *Journal of Creative Behavior,* 1971, pp. 19-36.

Parsons, T., and Platt, G. *The American Academic Profession: A Pilot Study.* Washington, D.C.: National Science Foundation, 1968.

Patrick, H., and Rosovsky, H. *Asia's New Giant: How the Japanese Economy Works.* Washington, D.C.: Brookings Institution, 1976.

Pechman, J. A. "The Distributional Effects of Public Higher Education in California." *Journal of Human Resources,* Summer 1970, pp. 1-10.

Pechman, J. A. "Note on the Intergenerational Transfer of Public Higher Education Benefits." In T. W. Schultz (Ed.), *Investment in Education.* Chicago: University of Chicago Press, 1972.

Perella, V. C. "Employment of Recent College Graduates." *Monthly Labor Review,* February 1973, pp. 41-51.

*Perry, W. G., Jr. *Forms of Intellectual and Ethical Development in the College Years.* New York: Holt, Rinehart and Winston, 1970.

*Peterson, R. E., and Uhl, N. P. *Institutional Goals Inventory.* Princeton: Educational Testing Service, 1975.

Peterson, R. G. "Higher Education's Social Contract to Serve the Public Interest." *Educational Record,* Fall 1975, pp. 250-256.

*Phenix, P. H. *Education and the Common Good.* New York: Harper & Row, 1961.

Plato. *The Republic.* (D. Lee, Trans.; 2nd ed.) Middlesex, England: Penguin Books, 1974.

Powel, J. H., Jr., and Lamson, R. D. *An Annotated Bibliography of Literature Relating to the Costs and Benefits of Graduate Education.* Washington, D.C.: Council of Graduate Schools, 1972a.

Powel, J. H., Jr., and Lamson, R. D. *Elements Related to the Determination of Costs and Benefits of Graduate Education.* Washington, D.C.: Council of Graduate Schools, 1972b.

Powers, J. *An Inquiry into the Effects of a College Education on the Attitudes, Competencies, and Behavior of Individuals.* Claremont, Calif.: Claremont Graduate School, 1976.

*President's Commission on Higher Education. *Higher Education for American Democracy.* New York: Harper & Row, 1947.

*President's Commission on National Goals. *Goals for Americans.* Englewood Cliffs, N.J.: Prentice-Hall, 1960.

Procter and Gamble. Survey of Attitudes Toward Education, 1976.

Psacharopoulos, G. *Returns to Education.* New York: American Elsevier, 1973.

Psacharopoulos, G. "College Quality as a Screening Device." *Journal of Human Resources.* Fall 1974, pp. 556-558.

Psacharopoulos, G. *Earnings and Education in OECD Countries.* Paris: Organization for Economic Cooperation and Development, 1975.

Quinn, R. P., and Baldi de Mandilovitch, M. S. *Education and Job Satisfaction: A Questionable Payoff.* Ann Arbor: Survey Research Center, University of Michigan, 1975.

Quinn, R. P., and others. *Survey of Working Conditions.* U.S. Department of Labor, Employment Standards Administration. Washington, D.C.: U.S. Government Printing Office, 1971.

Rainwater, L. *What Money Buys: Inequality and the Social Meaning of Income.* New York: Basic Books, 1974.

Reich, C. A. *The Greening of America: How the Youth Revolution is Trying to Make America Livable.* New York: Random Press, 1970.

*Religion in Education Foundation. *The Educational Situation as a Milieu for Maturing.* Santa Barbara, Calif.: Values Colloquium IV, May 14-17, 1970.

Rever, P. R. *Open Admissions and Equal Access.* Iowa City: American College Testing Program, 1971.

Ribich, Thomas I. *Education and Poverty.* Washington, D.C.: Brookings Institution, 1969.

Rivlin, A. "Measuring Performance in Education." In Milton Moss (Ed.), *The Measurement of Economic and Social Performance.* New York: National Bureau of Economic Research and Columbia University Press, 1973.

Rivlin, A. "Income Distribution—Can Economists Help?" *American Economic Review,* May 1975a, pp. 1-15.

Rivlin, A. "Why Can't We Get Things Done?" *The Brookings Bulletin,* 1975b, *9* (2), 5-9.

*Robbins, L. *Higher Education.* Report of the Committee Appointed by the Prime Minister under the Chairmanship of Lord Robbins. London: Her Majesty's Stationery Office, Cmnd. 2154, 1963.

*Robbins, L. *The University in the Modern World.* London: Macmillan, 1966.

Rock, D. A., Centra, J. A., and Linn, R. L. *The Identification and Evaluation of College Effects on Student Achievement.* Princeton: Educational Testing Service, 1969.

*Rockefeller, J. D., 3rd. *The Second American Revolution.* New York: Harper & Row, 1973.

Roper, B. W. *Trends in Public Attitudes Toward Television and Other Mass Media.* New York: Television Information Office, 1975.

Roskens, R. W. *The Relationship Between Leadership Participation in College and After College.* Iowa City: University of Iowa Press, 1958.

Rossi, P. H., and Williams, W. *Evaluating Social Programs.* New York: Seminar Press, 1972.

Ruskin, J. *Unto This Last.* London: Allen & Unwin, 1960.

Russell, J. E. *Change and Challenge in American Education.* Boston: Houghton Mifflin, 1965.

*Ryan, J. J. *The Humanization of Man.* New York: Newman Press, 1972.

Ryder, N. B., and Westhoff, C. F. *Reproduction in the United States, 1965.* Princeton: Princeton University Press, 1971.

*Salk, J. "Values and Education." Unpublished paper prepared for the Lilly Endowment, Inc., 1976.

Samuelson, P. A. "Economics of Forestry in an Evolving Society." *Economic Inquiry,* December 1976, pp. 466-492.

*Sanford, N. (Ed.). *The American College.* New York: Wiley, 1962.

Sanford, N., and Katz, J. "The New Student Power and Needed Educational Reforms." *Phi Delta Kappan,* April 1966, pp. 397-401.

*Sanford, N. *Where Colleges Fail.* San Francisco: Jossey-Bass, 1969.

Schelling, T. C. "The Life You Save May Be Your Own." In S. B. Chase, Jr., (Ed.), *Problems in Public Expenditure Analysis.* Washington, D.C.: Brookings Institution, 1968.

Schiller, B. R. "Equality, Opportunity, and the 'Good Job'." *The Public Interest*, Spring 1976, pp. 111-120.

Schrag, P. "End of the Impossible Dream." *Saturday Review*, September 19, 1970, pp. 68-96.

Schramm, W. L., and others. *Knowledge and the Public Mind: A Preliminary Study of the Distribution and Sources of Science, Health, and Public Affairs Knowledge in the American Public.* Mimeograph. Stanford: Institute for Communications Research, Stanford University, 1967.

Schultz, T. W. "Education and Economic Growth." In *Social Forces Influencing American Education.* Chicago: National Society for the Study of Education, 1961.

Schultz, T. W. "Rise in the Capital Stock Represented by Education in the U.S., 1900-57." In S. Mushkin (Ed.), *Economics of Higher Education.* Washington, D.C.; U.S. Government Printing Office, 1962.

Schultz, T. W. *The Economic Value of Education.* New York: Columbia University Press, 1963.

*Schultz, T. W. *Investment in Human Capital.* New York: Free Press, 1971.

Schultz, T. W. *Investment in Education: The Equity-Efficiency Quandary.* Chicago: University of Chicago Press, 1972.

Schultz, T. W. "The Value of the Ability to Deal with Disequilibria." *Journal of Economic Literature*, September 1975, pp. 827-846.

*Schumacher, E. F. *Small Is Beautiful.* New York: Harper & Row, 1973.

Schuman, H., and Harding, J. "Prejudice and the Norm of Rationality." *Sociometry*, September 1964, pp. 353-371.

Schumpeter, J. A. *Capitalism, Socialism, and Democracy.* New York: Harper & Row, 1950.

Schwebel, M. *Who Can Be Educated?* New York: Grove Press, 1968.

Selvin, H. C., and Hagstrom, W. O. "Determinants of Support for Civil Liberties." *British Journal of Sociology*, March 1960, pp. 51-73.

Sewell, W. H., and Hauser, R. M. *Education, Occupation, and Earnings.* New York: Academic Press, 1975.

Shannon, J. A. *Science and the Evolution of Public Policy.* New York: Rockefeller University Press, 1973.

Sharp, L. M. *Education and Employment.* Baltimore: Johns Hopkins University Press, 1970.

*Shils, E. "The Academic Ethos Under Strain." *Minerva*, Spring 1975, pp. 1-37.

Silver, M. "An Econometric Analysis of Spatial Variations in Mortality by Race and Sex." In V. Fuchs (Ed.), *Essays in the Economics of Health and Medical Care.* New York: National Bureau of Economic Research and Columbia University Press, 1972.

Silvey, H. M. "Changes in Test Scores After Two Years in College." *Educational and Psychological Measurement*, Autumn 1951, pp. 494-502.

Singer, S. "Review and Discussion of the Literature on Personality Development During College." In Joseph Katz (Ed.), *Growth and Constraint in College Students.* Stanford: Institute for the Study of Human Problems, 1967.

*Skinner, B. F. *Beyond Freedom and Dignity.* New York: Knopf, 1971.

Smith, A. *An Inquiry into the Nature and Causes of the Wealth of Nations.*

(E. Cannan, Ed.) New York: Modern Library, 1937. (Book V, Chap. 1, Art. 2.)

Smith, J. D. (Ed.). *The Personal Distribution of Income and Wealth.* New York: National Bureau of Economic Research and Columbia University Press, 1975.

*Smith, J. E. *Value Convictions and Higher Education.* New Haven: Edward W. Hazen Foundation, 1958.

Smith, J. P., and Welch, F. R. *Black/White Male Earnings and Employment, 1960-1970.* Santa Monica, Calif: Rand Corporation, 1975.

Solmon, L. C. "Meeting Demands for Increased Academic Productivity." *Educational Record,* Summer 1973a, pp. 198-203.

Solmon, L. C. "Proposal to the U.S. Office of Education for a Study of the Social Impacts of Higher Education." Paper prepared for the National Academy of Sciences, Washington, D.C., 1973b.

Solmon, L. C. "The Relation between Schooling and Savings Behavior: An Example of the Indirect Effects of Education." In F. T. Juster (Ed.), *Education, Income, and Human Behavior.* New York: McGraw-Hill, 1975.

Solmon, L. C. *The Utilization of Undergraduate Education in Careers.* Unpublished. Higher Education Research Institute, University of California, Los Angeles, 1976.

*Solmon, L. C., and Taubman, P. *Does College Matter?* New York: Academic Press, 1973.

Solmon, L. C., and Wachtel, P. "The Effects on Income of Type of College Attended." *Sociology of Education,* Winter 1975, pp. 75-90.

*Southern Regional Education Board. *Priorities for Postsecondary Education.* Atlanta, 1976.

*Spaeth, J. L., and Greeley, A. M. *Recent Alumni and Higher Education.* New York: McGraw-Hill, 1970.

Spender, S. *The Year of the Young Rebels.* New York: Random House, 1969.

Stern, D. *Implicit Prices of Nonpecuniary Job Characteristics.* Unpublished paper, Yale University, 1975.

Stern, G. G. *Studies of College Environments.* Syracuse: Syracuse University Press, 1966.

Stern, G. G. *People in Context: Measuring Person-Environment Congruence in Education and Industry.* New York: Wiley, 1970.

Stiglitz, J. E. "The Theory of 'Screening,' Education, and the Distribution of Income." *American Economic Review,* June 1975, pp. 283-300.

Stockwell, E. G. "A Critical Examination of the Relationship Between Socioeconomic Status and Mortality." *American Journal of Public Health,* June 1963, pp. 956-964.

Strumpel, B. (Ed.). *Subjective Elements of Well-Being.* Paris: Organization for Economic Cooperation and Development, 1974.

Strumpel, B. *Economic Means for Human Needs.* Ann Arbor: Institute for Social Research, University of Michigan, 1976.

Strumpel, B., and others. *Surveys of Consumers 1972-73.* Ann Arbor: Institute for Social Research, University of Michigan, 1975.

Sutherland, E. H. *White Collar Crime.* New York: Dryden Press, 1949.

*Szczepanski, J. *Higher Education in Eastern Europe.* New York: International Council for Educational Development, 1974.

Taubman, P. *Schooling, Ability, Nonpecuniary Rewards, Socio-economic Background, and the Lifetime Distribution of Earnings* (Working paper No. 17). New York: National Bureau of Economic Research, 1973.

Taubman, P. "The Determinants of Earnings: Genetics, Family, and Other Environments; A Study of White Male Twins." *American Economic Review.* December 1976a, pp. 858-870.

Taubman, P. "Earnings, Education, Genetics, and Environment." *Journal of Human Resources,* Fall 1976b, pp. 447-461.

*Taubman, P., and Wales, T. *Mental Ability and Higher Educational Attainment in the Twentieth Century.* Berkeley: Carnegie Commission on Higher Education, 1972.

Taubman, P., and Wales, T. *Higher Education and Earnings.* New York: McGraw-Hill, 1974.

Tavris, C. "What Does College Do for a Person? Frankly Very Little." A conversation with Theodore Newcomb. *Psychology Today,* September 1974, pp. 73-80.

*Taylor, H. *On Education and Freedom.* New York: Abelard-Schuman, 1954.

*Taylor, H. *Students without Teachers.* New York: McGraw-Hill, 1969.

Taylor, H. "Manning the Barricades from Berkeley to Bombay." *Change,* April 1975, pp. 30-33.

*Tead, O. *The Climate of Learning.* New York: Harper & Row, 1958.

Terleckyj, N. E. (Ed.). *Household Production and Consumption.* New York: National Bureau of Economic Research and Columbia University Press, 1975a.

Terleckyj, N. E. *Improvements in the Quality of Life.* Washington, D.C.: National Planning Association, 1975b.

Terleckyj, N. E. *State of Science and Research: Some New Indicators.* Washington, D.C.: National Planning Association, 1976.

Thaler, R., and Rosen, S. "The Value of Saving a Life: Evidence from the Labor Market." In N. E. Terleckyj (Ed.), *Household Production and Consumption.* New York: National Bureau of Economic Research and Columbia University Press, 1975.

Thistlethwaite, D. L. "The Impact of the Episodes of May 1970 upon American University Students." *Research in Education,* 1973, pp. 225-243.

Thurow, L. G. *Generating Inequality: Mechanisms of Distribution in the U.S. Economy.* New York: Basic Books, 1975.

Toffler, A. *Future Shock.* New York: Random House, 1970.

*Trent, J. W., and Medsker, L. *Beyond High School: A Psychosociological Study of 10,000 High School Graduates.* San Francisco: Jossey-Bass, 1968.

Trilling, L. "The Uncertain Future of the Humanistic Educational Ideal." *American Scholar,* Winter 1974-75, pp. 52-67.

Trow, M. "Reflections on the Transition from Mass to Universal Higher Education." *Daedalus,* Winter 1970, pp. 1-42.

Trow, M. "Higher Education and Moral Development." In *Proceedings of the 1974 ETS Invitational Conference.* Princeton: Educational Testing Service, 1974a.

*Trow, M. "Reflections on the Relation between the Occupational Structure and Higher Educational Systems." In *Higher Education: Crisis and Support.* New York: International Council for Educational Development, 1974b.

Trow, M. (Ed.). *Teachers and Students.* New York: McGraw-Hill, 1975.

Trow, M. *Aspects of American Higher Education, 1969-1975.* Mimeograph. Berkeley: Carnegie Council on Policy Studies in Higher Education, 1977.

Tunis, J. R. *Was College Worth While?* New York: Harcourt Brace Jovanovich, 1936.

*Ulich, R. *Three Thousand Years of Educational Wisdom.* (2nd ed.) Cambridge: Harvard University Press, 1968.

Upton, M. "Quality in Higher Education." *North Central Association Quarterly,* Spring 1963, pp. 307-314.

U.S. Bureau of the Census. Current Population Reports, series P-20, No. 263, 277. Washington, D.C.: U.S. Government Printing Office, 1975.

U.S. Bureau of the Census. *Statistical Abstract of the United States.* Washington, D.C.: U.S. Government Printing Office, Annual.

U.S. Bureau of Labor Statistics. *Survey of Consumer Expenditures, 1960-61.* Supplement 2 to BLS Report No. 237-93. Washington, D.C.: U.S. Government Printing Office, 1966.

U.S. Department of Health, Education, and Welfare (National Center for Health Statistics). *Divorces: Analysis of Change.* Washington, D.C.: U.S. Government Printing Office, 1969a.

U.S. Department of Health, Education, and Welfare. *Toward a Social Report.* Washington, D.C.: U.S. Government Printing Office, 1969b.

U.S. Department of Health, Education, and Welfare (National Center for Education Statistics). *National Longitudinal Study of the High School Class of 1972.* Washington, D.C.: U.S. Government Printing Office, 1975a.

U.S. Department of Health, Education, and Welfare (National Center for Education Statistics). *One and One-Half Years after High School Graduation: The Class of 1972.* Bulletin No. 21. Washington, D.C.: U.S. Government Printing Office, June 16, 1975b.

U.S. Department of Health, Education, and Welfare (National Center for Education Statistics). *The Condition of Education.* Washington, D.C.: U.S. Government Printing Office, 1975c, 1976.

U.S. Department of Health, Education, and Welfare (National Center for Education Statistics). *Digest of Education Statistics.* Washington, D.C.: U.S. Government Printing Office, Annual.

U.S. Department of Health, Education, and Welfare. *Projections of Educational Statistics to 1983-84.* Washington, D.C.: U.S. Government Printing Office, 1975.

Vaizey, J. *The Economics of Education.* Glencoe, Ill.: Free Press, 1962.

Van den Haag, E. *Education as an Industry.* Privately published. New York, 1956.

*Van Doren, M. *Liberal Education.* Boston: Beacon Press, 1959.

Veblen, T. *The Theory of the Leisure Class.* New York: Random House, 1931.

Verba, S., and Nie, N. *Participation in America: Political Democracy and Social Equality.* New York: Harper & Row, 1972.

Verry, D. W., and Layard, P. R. G. "Cost Functions for University Teaching." *Economic Journal,* March 1975.

Veysey, L. R. *The Emergence of the American University.* Chicago: University of Chicago Press, 1965.

Wachtel, P. "The Returns to Investment in Higher Education: Another View." In F. Thomas Juster (Ed.), *Education, Income, and Human Behavior.* New York: McGraw-Hill, 1975.

Wachtel, P. "The Effect on Earnings of School and College Investment Expenditures." *Review of Economics and Statistics,* August 1976, pp. 326-331.

*Walcott, F. G. *The Origins of Culture and Anarchy: Matthew Arnold and Popular Education in England.* Toronto: University of Toronto Press, 1970.

*Walizer, M. H., and Herriott, R. E. *The Impact of College on Students' Competence to Function in a Learning Society.* Iowa City: American College Testing Program, 1971.

Wallhaus, R. A., and Micek, S. S. *Higher Education Program Assessment Profiles.* Boulder: Western Interstate Commission for Higher Education, 1972.

Walsh, W. B. *Theories of Person-Environment Interaction: Implications for the College Student.* Iowa City: American College Testing Program, 1973.

*Weatherford, W. D. (Ed.). *The Goals of Higher Education.* Cambridge: Harvard University Press, 1960.

Wedge, B. M. *Psychosocial Problems of College Men.* New Haven: Yale University Press, 1958.

Weisbrod, B. A. *External Benefits of Public Education: An Economic Analysis.* Princeton: Princeton University Industrial Relations Section, 1964.

*Weisbrod, B. A. "Education: Private and Social Benefits." *Journal of Human Resources,* 1966, pp. 268-272.

Weisbrod, B. A., and Karpoff, P. "Monetary Returns to College Education, Student Ability, and College Quality." *Review of Economics and Statistics,* 1968, pp. 491-497.

Weiss, P. *Sport, a Philosophical Inquiry.* Carbondale: Southern Illinois University Press, 1969.

Welch, F. "Labor Market Discrimination: An Interpretation of Income Differences in the Rural South." *Journal of Political Economy,* June 1967, pp. 225-240.

Welch, F. "Education in Production." *Journal of Political Economy,* January-February 1970, pp. 35-49.

Welch, F. "Human Capital Theory: Education, Discrimination, and Life Cycles." *American Economic Review,* May 1975, pp. 63-82.

Whelpton, P. K., Campbell, A. A., and Patterson, J. E. *Fertility and Family Planning in the United States.* Princeton: Princeton University Press, 1966.

White, R. W. *Lives in Progress* (2nd ed.). New York: Holt, Rinehart and Winston, 1966.

*Whitehead, A. N. *The Aims of Education.* New York: New American Library, 1949.

Wiles, P. "The Correlation between Education and Earnings: The External-Test-Not-Content Hypothesis." *Higher Education,* 1974.

*Wirtz, W. *The Boundless Resource.* New York: Dutton, 1975.

*Withey, S. B. *A Degree and What Else? Correlates and Consequences of a College Education.* New York: McGraw-Hill, 1971.

Withey, S. B. "Quality of Life as an Education Outcome." In Educational Testing Service (ETS), *Educational Indicators: Monitoring the State of Education.* Princeton: ETS, 1975.

Witmer, D. R. "Is the Value of College Going Really Declining?" *Change,* December 1976, pp. 46-47, 60-61.

Wolfle, D. *The Home of Science.* New York: McGraw-Hill, 1972.

Woodward, C. V. "The Erosion of Academic Privilege and Immunities." *Daedalus,* Fall 1974, pp. 33-37.

Wren, S. C. *The College Student and Higher Education Policy: What Stake and What Purpose?* New York: Carnegie Foundation for the Advancement of Teaching, 1975.

*Yale College. *Report of the Study Group on Yale College.* New Haven: Yale University, 1972.

Yankelovich, D. *Changing Youth Values in the '70s.* New York: John D. Rockefeller 3rd Foundation, 1974a.

Yankelovich, D. *The New Morality: A Profile of American Youth in the 70's.* New York: McGraw-Hill, 1974b.

Young, A. M. "Labor Market Experience of Recent College Graduates." *Monthly Labor Review,* October 1974, pp. 33-40.

Young, A. M. "Students, Graduates, and Dropouts in the Labor Market, October, 1974." *Monthly Labor Review,* August 1975a, pp. 33-36.

Young, A. M. "Going Back to School at 35 and Over." *Monthly Labor Review,* December 1975b, pp. 47-50.

*Zhamin, V. *Education in the USSR: Its Economy and Structure.* Moscow: Novosti Press Agency Publishing House, 1973.

Name Index

Subject Index